THE GOLDWATCHER

Demystifying Gold Investing

JOHN KATZ AND FRANK HOLMES

John Wiley & Sons, Ltd

Email (for orders and customer service enquiries): cs-books@wiley.co.uk
Visit our Home Page on www.wiley.com

Other Wiley Editorial Offices

John Wiley & Sons Inc., 111 River Street, Hoboken, NJ 07030, USA

Jossey-Bass, 989 Market Street, San Francisco, CA 94103-1741, USA

Wiley-VCH Verlag GmbH, Boschstr. 12, D-69469 Weinheim, Germany

John Wiley & Sons Australia Ltd, 42 McDougall Street, Milton, Queensland 4064, Australia

John Wiley & Sons (Asia) Pte Ltd, 2 Clementi Loop #02-01, Jin Xing Distripark, Singapore 129809

John Wiley & Sons Canada Ltd, 6045 Freemont Blvd. Mississauga, Ontario, L5R 4J3 Canada

Wiley also publishes its books in a variety of electronic formats. Some content that appears in print may not be available in electronic books.

Library of Congress Cataloging-in-Publication Data
Katz, John, 1934–
    The goldwatcher : demystifying gold investing / John Katz and Frank Holmes.
      p. cm.
    Includes bibliographical references and index.
    ISBN 978-0-470-72426-2 (cloth)
1. Gold–Purchasing.   2. Investments.   I. Holmes, Frank, 1955-   II. Title.
HG293.K38 2008
332.63′28–dc22
                                                            2008015115

British Library Cataloguing in Publication Data
A catalogue record for this book is available from the British Library

ISBN 978-0-470-72426-2 (H/B)

Typeset in 11.5/13.5 pt Bembo by SNP Best-set Typesetter Ltd., Hong Kong
Printed and bound in Great Britain by CPI Antony Rowe, Chippenham, Wiltshire

JK

John and Adrienne Katz dedicate John's contribution to this book to Lola, Scarlet, Jake, Jesse, little Miss D to be, their lovely parents and the memory of our lovely parents.

FH

To Sorcha, Joshua and Nigel, for their love and support during my many days and nights away searching for opportunities around the globe.

Contents

PART TWO – GOLD INVESTING STRATEGIES BY FRANK HOLMES

Foreword

Dr. Marc Faber, author of 'Tomorrow's Gold' and 'The Great Money Illusion', is the Hong Kong-based publisher of the Gloom, Boom and Doom Report, a monthly commentary on global market conditions and monetary policy. A former managing director at Drexel Burnham Lambert, he now heads Marc Faber Limited, an investment advisor and fund management firm known for its contrarian approach to investing.

Years from now, the events of late 2007 and early 2008 will be remembered as a classic case study of the flawed thinking by governments that choose to use monetary policy to try to sustain an unsustainable economic bubble, and how that action broadens and deepens the pain when the bubble inevitably bursts. And the bubble always bursts.

The old image of cranking up the printing press to increase money supply is outdated in the digital age. Now computer keystrokes can create dollars or euros or yen by the billions, and then move them around the globe at cyberspeed. But advances in technology and global finance have not changed the basic economic principle represented by the printing press: when central banks can churn out paper money at will, the value of this paper is highly suspect.

Paper money can be valued, of course. The question is, 'Against what?' It would seem that cash is losing its purchasing power at an accelerating rate against other assets because of expansionary monetary policies. You can print money, you can increase the supply of bonds, you can increase the supply of equities through new issues, but you simply cannot increase the supply of oil endlessly, nor of copper, nor of gold.

Certainly not of gold.

Since 2000 gold and precious metals have significantly outperformed other financial assets. And the worse the economic and financial conditions of the United States and other countries become, the more value cash will lose against hard assets, which have now become the world's 'new money'. In an environment of monetary debasement – that is, when cash loses rapidly its purchasing power – all goods, services and assets become currencies. It is during these times that investors and savers realise that the only way to protect their purchasing power is to move away from paper assets.

The problem is that the US Federal Reserve, after having built up a massive financial sector through its easy money policies over the last quarter-century, does not have the will to clean up the financial mess it created. Rather, it is dealing with its fiscal ailment by simply accelerating the rate at which it prints paper money.

The Fed, led by its Chairman Ben Bernanke, is following an asymmetrical monetary policy. Bernanke and his crew let asset bubbles develop, and then when the marketplace tries to correct those bubbles through price declines, the Fed barges in to keep those overinflated assets aloft. It is an utterly illogical monetary policy that over the long run will backfire and devastate the global economy.

In the third quarter of 2007, the US money supply increased at an annual rate of 18% as the Fed rushed to cut interest rates to provide liquidity in response to the widening mortgage debt crisis. By following this expansionist monetary policy, the Fed is creating a massive glut of dollars that add to global liquidity, which stokes global inflation and leads to global bubbles.

The Fed followed a similar loose-money policy in the late 1990s, which as we all remember culminated with a technology-led stock bubble that abruptly burst in 2000. It seems that the current crop of American central bankers learned little to nothing from their predecessors' mistakes a decade ago. How can a responsible central bank cut interest rates and pursue an expansionary monetary policy when the stock market is near an all-time high, when the dollar is staggering and when food and commodity prices are going through the roof? If these conditions were found in virtually any other country, the prescription from the World Bank or International Monetary Fund would be to tighten monetary policies and to raise interest rates.

These risks are not limited to the United States, of course. If the dollar continues to lose ground against the euro, I foresee that at some point the European Central Bank would feel tremendous political pressure to cut interest rates to try to lower the value of the euro against the dollar. At that point, everyone around the world would also have to cut rates, no matter how illogical and irresponsible such a move might be. This would, in effect, trigger a competitive devaluation, a global race to the monetary bottom.

There is a very real danger that the whole world will go into hyperinflation and that paper money will be rendered worthless. This would create what I call the 'Zimbabwe-ization' of the world. It's almost mind-boggling to think that little more than a quarter-century ago, a Zimbabwean dollar was worth about one and a half US dollars. But years of inept monetary policies have destroyed that country's currency: the official exchange rate was 30000 Zimbabwean dollars to one US dollar in late 2007, but the black market rate was near 2000000:1 and worsening each day.

Mr. Bernanke's philosophy, like that of Alan Greenspan before him, is that monetary policy should target core inflation. In other words, the rate of inflation if you don't count energy or food prices. Using core inflation to structure monetary policy is fundamentally flawed because it is designed to underreport true inflation – energy and food are far from free these days. I'm convinced that most Americans are facing a rate inflation of at least 5 to 6% per annum, and for some it is 9% and even 10%. Nobody enjoys the 'official' rate of inflation of 4%.

The Fed's policy of monetary manipulation to keep asset prices up at all costs by use of artificially low interest rates means an era of continuous depreciation has arrived. Cash, once perceived as reasonably safe, has actually become quite a dangerous asset class due to its depreciation not only against asset prices but also against consumer prices.

In fact, I would argue that because of artificially low interest rates around the world, paper currencies have lost one of their principal functions, which is to be a store of value. Paper currencies have essentially become confetti! People will eventually realise that these confetti, deposited in a bank or loaned out at a low interest rate, are of little enduring value, and when that happens, they will get rid of that paper and store their value in real estate, commodities, equities and collectibles to avoid becoming 'penniless billionaires,' as so many Zimbabweans find themselves.

An exchange of cash into assets would lead to speculation by those who leverage their purchasing power with funds borrowed at the artificially suppressed interest rates. The increase in leverage, of course, would drive asset prices even higher, and the upward spiral would continue.

Now, someone could argue that there is nothing wrong with asset prices appreciating. I completely agree – provided that asset prices are indeed increasing because of favourable fundamental factors. On the other hand, if asset prices skyrocket because of excessive liquidity, the result is unsustainable asset bubbles that end in pronounced economic pain.

And if these decorative monetary confetti are no longer a store of value, they are also ill-suited to serve as a unit of accounting. The irresponsibility by central bankers makes it clear that we need to trade in the dollar and other paper currencies for an alternative that would serve as a unit of account to measure economic growth in the world and as a dependable store of value. In my opinion, this currency should be gold.

I don't mean to suggest that commodities cannot also decline in value. It should be clear, however, that the supply of paper money can be increased ad infinitum, whereas the supply of hard assets is extremely limited. I'm not particularly skilled at moving assets around to ensure they retain their value, so my tendency would be to stick to gold.

You as an investor are now faced with a monumental choice. Either you believe that the expansionary monetary policies of central banks will lift asset prices further, or you take the strongly contrarian view that this artificial creation will not work and that the world is heading toward a deflationary recession.

How would gold perform in a deflationary global recession? Initially gold could come under some deflationary pressure as well, but once the realisation sinks in as to how messy deflation would be for countries and households carrying too much debt, its price would likely soar.

Therefore, under both scenarios – stagflation or deflationary recession – gold and gold equities, and to a lesser degree other precious metals, should continue to perform better than financial assets.

List of Charts and Tables

Charts

Tables

Acknowledgements

The backbone of my analysis is based on the opinions of a range of money managers, financial commentators and economists who continuously publish their opinions and analysis. My special appreciation to the commentators I quote and to Frank Holmes – both for his contribution to investing in gold mining companies and for the indispensable analysis and information on gold that he and his team publish continuously. Sincere thanks also to Dr. Marc Faber for contributing the foreword and Neil Behrmann, Editor of Exchange Traded Gold; Jessica Cross and Matthew Turner of Virtual Metals; Nick Laird of Sharelynx; Larry Martin of Eagle Wing Research and Lawrence Chard of Tax Free Gold for their valued contributions.

Writers rely on the support of friends and associates. Some generously share their knowledge and insight on key issues. And some have faith in us even when a challenge is daunting. I faced such a challenge while writing this book in 2007. The US credit crisis emerged as the most menacing threat to investors and society since the Great Depression of the 1930s. In response I had to revise content. At that late stage changes involved timetable disruptions and additional work for the publisher. Yet everyone at Wiley afforded me the opportunity to contribute material that was both challenging to write and necessary. My sincere thanks for that opportunity – and for the support Caitlin Cornish and her colleagues have given since she commissioned The Goldwatcher. Sincere thanks also to Terry Badger, Communications Director of US Global Investors, for his steady assistance from commencement until all edits were complete. And my sincerest thanks to Adrienne, Herbert, Tony and everyone who encouraged me with friendship, advice, and often love beyond anything I deserve.

John Katz

I would like to thank the very capable investment team at U.S.

Global Investors, with a special thanks to research director John Derrick and gold analyst Ralph Aldis.

Thanks also to the U.S. Global board of directors who supported my vision for the company during the often challenging 1990s: Jerry Rubinstein, Roy Terracina and Tom Lydon. Likewise to the current senior management team, which has been indispensable in building U.S. Global into a vital and versatile enterprise.

Terry Badger, the communications director at U.S. Global, for the curiosity, enthusiasm and commitment to learn about the world of gold investments and for his help with research and editing.

I would also like to acknowledge some of the many people who have taught me the ropes in the investment business and those who continue to teach me valuable and lasting lessons about what's really important in this busy life: Frank Giustra, Marc Faber, Seymour Schulich, Pierre Lassonde, Ned Goodman, Gene McBurney, Mike Wekerle, Mike Vitton, Lukas Lundin, Ian Mann, Nash Jiwa, Paul Reynolds, Chantal Gosselin, Andrew Groves, Ron Woods, Ed Godin, Robert Friedland and Serafino Iacono.

Many others have helped me make adjustments after my move from Toronto to Texas: the U.S. Global fund trustees, Martin Weiss, Mary Anne and Pamela Aden, Mark Skousen, Bill Bonner, Ken Kam, Bob Bishop, Doug Casey, Jim Dines, Jay Taylor, Steve Dattels, Paul Robertson and Paul Stephens, to name but a few.

And finally, my gratitude to Susan McGee, U.S. Global Investors' president and general counsel, and my longtime assistant June Falks, both of whom work hard to keep me on task and on time.

Frank Holmes

PART ONE
DEMYSTIFYING THE GOLD PRICE

John Katz

1

Introduction: Why Gold?

'The recognition of risk management as a practical art rests on a simple cliché with the most profound consequences: when our world was created, nobody remembered to include certainty. *We are never certain; we are always ignorant to some degree.*'

Peter L. Bernstein: Against the Gods – The Remarkable Story of Risk

'We have entered the third millennium through a gate of fire.'

Nobel Laureate Kofi Annan, United Nations Secretary General 2001

Unbiased Research

How do you decide if and when you should buy gold when opinions on its future value can be poles apart? Pundits at one extreme forecast an inevitable dollar crash that ends with a 'bonfire' of all paper currencies and global financial meltdown. Gold, they say, will be the most sought after asset on the planet and it is going to be priceless. Sceptics at the other extreme say it belongs 'on the neck, in teeth and on the pinkie'. But it is obsolete in the information age and past its sell by date as a monetary asset. They say it won't be worth much to anyone except a jewellery manufacturer or a dentist. Most commentators call it a safe haven investment. But many brokers with experience of gold rush frenzies that ended in tears remind us that the system of outright gambling in financial markets, politely called spread betting, was invented to give punters a chance to play the volatile gold price. In their opinion gold is a speculative punt and is not an investment.

Opinions at the extremes tend to be flawed. As an unbiased analyst I am neither gold bull nor bear, pundit nor sceptic. Working from the grey area between the extremes I have analysed when owning gold makes sense and when it doesn't and when gold prices do or don't make sense. Answers to key questions raised are not always clear cut. But there is no doubt about why the mythical treasure at the end of the rainbow is always a pot of gold and never a few truckloads of copper, zinc, coffee or anything else. Gold is the great universal consolidator of value. A million dollars of gold priced at $600 an ounce weighs only 104 pounds and will fit in a safe deposit box. A single 400 ounce gold bar is worth $240 000. A kilogram about the size of a golf ball $21 000. A one ounce gold coin $600. Even a five gram slither, marketed with a certificate of authenticity, is over $100.

This book has origins in research on investments insulated against financial market risks. The research started in September 2001 shortly after the 9/11 terrorist attacks in the US. Gold was on the agenda as a legendary safe haven in troubled times and, subject to price, it still is. In Part One of this book 'Demystifying the Gold Price' I review what motivates people and organisations to own gold, who buys it and the factors that influence how much they are prepared to pay. Gold used to be officially 'the measure of all exchangeable value' and 'the scale to which all money prices are referred'.[1] Over the twentieth century, as the US became the global superpower, the dollar assumed more and more of gold's traditional role in the international monetary system. After US President Richard Nixon severed all links between the dollar and gold in 1971 the dollar also usurped gold's role as the universal measure of value. Gold is now another alternative investment with a different risk reward profile to financial assets. Owning it in good times can be as rewarding as watching paint dry. But, because it comes into its own whenever there is uncertainty, owning some gold is something to keep in mind when we make risk management plans.

Nowadays, of course, we can introduce hedge funds and other modern investments into our portfolios. Indeed the world's top financial brains have been producing a seemingly endless stream of derivatives and other financially engineered structures that not only reduce risk exposure but are expected to make us money at the same time. Among the brilliant academic economists now also engaged in hedge fund management is Andrew W. Lo, Finance Professor at the prestigious Massachusetts Institute of Technology's Sloan School of Management. Working at the cutting edge of information technology he is devising a programme that will simplify risk management. All you will have to do is punch a range of information personal to you into a computer with data on the risks you can and can't tolerate. An algorithm will then tailor a portfolio for you suitably hedged against unwanted risks. The Professor acknowledges his plans still sound like science fiction and it will be ten years before his programmes are up and running.[2] To be sure technology has already revolutionised the way we invest and will continue to. But, when it comes to making the strategic decisions, we will remain in the driver's seat. Just as we are when we drive a car with automatic cruise control. The cruise controller doesn't decide whether to travel on an A or B road or whether to drive at fifty or seventy miles an hour. We do.

While the Professor empowers his computers we can and must empower ourselves to manage risk more effectively. By understanding the challenges we are facing in the twenty-first century we can position ourselves to deal with any adverse consequences. This book is a compilation of analysis and information on twenty-first century financial risks and on gold as an alternative investment that can limit risk exposure. Commentary and analysis that follows is supported by links to reliable sources of current information. But there is no link to any information source on when an unexpected crisis is going to happen. Even the Professor's algorithms will never have that link. The legendary billionaire investor Warren Buffett has repeatedly warned that derivatives are weapons of financial mass destruction. But nobody can tell if or when the multi trillion dollar derivatives market will be further disrupted by another unexpected crisis. Or when anything else unexpected will happen. Warren Buffett, Andrew Lo, you and I, along with everyone else on the planet, will find out about an unexpected crisis at the same time after it has happened. But some of us will have made better plans than others to deal with the consequences. Remember it was only ten years ago when the hedge fund Long-Term Capital Management run by Nobel Prize winning economists collapsed. Roger Lowenstein's book *When Genius Failed*, details how a group of élite investors engaged with financial derivatives created a trillion dollar hole in the international banking system that brought world financial markets to the brink of imploding.[3]

If ever a derivatives crisis or other mishap roils financial markets again hedge fund protection could prove to be as useless as holding all your eggs in a basket in your right hand when you trip over your left shoe lace.

The Stateless Money Franchise

I first heard gold spoken about as a 'franchise' from an advertising professional who told me I would understand it better if I looked less at economics textbooks and tried more to understand why people everywhere in the world trusted it. She urged me to focus on the remarkable franchise that comes with the word gold through its umbilical links with money and wealth. I could agree with her about these links. But I asked if she wasn't over egging the symbolism of a single word. No, she replied, the word gold in marketing and advertising is magic. Only economists think of the gold standard as a monetary arrangement that no longer applies. In the real world the gold standard has always been shorthand for the finest qualities for anything and everything from personal ethics to butter on a supermarket shelf or Rolls Royce jetliner engines. Then, to dispel my doubts about the commercial power of a single word, she reminded me of the time when, with a word, the jewellery tycoon Gerald Ratner torpedoed the share price of his company and ended his career as chief executive. While telling his success story to an audience of marketing professionals he quipped that some of the cheap wares sold in his shops were crap. Wallmart, she assured me, sell similar cheap jewellery ranges to those Mr Ratner mentioned. But they are enormously successful because they don't sell crap. She urged me to look at their web site and see for myself how they engage the magic of gold to embellish their cheap jewellery. And, yes, they do associate their wares with the mystique of gold. The jewellery they sell is made from 'the oldest precious metal known to humankind, with lustre and remarkable properties that have allowed it to be crafted into the world's most coveted and exquisite jewellery'.[4] Nevertheless for about $20 they offer two pairs of '10 karat shiny yellow gold ear ring hoops'. That's how the masters engage the gold franchise to market trinkets made from thin metal tubes with a little gold content. Their marketing is so successful that they were at one time the biggest distributors of gold in the United States, the second biggest user of gold in the world. India is the biggest.

   Gold has unique properties that underpin demand for jewellery, gold as an investment and its stateless money franchise. France's President General Charles de Gaulle spoke flamboyantly about these qualities in a campaign he launched in 1965 against dollar hegemony. Gold backing for the dollar was eroding. It no longer looked like the 'better than gold' global currency it was at the end of World War II when the US owned 80% of the world's monetary gold. Instead it was starting to resemble Mr Ratner's jewellery. President Richard Nixon's Treasury Secretary John Connally said as much when he told European bankers: 'The dollar is our currency but your problem.' Campaigning for a return to the classic gold standard De Gaulle declared: 'There cannot be any other criterion, any other standard than gold. Oh yes! Gold which never changes its nature, which can be shaped into bars, ingots or coins, which has no nationality and which is eternally and universally accepted as the unalterable fiduciary value par excellence.' The General's campaign failed soon after it was launched. Whatever weaknesses there were with the dollar he had no viable alternative to offer to dollar hegemony. But he had one lethal weapon in his armoury. He was entitled under the post World War II Bretton Woods arrangements to demand that settlements of balances with the United States must be made with gold. In 1971, when demands from France and other European countries were draining America's gold reserves, Nixon summarily severed all links between the dollar and gold. In the jargon of the day he 'closed the gold window' and consigned the last remnants of the monetary gold standard to history. Currencies started to trade in open markets independently of each other. Gold, no longer money or a currency, started to trade as a commodity. But it is often still labelled a quasi currency or stateless money. I prefer the stateless money label because it associates gold with its role as a universally recognised store of value over thousands of years.

The heyday of dollar hegemony came at the end of the 20th century with the Pax Americana after the Cold War ended. Peter Bernstein's classic book *The Power of Gold – the History of an Obsession* was published in 2001.[5] Cynical on gold's traditional monetary role surviving into the twenty-first century Bernstein concluded:

> the most striking feature of this long history is that gold led most of the protagonists of the drama into the ditch. . . . Midas . . . Croesus . . . Charles de Gaulle, and the gold bugs of the 1980s all were fools for gold, chasing an illusion. . . . Gold and its surrogates make sense only as a means to an end, to beautify, to adorn, to exchange for what we need and really want.

After the millennial stock market collapse and 9/11 Bernstein changed tack. Acknowledging in a 2002 interview that he never thought he would again recommend investors to hold positions in gold he went on to say:

> Gold has this magic quality in the worst of times as a store of value because it is stateless money . . . Gold strikes me as an extraordinary asset as a hedge to-day. You can't hedge using the US dollar because if anything is going wrong that's the thing that is going to be going the most wrong. That is what you would want to have gold for.

In 2005 Bernstein again publicly advised investors to hedge against hyperinflation with gold and in February 2008, in a video interview with the Financial Times when gold was already trading above $900 he again endorsed its utility as a hedge against extreme outcomes.[6,7,8]

The most ringing recent endorsement of gold's stateless money franchise came from Alan Greenspan in 1997 when, as Chairman of the US Federal Reserve, he was the world's most powerful central banker. In testimony to a Congressional Committee he advised against selling any of America's gold in Fort Knox because 'gold still represents the ultimate form of payment in the world. Fiat money in extremis is accepted by nobody. Gold is always accepted.'

Crisis and Financial Market Risk Insurance

It is highly improbable, but not impossible, that in our lifetimes we will experience the unthinkable. A terrorist, military, economic, nuclear, environmental or financial market disaster that disrupts banking and civic systems and leaves us dependant for survival on owning something that can readily be exchanged for things we need to survive. In that situation nothing will be as useful as gold.[9] We know that over the centuries owning some in times of crisis saved many families from starvation and despair. Calamities in the twentieth century included two World Wars, the Cold War with the threat of nuclear confrontation, serial regional wars and several episodes of hyperinflation. The best remembered hyperinflation was in the German Weimar Republic in 1923 when the value of the currency was totally obliterated. Economic and social chaos followed. In its wake came the Nazis and World War II. Currently post Saddam Iraq is experiencing inflation of over 70% with its new currency – and that is after decimation in the value of its old currency only a few years ago. Zimbabwe is experiencing hyperinflation of over hundreds of thousands percent. Granted, comparing Iraq or Zimbabwe with a major international power like Germany is not comparing apples with apples. But Iraq has amongst the world's largest oil reserves and should be prospering. Zimbabwe is richly endowed with resources and was prospering until a few decades ago.

Most of us find it unthinkable that anything catastrophic will happen to us. We don't warm to the idea of hoarding gold as protection against our paper money becoming worthless. Yet, as risks to our personal safety and financial security have magnified since 9/11, we would probably consider some crisis insurance if it was on offer from a conventional insurer. To give effective protection the insurer will have to be in a position to settle claims instantly after a crisis and, if necessary, to settle in gold or another precious metal. Preferably gold. No insurer could guarantee that. And if promises on those lines were made in the sales puff the policy small print would certainly provide otherwise. For insurance against the unthinkable we have to own and possess gold. Stateless money that will keep its value even in the worst of times. Keeping even a small amount in your personal control will afford instant protection whenever you need it. Larger holdings in secure warehouses in any of the world's major financial capitals can be arranged with organisations that simplify all aspects of buying, storing and selling at low costs.[10]

You know your circumstances and must assess how you would deal with the consequences of an unthinkable disaster. I can't call the odds for you. The eccentric seventeenth century French mathematician and philosopher Blaise Pascal is remembered for his studies on gambling and calling the odds for a wager on the existence of God. He argued that you have to think about the consequences when you die if you made the wrong choice in your lifetime about the existence of

God. If there is no God it will be immaterial if you lived your life sinfully or righteously. But if God exists the difference will be profound. You will have the possibility of salvation if you lived a righteous life. But if you lived a sinful life you face eternal damnation. Needless to say salvation is preferable to damnation. Pascal abandoned high living, philosophy and mathematics and went live in a monastery.[11] His wager has been ridiculed in a religious context. But his conclusion that the best bet is the one that protects you from dire consequences is worth taking on board. Pascal was concerned with eternal damnation. We are concerned with poverty, distress and even starvation for our families.

If you own gold bought as insurance you can sell it if the time comes when you expect blue skies will be with you for the rest of your life. The insurance may even be free if you get more than it cost to buy and hold. If you get less, the loss will represent the cost of the security that came with owning it. Or, instead of selling, you could bequeath it to your heirs for their protection.

A Niche Investment

As a scarce natural resource gold is a small niche investing opportunity in a gigantic $150 trillion pool of financial assets.[12] As it lasts forever and does not degrade, almost all the 150 000 tonnes of gold mined since the days of the Pharaohs are believed to still exist somewhere on the planet as jewellery, bullion, coins, artefacts or scrap (to convert tonnes to ounces, etc., see page 275). If it was re-smelted into flat tightly stackable bars it would all fit in a square cube with about 18 meter sides. That is all six sides each about three meters shorter than the length of a tennis court. Priced at $600 an ounce the cube will be worth about $3 trillion. Fabricated gold objects and scrap are constantly re-smelted back into bullion and traded back onto the market. If the price is tempting enough it is guesstimated that as much as half the world's above ground gold stock could find its way back to the market and then be accessible to investors. This half includes gold in the manufacture and supply chain of jewellery manufacturers and other fabricators, gold bullion in storage vaults held for national treasuries, central banks, organisations, gold funds, companies and individuals as well as similar items and personal jewellery and ornaments kept in safe deposit boxes, jewel boxes or under mattresses. But regardless of how high the gold price might climb the other half of the world's stock of mined gold is not going to find its way back to the market. This half includes national and artistic treasures, religious artefacts, jewellery masterpieces, heirlooms and treasured personal possessions. If the broad-brush estimates used above are reliable, all the above ground gold in the world potentially accessible to central banks and investors is worth about $1.5 trillion.[13] About 1% of the pool of financial assets. Financial assets are growing at over 7% a year and are expected to reach $200 trillion by 2010. Mining only adds 2% to 2.5% a year to the world's gold stock. By 2010 it may be worth $2 trillion. Still only about 1% of financial assets. Over the years the disparity in growth rates and the law of large numbers will widen the gap between the value of the pool of global financial assets and the world's stock of gold.

Scarcity keeps gold valuable. Unlike paper money it can't be printed to order. Currencies not backed by precious metals or other 'specie' have a bad record of ending up worth less and less over the years and eventually even ending up worthless. The dollar lost over 98% of its purchasing power in the twentieth century. Other major currencies fared no better. The Nobel Laureate Economist Professor Robert Mundell tells us currency erosion is nothing new. After kings and other potentates first introduced coins as substitutes for ingots of precious metals over two millennia ago it did not take long before they started to water down their precious metals content. Mundell concludes 'the conventional wisdom that coins were first stamped to confirm their weight and thus provide a convenience for their subjects is sheer nonsense . . . the earliest function of coinage was profit for the state'. The ancients, he notes, 'succumbed to the fiscal temptation of replacing intrinsic money with overvalued currency. But they did not know when to stop. How far could the precious metals be replaced without running the risk of inconvertibility, depreciation and inflation?'[14] Questions on rather similar lines to those being asked again about the dollar and other fiat currencies.

Squaring a Valuation Circle

Gold's safe haven credentials in times of hyperinflation are not in question. But it is a myth that it is always a safe haven and always a good hedge against inflation. Unless prices are rising rapidly over short time frames it can be a poor indicator of inflation and, if it is bought at an unrealistic price, it can't be a safe haven. Consider the plight of anyone who still holds gold bought in 1980 when a speculative frenzy catapulted prices to peak above $850. Allowing only for consumer price inflation they will need almost $2000 in 2006 to recover the $850 paid in 1980, without any return on capital for over a quarter of a century. Almost $10 000 will be needed if, instead of a consumer price index, the Dow Jones Industrial Average is the comparative yardstick. The Dow was under 1000 in 1980 and closed above 23 000 at the end of 2007. Gold looks even more like the poor relation if real estate prices in London, California or other favoured locations are used for comparison. Well over $25 000 will be needed to match an outlay of $850 in 1980.

As gold is a sterile asset that pays no interest, yields no dividends and costs money to keep, there is a valuation circle to square before it can qualify as an investment – unless it is bought at a price low enough for a realistic prospect of profit from a sale at a higher price. Otherwise the circle can only be squared if indirect benefits come with ownership. With gold jewellery benefits can be the pleasure of wearing it and transferring wealth with it. With gold bought as crisis insurance the benefit is obviously protection. And when it is introduced into a portfolio of financial assets the benefit comes from spreading risk by not having all your eggs in the same basket. A rising tide lifts all boats and when sentiment in financial markets is positive gold prices may also be strong. But when sentiment is negative money usually flows in the direction of gold and prices tend to rise. The gold price is expected to soar if financial markets run into serious trouble.

Leading Questions on Reasonable Prices

In India, China and other societies where it is still culturally associated with money, wealth, savings and security people may still be as unquestioning about gold as they are about religion. They just believe in it. If the price is a mystery – perhaps so much the better. Families traditionally accumulate savings by hoarding valuable gold jewellery, coins and gold bars and in many interpretations of Sharia law, regardless of what happens to the marriage, jewellery remains the property of the wife. It is not unusual for a bride in prosperous Saudi Arabia to wear a few kilograms of gold jewellery. But in the West we are not believers. We are sceptics. Investing can only make sense when prices are reasonable. We can speculate on an asset with a mysterious price. But we can't invest in it.

There are two sides of the gold coin for investors. One side is for gold as a commodity and the other for gold as a financial asset or stateless money. A useful perspective on the two sides of the coin comes from this unscientific remark made by Professor Andrew Lo: 'Physics has three laws that explain ninety nine percent of the phenomena and economics has ninety nine laws that explain three percent of the phenomena.' As a commodity, gold is in the physical domain where cause and effect relationships are transparent. Research on gold as a commodity is focused on the mining industry and demand from mainly jewellery manufacturers. But as a financial asset or stateless money it is in the domain of economics and macroeconomics where cause and effect relationships are opaque. The main research focus for this side of the coin is on the dollar. It has usurped gold's role in the monetary system and the US economy commands the world economic stage. Outcomes and expected outcomes for the dollar and the US economy are likely to affect the gold price and not vice versa. The tail can't wag the dog.

Part One 'Demystifying the Gold Price' includes this Introduction and a further nine chapters presented as essays with analysis and an associated leading question. The first five chapters are background information on gold and legacy global monetary arrangements from the twentieth century:

1 Introduction: Why Gold?
2 The Gold Mining Industry: *What gold price gives producers a worthwhile profit?*
3 Gold Supply and Demand: *Do central banks still need gold and does gold still need central banks?*
4 The Rise and Fall of the Gold Standard: *Did gold cause the great depression?* and
5 The Dollar Standard and the 'Deficit without Tears': *Is the dollar again America's currency and everyone else's problem?*

The next five chapters address the twenty-first century economic uncertainties that have come in the wake of 9/11. The distinguished French Arabist commentator Gilles Kepel described 9/11 at the time as a 'seismic event with incalculable consequences (that) exposed the fragility of the United States empire, exploded the myth of its invincibility, and called into question all the certainties and beliefs that had ensured the triumph of the American civilisation in the twentieth century'.[15] President Bush responded with vigorous military and economic initiatives.

6 The Economic Consequences of 9/11 and George W. Bush: *For how long will Asians go on lending for Americans to go on spending?*

Chapters 7, 8, 9 and 10 examine different scenarios that may play out on the world economic stage, how they can affect us, what we can do to insulate ourselves from adverse outcomes and when gold can be usefully introduced into our risk management strategies:

7 The End of Cheap Oil, 'Chindia' and Other Tipping Points to Instability: *Will alternative energy come to the rescue?*
8 Globalisation and Global Economic Rebalancing: *Can the International Monetary Fund avoid global financial meltdown?*[16]
9 Gold Prices: Inflation, Deflation, Booms and Busts: *Do trees grow to Heaven?*
10 Investing Choices: *What gold?*

There are times when owning physical gold is a suitable investment but physical gold is always sterile. By contrast gold mining shares can also be growth investments and owning shares that invest in gold mining shares can be more rewarding and more tax efficient than owning physical gold via shares in an Exchange Traded Fund. Part Two of this book written by Frank Holmes, the Chief Executive and Chief Investing officer of US Global Investors takes the reader through the day to day disciplines and processes of managing and optimising investments in gold mining shares. In the following chapters he includes analysis on gold fund strategies, supply and demand for gold, mining costs, investment timing, stock picking, investment monitoring and the resources that are needed to successfully manage investments in gold mining companies.

11 Inside US Global Investors
12 Investing in Gold Equities
13 Gold Mining: Opportunities and Threats

The Goldwatcher blog on www.thegoldwatcher.com will continue commenting on developments relating to the contents of this book and serving as a supplementary information resource with up to date data and information.

Credible Analysis and Commentary

The media buzzed with excitement when the gold price jumped to $535 in December 2005, its highest level in nearly twenty-five years. In an article in *The Guardian* newspaper headlined 'Gold Sparkles as Never Before' Pierre Lassonde, the President of Newmont Mining, one of the world's biggest gold mining companies and at the time the driving force behind the industry's marketing initiatives, commented 'the market is hot and it's going to get hotter'. Simon Weeks, the Chairman of the London Bullion Market Association, cautioned 'when the froth dies down I think people will take a step back and say we are overextended'. I was quoted in the same article commenting that the run up to $500 was expected. Financial assets tend to revert to mean and the long-term inflation adjusted average price for gold at the time was $540.[17] Yet there was chatter at the time that the next stop would be $1000. A target no analyst would take seriously without a major crisis as a catalyst.

Since January 1994 the London Bullion Market Association (LBMA) have sponsored and published annual forecasts from respected analysts on gold, silver, platinum and palladium with the analysts' reasons for their conclusions.[18] Twenty-nine analysts contributed to the LBMA forecast for 2007. Their averaged expected gold price was $720, about 16% higher than the $603 average chalked up in 2006. But there were big differences between the highs, lows and averages in the individual contributions.

The highest and lowest forecasts for 2006 were:

Analyst	High	Low	Average
Norman Ross: The Bullion Desk	$760	$520	$618
Jeffrey M Christian: CPM: New York	$580	$425	$479
Outcomes for 2006	$725	$525	$603

The 2007 forecasts by Norman Ross, the most bullish and accurate forecaster in 2006, and Jeffrey Christian, the most bearish, are revealing. Norman Ross remained bullish and forecast gold would trade in a range between $580 and $850 and average $716 over the year. This comment accompanied his prescient forecast:

> We remain manifestly bullish for gold. Over the last five years gold has notched up a successive 23%, 25%, 5%, 20% and now a 23% rise; for 2007 we expect the gold price to rise by a comparatively modest 18% with a possible spike to an all time high of $850. Whilst a weakening US dollar, stagnating mine production, buoyant oil prices, ongoing geopolitical tension and the spectre of inflation may provide a positive backdrop we expect that sentiment will also be supported by institutional investor demand growth . . . However the fragmentation of the gold market that follows in consequence may well lead to increasing problems with liquidity and thus price volatility is also expected to remain high.

Jeffrey Christian who was bearish in 2006 turned bullish for 2007. He forecast that gold would trade in a range between $550 and $850 over the year and average $616. In his opinion:

> The gold market remains very tight on a physical basis. Mine production is not increasing as rapidly as had been expected due to bottlenecks in starting new mines and expansions. These are coming on stream but they are coming more slowly than had been expected by the mining industry. Central bank sales meanwhile are declining as central banks have sold much of the gold they wish to sell. This tightening of supply has run into investment demand that has remained high, and risen, reaching record volumes in 2006. While investment demand may cool somewhat in 2007, investors are expected to find enough economic and political developments around the world to keep them interested in gold as a safe haven.

The average gold price in the forecasts made for the LBMA for 2008 is $860 and over half the analysts expect the price will at times be over $1000.[19]

Analysts are agreed on the tight supply and demand dynamic for gold. However there is no support among them for the conclusions published by the French investment bank Cheuveux in January 2006 that challenged the consensus belief that the world's central banks and monetary authorities still owned about 30 000 tonnes of gold they were free to deal with in any way they chose to.[20] Cheuveux's studies concluded that over half the disclosed central bank holdings were already allocated to forward sales commitments leaving unencumbered holdings of only about 15 000 tonnes. Cheuveux no longer publish analysis on precious metals and it has not been possible to update their opinions but they suggested in their report that gold prices could spike to $2000 or even higher if central banks were put under pressure by traders aware of their forward sales commitments, or if anxieties about the US economy grew and concluded with the astute observation that 'gold comes out of hiding when the risk of a financial crisis in terms of inflation or deflation rises'.

The annual LBMA forecast is a useful base for access to analysis on gold inside a current year and, as they publish their forecasts going back three years, we can also assess the consistency of any analyst. Credible analysis is also published by other accessible and at times more current sources. The US Funds Website covering funds managed by Frank Holmes is also a treasure chest of analysis and current information.[21]

US Deficits and Missions Possible and Impossible

Frustrated by economists who hedged their bets with the characteristic caveat '. . . on the other hand' American President Harry S. Truman once demanded 'give me a one armed economist'. From 2001 to 2006 President Bush never had that problem. His appointees were there to do his bidding. If they had other ideas their appointments ended. A few months before the November 2004 US Presidential elections, Martin Wolf, an associate editor of the *Financial Times* and its chief economics commentator expressed the concerns held by many economists about the Bush administration when he wrote:

> Let's be blunt about it. The US is now on the comfortable path to ruin. It is being driven along a road of ever rising deficits and debt both external and fiscal, that risk is destroying the country's credit and the global role of its currency . . . Politicians wait until crises hit. Statesmen foresee them and act to prevent them. What is the chance of such a statesman emerging after the election? Almost none, I fear.[22]

By mid 2006 not only was Bush's misguided 2003 announcement of 'mission accomplished' in Iraq tarnishing his image but economists were also convinced he would be unable to enlist the support of an internationally respected Treasury Secretary to steer the US off the road to ruin. In April 2005 Bush surprised markets with an announcement that he was nominating as Treasury Secretary Henry Paulson, the Chairman of investment bankers Goldman Sachs.

Paulson is no one armed economist. He would not have accepted the responsibilities of public office without assurances on his authority and the general expectations were that he commanded the skills and stature to negotiate internationally and domestically on behalf of the US. I first became aware of his exceptional talent in 2000 when I was commissioned by the *Sunday Business* newspaper to write an article on Goldman Sachs's first year as a public company. There was no doubt then about the direction in which he would steer the company and I expected that if anyone could get to grips with the runaway US deficits he would. However, by the end of 2007, Paulson was humbled by the investment banking crisis that came in the wake of the housing bubble deflating and was unable to secure bi-partisan support for initiatives to correct the nation's deficits and get the US economy back on a safe course.

We tend to underestimate the risks that come with US financial deficits. This extraordinarily revealing analysis on the risks was given in 2001 by Robert McTeer, at the time President of the Dallas Federal Reserve:[23]

> What is my opinion of the current account deficit? . . . To some extent, the world has long been willing to hold the excess dollars that we put out by buying more than we sell to the rest of the world. And we get sort of a free ride. Sort of like we're in a poker game and we never have to cash in our chips. . . . The problem will come when people change their mind about all that and they've decided, maybe suddenly, that the world has too many excess dollars. . . . I don't know exactly what would happen, but it wouldn't be good. But we've had the potential for that to happen for several years now and it hasn't. Most of the countries that own a lot of the dollar balances don't have any real incentive to trigger a crisis like that. They would perhaps be hurt as much as anybody else by such a crisis. What is it they say: 'If you owe the bank a little money, you've got a problem. If you owe it a lot of money, the bank's got a problem.' We might be in that situation.[24]

In 2004 Richard Fischer, Robert McTeer's successor at the Dallas Federal Reserve, also played down concerns in financial markets about the widening US current account gap. He said it reflected robust US consumption, a key factor driving export growth in the rest of the world, and asked:

Where would the world be if Americans did not live out their proclivity to consume everything that looks good, feels good, sounds good, tastes good? . . . We provide a service for the rest of the world. If we were running a current account surplus or trade surplus, what would happen to economic growth worldwide and what would be the economic consequences? So I think we are doing our duty there.

Though McTeer's and Fischer's comments were brash and unconventional for central bankers, and were certainly not the kind of remarks Paulson would have made, there were some truths in what they had to say. Now, as investors, we have to concern ourselves with what is bound to happen as Americans find they can't afford to 'live out their proclivity to consume everything that looks good, feels good, sounds good and tastes good' and when eventually McTeer's 'free ride' poker game comes to an end and the poker chips have to be accounted for. Will the US have the money to pay everything it owes, or be able to borrow if it hasn't got the funds to settle up, or will it just print dollars as necessary to clear the books? And what should we be doing now to protect ourselves from the vicious circle of value destruction that will follow if the US gets into funding difficulties?

The former US Comptroller General, the Hon. David Walker, has this advice to give: 'Keep in mind the passengers on the Titanic had a smooth ride and a great time until the very moment the ship hit the iceberg.' Walker is the public official responsible for auditing the US Federal accounts. He has added up the numbers and is anxious and militant. Multi trillion dollar debt burdens threaten America's role as the world's most powerful economy and prospects for the world economy and impose a 'birth tax' on future generations. From 2000 to 2005 explicit and implicit commitments by the US Government more than doubled from $20.4 trillion to $50.5 trillion.[25]

Most of us can't make any sense of $ signs followed by trailing banners of zeros. This analogy gives some insight into the enormity of the numbers: One billion seconds equals 32 years. One trillion seconds equals 300 centuries. Walker has been conducting a 'wake up campaign' to get public support for solving problems that won't be solved, 'until the majority of the people believe you have a problem that needs to be solved'. He is committed to making sure that no serious candidate for the US Presidency in 2008 will be able to duck financial realities in his or her electoral campaign. The best he expected from his initiatives before the next Presidential election was to 'slow the bleeding'. For someone warning that on its present course the US could go broke, it looked rather like rearranging the deck chairs on the Titanic. Since 5 January 2007 when President Bush's political opponents, the Democrats, took control of the US Senate and House, Walker's comments will have had more clout.

The Road to Global Economic Rebalancing

Questions about the solvency of the US have been asked before. Often. And we don't take them seriously. Whatever the challenges, we expect that the resilient US economy and the robust dollar will always come out on top. But Walker is not the only informed expert sounding the alarm. In a study published by The Federal Reserve Bank of St Louis in July 2006 Professor Lawrence J. Kotlikoff of Boston University warns against scoffing at the notion that the US could go broke. His analysis, in line with other credible research, warns that unless the US economy, and with it the world economy, is pulled back from the brink the unthinkable will happen. Kotlikoff's calculations reveal that providing for unfunded entitlement commitments and paying off the existing US deficit will require either an immediate doubling of personal and corporate income taxes, a two thirds cut in Social Security and Medicare benefits or some combination of the two. Fortunately he is not addressing an imminent crisis. His analysis, like Walker's, is intended to warn policymakers that the ship of state on its present fiscal course is heading for the rocks. It is not yet too late for course corrections by the United States and the world's other major economies.

On the positive side Paulson, Walker and other dedicated public office holders have enhanced influence with political power in the United States split between the Bush administration and legislature. The US is the global superpower, its economy has formidable strengths and the global economy has experienced above trend growth. The world's great powers are committed to economic growth and global institutions, including the International Monetary Fund, exist to support cooperation. Paulson, by profession an investment banker with a consummate knowledge of global capital markets, has skills in his profession and as a politician and statesman. He was expected to shine a spotlight on domestic and international commitments, initiate a programme of strategic co-operation with China, encourage currency re-alignments and open markets but he has so far been unable to secure bi-partisan cooperation on entitlement and fiscal reforms. And, again on the negative side, the US is no longer as it used to be the world's largest creditor. Instead it is the world's largest debtor, borrower and spender.

The appreciation of China's currency the US seeks may not be in China's or its own interests. Protectionist sentiment has been growing in the US. Parallel issues on world trade are unresolved. Domestic constituencies have radically different priorities to reconcile. Implementing major policy changes in the US now won't be possible until a new President is elected in 2008 with a clear mandate for change. And, for some time after the US 2008 Presidential elections, the fallout from wars in Iraq and Afghanistan and other conflicts in the Middle East will continue to destabilise the region and disrupt world oil supplies. With the euro now well established as an international currency, countries with vast international reserves also have an alternative safe haven currency to the dollar for the first time since the dollar came to dominate global currency markets over half a century ago.

If we look ahead over the next decade the probability of a global economy less dependent on a runaway US balance of trade deficit is high. But the probability of outcomes that don't result in a substantial dollar depreciation are extremely low. As are the chances of any quick fixes. The road to global rebalancing is likely to be a multi decade marathon with competitors fighting it out over the distance.

Why Gold Makes Sense Now

Analysis in Chapter 8 'Globalisation and Global Economic Rebalancing' reveals how the US current account deficit has more or less financed itself up to now. Central banks of dollar surplus countries have been buying the surplus dollars coming into their countries to prevent their domestic currencies from appreciating. Then, to earn interest on their money, they have recycled their dollars back into US dollar denominated investments. This explains why Robert McTeer could say ' . . . we get sort of a free ride. Sort of like we're in a poker game and we never have to cash in our chips.' But because the US can't keep on going deeper and deeper into debt forever the game can't go on forever. The day for settling up will inevitably come sooner or later. The advent of Sovereign Wealth Funds in dollar surplus countries will also have to be factored in to future expectations on creditors' intentions and plans to limit their losses on dollar holdings.

Gold bugs expect that when the time comes for settling up Dr Ben Bernanke, now the US Federal Reserve Board Chairman, will recklessly print money and pay whatever the nominal amount of the debt is with a devalued currency. They have been convinced this will happen since 2002 when, shortly after being appointed a US Federal Reserve Governor, Bernanke gave a speech titled 'Deflation: Making sure it won't happen here'. This sentence from his 5000 word speech was provocative: 'but the U.S. government has a technology called a printing press (or, today, its electronic equivalent), that allows it to produce as many U.S. dollars as it wishes at essentially no cost.' Bernanke certainly made it crystal clear that, if necessary to stop deflation taking hold, the US will print as much money as is necessary. Few economists will disagree it would be the right thing to do. However, while the idea that Bernanke is committed to an irresponsible course is wide of the mark, adverse developments following the US sub prime mortgage and associated unregulated shadow banking crisis suggest Bernanke will continue to find it necessary to print money to fend off deflation.

Bernanke's opinion in April 2005 that the time for settling up with international creditors was not imminent. In a speech 'The Global Saving Glut and the U.S. Current Account Deficit' he made the case that over the past decade globalisation and a 'global saving glut' have been behind the increased US current account deficit. In his opinion the US deficit was 'the tail of the dog' responding to globalisation, rising asset prices worldwide and increased personal incomes and savings. But he also emphasised that 'the current pattern of international capital flows – should it persist – could prove counterproductive. Most important, for the developing world to be lending large sums on net to the mature industrial economies is quite undesirable as a long-run proposition.' His conclusion, particularly after the word 'however,' is worth taking on board: '[f]undamentally, I see no reason why the whole process should not proceed smoothly. *However,* the risk of a disorderly adjustment in financial markets always exists, and the appropriately conservative approach for policymakers is to be on guard for any such developments.'[26]

As investors and savers we are also policy makers and must be 'on guard' for developments that affect us. In his Global Savings Glut speech Bernanke acknowledged that to repay foreign creditors, as it must someday, the United States would need 'large and healthy export industries'. Surely that will be a mission impossible without a substantial fall in the exchange rate of the dollar. And can we afford to bet on no 'disorderly adjustment' roiling financial markets – or should we take 'an appropriately conservative approach'? Martin Wolf has warned of 'a brutal and sudden correction' if at any time the rest of the world decides that its holdings of dollar claims are excessive. In his opinion: 'the chance of a hard landing, with unpredictable political consequences in the United States and among its creditors though not 100% is not zero either'.[27]

Owning some gold bought at a reasonable price can be useful to spread risks and insulate assets from damage caused by a financial crisis. In 1934 when gold was still the universal measure of value and the US Treasury could not meet its commitments President Franklin D. Roosevelt devalued the dollar to gold by 47%. After President Richard Nixon ran into trouble in 1971 and reneged on all commitments to gold the market price of an ounce of gold rose within a decade from an average of $35 to over $600. Nixon imposed a surcharge of 15% on all imports to force negotiated dollar devaluations of more than 20% against other currencies. In 1985 President Ronald Reagan's Treasury Secretary James Baker negotiated the Plaza Accord with Germany, France, Britain, Canada and Japan that made it possible for the floating dollar to fall 30% over the next two years. The current round of global rebalancing may be resolved with a 'soft landing' but, if history is anything to go by, the dollar and other currencies are on course to losing purchasing power.

Should we be looking back at history? After all the author Thomas Friedman sees globalisation as having changed the world so radically that he has written a best selling book titled *The World is Flat*. The chapter in his book 'The Unflat World' explains that, actually, everything hasn't changed. Here is a key paragraph:[28]

> But another barrier to the flattening of the world is emerging . . . a natural resource constraint. If millions of people from India, China, Latin America and the former Soviet Union who were living largely outside the flat world start to walk onto the flat world playing field at once – and all come with their own dream of owning a car, a house, a refrigerator, a microwave and a toaster – we are going to experience either a serious energy shortage, or worse, wars over energy that would have a profoundly un-flattening effect on the world.

Insight into the Post 9/11 World and the Jihad against America

To better understand 9/11 and its aftermath we have to look beyond Osama bin Laden and Al Qaeda. The US had enemies in many quarters prior to 9/11 including the scattered community of 'Afghan Arabs' who joined the Afghan jihad against Soviet Russia in the 1980s. It's ironic that they were funded largely by the CIA and others to join the Afghan Mujahideen but, after Soviet Russia was defeated, they were totally ignored. I draw attention to them because they are among elements that were dangerous before 9/11 and still are.

In his book *Taliban*[29] Ahmed Rashid, a journalist who has covered Afghanistan for over a quarter of a century, tells us that between 1982 and 1992 some 35 000 Muslin radicals from 43 Islamic countries in the Middle East, North and East Africa, Central Asia and the Far East joined forces with the Afghan Mujahideen fighting a guerrilla war against Soviet Russia. Tens of thousands more foreign Muslim radicals came to study in madrassas in Pakistan. Eventually according to some estimates as many as 100 000 Muslim radicals came in contact with jihadists in Pakistan and Afghanistan. It's worth pausing here for a moment and noting that among the 100 000 radicals were a significant number of potential warriors in a holy war, Mujahideen, terrorists, insurgents or whatever else they may be called at different times.[30] In Afghanistan the camps where they lived, studied and trained became virtual universities for Islamic radicalism. Yet neither the CIA nor the intelligence organisations of other countries funding the Afghan jihad against Soviet Russia considered the consequences of bringing together thousands of radicals from all over the world until, as Rashid reminds us, American citizens 'woke up to the consequences when Afghanistan-trained Islamic militants blew up the World Trade Centre in New York in 1993, killing six people and injuring 1000'.

Funding for the Afghan jihad came from several sources – mainly Saudi Arabia, Pakistan and the United States through the CIA. Saudi Arabia supported the jihadists for religious reasons and as a way to get disgruntled radicals out of their own communities. Pakistan funded them to cement its position at the centre of the Islamic world and the United States funded them so that they, instead of American soldiers, would fight the Soviet Union.[31] Robert Gates, a former Director of the CIA and now the United States Defense Secretary, writes in his book *From the Shadows* that in 1985–1986 'we began to learn of a significant increase in the number of Arab nationals from other countries who had travelled to Afghanistan to fight in the Holy War against the Soviets . . . We examined ways to increase their participation, perhaps in the form of some sort of international brigade but nothing came of it.' It's not surprising nothing came of that idea but the following comment from Mr Gates beggars belief: 'Years later, these fundamentalist fighters trained by the Mujahideen in Afghanistan would begin to show up around the world, from the Middle East to New York city, still fighting their Holy War – only including the United States among their enemies. Our mission was to push the Soviets out of Afghanistan. We expected post-Soviet Afghanistan to be ugly, but never considered that it would become a haven for terrorists worldwide.'[32] Did Mr Gates really think the band of religious zealots fighting the Soviets were modelling themselves on a Boy Scout Brigade committed to upholding Western values of liberal democracy? Surely not.

Gilles Kepel tells us the militant Islamic Palestinian University Professor Abdallah Azzam was a key figure among the Afghan Arabs. Mr Gates and everyone engaged in the issue must have known that Azzam, funded again directly by Saudi Arabia and indirectly by the CIA, had founded a 'Bureau of Services Maktab al-Khidamat', for the foreign Mujahideen in 1984. Azzam made no secret of his extreme views. He was a spiritual father of the global jihad with a mission to educate and promote the cause of militant Islam. His publication *Al Jihad*, distributed throughout the Arabic-speaking world, was translated into English and other European languages.

Azzam decreed that defending the land of Muslims was each man's most important duty and the faithful committed a *capital sin* if they did not participate in the Afghan Holy War. After victory in Afghanistan, he wrote, 'the jihad will remain an individual obligation until all other lands which formerly were Muslim come back to us and Islam reigns within them once again. Before us lie Palestine, Bukhara, Lebanon, Chad, Eritrea, Somalia, the Philippines, Burma, South Yemen, Tashkent, Andalusia . . . Our presence in Afghanistan today does not mean that we have forgotten Palestine. Palestine is our beating heart. It comes even before Afghanistan in our minds, our feelings and our faith.'[33] His long-term goal was the re-establishment of the Islamic Caliphate. In 1924, the Ottoman Sultan was relieved of his role as Caliph of the Islamic world by Turkish arch-secularist Mustapha Kemal, bringing an end to any sort of central authority in Islam. Muslims, in Azzam's opinion, should not wait for the re-establishment of the

Caliphate to pursue jihad. On the contrary jihad was the 'safest path' for the establishment of the universal leadership of the Caliphate.[34]

Osama bin Laden first met Azzam when he was taught by him at a University in Saudi Arabia. Though from time to time there were disagreements between them they worked closely together in Afghanistan and, after Azzam's assassination in 1987, bin Laden took responsibility for Azzam's organisation, the precursor to Al Qaeda. In 1998 religious groups associated with bin Laden and Al Qaeda endorsed Azzam's fatwa: 'The ruling to kill the Americans and their allies – civilians and military – is an individual duty for every Muslim who can do it in any country in which it is possible to.' Bin Laden, obviously seeking access to weapons of mass destruction, declared: 'It would be a sin for Muslims not to try to possess the weapons that would prevent infidels from inflicting harm on Muslims. Hostility towards America is a religious duty and we hope to be rewarded for it by God.' In the early 1990s Egyptian intelligence reported that he was training a thousand militants, a second generation of the Arab Afghans, to bring about an Islamic revolution in Arab countries.

Filling in the dots between Azzam, bin Laden, Al Qaeda and 9/11 reveals a sequence of events that, if written in a novel, would be dismissed as too fanciful to be credible. The tale includes the activities of a cocaine smoking, womanising US Congressman and committee chairman Charlie Wilson who played a unique role in garnering support for the Afghan Mujahideen. The film Charlie Wilson's War released in 2008 is based on the book *Charlie Wilson's War*.[35] A Faustian pact that was also made when Richard Perel, Under Secretary of Defense in Ronald Reagan's government, committed support for the Afghan rebels while Osama bin Laden and Ayman al-Zawahiri were in training camps in Pakistan and Afghanistan undergoing a makeover as freedom fighters against the Soviet army. In a recent interview Gilles Kepel commented that Americans don't want to be reminded that help from the Reagan administration made jihadism possible, then and now, and jihadists don't like to be reminded that without the shoulder borne Stinger Missiles supplied by the US the Soviet forces would never have been defeated.[36]

The above comments on the jihad against America are important for investors. When George Bush is no longer in office a new President may have the charisma to inspire a new understanding with militant elements still committed to a jihad against 'the great Satan'. But, even after George Bush's many misjudgements, let's remember that since 9/11 the US has been at war and it's not a war that it started. In managing our affairs we have to draw the line between the pre 9/11 world when the US was at peace and the post 9/11 world with the US at war, and currencies of countries engaged in war tend to be weak.

2

The Gold Mining Industry

What gold price gives producers a worthwhile profit?

Gold Mining Past and Present

An element in the earth's crust as old as the planet, gold has been mined and crafted by artisans since antiquity. It is soft, malleable, can be drawn into fine wire and hammered into incredibly thin sheets of gold leaf. Since the beginnings of recorded history priests, kings, and other privileged leaders have cherished it as a symbol of power and have controlled the mining of gold in their domains. It's estimated that in Biblical times about 30 000 ounces of gold were mined annually for ornamentation, jewellery, religious artefacts, tomb decoration and the like. The Bible has over four hundred references to gold.

In *The Power of Gold*[1] Peter Bernstein reminds us that when Moses came down from Mount Sinai he found his people 'in delirium worshipping a golden calf' and, in a fit of rage, he smashed the tablets with the Ten Commandments. Bernstein also describes religious and ceremonial use of gold in ancient times as 'a medium for advertising power – wealth, eminence and proximity to the gods'. Nowadays, with citizen journalism, they wouldn't have got away with that masquerade. Slave mine workers lived and worked in appalling and brutal conditions and were worked and whipped to death.

The Chronology in the Fact Book traces the history of gold from the 5th millennium BC when it was first used in Mesopotamia for the manufacture of 'sacred, ornamental and decorative instruments' through to the twenty-first century. The first coins that became the standard for worldwide trade and commerce were minted by Croesus, the ruler of ancient Lydia, modern day western Turkey. Augustus (31 BC–AD 14) was the first Roman Emperor to mint the gold aureus coins that contributed to the dynamic expansion of the Roman economy.

Because it is imperishable and has always been valuable almost all the gold ever mined is thought to exist above the ground in some processed state somewhere in the world. Estimates made of above ground gold accumulated over the last few centuries are 39 million ounces at the beginning of the nineteenth century; 226 million ounces at the beginning of the twentieth century; and 3 billion ounces by the beginning of the twenty-first century.[2]

It's estimated that gold mined from 1800 to 1850 totalled 1500 metric tonnes. Production surged after 1850 following new gold discoveries in the US and Australia and widespread adoption of the gold standard. By 1900 10 500 metric tonnes had been mined. Production surged again when gold from South Africa's mines came onto the market at the end of the nineteenth century and the beginning of the twentieth century.

Detailed production and demand information prepared by the gold historian and author Timothy Green on gold production and the monetary role of gold in the nineteenth and twentieth centuries is accessible on the web site of the World Gold Council.[3] These comments are from his study on gold mining capacity and monetary demand in the nineteenth century:

> This growth coincided with an era of rapid expansion in industry, trade and international banking, which gold helped to finance. The relative abundance of gold also made possible the development of the international gold standard in all major nations save China, with gold coin forming a significant part of the monetary circulation in many countries. Previously it had only been in Britain that the true gold standard ruled. 1850 is the watershed. Suddenly governments, their treasuries or central banks had unprecedented flows of gold from America and Australia, which could fill their reserves or enable their mints to make gold coins, which found their way into the pockets of millions of people world-wide, replacing the silver coins that had predominated before. A host of nations nailed the gold standard to their mast, led by Germany in 1871, followed by most European countries including France, Belgium and Switzerland by 1878. The United States dithered between a gold and a bimetallic (gold and silver) standard until 1900.

When production from new gold discoveries in the US and Australia came onto the market in the nineteenth century most countries were on a bimetallic silver and gold standard or a silver standard. Green notes that the increased supply of gold from the new discoveries underpinned worldwide acceptance of the gold standard:

Ultimately, fifty-nine countries were on a gold or gold exchange standard; only China, among major nations, remained loyal to silver. In practical terms, to accommodate the widened standard, central bank stocks of gold rose by 70% during the 1890s and at the end of the century with the shadow of war . . . many central banks and treasuries built war chests. Official reserves in France, Germany and Russia doubled between 1900 and the end of 1913; in the US they quadrupled. . . . War was a real challenge, the first true test for the gold standard. War is expensive and governments knew they would need the gold.

Green describes the gold standard as 'going into limbo' during World War I and, after the war, governments wanting to keep gold 'firmly in their own hands, not those of their citizens'. In the inter-war years between 1918 and 1939 Europe was traumatised by war, Russia succumbed to a revolution and in 1925 Britain unwisely reinstated the gold standard at the pre-war parity to gold. Unsettled conditions led to a fall in the demand for gold bullion and by 1930 gold production fell from around 700 tonnes to 500 tonnes a year.

By 1930 South Africa accounted for 53% of the world's newly mined gold. The production was destined mainly for central banks. Later in the 1930s the fragility of the inter-war monetary relationships, the Wall Street crash of 1929, the failure of Austria's Credit Anstalt Bank in 1931 and the suspension of the gold standard by Britain in 1931 led to a surge in private hoarding of gold encouraged by concerns over the security of paper money and the prospect of another war.

President Franklin D. Roosevelt was elected to office in the US in 1933 when the country was in the grip of a deflationary depression. In 1934 he raised the official price for an ounce of gold by 69.33% from $20.67 to $35 and committed the US to buy or sell gold at the $35 parity. At the appreciably higher $35 price gold production soared, doubling to a new record of 1200 tonnes by 1940. The US Treasury became the main destination for both newly mined gold and gold held by other central banks. Green calculates that 'Before the gold price rise to $35 the US held 6,070 tonnes, by 1938 it had 11,340 tonnes and by 1942 20,205 tonnes with the ultimate peak just over 22,000 tonnes in the late 1940s and early 1950s (being 75% of all monetary gold by then and half of all gold ever mined.)' In the post World War II years, as prosperity returned, West Europe's central banks also increased their gold holdings substantially. About 1000 tonnes a year of gold was mined worldwide in the 1950s, the first decade after World War II. From the 1960s production rose steadily reaching about 2400 tonnes in the 1990s.

The following chart illustrates world production and declining world reserves. Reserves are based on the following estimates made by the US Government Minerals services:[4]

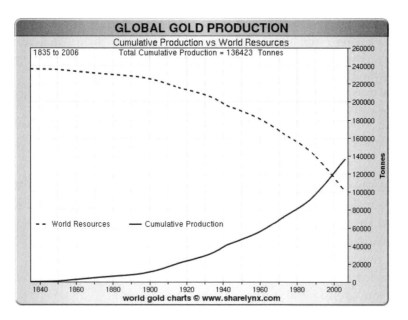

Chart 2.1 Global gold production.

Rising Costs and Declining Production

Annual gold production peaked in 2001 at 2650 metric tonnes. By 2006 it fell to 2475 metric tonnes, 6.6% off the peak. For 2008 production is forecast at about 2400 tonnes. In the following chapter, 'Gold Supply and Demand' we review the changes in sources of demand for newly mined gold after it was officially demonetised in 1971. Initially jewellery manufacturers took the place of central banks as the principal users. Over recent years investment demand has been growing with concerns over current economic uncertainties. At the same time Exchange Traded Funds (ETFs), discussed fully in the following chapter, have developed an easy and economic way for investors small and large to buy, hold and sell gold. The World Gold Council have reported that gold ETFs already hold more than 700 tonnes of gold at a current value of over $20 billion. In the third quarter of 2007 investing even overtook jewellery as the largest buyers of gold. That position is unlikely to be maintained but it's significant that it occurred.

In Chapter 13, 'Gold Mining Opportunities and Threats', Frank Holmes reviews production potential and discusses the spectrum of challenges facing gold miners. They include rising costs and risks involved in the long and uncertain process of exploration, discovery and commissioning a gold mine. Many people still have the image of gold mining as a fantasy sequence with windfall discoveries, get rich quick stories and the like. A century ago that may have been the case. Now and then prospectors and mining promoters still strike it rich and fortunes are made – and lost. But there's no more romance in gold mining now than quarrying stone. Mining involves long term investment and substantial capital.

South Africa

South Africa's output has fallen off by 41% over the last ten years. Until it was overtaken by China at the end of 2007 it was entrenched as the world's largest producer. There is little public information on China's gold resources but South Africa still has vast unmined proven reserves deep under the ground. Estimates of global gold reserves reflected in the following table point to South Africa as having about a third of the world's known reserves.

Table 2.1 World mine production, reserves and reserve base.

GOLD

World Mine Production, Reserves, and Reserve Base:

	Mine production		Reserves[7]	Reserves base[7]
	2005	2006[e]		
United States	256	260	2,700	3,700
Australia	262	260	5,000	6,000
Canada	119	120	1,300	3,500
Indonesia	225	240	1,200	4,100
Peru	140	145	1,800	2,800
Russia	208	210	3,500	4,100
South Africa	169	162	3,000	3,500
Other countries	295	270	6,000	36,000
World total (rounded)	793	840	[8]17,000	[8]26,000
	2,470	2,500	42,000	90,000

World Resources: An assessment of U.S. gold resources indicated 33,000 tons of gold in identified (15,000 tons) and undiscovered resources (18,000 tons). [9] Nearly one-quarter of the gold in undiscovered resources was estimated to be contained in porphyry copper deposits. The gold resources in the United States, however, are only a small portion of global gold resources.

http://minerals.usgs.gov/minerals/pubs/commodity/gold/gold_mcs07.pdf.
(Courtesy of world gold charts © www.sharelynx.com)

South Africa's unmined gold reserves include deposits described as marginal because they are deep underground and the grade at times is also so low that mining can only be profitably undertaken when the gold price is high, or when an established mine is already working around the same deposit and covering all overhead costs. In that situation receipts over and above the direct cash costs of working the marginal deposit are treated as profit.

However gold mining in South Africa is anything but a low cost operation. Many South African mines are already working reefs as deep as 5000 metres below the ground. The costs of mining in these conditions are exceptionally high as beyond the high costs of access in and out of the shafts for men, machinery and materials substantial additional costs are incurred for safety and ventilation. In a comment on oil prices later in this book I quote Matthew Simmons, an investment banker servicing the energy industry, who contends that from his perspective for most of the twentieth century oil was too cheap to reward producers adequately and at times it was almost free. I believe that until the link between gold and the dollar pegged at $35 an ounce in 1934 was severed in 1971, a similar conclusion would not apply in relation to gold mining in South Africa and it would not be out of place in relation to the depressed low gold price through most of the 1980s and 1990s.

Prospects for mining South African marginal resources were more promising a few years ago when the South African Rand fell in value to Rand 12/1$. But since then the South African Rand has recovered to about Rand 7/1$. Even if the pundits who forecast a gold price of $2000 or $3000 an ounce are right, prospects for mining marginal deposits will depend on what the dollar will be worth at the time the mining is undertaken. If R1 = $1 a gold price of $2000 or $3000 won't help. $10 000 might!

The Bear Market for Gold in the 1980s and 1990s

Gold prices were depressed by central bank sales and forward sales committed by producers hedging against price volatility over the 1980s and 1990s. At the end of 1999 a sales quota agreement orchestrated by the World Gold Council, The Central Bank Gold Agreement that has become known as 'The Washington Agreement', was adopted by European central banks with significant gold holdings. To stabilise the market the banks committed themselves not to reduce their gold holdings in excess of volumes the market could absorb without disruption.

Because they own about 30 000 tonnes of gold central banks are as important in the gold supply demand equation as gold miners. The Washington Agreement and other factors affecting supply and demand are discussed fully in the following chapter, 'Gold Supply and Demand'. What's important about the quota sales agreement from a mining perspective is that prior to the agreement there was little incentive for gold mining companies to fund large exploration budgets because prices were too low to warrant the high costs and risks of exploration and the high levels of investment that would be required to bring new deposits to production. Since the Washington Agreement exploration budgets were increased and with the surge in gold prices since 1971 substantial funds have been invested in exploration. The potential for new sources of gold is discussed by Frank Holmes in Chapter 13 'Gold Mining Opportunities and Threats'.

Rising Mining Costs and South Africa's Marginal Resources

Market participants tend to take a view on future gold prices in relation to what gold will be worth to buyers. Typically when investors and speculators are active buyers market prices rise. Then, when they are sellers, prices fall to levels the grass roots jewellery industry will support. However, with little prospect of substantial production increases and every chance of demand growth, we must consider the prices that reward producers. In Part Two analysis by Frank Holmes reveals rising costs and falling production from the world's traditional producers and it appears that different prices will reward producers in different situations, regions and geologies.

My knowledge of the gold mining industry relates to South Africa and recent discussions I have had with executives of gold mining companies owning substantial marginal resources. Their position appears to be that they stand to be well rewarded with prices above $600 on present values of the dollar but, before making substantial commitments to mining infrastructure, they will need to have confidence that gold prices above $600 are entrenched. From investments being made and plans announced prospects for exploitation of marginal deposits were promising. However in January 2008 gold production in South Africa suffered when the country's electricity provider Eskom found itself forced to impose cuts in services. The Goldwatcher blog www.thegoldwatcher.com will monitor and report on developments in this important issue.

3

Gold Supply and Demand

Do central banks still need gold, and does gold still need central banks?

Part One: Introduction to Gold Exchange Traded Funds

A New Dynamic in the Supply and Demand Equation

Contributed by Neil Behrmann, Editor: Exchange Traded Gold – www.exchangetradedgold.com and MarketPredict.com – www.marketpredict. com Copyright Neil Behrmann

Copyright Neil Behrmann

History of ETFs

The surge in investment in gold Exchange Traded Funds (ETFs) has exceeded analyst expectations by a wide margin. The growth of this gold product has been extraordinary. It is arguably the most significant gold investment development since gold futures and options trade began on New York's COMEX in the early seventies.

LyxOR Gold Bullion Securities (GBS) was the pioneer fund and began trading in Australia in March 2003. By the time GBS was listed in London at the end of that year, it held only a few hundred thousand ounces in trust on behalf of investors. When StreetTRACKS Gold Shares (GLD) was ready for launch in New York in mid October 2004, the amount of GBS gold holdings had risen to almost 2 million ounces worth around $900 million.

The listing of GLD on the New York Stock Exchange on 18 October 2004, defied negative expectations of some analysts, who did not believe that ETFs would have much impact on gold investment demand. The product took off and by the second quarter of 2005, bullion holdings of gold ETFs had jumped to 8 million ounces. Investment in gold ETFs surged further during the next stage of the gold bull market. Barclays' 'ishares' COMEX Gold Trust was launched in 2005. As the gold price soared from around $425 an ounce in the second quarter of 2005 to a peak of $731 an ounce early May 2006, total global gold ETF holdings rose to around 15 million ounces. By late October November 2007, bullion inventories of GLD, the market leader by far, and other products had reached around 25 million ounces worth $19 billion. 'StreetTRACKS gold has proved to be one of the fastest growing ETFs in the history of the product,' according to Dodd Kittsley, the director of ETF research at State Street Global Advisors.

Encouraged by the flows, London based ETF Securities, which has a gold product, launched numerous Exchange Traded Commodities on the London Stock Exchange in 2007, ranging from energy and base metals to soft commodities and grains. Assets and volume of trade, however, are tiny in relation to GLD.

The growth in ETF gold holdings has not been strictly correlated to movements in the bullion price. Indeed, during the extensive speculation which drove the bullion price up by 33 per cent from around $550 late March, towards the May top of $731, ETF gold holdings rose by only a few hundred thousand ounces. This contrasted with a surge in the open interest on Comex, the New York futures and options exchange. The small increase at the time illustrated that gold ETFs attracted medium and long term gold investors wary of speculative runs and not prepared to chase prices. When gold tumbled in volatile conditions in May and June of 2006 Gold ETF investors didn't dump their gold. ETF holdings fell back by less than 5 per cent. Moreover when gold had another leg downwards to around $560 during the Northern hemisphere summer months of that year, investors buying caused ETF gold holdings to rise to around 16 million ounces. By the early winter they were above 17 million ounces. Similar trends were evident during general market downturns during the northern hemisphere 2007 summer credit crisis. Bargain hunters at the time recognised an opportunity as the price recovered sharply to around $760 an ounce late October 2007.

Major gold ETF liquidity

The gold ETF market is now exceedingly liquid. Large and small investors can easily trade in and out of gold ETFs as each share comprises one tenth of an ounce of gold. GLD, for example, averaged $433 million a day in the third quarter of 2007 with institutions, individual investors and hedge funds all active. Morgan Stanley predicts that total global exchange traded fund assets under management will soar to $2 trillion in 2011 compared with $500 to $600 billion in 2007.

Kittsley of State Street has a more conservative estimate of $1 trillion to $2 trillion in five years' time. Growing numbers of institutional and retail investors are investing in ETFs following positive regulatory changes. Unlike futures and options, a purchase of a Gold ETF can avoid leverage and margin calls.

New ETFs, including gold products are being launched on exchanges around the world. This indicates that the Gold ETF share of the global gold investment pool will continue to increase. While ETFs suit individual investors each investor or trader must make their own decisions on timing and take advice, similarly to dealings in other securities.

Gold holdings of ETFs cannot be strictly compared with central bank and other official gold reserves as they are private sector investments. Nevertheless the current size of Gold ETF holdings now exceed central bank reserves of the European Central Bank, Netherlands, China, Russia, UK and numerous other countries. The official figures are gleaned from 2006 IMF and World Gold Council sources and ETF Gold, October 2007.

Buyers of gold ETFs

Gold ETFs are effectively being used for asset allocation purposes, placing a proportion of total portfolios to physical gold. Historical inventory patterns of gold ETFs indicate that the majority of investors are there for the medium to long haul, rather than day to day speculation. It is difficult to gauge the exact percentage flowing to institutions. Research of Exchange Traded Gold Newsletter, however, indicates that private banking clients, institutional and mutual funds dominate gold ETFs European investment register. Market professionals, including hedge funds, account for only 10 to 15 per cent of the total. It must be stressed, however, that although ETF gold investment has been exceedingly rapid, the 25 million ounce or 780 metric ton holdings are only a fraction of the estimated 4.9 billion ounces of above ground central bank, investment and jewelry inventories.

Gold acting as a safe haven, inflation and currency hedge

Worried investors bought gold as a safe haven during the sub prime and credit crisis of 2007. Gold ETFs were an indicator. Stocks of gold exchange traded funds steadily rose during the sub prime and junk bond credit crunch and stock market slide. From June to October 2007 when Bear Stearns' hedge fund debacle precipitated the financial turmoil, bullion stocks of gold ETFs rose to 25 million ounces worth $19 billion from pre crisis levels of 20.8 million ounces. The small increase was significant during that credit crunch period. Hedge funds and other speculators were dumping corporate bonds, equities and commodities to repay bank borrowings and meet withdrawals of disenchanted investors. Gold itself was not immune from the panic. Stressed hedge funds had to sell liquid assets and gold falls into that category. Thus after rising from $659 an ounce at the end of May to $684 towards the end of July, it fell back to $653 during the tense market period of August 2007. Despite those sales, gold volatility was much lower than stock markets and in dollars, euros and pounds gold traded in a narrow range of 3 to 4 percent.

While hedge funds, commodity trading advisors and other speculators were selling, it was evident that other investors sought safe havens. Prices of US Treasury, European and Japanese sovereign bonds rose. Money also shifted into gold. Indeed in recent years wealthy US, European, Middle Eastern, Asian, South American and other investors, who have been concerned about a credit binge, excess speculation, inflation and a potential financial and economic crisis built up holdings of physical gold in bullion and private banks. Those flows were difficult to quantify in the global gold market. The bulk of trading takes place through bullion banks in London, Zurich, New York, Tokyo and Hong Kong. The bullion and private banks don't publish their gold inventories.

The trend of Gold ETF stocks, however, can be used as a pointer. Gold ETFs are a tiny proportion of the gold market, but their stock movements are transparent and generally indicate intentions of medium and long term investors rather than speculators. Since the end of 2003, they more than doubled to 25 million ounces or almost 800 metric tons, helping boost gold to a new Millennium peak of $760.

ETF gold stocks are also a safe haven indicator. Since each gold ETF share comprises one tenth of an ounce of gold, an investor who buys 1000 shares in New York Exchange listed StreetTracks Gold Shares, for example, is buying 100 ounces of gold. StreetTracks, Lyxor Gold Bullion Securities and other gold ETFs are trustees on behalf of investors for physical gold bullion deposited in dedicated banks. This gold is held in 'allocated accounts'. This means that the gold is held on behalf of gold ETF investors. They are the sole owners. The gold bars that are deposited in the banks' vaults, are numbered and placed on shelves. They are labelled and are the property of the individual gold ETF owner. Even though the gold is held on the bank's premises, it is neither the property of the bank nor the liability of the bank. The bank is the safe keeper. Thus if the bank fails, its creditors cannot claim the gold as part of the bank's assets. Ordinary bank deposits, unallocated gold, which is kept in a pool on the bank's premises and gold futures and options derivatives, do not have this security.

Investors who fear a systemic financial collapse and possible bank failures are thus prepared to pay higher storage and insurance fees of allocated bank accounts. The fees vary according to the amount of gold that the bank stores, but are obviously higher for medium and smaller holdings. In contrast, gold ETFs charge 0.4 per cent annual management fees. They include storage and other expenses and are the same for big or small investors.

Stock movements of gold ETFs illustrate that long term investors are holding on to their gold. Some believe that central bank infusion of money to calm banker fears could ultimately lead to higher inflation. Others contend that a holding in gold is a good diversification policy during times of heightened risks. Whatever the reasons, a decision to hold their gold in separate allocated accounts for a storage fee or via gold ETFs, is a further safeguard.

Flexible gold ETFs can also yield income

The surge in the demand for Gold Exchange Traded Funds illustrates not only the move into gold, but also the growing realization that ETFs are a useful cost effective and flexible way to trade bullion.

Since the market has grown rapidly and is now much more liquid, hedge funds and other sophisticated investors are going long and short in gold ETFs. A window is thus open for institutions and other long term investors to lend the securities and earn interest. A major disadvantage for pension funds that invest in commodities is that they do not yield income. The price of metals or other commodity holdings must appreciate more than the dealing costs, storage, insurance and other expenses. But if pension funds, other institutions and investors have gold ETF holdings, they can lend out the security like any stock. The Gold ETF is thus a useful asset for pension funds as the interest on the security loans helps fund the cost of holding the asset

Depending on the level of general interest rates, the annual lending rate for gold ETFs has ranged from 1% to 2.5% and is higher than individual shares, according to brokers who deal in ETFs including the gold products. The rate, which is five times the annual ETF management fee of 0.4%, thus also offsets costs. It is also higher than the lease rate on physical gold. Meanwhile the gold backing of the ETF remains safely in the vaults, specifically allocated to the investor. The gold can thus be held as a long term investment in terms of an asset allocation diversification policy. It is still an open question whether lending can take place on a large scale. The market is now sufficiently liquid for hedge funds and other sophisticated players to actively trade in large blocks. Illustrating the extent of liquidity in this new market, total investment in StreetTRACKS Gold Shares (GLD), for example, was 19 million ounces worth almost $15 billion. Since each gold ETF is backed by around 1/10 of an ounce of gold, the number of shares of GLD alone is now around 190 million with a market capitalization of around $15 billion. Daily trading in GLD averaged between 10 to 20 million shares or $400 million to $1 billion a day towards the end of 2007, according to brokers. In both value and volume terms, GLD, which only came to the market in 2004, has become a much more active stock on the New York Stock Exchange than long standing leading gold mines. Gold mining stocks will remain popular with investors when bullion is in an upward trend. Investors are attracted to the mine as operational leverage causes the shares to increase by a greater factor than the gold price. Exploration and ore results also add spice. When gold declines, however, mining stocks fall by a greater proportion than bullion. Operational and financial leverage of mines can enhance profitability but also introduce risks. These include changes in currency values that affect profits, corporate governance risks, geological forecasting mistakes, political risk in Third World nations, energy and other operating costs, depletion of reserves and losses from hedging at lower than market prices. In contrast gold ETFs rise and fall in tandem with the gold price.

GLD volumes have grown rapidly as an increasing number of individual and institutional investors prefer the ETF because it is 100% correlated to bullion. They have also found that GLD is easily accessible for trading purposes. They can go long and short with narrow spreads and low dealing costs attractive for investors. According to Kittsley of State Street Global Advisors, GLD's average bid–ask spread has been the narrowest of any commodity-based ETF and has been tighter than that of most large cap stocks in the US. GLD's average spread has been $0.02, equivalent to 20 cents an ounce. This compares with recent spreads in the over the counter spot gold market of $1 to $1.50 per ounce for deals of 5 000 to 10 000 ounces.

Institutions and other investors can be flexible with their gold ETFs and lend and withdraw the loans at swift notice, depending on their own investment needs and changing investment and asset allocation strategies. A table with daily volumes of traded shares follows:

Table 3.1 Daily trading volume comparisons.

	Daily volume ($m)	Daily volume (shares million)	Market capitalisation ($billion)
Microsoft	2459	90	233
ExxonMobil	1225	20	354
Citigroup	792	16	240
General Electric	786	25	346
Bank of America	727	14	217
StreetTRACKSGLD	**750**	**12**	**190**
Newmont Mining	347	8	22
Goldcorp	178	7	10
Barrick Gold	149	6	24
Anglogold Ashanti	71	1.4	12
Gold Fields	60	3	10

Daily volumes in terms of value are based on published trade on the New York Stock Exchange in May 2006. Volumes of shares traded are based on averages in the three months ended May 2006 (Source Stock Exchange statistics and Yahoo Finance) StreetTRACKS GLD in October 2007.

Exchange traded gold risks

Since Exchange Traded Gold is 100 per cent correlated with gold, it is obviously subject to the same risks as bullion. So far gold ETFs have grown rapidly in a benign environment, notably a lengthy and extensive gold bull market. By October 2007 gold had trebled from its market depression of around $250 in 2001. The test is how the product performs in a bear market. So far, as narrated above, gold ETFs have been resilient in the face of market corrections within the bull market. Despite price declines in gold ETF inventories were minimal in percentage terms. The test whether ETF investors are committed holders will come in the event of a lengthy gold bear market.

The biggest gold price risk and therefore gold ETF risk, is recession and a decline in all asset classes. Yet statistics show that gold is generally not correlated to stocks and other assets. In practice, however, the gold price has slipped during general market downturns. There is also another direct risk to gold ETFs as if hedge funds and other speculators are forced to dump overvalued copper, zinc, lead and other commodities they may find base metals markets less liquid than gold and, to raise cash for margin calls, may sell the more liquid commodity, notably bullion. Price falls in the past have shown that this happens.

In the third quarter of 2007 the European Central Bank, the Federal Reserve Bank, the Bank of Japan and several Asian central banks pumped hundreds of billions of dollars into illiquid financial markets. This prime pumping was the major economic and financial reason for the surge of gold prices during that time. By providing loans to vulnerable banks, the central banks allayed concerns of counterparty banks to some degree. But the move was only the first step. The underlying problems are still very serious. The next step is how central banks, regulators and investors deal with parallel crises. The first relates to excessive loans on residential real estate and rising defaults. Alongside this problem is an acute crisis of overextended banks and the $2 trillion global hedge fund industry. Leverage, or borrowings of thousands of hedge funds raises their market exposure to an estimated $4 trillion. It has been reported that banks have been pulling back credit to some funds and investors have withdrawn money.

Economists and other analysts believe that reckless bank lending and the unwinding of hedge funds' leveraged positions are one of the root causes of the 2007 credit crisis, the worst since the failure of the hedge fund Long Term Capital Management in 1998. There could still be considerable volatility and currency turmoil in the coming year or two. Little wonder that some investors have bought gold ETFs as on the face of it, uncertainties are bullish for gold. But much depends on the level of gold prices and the possibility of a sharp decline in jewelry and other physical demand. The potential risks of a precious metals and general commodities bubble remain. Caveat Emptor!

Part Two:
Supply and Demand Fundamentals and Swing Factors

Supply and Demand Fundamentals

In Chapter 12 Frank Holmes presents his analysis of the factors 'driving gold'. The web site of the funds he manages frequently publishes webcasts for investors and a weekly report on current events and developments following a SWOT formula – Strength, Weaknesses, Opportunities and Threats. Investors will be in a position to evaluate his analysis now and respond to the current information addressed by US Global Investors in their weekly analysis.[1]

The world's major economic concerns now relate to levels of US borrowings and associated global economic imbalances. Former British Prime Minister Harold Macmillan famously responded 'Events, dear boy, events' to a question on the principal danger his Government faced. The economic historian Niall Ferguson adds that the dictum applies 'to all who borrow money . . . with especial force to a government with a large amount of short-term debt'.[2]

The strong supply and demand fundamentals for gold over the last fifteen years are reflected in the following chart and table. The chart illustrates the supply gap between newly mined gold and market demand from 1981 to 2005 and the table details world supply and demand from 2003 to estimates for 2008.

The gap between supply and demand continues to widen. In Chapter 12 Frank Holmes addresses the plateau reached in gold mine production below its peak and the long and uncertain path to bringing new mines to production. In 2007 high mining costs resulted in South Africa losing the position it held since 1902 as the world's largest producer and in 2008 mines in South Africa were unable to work continuously as a result of the national power supplier ESKOM not having the capacity to supply the needs of the growing economy. As many mines in South Africa work at depths of as much as 5000 metres below the ground power is needed not only for the usual industrial needs but also for ventilation, cooling, transporting men and materials and safety underground. It's already known that the power outages have resulted in lower mine output. They will continue to – but at this stage it's not known the extent to which production will be lost and it will probably not be known for some time.

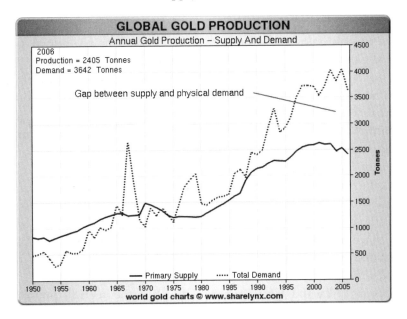

Chart 3.1 Annual gold supply and demand gap.
(Source: world gold charts © www.sharelynx.com)

Table 3.2 Virtual metals gold supply and demand analysis from 2000 to forecast 2008.

World total supply and demand (tonnes)						
	2003	2004	2005	2006	2007e	2008f
Supply						
Mine supply	2512	2351	2411	2387	2413	2414
Scraps recycling	900	1100	938	1057	991	917
Hedging	196	69	84	40	42	25
Central Bank sales	571	464	616	379	583	495
Total supply	4171	3983	3947	3845	4016	3751
Demand						
Jewellery fabrication	2808	2878	2996	2276	2257	2334
Legal tender coins	85	91	101	102	90	92
Electronics	310	332	357	372	403	416
Other end uses	315	350	393	315	311	313
ETFs	33	125	192	253	241	178
Central bank purchases	39	61	39	132	54	61
Dehedging	529	524	223	482	442	235
Total demand	4119	4382	4304	3912	3796	3628
Residual						
Supply less demand	52	(378)	(357)	(70)	220	123

(Courtesy Virtual Metals, www.virtualmetals.co.uk)

For over twenty years the jewellery industry alone has accounted for some 70% of gold sales and absorbed more than all newly mined gold. The World Gold Council and the gold mining industry are also engaged in sponsoring initiatives to develop industrial uses for gold. It's already extensively used in the semi-conductor industry. In December 2007 progress was announced on the potential for gold in the motor vehicle catalyst market where it appears to have utility with emissions from diesel engines.[3] The developments are at an early stage but, if they are successful, as diesel vehicles become more popular there is the potential for significant extra demand in an already tight market. About 120 tonnes of platinum were used in auto catalysts in 2007. With no realistic prospect of an increase in mined gold the pattern will continue unless investment demand either falls or drives the gold price to a level that undermines the economics of the jewellery industry. In markets where demand for gold is surging and growth potential is almost unlimited many of the factors that drive investor demand also drive jewellery demand. This applies in India and China where a third of the world's population live and where incomes have been and continue to rise dramatically. Gold also enjoys traditional support in Middle East countries enjoying exceptional prosperity with current high oil prices. And demand for gold is strong in the developed West with investors seeking to insulate themselves from risks associated with fiduciary money. In a nutshell: there is now global interest in gold's stateless money franchise.

Growing Investor Demand

In their report on demand to the end of September 2007 The World Gold Council reported exceptionally strong demand.[4] Their headline comments read:

> A surge in investor interest on top of robust jewellery demand made Q3 2007 a further quarter of strong demand for gold. Total identifiable demand reached a new record in dollar terms at $20.7bn, up 30% on a year earlier; in tonnage terms the rise was 19%. Jewellery demand rose by 6% in tonnage terms over Q3 2006 and by 16% in dollar terms. However, identifiable investment demand was nearly double year-earlier levels in tonnage terms due to a record inflow into Exchange Traded Funds and similar products. The rise in dollar terms was 115%.

According to the report investment demand overtook jewellery demand for the first time:

September saw a surge in investor interest following the financial crisis and further encouraged by the falling dollar and inflationary fears. With the price rising rapidly jewellery buyers in many Asian and Middle East countries held back as they typically do in times of volatile prices. The supply of gold was more plentiful than in recent quarters. Total supply was 16% higher than a year earlier (tonnage terms). This was not due to any increase in mine production, which was effectively unchanged from year-earlier levels, but to a sharp reduction in de-hedging by mining companies and to higher central bank sales. In addition there was some increase in the supply from scrap. The rise in supply helps to explain the rise in demand in tonnage terms as demand grew to match supply. It does not explain the 9% rise in the quarterly average price compared to one year earlier. The fact that the price rose even with a substantial increase in supply is testament to the underlying strength of demand for gold. Part of this strength is the longer term rise in investor interest which has been one of the features of the bull market in gold which started in 2001. . . . Industrial and dental demand in Q3 was relatively subdued, little changed from year-earlier levels. The largest industrial use of gold is in electronic components where demand for gold and other materials was affected by an oversupply of semi-conductors and integrated circuits at the beginning of the quarter.

The rising gold price to the end of 2007 reflecting the strong supply and demand conditions over the year is reflected in the following chart:

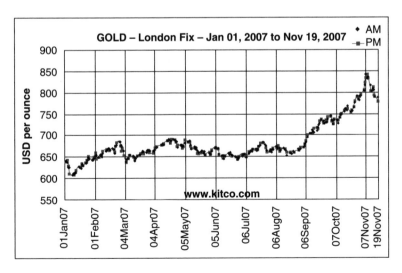

Chart 3.2 Gold price January 2007 to December 2007.

Swing Factors Affecting Supply and Demand

With annual demand for gold of about 4000 tonnes and newly mined gold accounting for about 2400 tonnes the gap of about 1500 to 1600 tonnes a year has been met by:

1. Central bank sales;
2. Gold bullion held by investors recycled back into the market;
3. Recycled scrap including privately owned jewellery and artefacts;
4. Mining companies de-hedging.

Central banks gold holdings

Table 3.3 Total tonnes of gold owned by all countries and organisations: 30,163.2 tonnes.

Countries & organisations owning over 1000 tonnes:		
1	United States	8 133.7
2	Germany	3 417.7
3	IMF	3 407.0
4	France	2 658.4
5	Italy	2 451.9
6	Switzerland	1 242.0
Sub total		21 310.5

Countries & organisations owning over 100 tonnes:		
7	Japan	765.1
8	Netherlands	641.0
9	China	600.0
10	Russia	407.5
11	Portugal	382.6
12	India	357.7
13	Venezuela	356.8
14	United Kingdom	310.4
15	Lebanon	268.8
16	Austria	281.8
17	Spain	281.5
18	Belgium	227.7
19	BIS estimated	190.0
20	Algeria	173.6
21	Sweden	152.7
22	Libya	143.7
23	Saudi Arabia	143.1

Table 3.3 (Continued)

Countries & organisations owning over 1000 tonnes:

24	Philippines	140.3
25	South Africa	124.1
26	Turkey	116.0
27	Greece	112.3
28	Romania	104.8
29	Poland	103.0
Total over 100 tonnes		24 305.8

The above table details gold holdings by the world's central banks, the United States Treasury and parastatal monetary organisations including the International Monetary Fund and the Bank for International Settlements. Together all central banks own about 30 000 tonnes of gold. Enough gold to service total demand of 4000 tonnes a year for over seven years.

Under pressure of sales by European central banks the gold price fell to a trough of $252 in July 1999. The price stabilised after the 'Washington Agreement' was reached between 15 European central banks after September 1999. The agreement set a sales quota of 400 tonnes a year – a volume that the market could absorb and indeed needed. The following chart reflects the strong price rise when the quota agreement was announced in 1999.

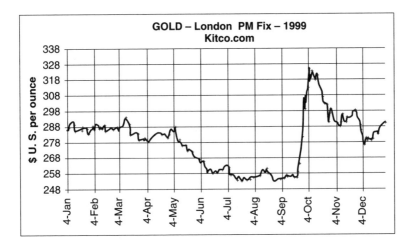

Chart 3.3 Gold price January to December 1999.

The Washington Agreement

The Central Bank quota sales agreement has become known as the Washington Agreement though its correct name is the Central Bank Gold Agreement. It was orchestrated by the World Gold Council and announced on 26 September 1999 for an initial tenure of five years covering monthly sales of 400 tonnes. In 2004 the agreement was extended to September 2008 with the quota increased to 500 tonnes. The tenure of the current agreement expires in September 2008. It's expected that it will be renewed but, if the gold price is sufficiently high, central bankers may decide to take advantage of a favourable market.

At the time of writing, the United States, the world's largest holder of gold with 8133 tonnes, the International Monetary Fund, the third largest holder with 3407 and Japan, the seventh largest holder with 765 tonnes were not party to the agreement. The United States and Japan have indicated that currently they do not intend to sell gold and the IMF has sold gold and intends to sell more. Current indications are that 400 tonnes will be sold in 2008.

The World Gold Council describe the Washington Agreement as an explicit signed agreement but in law only a gentleman's agreement that does not have the legal force of an international treaty.[5] A crucial element of the agreement is that the parties undertook not to expand their gold leasing activities or their exposure to other derivatives trades relating to their gold holdings over the currency of the agreement. These curbs on bank leasing and selling options have helped underpin the gold price recovery over recent years. The World Gold Council indicated when the agreement was announced that if the restrictions against leasing or granting options on gold are complied with, more than 26 000 tonnes of gold has been taken off the market. This completely changed the supply demand dynamic for gold.

However calculating the exact quantity of gold held by central banks is not an exact science. The data is not officially correlated or published in any report published in the public domain. Data used by analysts relies on estimates made by Gold Fields Mining Services, Virtual Metals and other organisations who monitor and report on the gold mining industry.[6,7] There are also questions on the extent to which central bank gold holdings have already been committed through derivatives and other forward sales obligations. The Gold Anti Trust Action Committee 'GATA' have alleged a conspiracy involving national treasuries, central banks and private sector banks acting covertly in concert to depress the gold price. They challenge all published data and campaign vigorously to expose the conspiracy. Their most recent initiative was a full page $260 000 advertisement in the *Wall Street Journal* in February 2007 setting out their claims.[8]

Central Bank holdings and the Washington Agreement are arguably the most important factors in the supply–demand equation for gold. GATA have run a tenacious campaign to expose a gold price suppression conspiracy. Among those who believe that politicians and governments will stop at nothing to achieve whatever ends suit them they have a dedicated following and their arguments also attract some support from more conventional analysts. The difficulty I have with conspiracy theories is the number of people that have to be corrupt, engaged in the conspiracy and relied on to keep the secret. The Goldwatcher web site will continue to update all developments relating to central bank gold holdings, including the GATA conspiracy claims.[9]

Exchange Traded Funds and Sovereign Wealth Funds

As Neil Behrmann explains in Part 1 of this chapter the World Gold Council's promotion of Gold Exchange Traded Funds has made investing in gold as straightforward as buying a share in a company and thus accessible to the investing community by and large, ranging from major funds to retail investors. He also explains that no one really knows who buyers of shares in the funds are. I have no tangible information that supports my view that current strong gold prices are being supported by Sovereign Wealth Funds. But I sense that they are.

If China or any other country were to start building up their gold bullion holdings using their official reserves they would be expected to report the gold they acquired as reserve assets to the IMF. Gold prices would soar on the news and make any further purchases more expensive. But Sovereign Wealth Funds don't have to report what they own to the IMF – or anyone else. As they are not likely to declare their holdings we are left to speculate. A comment in the US Funds report of 23 November on ETFs disclosed this information:

- The World Gold Council reported that gold ETFs now hold more than 700 tons of gold at a current value of slightly less than $19 billion. A well-known fund manager in this space noted, 'It's the privatization of central bank gold reserves.'
- Morningstar highlighted several non-gold funds that had taken large positions in gold bullion via ETFs and noted that all of these funds sported year-to-date returns in the top-10 percent of their categories.

On my reading of the comment the phrase 'the privatisation of central bank gold reserves' doesn't necessarily mean that Sovereign Wealth Funds have become proxy buyers for their central banks. But it could. And the privatisation of central bank gold reserves would be consistent with recognition of gold's stateless money franchise.

Do Central Banks Still Need Gold and does Gold Still Need Central Banks?

The world banking system functions now without gold. That doesn't mean gold is not a useful asset for them to hold – particularly when currencies are unstable. But if central banks were to start offloading gold as they did in the 1980s and 1990s the supply–demand balance would swing from undersupply to oversupply. In a speech 'The International Monetary System in the 21st Century: Could Gold Make a Comeback?' Robert Mundell said:[10]

> There will also be a role for gold. The total amount of gold mined since the days of Nefertiti is about 3.5 billion ounces (120,000 tons). One billion ounces is in the central banks, more than another billion ounces is in jewelry, and the rest is in speculative hoards. This last holding is why Alan Greenspan says he looks at gold whenever he gets a chance. I look at three things for signs of inflation in the economy: I look at the money supply, I look at interest rates, and I look at gold. . . . The stock of gold in the world is going to maintain itself as a viable reserve asset for a long time to come.

The above extract from Mundell's comments has been widely quoted. However he went on to say:

> But I do not think that we will see the time when either of those two great economic powers, the United States and the European Union, will ever again fix their respective currencies to gold as they have in the past. More likely, gold will be used at some point, maybe in 10 or 15 years when it has been banalized among central bankers, and they are not so timid to speak about its use as an asset that can circulate between central banks. Not necessarily at a fixed price, but a market price.

Mundell's speech was made over ten years ago and mentioned a ten to fifteen year time frame before gold was 'banalized' and trading at a market price. Were it not for the quota agreement that restricts sales by central banks a strong case could be made that gold is indeed now trading at a market price. However, in the light of present economic uncertainties, it's likely that central banks will not be interested in selling their gold – other than at very tempting prices. The likelihood is that central banks and gold will continue to need each other for the foreseeable future.

4

The Rise and Fall of the Gold Standard

Did gold cause the great depression?

Introduction: The Stateless Money Franchise

> GOLD is a hardy perennial. . . . It provides a psychological and material safe haven for people all around the world, and its invocation still produces deep-seated visceral reactions in many. It is not surprising, then, that when economic conditions are unfavourable, proposals to strengthen the role of gold in the monetary system find an audience much wider than the 'gold bugs' who have always seen the demise of the gold standard as the negative turning point in Western civilization.
>
> Harvard Professor R. N. Cooper – 1982[1]

With a soaring gold price and weak dollar gold bugs are buzzing on web sites, publishing articles and writing books calling for a return to gold. And, to be sure, there is more than enough economic and geopolitical anxiety to keep them buzzing. Congressman Ron Paul, a sound money advocate and maverick contender for nomination as the Republican Presidential candidate in 2008, attracted an astonishing amount of funding for his campaign. He didn't make a return to the gold standard a campaign promise but has consistently argued that the US Constitutional calls for its currency to be minted in gold or silver coin. That position is not too far from calling for a bimetallic gold and silver standard. However I start from the premise that there is no prospect of a restoration of the gold standard or any other monetary standard backed by a commodity. The world has adopted a monetary system based on national currencies supported by commitments to keep their value essentially by controlling inflation.

James Burton, the chief executive of the World Gold Council and the gold mining industry's spokesperson, was asked in a question and answer session arranged by the *Financial Times* early in 2007 if he thought a return to a type of gold standard was possible in the foreseeable future. He answered with an unqualified 'No'. 'The gold standard' he explained 'was appropriate to the second half of the 19th century but circumstances are now different'. James Burton's opinion is in line with the approach of mainstream economists and commentators that the gold standard is history. However that is very different to the view taken by many commentators only a decade ago that gold's stateless money franchise was history.

A decade ago the *Financial Times* published a feature on gold as 'nothing more than another commodity and a bad investment'. By January 2008 the *Financial Times* recognised the reality of gold's stateless money franchise and wrote about gold as 'the new global currency':

> A better way to think of gold may be as central bankers used to before America dropped the gold standard: not as a commodity, but as another currency. As long as the dollar stays weak, gold's bull run will last. The arguments for further gains in the gold price are compelling. It looks cheap, despite climbing from a low of about $250 a troy ounce in 1999, when central banks were selling reserves. The UK's decision back then to sell 60 per cent of its official holdings looks particularly poor judgment. Prices have a long way to go before they approach the inflation-adjusted record touched in 1980 when Soviet tanks invaded Afghanistan. At Monday's $859, gold was trading at less than half that level. It could top $1,000 and still be at the lower end of what some analysts argue is a safe haven range.[2]

Unfinished Business

Twenty-first century monetary arrangements are a legacy from twentieth-century systems and institutions including the International Monetary Fund and the gold standard. Until 1971 a gold exchange standard survived at the core of the International Monetary Fund and the international monetary system. The reader will find an informed and insightful analysis of the transition from a gold standard to what we now call the dollar standard in Robert Mundell's 1999 Nobel Laureate Awards Speech *A Reconsideration of the 20th Century* – a century he characterises as 'The American Century'.[3] Mundell was awarded the Nobel Prize for the analysis he published in the 1960s that contributed to the framework for the introduction of the euro currency. Apart from his brilliance as an economist and scholar he experienced the economic disruption of the 1970s and 1980s and contributed to solutions.

In his Nobel Prize lecture Mundell noted extreme changes over the century. 'The early years were a benign continuation of the pax of the 19th century . . . a calm before the storm followed by World War I, communism, hyperinflation, fascism, depression, genocide, World War II, the atom bomb and the occupation of Eastern Europe.' He explains how the dollar came to 'elbow' gold out and assume dominance in the monetary system. He concluded that monetary stability had improved since the 1970s and 1980s, but there was still ' . . . unfinished business'. The most important is the dysfunctional volatility of exchange rates that could sour international relations in time of crisis. The absence of an international currency is the other.

The global economic situation has deteriorated dramatically since 1999 and Mundell's 'unfinished business' warning has more resonance now than it had then. Dysfunctional exchange rates and the absence of an international currency are of course interrelated. Together they support a global perception that while the dollar and to an extent the euro are global currencies for trade and commerce, gold's role as an international store of value remains entrenched.

The Gold Standard and the Gold Exchange Standard

The gold exchange standard that survived until 1971 was watered down from The Classic Gold Standard, a monetary system where gold was money and national banknotes and coins were tokens freely exchangeable into gold by national central banks for anyone and everyone. Supported by the global hegemony of the British Empire the classic gold standard reached its heyday of the Pax Britannica between 1870 when the Napoleonic Wars ended and 1914 when World War I started. In order to be free to print money as necessary to fund the war the belligerents in the conflict suspended convertibility of their currencies into gold before the war started. Following the devastating casualties and costs of the war the social, economic and political landscape of the world changed. Eight million men were slaughtered in combat and fifteen million were wounded, many so severely that they were invalids for life. Attempts were made to restore the classic gold standard in the years between the end of World War I in 1918 and the outbreak of World War II in 1939 but conditions were so changed after the war that widespread re-introduction of the gold standard could not be achieved.

The US retained convertibility of the dollar into gold until 1933. But after 1914, with few exceptions, most domestic currencies could no longer be exchanged for gold. America emerged from the war in the strongest financial position of all the belligerents and, over the years as its economic and military might and global hegemony grew, a dollar standard evolved from the gold standard and the dollar came to usurp gold's role as universal money. When the 1944 Bretton Woods Accords defined the structure for the post World War II international monetary system the dollar even became the numeraire for the International Monetary System. Yet, until gold was demonetized by US President Richard M. Nixon in 1971, it remained at the centre of the international monetary system and foreign treasuries retained the right to oblige the US to settle accounts in gold instead of dollars.

Following the demonetization of gold in 1971 the decade of the 1970s is remembered as *the great inflation* with several years of double digit inflation. With such high inflation it's not surprising that a return to the gold standard was a political issue in the 1980s. We can get a sense of issues that might be debated if a return to gold was being considered now by reviewing opinions on gold in the run up to the 1979 US Presidential elections. The election was contested by President Jimmy Carter and California Governor Ronald Reagan.

Gold in 1980 and in 2008

In 1980 US President Jimmy Carter was in his last year of office, unpopular and unlikely to be re-elected. Inflation was out of control. There were serious geopolitical tensions. The Soviet Union was invading Afghanistan. In January 1979 the pro-American Shah had been forced to flee Iran. In February Ayatollah Khomeini returned from exile. On 1 April Iran declared itself an Islamic Republic. Within a year of the Iranian revolution fuel shortages were experienced and crude oil prices surged from $15.85 to $59.50 a barrel, the equivalent of $140 in 2007 dollars allowing for consumer price inflation.[4] On 4 November militant Islamic students demanded the extradition of the Shah from the US where he was being treated for cancer to stand trial in Iran, stormed the US embassy in Teheran and held more than 90 people hostage. Iran's revolutionary guards and the police did nothing to stop the embassy siege. Iranian television indicated support by broadcasting live pictures. Ayatollah Khomeini also voiced his support. In April 1980 a US mission to rescue the hostages failed. The embassy hostage siege lasted 444 days and only ended in January 1981.[5]

In January 1980 the gold price spiked to above $850. The average gold price for the year was $612.56 − equivalent to about $1500 in 2007 money adjusted for inflation.[6] As can be seen from the following chart the gold price reflected current political, economic and geopolitical anxieties.

Geopolitical risks with Iran are more menacing now than they were during the 1980s hostage crisis. The failed invasion of Iraq continues to drain the US financially. Crude oil has traded at almost $100. Gold has traded at over $900. The

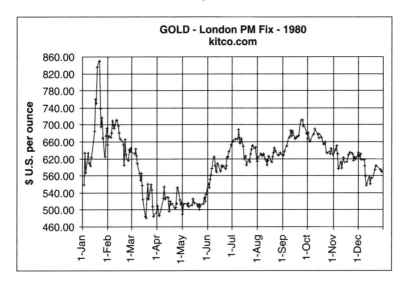

Chart 4.1 Gold price – 1980.
(Chart courtesy of Kitco: http://www.kitco.com)

dollar has been sinking. Upsets in markets overdosed with finance remind us that global contagion puts us all at risk. In a worst case scenario a global currency crisis could end with all fiduciary money collapsing like a deck of cards. Will we hear calls again for a return to gold to stabilise the international monetary system?

Time Magazine on **Bring Back the Gold Standard**

Journalists were still well informed on the gold standard in the 1980s when a *Time Magazine* article titled 'Bring Back Gold' published on 22 June 1981 canvassed the realities of a gold standard. The article opened with the comment that while gold had not been used to settle accounts between central banks for a decade 'it still remains the barometer of world tension . . . nervous people stash away Kruger Rand coins or gold jewellery at the first sign of any political or economic unrest'.[7]

Time reported that a group of conservative economists were trying to bring gold back as the anchor of the world's monetary system, the position it held during the late nineteenth and early twentieth centuries and a relentless chorus of hard money advocates were demanding their money be made as good as gold again. An adviser to Ronald Reagan was reported saying: 'I am convinced that we will be back on the gold standard within ten years . . . The basic requirements of a gold standard are that a unit of money be defined by a specified amount of gold and that the central bank will convert money into gold. The gold standard then becomes a mechanism for controlling the money supply, and thus inflation, by linking the growth of currency to a commodity that is scarce, only slowly increasing in supply and indestructible.' Some supporters were reported as favouring a 'fractional' gold standard in which money would be only partially covered by Government gold stocks. This would not entirely remove the Federal Reserve's role in monetary policy, but would restrain its powers to issue paper money.

In the run up to the 1980 presidential election the Republican platform hinted at endorsing 'hard' money and Ronald Reagan made some pro-gold statements. But there were doubts on whether he was seriously interested in seeing the gold standard reinstated. One commentator noted 'This commission is a very considered manoeuvre by the Reagan Administration to allow conservatives to have their day. It is a way of diffusing sentiment – a masterful stroke.' And Congressman Ron Paul, who sought nomination to run as President again in 2008, pointed out: 'The important thing is that we're finally talking about it. Sooner or later, it will all dawn on people.' But the gold advocates won few converts among economists. Opponents argued that a gold system would be too rigid for the modern international economy. One was quoted as saying: 'To tie the world economy to an asset that represents such a small part of the total monetary system is really impossible. You could as well stabilize the world economy on the cabbage standard. It is absurd.'

The *Time* article closed with these excellent comments on the gold price that, with the benefit of hindsight, demonstrate that well informed commentators can make sensible predictions:

> Probably the most difficult part of any return to gold would be to establish a suitable price for the yellow metal. In the past decade, gold has been as low as $35 per oz., but in January 1980 it hit $850 per oz. If world leaders fixed the price of gold too low, it could result in a severe depression, because there would not be enough cash to keep the economy running smoothly. If the price was set too high, it could cause more inflation, because the gold would have created too much cash and credit. Roy Jastram, a professor of business administration at the University of California at Berkeley, has studied the world prices of gold and other commodities going back to 1560. He concluded that the historic price of gold, in relation to the prices of those other products, would now be about $250 per oz. Some gold bugs, though, insist that the price under a new gold standard should be as high as $1,500 per oz.

Jastram was on the money. His study *The Golden Constant: The English and American Experience* was published in 1977.[8] At the time of writing, gold was trading at about $740 and about $700 would be needed to replace the purchasing power of Jastram's $250 calculated price for gold in 1979. By contrast the $1500 the gold bugs proposed in 1980 would have equated to over $4000 in 2007!

Robert Mundell on Gold at $10 000

Robert Mundell also called for a return to gold in the run up to the 1980 Presidential elections. His call was published in the *New York Times* on 18 October 1980 headlined: 'Gold at $10 000 – Robert A. Mundell, a Professor of economics at Columbia University and an advisor to the Reagan camp argues for the standard.'[9,10]

Mundell's plea was impassioned but included a useful explanation of how the gold standard worked. He wrote:

> At current rates of inflation, the dollar price of an ounce of gold will push into the $5 000 to $10 000 range within a generation and consumer prices generally will double every five to ten years in the United States. This disastrous inflation will provoke a reaction in Washington. . . . As usual, the government will confuse symptom with cause, and probably forget that inflation's origins lies in the breakdown of the gold standard and the lack of constraints on money creation by the Federal Reserve System, the greatest engine of inflation ever created by man. Since Roman times, at least one currency has been linked to gold, and there has always been a link between the supply of money and the price of commodities. But on August 15th, 1971, Richard M. Nixon suspended gold convertibility. Monetary restraint then rested only on the limits self-imposed by central bankers and their political bosses, a flimsy reed on which to base monetary stability.
>
> The stability of prices under the gold standard rested upon control of the global quantity of money. Under a pure gold standard, a central bank would sell gold for old currency when its balance of payments was in deficit and its currency was weak on the exchanges, thus contracting the supply of currency. Similarly, when its balance of payments was in surplus and its currency was strong, it bought gold with new currency, thus expanding the supply of national currency and preventing undue appreciation on the exchanges thus contracting the supply of currency. When several countries were on the gold standard the expansions and contractions balanced out. There would be no significant change in global spending and therefore no systematic tendency for inflation or deflation in the world as a whole.

Mundell went on to explain how gold came to be undervalued in the world monetary system, how the Federal Reserve 'gunned the money supply' causing deficits to escalate and how Europe's demands for payments in gold gave Mr Nixon an excuse for suspending gold convertibility. He concluded:

> In short, in the 1970s, money became an elastic and accommodating factor, no longer held in check by an impersonal, neutral force. Thus when oil prices quadrupled in 1973–4, the result was inflationary finance in the Eurodollar market by the Federal Reserve. The international gold standard has acted in the

past as a catalyst for peace and order and can do so again. Whatever administration comes to power after November elections should make a return to it the major task of the 1980s. Democracy will not survive galloping inflation.

The Official US Enquiry into Restoring the Gold Standard in 1982

The Gold Commission mentioned in the *Time* article completed its findings in 1982. Their deliberations were contentious. But they didn't recommend a return to the gold standard. Following the publication of their report the Washington-based Brookings Institution commissioned research on their findings and on prospects for gold with Harvard Professor Richard N. Cooper and other eminent economists. Their conclusions were published in a Brookings Report titled *The Gold Standard: Historical Facts and Future Prospects.*[11]

Among the findings in the report the following conclusions illustrate why a return to a gold standard was not a realistic prospect in the 1980s and why it won't be now:

1 A regime of gold convertibility with constrained monetary demand could be made to function technically, but there are doubts whether it could function politically. Politicians and central bankers would be inclined to take all steps necessary to prevent financial distress and the public would probably think of a restored gold standard as a fair weather vessel, likely to capsize and be abandoned in the first storm.

2 An element of gold backing for a currency does not necessarily assure monetary discipline. The dollar had gold backing for many years and, during most of that period, the gold reserve requirements were not complied with. They were lowered whenever necessary and eventually they were removed. The ceiling on US borrowings provides a comparable restraint on government borrowing. The ceiling is there in principle but is regularly overridden by other considerations.

3 In view of the huge sums of money involved it would not be feasible to even consider convertibility for all liquid US Federal Reserve claims outstanding unless the gold price was appreciably increased. However, with an appreciably higher price, gold production would increase substantially and the authorities would also find themselves flooded with hoarded gold coming back onto the market.

4 From analysis it appeared that much of the gold standard's historic utility was because it effectively fixed rates of exchange between currencies. The authors thought it unlikely that the United States or other countries would be interested in returning to fixed exchange rates.

Overview on the Gold Standard

Gold has been used as a store of value and as a means of payment since ancient times. The oldest known gold coins date from the sixth century BC. Under the classical gold standard money was gold and gold was money. National coins and banknotes were only tokens for specific weights of gold. Gold was freely coined and a significant amount of gold coin was in circulation. Exchange rates didn't vary and central banks and treasuries of countries subscribing to the gold standard were always ready to exchange token coins and bank notes for gold and to buy or sell gold at the price fixed by weight. Gold could be freely imported and exported and settlement between countries was in 'specie' – jargon for gold coin or, if silver was the standard, silver coin.

Under a gold standard a country experiencing a balance of payments deficit loses gold and its money supply decreases, both automatically and by policy in accordance with the 'rules of the game'. Money supply contracts and the price level falls, thereby increasing exports and decreasing imports. Similarly, a surplus country gains gold, the money supply increases, money income expands, the price level rises, exports decrease and imports increase. In each case, balance of payments equilibrium is restored via the current account. This is called the price specie-flow mechanism. To the extent that wages and prices are inflexible, movements of real income in the same direction as money income occur; in particular, the deficit country suffers unemployment but the payments imbalance is nevertheless corrected. This was one reason for the stability of the classical gold standard. Another was that there was always absolute private sector credibility in the commitment to the fixed domestic currency price of gold.

Until the late nineteenth century most countries were on a gold and silver bimetallic standard with occasional periods of inconvertible paper money. A detailed study of the gold standard and a note on the bimetallic standard can be found on the eh.net web site.[12] The gold standard was never universal. Belgium switched from bimetallism to silver in 1850 on the grounds that gold was too unstable to provide the basis for the currency. The US adopted a de facto gold standard with resumption of specie payment on Civil War paper money greenbacks in 1879 and formally went on to gold with the Gold Standard Act of 1900. Some countries, including China and Mexico, remained on silver.

The British sterling currency was originally based on a £ representing a pound in weight of silver. The United Kingdom was on a full legal gold standard from 1816 and a de facto gold standard from 1717 when Sir Isaac Newton, Master of the Mint at the time, accidentally established a de facto gold standard by not depreciating gold enough when he set the official price of the guinea at 21 shillings.

Only Britain and Portugal were on the gold standard in 1850. Following the end of the Napoleonic Wars with the influence of Britain in all spheres including global finance and trade growing by 1880 the US and almost all of Western Europe had adopted gold. The timing of the swing to gold was also influenced by the California gold rush in the mid-nineteenth century when new production increased the world gold supply and caused a fall in the relative price of gold.

The 'classical international gold standard' is defined as the time during which all four core or centre countries – the United Kingdom, the United States, France and Germany – were on the gold standard. It only lasted until 1914 and, as previously mentioned, its widespread adoption was to a great extent associated with the hegemony of the British Empire. After the belligerents suspended convertibility of their currencies into gold to be free to print money as necessary to pay for the war and after the overwhelming economic, social and political consequences of World War I, attempts to revive the gold standard in the inter-war years and curb monetary expansion were destined to fail.

Turning Points

The approach I have taken to headlining the gold standard by reviewing turning points in history is a sterile and minimal approach constructed for a book focused on investing in the twenty-first century. The message I seek to convey is that a traditional monetary system based on a gold standard with strengths and vulnerabilities was displaced by a monetary system based essentially on a dollar standard. The dollar standard has been robust but it also has vulnerabilities. Vulnerabilities that are being stress tested now with outcomes that are bound to affect us all. But headlining history doesn't do justice to the subject. To an extent this is because headlines exclude the interplay between the giant personalities, movers and shakers engaged in politics and finance who over the nineteenth and twentieth centuries were instrumental in implementing and devising the monetary systems we have inherited. In the same way that the long-serving Chairman of the US Federal Reserve, Alan Greenspan, exerted global influence over latter decades, over earlier decades central bankers in the US, the United Kingdom and elsewhere also wielded great influence and power. Influence that should be considered when we review the momentous decisions of their times to see what lessons we can learn from them.

Winston Churchill referred to bringing Britain back onto gold in 1925 at the pre World War I parity as the greatest blunder of his life. On 4 May 1925 when he announced to Parliament that he proposed a return to the gold standard he introduced his speech with this caveat: 'I do not pose as a currency expert. It would be absurd if I did. No one would believe me.' Everyone knew he was acting on the advice of the long-serving Governor of the Bank of England,

Montague Norman. A banker with a reputation for 'godlike aloofness and tantalising omniscience' known for 'the high Priest of the City's dogma that the power of Britain had been founded on gold . . . an article of faith as unassailable as the universal belief of mankind before the time of Copernicus and Galileo that it was the sun which moved not the earth'. In 1926, within a year of the return to gold a general strike nearly paralysed Britain. By 1931 Britain went off gold again when the Bank of England was forced to ask the Government to relieve it of the obligation to provide gold bullion on demand. In *The Power of Gold* Peter Bernstein describes the painful and protracted death of the great Victorian classic gold standard and comments:

> The notion that gold would make everything come out all right was a notion that was upside down: gold would make everything come out all right only when everything was all right in the first place. That was the real meaning behind Disraeli's assertion in 1895 that Britain's gold standard was a consequence, rather than the cause, of her commercial prosperity.[13]

The reader interested in looking at a picture instead of a sketch can do no better than to get his or her hands on a copy of Peter Bernstein's book *The Power of Gold – The History of an Obsession* and read it from cover to cover.

How the Gold Standard Fared

In the Brookings study, Professor Cooper discusses how the classic gold standard actually fared. He found that the idealised gold standard as it appears in textbooks gives a picture of 'automaticity and stability with a self-correcting mechanism assuring rough stability of prices and balance in international payments'. But he finds the actual gold standard could hardly have been further from the representation. It was generally deflationary and the first period of the classic gold standard, from 1880 to 1914, went down in history as the great depression until the second period, from 1918 till 1934, ended with the Great Depression of the 1930s. Cooper concluded that with a dose of nostalgia, the gold standard period looks somewhat better to us than it did to contemporaries.

Price stability was also not attained, either in the short run or in the long run. Stability in the sense of a return to earlier levels of prices over longer periods can only be inferred by 'judicious choice' of the years chosen for comparison. If 1822, 1856, 1877, late 1915 and 1931 were chosen the US wholesale price level appeared unchanged. But between these dates there were great swells and troughs as can be seen from the following Brookings chart accompanying their report:

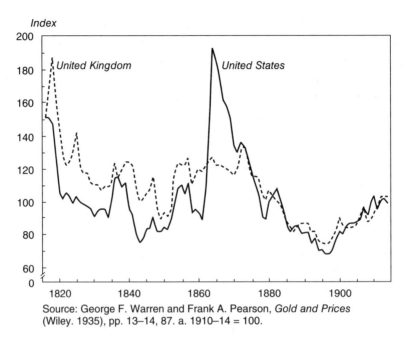

Source: George F. Warren and Frank A. Pearson, *Gold and Prices* (Wiley. 1935), pp. 13–14, 87. a. 1910–14 = 100.

Chart 4.2 Wholesale price indexes in the United States and the United Kingdom 1816–1914.
(Reproduced by permission of the Brookings Institute)

US Fed Chairman Ben Bernanke and the Great Depression

Ben Bernanke finds that understanding the Great Depression is the holy grail of macroeconomics. Not only did it give birth to macroeconomics as a distinct field of study but, to an extent that is not always fully appreciated, 'the experience of the 1930s continues to influence macroeconomists' beliefs, policy recommendations, and research agendas'. He acknowledges that he is a Great Depression buff in the same way people are Civil War buffs and says the Great Depression is to economic policymaking what the voyage of the Titanic was to ocean navigation. Both disasters could have been avoided if there had been more knowledge at the time on how to avoid them. A distinguished academic economist before he was appointed a Federal Reserve Board Governor in 2002 Bernanke traces his interest in the Great Depression to a visit to his grandmother when he was a small child.

The young Bernanke sat with his grandmother on her front porch listening to her describe life during the 1930s. She was proud, she told him, that she could buy new shoes for her children every year when many neighbourhood children went to school in tattered shoes or barefoot. 'Why didn't their parents just buy them new shoes?' young Ben asked. The answer was their fathers had lost their jobs when the shoe factories closed. 'Why did the factories close down?' The answer was because nobody had any money to buy shoes. Many years later when he was already an academic Bernanke recounted in a textbook that the circularity of her logic worried him. It raised important unanswered questions about the depression. Why was there so much unused capacity and so much unmet demand? Bernanke argues that the events that led to the Great Depression were a result of the Federal Reserve focusing on preserving the gold value of the dollar after the 1929 Wall Street crash instead of stimulating the economy to break a vicious cycle of recession, depression and deflation.[14]

In his role now as the Fed Chairman Bernanke has declared that his strategy is to ensure there will always be enough liquidity in the monetary system to maintain stability. In 2000, while he was still Professor of Economics and Public Affairs and Chair of the Department of Economics at Princeton University, the *Journal of Foreign Policy* published this contribution from him spelling out his views:[15]

> A collapse in US stock prices certainly would cause a lot of white knuckles on Wall Street. But what effect would it have on the broader US economy? If Wall Street crashes, does Main Street follow? . . . After the 1929 crash, the Federal Reserve mistakenly focused its policies on preserving the gold value of the dollar rather than on stabilizing the domestic economy . . . Central bankers got it right in the United States in 1987 when they avoided deflationary pressures as well as serious trouble in the banking system. In the days immediately following the October 19th crash, Federal Reserve Chairman Alan Greenspan—in office a mere two months—focused his efforts on maintaining financial stability . . . Reassured by policymakers' determination to protect the economy, the markets calmed and economic growth resumed with barely a blip. There's no denying that a collapse in stock prices today would pose serious macroeconomic challenges for the United States. . . . History proves, however, that a smart central bank can protect the economy and the financial sector from the nastier side effects of a stock market collapse.

The Crash of 1929 and the Great Depression

Responses by the Fed and the Hoover administration after the 1929 Wall Street crash were the opposite of what Bernanke believes they should have been, contributed to deflation and magnified a recession into the Great Depression. US President Herbert Hoover, who took office in March 1929 six months before the Wall Street crash, made bold statements in his inaugural address and gave a hint of his views on excessive speculation. He spoke of emerging from the losses of the Great War with 'virility and strength', the US having contributed to the recovery and progress of the world and having 'reached a higher degree of comfort and security than ever existed before in the history of the world'. However he warned 'all this majestic advance should not obscure the constant dangers from which self-government must be safeguarded. The strong man must at all times be alert to the attack of insidious disease.'[16]

What was the insidious disease? Presumably the 'American Wave of Optimism' Hoover later referred to in his memoirs.[17] Speculation, exuberant stock market prices and a speculative bubble.

The Hoover administration and the Federal Reserve took their policy line from the so-called 'liquidationists' who regarded a depression as economic penance for the excesses of the 1920s. Hoover's Treasury Secretary Andrew Mellon advised him to:

> Liquidate labour, liquidate stocks, liquidate the farmers, liquidate real estate . . . It will purge the rottenness out of the system. High costs of living and high living will come down. People will work harder, live a more moral life. Values will be adjusted, and enterprising people will pick up the wrecks from less competent people.

Believing that his 'medicine' was right Mellon continued to reassure Hoover and Hoover reassured the public that if the principles of orthodox finance were faithfully followed, recovery would surely be the result. Prominent economists advised against remedial measures which work through money and credit, storing up trouble for the future. Elements of the press were also inclined to follow the same line. An entertaining and rather extreme editorial from the *Commercial and Financial Chronicle*, of 3 August 1929 titled 'Is Not Group Speculating Conspiracy, Fostering Sham Prosperity?' complained of the economy being replete with profligate spending including: (a) The luxurious diversification of diet . . . (b) luxurious dressing . . . more silk and rayon . . . ; (c) free spending for automobiles and their accessories, gasoline, house furnishings and equipment, radios, travel, amusements and sports; (d) the displacement from the farms by tractors and autos of produce-consuming horses and . . . (e) the frills of education to thousands for whom places might better be reserved at bench or counter or on the farm.[18]

Roosevelt and the Birth of the Gold Exchange Standard

Franklin D. Roosevelt scored a landslide victory over Hoover in the elections at the end of 1932. In his inaugural speech on 3 March 1933 he couldn't speak about majestic advances, virility, strength, comfort or security. For him, 'the withered leaves of enterprise' were everywhere. The economy was being devastated. Bank closures were sweeping the country. Industrial production and employment were slumping. Yet Roosevelt famously assured Americans they had nothing to fear but fear itself.[19] Then he went on to describe the effects of the deflation on the economy:

> Values have shrunken to fantastic levels; taxes have risen; our ability to pay has fallen; government of all kinds is faced by serious curtailment of income; the means of exchange are frozen in the currents of trade; the withered leaves of industrial enterprise lie on every side; farmers find no markets for their produce; the savings of many years in thousands of families are gone . . . More important, a host of unemployed citizens face the grim problem of existence, and an equally great number toil with little return. Only a foolish optimist can deny the dark realities of the moment.

Dark realities indeed. Within a few days of taking office Roosevelt was forced to order a nationwide five day banking holiday to try and save the banks that still had their doors open. A wave of runs on banks and liquidations had already closed over half the country's banks. Later in his first fireside chat he explained how the banking crisis developed and how it was being resolved:

> Undermined confidence had led to a general rush by a large number of people to turn bank deposits into cash. The soundest banks didn't have enough money to meet the demand without selling assets at panic prices. By the afternoon of March 3 1933 scarcely a bank in the country was open to do business and proclamations temporarily closing them had been issued by the Governors in almost all the states.

Roosevelt issued the proclamation providing for the nationwide bank holiday as a first step in the government's reconstruction of the financial and economic fabric. The bank holiday afforded the government the opportunity to stabilise the banking system and supply additional currency to the banks. In his speech he assured the public new currency was being printed and would be sent out by the Bureau of Engraving and Printing in large volume to every part of the country.

In his second fireside chat on 7 May Roosevelt addressed the ravages of deflation, disclosed huge over commitments on gold obligations that had been made and gave a hint that a currency devaluation would follow so that 'those who have borrowed money will, on the average, be able to repay that money in the same kind of dollar which they borrowed'.

Almost everyone today has been concerned at times with inflation. We have never experienced deflation and hopefully we never will. Roosevelt's speech sheds light on why policy makers now are more concerned about deflation than inflation and why they should be. The extract that follows is laden with information explaining deflation and the origins of the gold exchange standard. The extract is lengthy, it deals with the government's over commitment on gold obligations and carries messages we all need to take on board again now, including the prospect of mass mortgage foreclosures. Comments of special interest are underlined:

Two months ago we were facing serious problems. The country was dying by inches. It was dying because trade and commerce had declined to dangerously low levels; prices for basic commodities were such as to destroy the value of the assets of national institutions such as banks, savings banks, insurance companies, and others. These institutions, because of their great needs, were foreclosing mortgages, calling loans, refusing credit. Thus there was actually in process of destruction the property of millions of people who had borrowed money on that property in terms of dollars which had had an entirely different value from the level of March, 1933. That situation in that crisis did not call for any complicated consideration of economic panaceas or fancy plans. We were faced by a condition and not a theory.

There were just two alternatives: The first was to allow the foreclosures to continue, credit to be withheld and money to go into hiding, and thus forcing liquidation and bankruptcy of banks, railroads and insurance companies and a recapitalizing of all business and all property on a lower level. This alternative meant a continuation of what is loosely called 'deflation', the net result of which would have been extraordinary hardship on all property owners and, incidentally, extraordinary hardships on all persons working for wages through an increase in unemployment and a further reduction of the wage scale. . . .

Much has been said of late about Federal finances and inflation, the gold standard, etc. Let me make the facts very simple and my policy very clear. In the first place, government credit and government currency are really one and the same thing. Behind government bonds there is only a promise to pay. Behind government currency we have, in addition to the promise to pay, a reserve of gold and a small reserve of silver. In this connection it is worth while remembering that in the past the government has agreed to redeem nearly thirty billions of its debts and its currency in gold, and private corporations in this country have agreed to redeem another sixty or seventy billions of securities and mortgages in gold. The government and private corporations were making these agreements when they knew full well that all of the gold in the United States amounted to only between three and four billions and that all of the gold in all of the world amounted to only about eleven billions.

If the holders of these promises to pay started in to demand gold the first comers would get gold for a few days and they would amount to about one twenty-fifth of the holders of the securities and the currency. The other twenty-four people out of twenty-five, who did not happen to be at the top of the line, would be told politely that there was no more gold left. We have decided to treat all twenty-five in the same way in the interest of justice and the exercise of the constitutional powers of this government. We have placed every one on the same basis in order that the general good may be preserved. Nevertheless, gold, and to a partial extent silver, are perfectly good bases for currency and that is why I decided not to let any of the gold now in the country go out of it.

A series of conditions arose three weeks ago which very readily might have meant, first a drain on our gold by foreign countries, and secondly, as a result of that, a flight of American capital, in the form of gold, out of our country. It is not exaggerating the possibility to tell you that such an occurrence might well have taken from us the major part of our gold reserve and resulted in such a further weakening of our government and private credit as to bring on actual panic conditions and the complete stoppage of the wheels of industry.

The Administration has the definite objective of raising commodity prices to such an extent that those who have borrowed money will, on the average, be able to repay that money in the same kind of dollar which they borrowed.

Roosevelt made good on his promise to devalue the dollar to gold in 1934 and raised the dollar price of gold from $20.67 to $35 per ounce. The devaluation restored nominal solvency to the US Treasury and realigned the value of securities pledged to banks and other lenders. He also committed the United States to buy or sell gold to foreign official holders at the new $35 price. A commitment that remained in force until 1971 and became the cornerstone for dollar dominance in the international monetary system and for the gold exchange standard.

In 1933, to arrest the drain on the nation's gold reserves and to stop gold hoarding, Roosevelt also introduced legislation that abrogated all gold clauses in contracts, banned all export of gold and required that gold held domestically be turned over to the government in exchange for gold certificates. Legislation was also introduced that criminalised private ownership of gold except personal jewellery and gold for use by artisans. Under these arrangements owners of gold were treated unfairly. When their gold was surrendered to the Treasury in 1933 the price was $20.67 an ounce. However when the owners were compensated the gold price was already $35 an ounce. Yet they were only paid $20.67 and they sustained the devaluation loss. The unfair compensation remains a source of contention. The Nobel Laureate economist, the late Milton Friedman, went as far as to say 'one can hardly imagine a measure more destructive of the principles of private property on which a free enterprise society rests'.

Friedman has also challenged the rationale given for prohibiting private ownership of gold as conserving gold for monetary use. He maintained:

The nationalisation of gold was enacted to enable the government to reap the whole of the 'paper' profit from the rise in the price of gold – or perhaps, to prevent private individuals from benefiting. The abrogation of the gold clause had a similar purpose. And this too was a measure destructive of the basic principles of free enterprise. Contracts entered into in good faith and with full

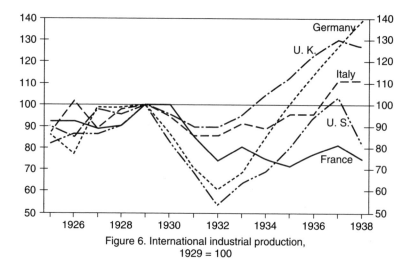

Figure 6. International industrial production,
1929 = 100

Chart 4.3 Industrial production 1925 to 1938. United States, United Kingdom, France, Italy and Germany.
(Chart courtesy of eh.net)

knowledge on the part of both parties to them were declared invalid for the benefit of one of the parties![20]

To this day Roosevelt's ban on private ownership of gold, only lifted in 1975, encourages people all over the world to recognise gold as a protection against government interference. Consider Milton Friedman's charge that there was no difference between Roosevelt's nationalisation of gold at an artificially low price and Fidel Castro's nationalisation of land and factories at an artificially low price. After all, Friedman asks 'on what grounds of principle can the US object to the one after having itself engaged in the other?'[21]

While owners of gold may have been treated unfairly, Roosevelt's actions broke the vicious circle of bank failures and value destruction and the US economy started to recover. The following chart illustrates the precipitous fall in industrial production that started in 1929 in the US and Europe and the recoveries in economic activity that followed, generally after countries abandoned commitments to the gold standard.

The Post World War II Bretton Woods Accord, the Dollar and the IMF

In 1944, a few months after the D-day invasion of Europe started, but before the war in Europe ended, representatives of 44 countries met in the Bretton Woods resort town of New Hampshire at the invitation of the United States. At the meeting a new economic post war economic framework was agreed and adopted.

The wealth and power of the US was formidable at the end of World War II. It owned over 70% of the world's gold, was the world's principal creditor, the strongest military power and an exporter of oil. From its position of strength it set the Bretton Woods Agenda.

Peter Bernstein writes in *The Power of Gold* that most of the designs for the new arrangements came from John Maynard Keynes representing the British Treasury and his counterpart Harry White of the US Treasury Department and:

> ... the broad outlines of what was necessary were easy to define: the cascade of tragic errors in the 1920s and 1930s provided the leaders with a blueprint of what not to do ... Instead of exacting reparations, the Allies carried on vigorous financial and political efforts to bring Germany, Italy & Japan into the mainstream of democratic society. Instead of insisting on repayments for the huge amounts of military aid the United States had provided during the war, Americans only gave lip service to demanding repayment. Instead they converted most of their contribution to the Allied War effort into gifts – and then added the prodigious assistance of the Marshall Plan and other substantial aid programmes on top of that. Instead of a world where each nation stubbornly pursued its own self-interest, the United Nations was created to manage a world of international co-operation.[22]

Robert Mundell gives this nuanced, slightly different and doubtless well informed account of the background to Bretton Woods outcomes:[23]

> In 1944 President Roosevelt told Treasury Secretary Henry Morgenthau to make plans for an international currency after the war. US Treasury economists remember that Harry Dexter White and the staff at the US Treasury actually made a plan that involved the creation of a world currency to be called the *unitas*. A comparable plan that included a world currency called *bancor* was made by Lord Keynes, in London. However before the plan could be debated the Americans had second thoughts and kept silent.

Thus, according to Mundell, Bretton Woods did not create a new international monetary system; it kept the system and dollar/gold parity that had been in place since 1934 when Roosevelt revalued gold at $35/oz. Mundell says it is wrong to speak of a 'Bretton Woods system': The conference at Bretton Woods did not create a new international monetary system. It created two new international institutions, the IMF and the World Bank to manage interdependence in the international financial system. In his view the IMF has been correctly described as 'an episode in the history of the dollar'.

The US dollar took centre stage at Bretton Woods and provided the system's link to gold, became the world's reserve currency and the standard measure of value – the numeraire for the system. It was to be more than *as good as* gold. It was to be *better than* gold. Gold costs money to store and yields no interest or dividends. By contrast owners of dollar securities would earn interest. Backed by a US commitment to convert dollars into gold for official holders it was expected that other countries would hold dollars rather than gold.

The Bretton Woods arrangement governing foreign exchange was a gold exchange standard that provided:

1 The dollar was to be convertible into gold for official holders and the US was obliged to buy or sell gold at $35 per ounce;
2 Member countries were expected to maintain 'stable but adjustable' par values for their currencies within margins of 1% on either side of par value. In the event of 'fundamental disequilibrium' and with the approval of the IMF, par values could be changed; and
3 Currencies other than the US dollar were convertible into the dollar or gold at fixed rates.

To promote stability the IMF was funded with resources to make loans to countries with balance of payments difficulties. After a transitional period member countries were expected to eliminate exchange restrictions on international trade and current account transactions, and make their currencies 'convertible' for non-residents so that they could exchange their funds into currencies of their choice.

The Bretton Woods agreement was negotiated in 1944 and the International Monetary Fund opened for business in 1946. But the financial difficulties of the early post war years were far more severe than had been expected and the system did not become fully operational for a number of years. During this period a dollar shortage developed, the IMF was put on hold and the Marshall Plan was funded to accelerate economic revival in Europe. It took until 1958 before European nations were in a position to accept their IMF obligations.

As strength was restored to the European and Japanese economies in the 1950s and their balance of payments positions improved they started to build up their gold reserves. At the same time the US balance of payments position started to weaken and, with foreigners acquiring more dollars than they were spending over the decade, the world dollar shortage turned into a dollar glut. In 1950 the US had gold backing for 20% of the dollars circulating domestically and abroad. By 1956 it was down to 16%, by 1962 it was down to 11%, and by 1969 down to 5%. By late 1960, less than two years after the European nations had accepted, countries were already anxious about their 'excess' dollar holdings and sought to exchange them for gold and when this happened the US experienced the first of many gold crises.

The Triffin Dilemma and the Gold Pool

Testifying before the US Congress in 1960, the Yale economist Professor Robert Triffin exposed a fundamental problem in the Bretton Woods international monetary system. If the United States stopped running balance of payments deficits, the international community would lose its largest source of additions to reserves. The resulting shortage of liquidity could draw the world economy into a contractionary spiral leading to instability. If US deficits continued, a steady stream of dollars would continue to fuel world economic growth. However, excessive US deficits (a dollar glut) would erode confidence in the value of the US dollar. Without confidence in the dollar, it would no longer be accepted as the world's reserve currency. The fixed exchange rate system could break down, leading to instability. Triffin proposed the creation of new reserve units. These units would not depend on gold or currencies, but would add to the world's total liquidity. Creating such a new reserve would allow the United States to reduce its balance of payments deficits, while still allowing for global economic expansion. In 1969, following Triffin's recommendations, an international agreement was reached to introduce a new IMF reserve asset, Special Drawing Rights (SDRs). They were intended to supplement the US dollar and provide a mechanism for expanding international liquidity without requiring additional US payments deficits or additional dollar balances.

When Europe and Japan recovered and gained relative economic strength the United States faced more competition and commanded less authority over the monetary system. It no longer owned the lion's share of the world's monetary gold and its unique role as issuer of the world's reserve currency came under severe strain. As other nations' dollar holdings grew to a level far in excess of its own, its ability to convert officially held dollars into gold at $35 per ounce also weakened. By the beginning of the 1960s the free market price of gold started to test the pegged US$35 an ounce price. In 1961, with demand rising and US gold reserves falling, President Kennedy's Treasury Secretary Robert Roosa proposed that the US and Europe pool their gold resources to prevent the open market price creeping above $US35 an ounce. On his suggestion early in 1961 the central banks of the US, Britain, West Germany, France, Switzerland, Italy, Belgium, the Netherlands and Luxembourg set up the 'London Gold Pool'. Gold would be sold from the pool if high demand threatened to raise the price on the open market. Dramatic increases in private gold buying by hoarders, speculators and industrial users after 1966 exhausted the pool's supply. Members had to dip into their own gold reserves to meet the demand and, after a rush to purchase gold from November 1967 to March 1968, the gold pool was disbanded.

Vietnam, Charles de Gaulle, Richard Nixon and the End of the Gold Standard

Chronic US balance of payments deficits associated with the costs of funding the Vietnam War and expansive domestic social programmes compounded pressure on the dollar in the 1960s. Over the decade and again in the early 1970s the US incurred federal budget and balance of payments deficits. The following charts illustrate the rising money supply and declining US holdings; the surging US Balance of Payments deficit; and the surging Federal budget deficit.

A report titled 'That (early) 70s Show', published in March 2004 by Paul L. Kasriel, Director of Economic Research at Northern trust, notes similarities between current Fed actions and actions in the 1960s and 1970s, and questions whether similar outcomes will be seen again.[24] The first of the three following charts from the report shows increasing US monetary authority liabilities and decreasing gold stock – the action Robert Mundell described as the Fed 'gunning the money supply' in the *New York Times* article mentioned above. The second chart reflects the build-up of Federal deficits. The third chart reflects the build-up of Balance of Payment Deficits.

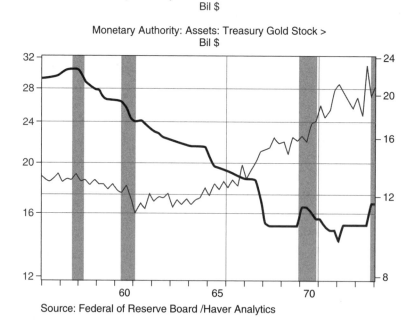

Source: Federal of Reserve Board /Haver Analytics

Chart 4.4 US monetary reserves and gold stocks 1955 to 1974.
(Courtesy Paul Kasriel/Northern Trust)

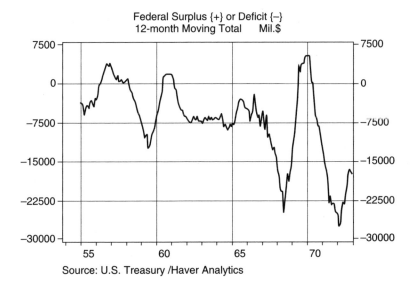

Chart 4.5 Federal surplus (+) or deficit (–) 12 month moving total mil $. (Courtesy Paul Kasriel/Northern Trust)

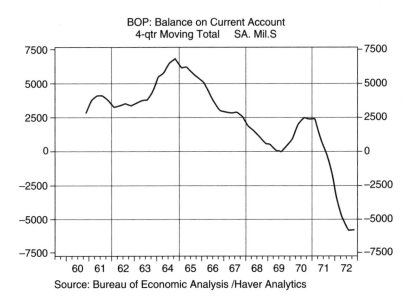

Chart 4.6 BOP: Balance on current account. (Courtesy Paul Kasriel/Northern Trust)

An historic turning point came in February 1965 when France's President Charles de Gaulle assembled an audience of a thousand journalists in the opulent and gilded Elysée Palace. The gathering was arranged for the world to hear him make a call for a return to a classic gold standard. In his speech de Gaulle echoed the words of the French economist Jacques Rueff, an implacable critic of the gold exchange standard, that entrenched the dollar as the world's principal international currency. The objection was that it gave the United States the 'exorbitant privilege' of settling its foreign debts in dollars rather than gold – a privilege Rueff described as the United States having discovered the 'marvellous secret of a deficit without tears'. Rueff concluded a dollar glut would to lead to a collapse of the world economy and a second Great Depression.

In his speech, Charles de Gaulle complained that the United States was not capable of balancing its budget. As a result, he explained, the US 'allows itself to have enormous debts. Since the dollar is the reference currency everywhere, it can cause others to suffer the effects of its poor management. This is not acceptable.' His conclusion was that there can be no criterion or standard other than gold: 'Gold that never changes, that can be shaped into ingots, bars, coins, that has no nationality, and that is eternally and universally accepted as the unalterable fiduciary value par excellence.'

Many commentators, including Peter Bernstein, accuse de Gaulle of dollar baiting. There is certainly some truth in their claims. But there were also grounds for serious concern over America's financial condition shared by Germany and other European states. Yet de Gaulle's campaign was a non starter. Nostalgia about 'the good old days' of the classic gold standard were misplaced. Europe had staged a rapid post war recovery funded and enabled by the US and neither de Gaulle, nor anyone else, could offer an alternative to dollar hegemony. De Gaulle lost the campaign for a restoration of the gold standard but he hadn't lost the war. Under the Bretton Woods agreements France could oblige the United States to settle dollar claims in gold and de Gaulle demanded that, in future, French dollar claims would have to be settled in gold. His actions hastened the end of the dollar and the International Monetary System's links with gold.

Faced with a relentless gold drain in August 1971 President Richard Nixon announced he was severing all links between gold and the dollar. In a broadcast message he played down the importance of gold and said he was acting to 'protect the position of the American dollar as a pillar of monetary stability around the world'. Over the previous seven years, Nixon complained, there had been a monetary crisis every year and 'in recent weeks, the speculators have been waging an all-out war on the American dollar'. As the strength of a nation's currency is based on the strength of its economy and America's economy was by far the strongest in the world, he announced he had directed the Secretary of the Treasury 'to take the action necessary to defend the dollar against the speculators . . . to suspend temporarily the convertibility of the dollar into gold or other reserve assets, except in amounts and conditions determined to be in the interest of monetary stability and in the best interests of the United States'. He also introduced price controls and imposed a 15% import tariff protection to cushion the US economy from the fall out from leaving gold and force revaluations on the currencies of countries exporting to the US.

Nixon went on to address the question of the effect of his actions on Americans and posed the question 'Now, what is this action – which is very technical – what does it mean for you? Let me lay to rest the *bugaboo* of what is called devaluation.' I can't tell you what the word bugaboo means. It's not in any dictionary I have access to. However in 1981 you would have needed over $200 to buy what $100 bought in 1971.[25] The world experienced the biggest peacetime inflation in history after Nixon 'closed the gold window' – the jargon used to describe ending the right of national treasuries to receive payment in gold instead of dollars. It wasn't all Nixon's fault. The price of a barrel of oil was about $3 in 1971. By 1974 it had quadrupled to $12.[26]

The severing of the dollar link to gold in 1971 and the movement to flexible exchange rates in 1973 removed constraints on monetary expansion. The dollar emerged as the only international money and, in the words of Robert Mundell:

> The US Federal Reserve could now pump out billions and billions of dollars that would be taken up and used as reserves by the rest of the world. Not only that, but US government Treasury bills and bonds became a new form of international money. Dollars became the reserves of new international banks producing money in the Eurodollar market and other offshore outlets for international money. The newly elastic international monetary supply was now made to order to accommodate the supply shock of the oil price spike at the end of 1973. The quadrupling of oil prices created deficits in Europe and Japan which were financed by Eurodollar credits, in turn fed by US monetary expansion. The Fed argued that its policy was not inflationary because the money supply in the United States did not rise unduly. The fact is that it had been exported to build the base for inflation abroad. As I showed in an article published in 1971, it is the world, not the national dollar base that governs inflation. US prices rose 3.9 times in the quarter century after 1971, by far the most inflation than at any other time in the nation's history.[27]

As we will see in the following chapter on the dollar standard, Mundell's comments on dollar liquidity boosting international reserves in the 1970s applies again to international reserve growth in the twenty-first century. The US current account deficit remains the font for global liquidity on a grander scale now than at any previous time even though the US, once the world's biggest creditor, is now the world's biggest debtor.

Charles de Gaulle's 1965 speech explained the difference between a classic gold standard and a gold exchange standard where some currencies enjoy the privilege of being treated as if they were gold. Over the last few centuries there haven't been pure gold standards. Generally National Treasuries and central banks have held enough gold to meet likely calls for conversion of currency into gold in the normal run of events. To fund their international commitments they have supplemented their gold holdings with currencies considered 'as good as gold'. De Gaulle's comments on the gold exchange standard explain the distinction between a gold standard and a gold exchange standard and why a gold exchange standard 'no longer tallied with the facts':

> It is common knowledge that, as a result of the Genoa Conference in 1922, this system had conferred upon two currencies, the pound and the dollar, the privilege of being automatically regarded as equivalent to gold for all international payments purposes. Other currencies were not so regarded. Later on, as the pound was devalued in 1931 and the dollar in 1933, it looked as if this major advantage was in jeopardy. But the United States came out of the Great Depression. Then the Second World War ruined European currencies by unleashing inflation. Now nearly all the gold reserves in the world were in the hands of the United States, which being supplier to the whole world had maintained the value of its national currency. Therefore it could seem natural that other states should include dollars or gold, indifferently, in their foreign-exchange reserves, and that balance-of-payments equilibrium should be achieved by transferring U.S. credit or currency as well as gold. The more so as the United States had no difficulty in settling its debts with gold if requested to do so. This international monetary system, the so-called gold-exchange standard, thus became common practice.
>
> Today, however, it seems that this system no longer tallies with the facts, and therefore its drawbacks are becoming increasingly burdensome . . . The circumstances that led to the gold-exchange standard in the past are indeed different now. The currencies of Western nations have been rehabilitated, so much so that the total gold reserves of the Six are now equal to those of the United States. They would be even higher if the Six determined to convert all their dollar holdings into gold. It is therefore clear that the convention under which the dollar is an international currency of transcendent value no longer rests on the initial basis, which was that the United States owned the major part of the world's gold. But there is more. The fact that many countries as a matter of principle accept dollars as well as gold to offset the U.S. balance-of-payments deficits leads to a situation wherein the United States is heavily in debt without having to pay. Indeed, what the United States owes to foreign countries it pays − at least in part − with dollars that it can simply issue if it chooses to.

Conclusion

To this day the US continues to settle its foreign debts with 'dollars that it can simply issue if it chooses to'. After the great inflation of the 1970s that followed when links between the International Monetary System and gold were severed it took until the 1980s before central bankers regained credibility as inflation fighters. The Cold War ended in the 1990s and, by the end of the twentieth century there were no challenges to the global hegemony of the United States and the dollar.

By 2008 the pendulum had swung in the other direction. A stock exchange bubble burst in 2000. The 9/11 attacks followed in 2001. The Iraq and Afghanistan wars, waged at great cost, failed to achieve their objectives. Oil prices soared to record levels. Inflation menaced. A housing bubble inflated and burst in the US. A global credit crisis led to losses the IMF expect to reach $1 trillion. Global banks are likely to bear about half the losses. Money market, pension and hedge funds, other institutional investors and insurance companies are expected to bear the other half. In the US and the UK the Fed and the Bank of England have already had to act as lenders of last resort and bail out banks to avoid systemic failure. The IMF have acknowledged that credit deterioration, a weakening economy and falling credit prices threaten the capital of systemically important financial institutions.[28,29]

The Austrian School of Economists, diehard advocates of the gold standard, warned this was going to happen. In their book 'the (current) housing boom and bust is only a symptom of a wider problem'. They attribute the severity of the Great Depression to 'the prevalence of the view that wage rates must at all costs be maintained in order to maintain the purchasing power of the consumer'. For them 'a recession is precisely what the economy needs the most. It is the equivalent of the drunk who needs time on the wagon'.[30]

Did gold cause the Great Depression? In the opinion of Milton Friedman, Ben Bernanke and several other economists excessive concern by the Fed over preserving the levels of the nation's gold reserves contributed to the onset of the Great Depression. Their opinions are challenged by others and whether or not gold caused the Great Depression is an academic question now. What we have to consider is whether the dollar standard might cause the next depression. It won't be because of a shortage of dollars. With a paper money currency a country can always print money. But excess money printing leads to other problems discussed in the following chapters.

5

The Dollar Standard and the 'Deficit without Tears'

Is the dollar again America's currency and everyone else's problem?

The closest analogy to the United States' position is that of a central bank issuing fiat money within its own national monetary domain. Although banknotes and coins may formally be liabilities of the central bank, in practise they never have to be redeemed, because the private sector's demand for domestic money is ongoing. Analogously, on an international scale, the collectivity that is the United States can issue to the rest of the world liquid claims on itself that 'never' have to be redeemed.

Professor Ronald I McKinnon, Stanford University 2000[1]

The Dangers of Uncharted Waters

A decade ago Robert Mundell gave a speech in which he questioned whether current international monetary arrangements still add up to a system. 'An international monetary system in the strict sense of the word' he said 'does not presently exist. Every country has its own system.'[2] It's not playing with words to debate whether we have an international monetary arrangement or a system. There was a regime change in the international monetary system when all links between gold, the dollar and global price levels were severed. Since then, with the dollar-centric international monetary system in uncharted waters, the stability of our fiduciary money, whether it is in dollars, yen, pounds or any other currency, can't be taken for granted. Whatever currencies we own will be affected by outcomes for the dollar. It's the kingpin in the system.

Until Richard Nixon closed the gold window in 1971 the international monetary system was indirectly linked to gold through fixed exchange rates with the dollar anchored to gold. It was an imperfect system but it was a system. After the gold window was closed a new monetary system was never devised – it happened. In December 1971 the Group of Ten OECD countries met in the United States to find a formula for new monetary arrangements. US Treasury Secretary John Connally chaired the meeting held at the Smithsonian Institution in Washington. The Group of Ten is made up of the eleven industrial OECD countries that have since after World War II consulted and cooperated on economic, monetary and financial matters. (The OECD is the successor to the Marshall Plan.)

The 'Smithsonian Agreement' reached in 1971 sought to formalise a business as usual continuity – except that the US would no longer be obliged to settle dollar debts in gold.[3] Gold, however, remained the numeraire in the system and, to establish a devaluation against other currencies, the US first devalued the dollar to $38 an ounce and then to $42.11, at which price it still values its gold holdings.

Mundell's opinion is that after the Smithsonian Agreement was reached:

> The world thus moved onto a pure dollar standard in which the major countries fixed their currencies to the dollar without a reciprocal obligation with respect to gold convertability by the United States. But US monetary policy was too expansionary in the following years and, after another ineffective devaluation of the dollar, the system was allowed to break up into generalised floating in the spring of 1973. Thus ended the dollar standard.[4]

What followed the end of the 'Smithsonian' dollar standard was in reality a global fiat money establishment with economic growth funded by credit expansion. The great inflation of the 1970s was a consequence of the rapid expansion of credit. Mundell finds that when the system broke down 'money supplies became more elastic, accommodating wage increases and the monopolistic pricing of internationally traded commodities'. As the price of oil rose in the 1970s the Eurodollar market expanded to finance the deficits of oil importers. From Eurodollar deposits of $221 in 1971 they 'exploded' to $2.35 billion in 1982. Inflation was worldwide and became a major problem in the US. Over twenty years from 1952 to 1971 US wholesale prices rose less than 30%. In the 11 years following 1971 they rose by 157%. In Italy and the UK prices more than tripled. Mundell cites the following Table of Consumer Price levels for G7 countries between 1950 and 1998:

Table 5.1 Consumer prices in G-7 countries, selected years, 1950–1998.

Country	1950	1971	1980	1985	1990	1998
United States	29.2	49.1	100	130.5	158.5	197.8
Japan	16.3	44.9	100	114.4	122.5	134.4
United Kingdom	13.4	30.3	100	141.5	188.7	243.6
Germany	39.2	64.1	100	121.0	129.4	144.8
Fance	15.6	42.1	100	157.9	184.2	213.7
Italy	13.9	28.7	100	190.3	250.6	346.3
Canada	28.4	47.5	100	143.0	177.9	203.7

Source: IMF International Financial Statistics (International Monetary Fund, various years).

Three consecutive years of double digit back to back inflation in the US from 1979 to 1981 led to the crisis situation Mundell described in his *New York Times* '$10 000 Gold' op-ed contribution quoted in the previous chapter.

In July 1978 former US President Jimmy Carter appointed Paul Volcker as Fed Chairman. Volcker first raised interest rates and, when that was not sufficient to control inflation, he took steps to control the money supply. Volcker succeeded in taming inflation but it took time for his measures to take effect and when inflation was soaring the gold price also soared. It rose from $380 in November 1979 to its brief legendary 21 January 1980 peak of $850 (equivalent to about $2000 in 2008 money). When later in 1980 interest rates in the US surged to over 20% money started to move from gold back to dollars and, by the last few days of February 1983, gold fell briefly to $105.

By the late 1980s and early 1990s there was general comfort that central bankers had the formula, authority and courage to tame inflation. However to this day 'the deficit without tears' remains the font for expansion of global liquidity.

There have, of course, been key monetary developments between 1973 when the Smithsonian Agreement ended and the regime of free floating exchange rates started. They include the Plaza Agreement when the Group of Ten cooperated to achieve an orderly dollar devaluation and the Louvre Agreement when they agreed to cooperate for a dollar revaluation and the introduction of the Euro currency in 1999. The Chronology details the dates and scope of these and other developments.

The focus of this book is on whether current economic crises could lead to anything akin to a re-run of either the Great Depression of the 1930s or the great inflation of the 1970s. The commentary on the rise and fall of the gold standard in the previous chapter and the deficit without tears in this chapter is intended to support:

1 A better understanding of deflation and the Great Depression of the 1930s;

2 A better understanding of the great inflation of the 1970s and inflation generally;

3 Recognition of economic and emotional factors that affect the gold price; and

4 A framework for interpreting developments that could lead to erosion of the value of the fiduciary fiat money we own.

In worst-case scenarios policy blunders, global tensions and other unfortunate events will trigger what Dr Marc Faber calls the 'Zimbabwiazition' of the dollar. For that outcome owning gold and precious metals is an imperative. But must the deficit without tears end in tears as Marc Faber expects it will? Or might the opinion of Professor Ronald McKinnon quoted at the beginning of this chapter that 'the collectivity that is the United States can issue to the rest of the world liquid claims on itself that "never" have to be redeemed' prevail?

Events will cast different complexions on the economic opportunities and threats we are going to confront. Beyond outlining factors recognised as influencing economic prospects in these chapters the Goldwatcher web site will post references to news, opinion and commentary on the content in this book, including hopefully commentary from readers.[5]

The United States current account deficit is in the region of $800 billion and is over 5.5% of GDP. To finance both the current account deficit and its own sizeable foreign investments the United States must import about $1 trillion of foreign capital every year. That's more than $4 billion every working day.[6]

The following table reflects global Current Account Balances in dollars in mid 2007:

Table 5.2 Global current account balances in dollars.

CURRENT A/C BALANCES BILLIONS US $	1996	2000	2004	2005	2006
Country or Region Industrial	31.1	–304.7	–296.5	–502.5	–607.3
United Sates	–124.8	–417.4	–640.2	–754.8	–811.5
Japan	65.7	119.6	172.1	165.7	170.4
Euro area (see note)	77.3	–37.0	115.0	22.2	–11.1
France	23.4	22.3	10.5	–19.5	.28.3
Germany	–14.0	–32.6	118.0	128.4	146.4
Italy	36.8	–6.2	–15.5	–28.4	–41.6
Spain	–1.4	–23.1	–54.9	–83.0	–108.0
Other	12.9	30.0	56.6	64.4	45.0
Australia	–15.4	–14.9	–38.5	–41.2	–40.9

Table 5.2 (Continued)

CURRENT A/C BALANCES BILLIONS US $	1996	2000	2004	2005	2006
Canada	3.4	19.7	21.3	26.3	21.5
Switzerland	22.0	30.7	50.4	61.4	69.9
United Kingdom	-10.5	-37.6	-35.4	-53.7	-88.3
Memo:					
Industrial excl. United States	155.9	112.7	343.7	252.3	204.2
Developing	-82.8	124.7	296.5	507.9	643.2
Asia	-40.2	77.0	172.4	245.1	352.1
China	7.2	20.5	68.7	160.8	249.9
Hong Kong	04.0	7.0	15.7	20.3	20.6
Korea	-23.1	12.3	28.2	15.0	6.1
Taiwan	10.9	8.9	18.5	16.0	24.7
Thailand	-14.4	9.3	2.8	-7.9	3.2
Latin America	-39.1	-48.1	20.4	34.6	48.7
Argentina	06.8	09.0	3.2	3.5	5.2
Brazil	-23.5	-24.2	11.7	14.2	13.6
Mexico	-2.5	-18.7	-6.7	-4.9	-1.5
Middle East	15.1	72.1	99.2	189.0	212.4
Africa	-5.2	7.2	0.6	14.6	19.9
Eastern Europe	-18.5	-31.8	-58.6	-63.2	-88.9
Former Soviet Union	5.2	48.3	62.6	87.7	99.0
Memo: Developing Asia Excluding China	-47.4	56.5	103.7	84.3	102.2
Statistical Variation	-51.6	-180.0	0.0	5.4	35.9

Commentators have opposing views on the consequences of the international current account imbalances reflected in the table. A traditional view sees the imbalances as a threat to global economic stability and a 'new paradigm' view seeks to explain them as a natural consequence of economic and financial globalisation. The traditional view argues that it will be hard to avoid an abrupt unwinding of the imbalances, a sell-off of dollar assets, a sharp increase in US interest rates and a hard landing for the global economy. The traditionalists argue that loose monetary and indulgent fiscal policies in the US must be reversed urgently. By contrast, the new paradigm view argues that over time the imbalances will be resolved smoothly through the normal functioning of markets.[7]

The dispute relates to the role of the dollar as universally accepted money and to the status of US Treasury securities as the world's premier risk free asset. Stanford Professor Ronald McKinnon, quoted above, argues that US Treasury securities are accepted as a risk free asset in the world's capital markets 'because the U.S. federal government owns the dollar-creating central bank (the Fed) and it can always create means of settlement on its own debt – whether held domestically or by foreigners . . . (and) under the world dollar standard, no other country can similarly create international money at will'.[8] He traces the origins of the dollar standard back to the 1944 Bretton Woods Accords when 'other nations declared official exchange rate parities against the dollar, making it the central numeraire for the system. The official monetary order did not create asymmetry among currencies' he contends, 'it simply recognised it. Thus was the dollar enthroned as international money. When the system of official exchange rate parities broke down in 1971, the dollar was not dethroned.' It's over 35 years since the Bretton Woods arrangements broke down and McKinnon asserts that the dollar is still the main currency used in the world's interbank forward spot and exchange markets, is still the currency of invoice for primary commodity trades and industrial goods and services and the main currency of denomination for international capital flows. Outside of Europe the dollar is also the prime intervention currency used by many governments who unofficially peg their currencies to the dollar. Further, all foreign central banks have extensive holdings of dollars and US Treasury securities in their official exchange reserves.[9]

The Traditional View

Richard Duncan, the author of *The Dollar Crisis – Causes, Consequences & Cures*,[10] is among the best known commentators who take the traditional view. He argues that since links with gold were severed in 1971 explosive growth in international monetary reserves spawned by dollar deficits have resulted in a global credit bubble that is going to burst. In the first chapter of *The Dollar Crisis*, 'The Imbalance of Payments', he writes 'during the three decades following the breakdown of the Bretton Woods international monetary system trade imbalances have flooded the world with liquidity causing economic overheating and hyperinflation in asset prices, initially within individual countries, and now on a global scale'. He finds the primary flaw of the dollar standard is that it lacks the adjustment mechanism that existed with the gold based Bretton Woods system or any other adjustment mechanism. As a result trade imbalances of 'unprecedented magnitude and duration' have developed and destabilised the global economy. The enormous balance of trade surpluses held by exporting countries in dollar denominated debt instruments have turned the United States into the most heavily indebted nation in history. To forecast the outlook for the global economy Duncan argued it was necessary to estimate the timing of two events:

1 A collapse in consumer spending in the United States that will lead to a recession after the US property bubble bursts; and
2 A correction of the US current account deficit.

The first condition was met in 2007 and, with a likely slowdown or even recession in the US, the second condition could be met in 2008.

Duncan focused on the US trade deficit for two reasons. First its extraordinary size and second because the US has been the only country able to finance its growing level of indebtedness to the rest of the world by issuing debt instruments payable in its own domestic currency. The following lines flesh out the basis of his prediction for an inevitable worldwide recession:

> When the US refused to abide by the rules of Bretton Woods by suspending the convertibility of dollars into gold, the adjustment mechanism that had previously prevented persistent imbalances ceased to function. As if by magic the constraints that had previously kept the trade deficits of the US in check seemed to just disappear.

Over the three decades since the collapse of Bretton Woods Duncan notes: 'The US has incurred a cumulative current deficit of more than $3 trillion (as at 2005). The effect of $3 trillion coming into the banking systems of the countries with a current account surplus against the US set in motion a process of credit creation just as if the world had discovered an enormous supply of new gold.' The surge of credit generated a worldwide credit bubble backed only by paper reserves and was characterised by economic overheating and severe asset price inflation. Because much of the credit cannot be repaid Duncan argues the credit bubble is precariously close to deflating and 'the economic house of cards built with paper dollars has begun to wobble'. Its fall, he concluded 'will once again teach the world why gold – not paper – has been the preferred store of value for thousands of years'.[11]

Duncan forecast that after the era of export-led growth ends and economic growth founded on domestic demand follows a global recession that will impact world trade, commodity prices, stock markets and government finances – a conclusion in line with the French economist Jacques Rueff's often quoted remark that asking the US to settle its deficits would be like giving a bald man a comb and asking him to comb his hair. He can't. But keep in mind that the traditional view on deficits and imbalances could be wrong. Jacques Rueff challenged the sustainability of dollar hegemony forty years ago. Since then the US and the global economies have prospered. So let's look at the new paradigm approach to global current account imbalances and see if we can find an acceptable explanation.

A New Paradigm: The Bretton Woods II Theory

Investors who only a few years ago experienced the new paradigm hype that pumped hot air to the Nasdaq stock exchange bubble will be sceptical of new paradigms. But it's foolish to ignore the Bretton Woods II theory on global current account imbalances just because it's a new paradigm. It's complex, contrarian and controversial but the Bretton Woods II theory has been supported by three grass roots positive factors:

1 It has explained current money flows and interest rates with reference to international trade patterns past and present;
2 Predictions on the consequences of international trade patterns made by the authors were prescient; and
3 The authors are credible and influential economists.

Bretton Woods II is the brainchild of Michael Dooley, a senior consultant to Deutsche Bank, David Folkerts-Landau, a Managing Director and global head of research for Deutsche Bank, and Peter Garber, a global strategist with the bank. For convenience they are often cited as D, F & G. Since 1992 Dooley has been an economics professor at the University of California Santa Cruz.[12] In view of the general interest in their work and the frequent revisions D, F & G compiled a 140 page compilation of their research and have made it accessible on line.[13]

For convenience I refer to the post World War II Bretton Woods agreements as Bretton Woods I. D, F & G argue that in 1944, when the Bretton Woods I agreements were made, the priority was to repair the physical devastation caused by the war and revive the economies of war torn Europe and Japan. At the time the US owned over 70% of the world's gold, had the wealth to underwrite post war reconstruction and economic revival and was in a position to ensure that it would be accomplished. In this relationship the US was the centre or core country and the war torn countries of Europe including Germany, France and Italy and Japan were the periphery.[14] A similar construction applied in the colonial relationships of the nineteenth and early twentieth centuries, when the colonial masters were the centre countries and the colonies were the periphery.

The 1944 Bretton Woods arrangements formally required countries to peg the exchange rates of their currencies to the dollar and maintain fixed rates of exchange. The periphery countries adopted an export-led recovery strategy, kept their labour costs low, introduced currency controls and kept their currencies undervalued. Further, to avoid fuelling domestic inflation, when payments for their exports were received, to the extent that it was possible, the funds were accumulated as dollar reserves. Over the years, as the economies of the old periphery recovered, they liberalised their currency policies and eventually joined and competed with the prosperous core countries and, when that stage was reached, the post World War Bretton Woods arrangements broke up. If we ask the question now whether hardships experienced after World War II when countries in the old periphery first adopted an export-led growth strategy were worth enduring the answer is obviously that they were. It didn't take long for the post war recovery initiatives to restore prosperity and, since then, the old periphery countries have gone from strength to strength.

While the cold war was still in progress D, F & G argue that when the old periphery countries joined the centre countries there were no candidates to make up a new periphery. But that all changed when the Cold War ended and emerging Asia became the new periphery. The countries in the new periphery now follow a similar export-led growth strategy, keep their labour costs low, their reserves in dollars and, when necessary to keep their currencies undervalued, they intervene in currency markets. The key twenty-first century global priority is China's plan to urbanise 200 million workers. But, as China can only absorb 10 million new workers a year, D, F & G argue that Bretton Woods II can last for 20 years supported by China alone and, in any event, other emerging countries will keep it going for decades.

D, F & G first published their opinions in 2003 as *An Essay on the Revived Bretton Woods System*. A short abstract introducing the essay reads:

> The economic emergence of a fixed exchange rate periphery in Asia has re-established the US as the center country in the Bretton Woods international monetary system. The normal evolution of the international monetary system involves the emergence of a periphery for which the development strategy is export-led growth supported by undervalued exchange rates, capital controls and official capital outflows in the form of accumulation of reserve asset claims on the center country. The success of this strategy in fostering economic growth allows the periphery to graduate to the center. Financial liberalisation, in turn, requires floating exchange rates among the center countries. But there is a line of countries waiting to follow the Europe of the 1950s/60s and Asia today sufficient to keep the system intact for the foreseeable future.[15]

A key concept in D, F & G's analysis of the current monetary system is that 'earned' US dollars have replaced gold as the ultimate reserve asset. The dollars are 'earned' when physical delivery of a consignment is made and a dollar invoice becomes payable. They also argue that money from the new periphery held in dollars in US banks serves as collateral to secure exporters' obligations. This argument has some resonance as China is still a communist country and property rights are not well protected. But it is most unusual for the debtor to provide collateral to the creditor. A normal security arrangement would be vice versa.

There is also concern about whether the pattern of savings flowing from developing countries to the United States, a phenomenon that has been described as money flowing uphill, can be sustained. Miranda Xafa, a member of the IMF's executive board, is one of those who believe it can. She has written:[16]

The '*Revived Bretton Woods*' view (Dooley et al. (2003, 2004) explains the paradox of savings flowing from developing countries to the United States, as well as the low global interest rates, through the export-led strategy pursued by Asian countries in order to channel domestic and foreign direct investment to the export industries . . . The result is persistent current account surpluses and reserve accumulation by Asian central banks, thus generating Bernanke's global savings glut and keeping interest rates low.[17] In this view, Asian countries with underdeveloped financial systems are better off exporting their savings to the United States by buying U.S. bonds, and re-importing some of these savings in the form of FDI (foreign direct investment). The accumulation of dollar assets by Asian central banks is effectively used as collateral for FDI. Contrary to conventional wisdom, this development strategy has permitted developing countries that are net *lenders* to grow rapidly by ensuring efficient intermediation of their savings and thus acquiring a world-class capital stock.

Nouriel Roubini's Criticism of Bretton Woods II

Among Bretton Woods II's many critics the most vociferous has been Nouriel Roubini, an economics Professor at New York University's Stern School of Business and the founder of the leading macroeconomics web site RGE monitor.[18] Since the Bretton Woods II theory was first published in 2004 Roubini has challenged every aspect of it.[19] He makes the case that the US must take steps to reduce its need for external financing before it exhausts the rest of the world's willingness to add to their dollar reserves. The rest of the world must also take steps to reduce its dependence on unsustainable growth in US domestic demand to support its own industrial growth. Otherwise the risks of hard landings for the US and global economy are bound to grow. Roubini envisions the path to a hard landing as: 'A sharp fall in the value of the US dollar, a rapid increase in US long-term interest rates and a sharp fall in the price of a range of risk assets including equities and housing.' A steep dollar fall in his opinion can also lead to a severe global economic slowdown, if not an outright recession.[20]

I was surprised to read at one stage that Roubini had second thoughts about Bretton Woods II. On 13 September 2007 he presented a seminar to staff at the IMF on 'The Risk of a U.S. Hard Landing and Implications for the Global Economy and Financial Markets'.[21] In response to a question on global financial imbalances he answered that he had thought the Bretton Woods II regime would unravel sooner rather than later, but what he *got wrong* 'was the willingness of the world's central banks not only to continue financing the US but to increase their financing' and 'the unravelling of something unsustainable has not occurred so far'. Roubini added he wasn't even sure whether a US hard landing would lead creditors to 'pull the plug' on the US in view of repercussions that would also damage their interests.

To an extent Roubini's re-think endorses D, F & G's conclusion that 'the US is being underwritten by Asia for the foreseeable future'. The following extract from D, F & G's analysis outlines why they find relationships between emerging Asia and the US are symbiotic:

> Asia's proclivity to hold US assets does not reflect an irrational affinity for the US. Asia would export anywhere if it could and happily finance any resulting imbalances. But the US is open. Europe is not. Europe could not absorb the flood of goods, given its structural problems and in the face of absorbing Eastern Europe as well. So Asia's exports go to the US, as does its finance – otherwise, a US, if faced with financing difficulties, might similarly tend toward more stringent commercial policy. Asian officials are unlikely to shift toward euro assets because of the depressing effect this would have on trade with the US. The irony here is that concern of investors in the capital account region about the risk/return in an increasingly indebted US is misplaced. The US is being underwritten by Asia for the foreseeable future.

The Deficit without Tears

It's interesting that in their first essay published in 2003 D, F & G included a reference to a 1965 interview with Jacques Rueff that appeared in the *Economist* magazine. The interview was conducted after President Charles de Gaulle launched his campaign for a return to the gold standard and included Rueff's comment on the United States 'having discovered the magic secret of running a deficit without tears'. This was Rueff's main complaint about the dollar standard mentioned in the *Economist* interview:

> When a country with a key currency runs a balance of payments deficit – that is to say, the United States for example – it pays the creditor country dollars, which end up with the latter's central bank. But the dollars are of no use in Bonn, or in Tokyo or in Paris. The very same day, they are re-loaned to the New York money market, so that they return to the place of origin. Thus the debtor country does not lose what the creditor country has gained. So the key currency country never feels the effect of a deficit in its balance of payments. And the main consequence is that there is no reason whatever for the deficit to disappear because it does not appear. Let me be more positive: if I had an agreement with my tailor that whatever money I pay him returns to me the very same day as a loan, I would have no objection at all to ordering more suits from him.

Ben Bernanke

Fed Chairman Ben Bernanke has given two speeches on his Global Savings Glut theory explaining America's current account deficit funded largely by emerging economies. First in March 2005 in the US and later in September 2007 in a Bundesbank lecture in Germany 'Global Imbalances: Recent Developments and Prospects'.[22] The table of global current account balances included with this chapter accompanied his September lecture. Bernanke's speeches tend to be lengthy academic discussions. Getting to the nub of what he is saying can be difficult. However he raises the question 'Are the current account imbalances that we see today a problem?' and answers 'Not everyone would agree that they are, for several reasons.' His answer invites the response that not everyone would not agree they are not, again for several reasons. The following are a few selected points taken from Bernanke's otherwise ambiguous comments:

1 Although the US current account deficit is not sustainable at its current level the cost of servicing debt owing to foreigners has to date not been onerous and the share of US assets in foreign portfolios does not seem excessive relative to the importance of the United States in the global economy.

2 The current pattern of external imbalances reflecting the export of capital from the developing countries to the industrial economies, particularly the United States 'may prove counterproductive over the longer term'.

3 The large US current account deficit can't persist indefinitely. The ability of the US to make debt service payments and the willingness of foreigners to hold US assets in their portfolios are both limited. 'Adjustment must eventually take place, and the process of adjustment will have both real and financial consequences.'

4 In the longer term, the developing world should be the recipient, not the provider, of financial capital.

In his 2005 speech Bernanke included a reference to D, F & G's analysis and the all important issue of foreign exchange interventions by emerging economies to promote export-led growth.[23] He has only mentioned D, F & G that one time. Their conclusions don't line up with his thesis that the surging US current account deficit funded by China and other developing economies 'is the tail of the dog; for the most part, passively determined by foreign and domestic incomes, asset prices, interest rates, and exchange rates, which are themselves in turn the products of more fundamental driving forces'.

Referring to the expansion of US housing wealth, Bernanke acknowledged 'much of it came from foreign money easily accessible to households through cash-out refinancing and home equity lines of credit'. However these are surely not conditions that were forced on Americans. One well known commentator has even suggested that the US current account deficit would be better described as caused by a global savings glutton than a global savings glut.

Miranda Xafa

Miranda Xafa's analysis on global financial imbalances is more crisp than Bernanke's rambles. She comes to the conclusion that an abrupt unwinding of dollar debts is highly unlikely and argues that there is no historical precedent of disorderly exchange rate adjustment in industrial countries that keep inflation under control and have a well-regulated financial system. She also argued that foreign appetites for US assets remained strong as a result of the unique role of the US as the 'banker of the world', offering liquid, low-risk low-return assets at the same time as American investors acquire higher yielding assets from the rest of the world.

In her opinion it's more appropriate to measure US debt against assets than against GDP. US net foreign liabilities amount to $2.5 trillion and household net worth amounts $55 trillion. If the United States were a company, she asks, who would worry about its debt-equity ratio of 4.5%? And who would refuse to extend new credit?

Miranda's Xafa's arguments were more convincing when her comment was published in May 2007 than they are at the time of writing. With the severe depreciation of the dollar it's arguable that the US is not keeping inflation in control. The sub prime mortgage and shadow banking crises also raise questions about whether the US economy is well regulated and ignoring the multi-trillion dollar unfunded social insurance obligations of the US discussed in the following chapter gives a false picture of the state of national solvency.

Obstfeld and Rogoff

While some well constructed arguments support benign outcomes for the US current account deficits other substantial arguments support disruptive outcomes. In a comprehensive paper *The Unsustainable Current Account Position* Professors Maurice Obstfeld and Kenneth Rogoff present detailed analysis on how global imbalances are likely to unwind.[24] On the subject of shocks that might trigger rapid depreciation of the dollar they noted 'One likely shock that might reverse the US current account is a rise in US private saving – perhaps due to a slowdown or collapse in real estate appreciation.' Their conclusions include this warning on derivatives: '. . . world derivatives markets have exponentially expanded in comparison with even ten years ago. With little reliable data on counterparty risk, there has to be concern that a massive dollar movement could lead to significant financial problems that are going to be difficult to foresee before they unfold (e.g. along the lines of the collapse of Long Term Capital).' Rogoff and Obstfeld's argument will be even stronger if, instead of Long Term Capital Management in their closing comment, we read 'The 2007 house price and sub prime mortgage debt crisis' and we also factor in the exponential growth of derivatives since 2004, the year when their report was published.

In a later paper, *America's Deficit the World's Problem*[25] Obstfeld wrote that even during the gold backed Bretton Woods I era the liquidity and risk structure of US deficit financing would 'give an emerging market finance minister sleepless nights'. The US portfolio is extensively leveraged, with foreign obligations four times the net external liability and foreign claims three times as big as the net liability. His concern was that in relation to other nations 'the US is short on debt instruments and long on equity instruments – the gross positions are not offsetting. Instead, they have very different risk and liquidity characteristics, that is, different payouts in different possible future states of the world.' Looking beyond statistical implications Obstfeld posed two serious challenges to the Bretton Woods II argument:

1 Why must the US run a deficit in order for China to accomplish its goals?
2 Will China be able to withstand the threat of US protection, which has already induced it to tax textile exports?

In Chapter 7, Tipping Points to Instability, we discuss financial derivatives in the context of the troubled shadow banking establishment that mushroomed in the US through the years of the Bush presidency and imploded in 2007.

Barry Eichengreen

Another highly respected monetary economist Professor Barry Eichengreen, also of the University of California, Berkeley, acknowledges the insightful analysis in the Bretton Woods II theory in a 2004 paper *Global Imbalances and the Lessons from Bretton Woods.*[26] However he finds a Bretton Woods II System a misleading way of thinking about prospects for the international monetary and financial systems in the twentieth century. He warned 'There may come a point where China and other Asian countries grow fed up with subsidizing the ability of the United States to buy up their corporations and to establish joint ventures on the cheap . . . this is what got Charles De Gaulle all hot and bothered when he complained of "America's exorbitant privilege" and the French decision to pull the plug on Bretton Woods.'

Eichengreen forecast that the end of the present international monetary regime was not far off and challenged benign outcomes suggested by others on several grounds. One was that the members of the periphery were more numerous and heterogeneous today than they were in the 1960s and 'collective interest can't be assumed'. He branded as dubious the assumption that Asian countries will work together to maintain the status quo as 'Asian policy makers are not ignorant about history and are seeking to build more diversified economies that rely on domestic demand as well as exports'.

Assessing the Risks of a Hard Landing for the Dollar

A difficulty with D, F & G's analysis is that while post World War II and post Cold War outcomes certainly underpinned American financial hegemony they have yet to publish on challenges to that hegemony playing and to other developments of overwhelming importance. The first is the Sovereign Wealth Funds that have been established by the world's dollar surplus countries including Middle East oil exporters and China. These are funds that will seek better returns on money than national central banks have achieved owning fixed income debt securities. $2.5 trillion has already been introduced into Sovereign Wealth Funds and it's only the beginning. Financial market forecasts are that over $10 trillion will be introduced within a decade. The second factor to be recognised is that ten years ago oil was hovering round $10 a barrel and by the end of 2007 it was testing $100. The flow of funds to oil exporting nations drains wealth away from the US, introduces inflation and adds to any vulnerabilities in the dollar standard.

As investors we can of course take a heroic view and accept palliative theories and comments in the press. We can even be convinced by the dubious logic that as oil accounts for a small percentage of GDP oil price rises aren't important. We can also comfort ourselves that neither a dollar crash nor a worldwide recession will be in the interests of any players in the global economy and, if serious problems develop, market participants, debtors and creditors will all cooperate to resolve them and we will be spared the ravages of worst-case scenarios. But, even if we are heroic enough to make all these assumptions we can't ignore geopolitical risks that get more menacing by the day.

We also can't ignore the danger of protectionism challenging global economic cooperation. Even Miranda Xafa in her stalwart defence of Bretton Woods II concludes 'it is policymakers, not market participants, who are more likely to upset the existing stable disequilibrium'.[27] And even D, F & G acknowledge that a geopolitical event could threaten the system: 'A blockage of oil through the Strait of Hormuz for example, would likely result in a global recession that easily generates a serious protectionist reaction. More directly, a geopolitical disturbance involving China would obviously portend the sudden end of the game.' And, on the subject of recession, the sub prime, securitised debt crisis and shadow banking crisis that erupted in 2007 must surely also be brought into the equation.

It is too early to decide if D, F & G are right, wrong or partly right. Their strongest argument is that the periphery countries have much to gain by keeping trading and financing patterns going until they have achieved their objectives. Michael Dooley has referred me to comments he recently published on a blog site where he writes:

> The US subprime mortgage fraud currently working its way through world financial markets has almost universally been interpreted as the shock that will finally bring the BW II system to an end (1). Our view is that the opposite prediction is warranted. That is, the Bretton Woods II system will continue to provide the favorable climate that will allow financial markets to recover from the losses generated by fraudulent valuations in a segment of the US mortgage market.
>
> The bottom line for us is that a general decline in the market value of US financial assets could threaten the BW II or any other international monetary system. But the BW II system itself generates levels of interest rates that make the spread of problems in one segment of the US market to a general collapse of asset prices much less likely. The US still generates safe assets for the world even when the US is the source of trouble for risk assets.
>
> The conventional argument has been that the BW II 'internal' problem is that investors will not continue to finance a US deficit in the face of expectations that the dollar will have to depreciate to generate exports needed to service the growing debt. The subprime problem is the most recent in a long line of shocks that have led to announcements of the death of BW II and a hard landing for the US economy . . . No international monetary system could withstand what Martin Wolf has called a 'huge blow to the credibility of the Anglo-Saxon model of transaction-oriented financial capitalism.' But an international monetary system that sustains low real interest rates in international capital markets and rapid growth in the periphery is well placed to withstand a run of the mill outbreak of fraud in US financial markets.[28]

However much is left unexplained. How will China and other periphery countries react to capital losses if the dollar keeps on falling? And will Bretton Woods II still work when national sovereign wealth funds seek out the best returns on their funds instead of their central banks lending to the US at subsidised rates?

This Won't be Fun

If we could be relatively sure that any disruptions in funding the US current account deficit would be slow and of the soft landing variety we need not be too concerned as the US current account deficit will always be 'a deficit without tears'. But can we be sure of a soft landing? Or are we at risk of finding ourselves like the ever frustrated Wile E. Coyote from the old Road Runner cartoons who would run off a cliff, take several steps in the air and then realise he was going to plunge down the precipice?

In July 2007 the economist Paul Krugman presented a paper, *Will There Be A Dollar Crisis?*[29] Reviewing the chances of a Wile E. Coyote moment Krugman finds 'the real question is not whether the dollar must eventually depreciate. It is whether the dollar must eventually depreciate at a rate *faster than investors now expect.*'

Krugman finds investors have been myopic and have not taken on board the *need* for a future dollar decline. 'So' he writes 'it seems likely that there will be a Wile E. Coyote moment when investors realize that the dollar's value doesn't make sense, and that value plunges.' The last words of his report carry the most telling part of his message: 'This probably won't be fun.' In a recent comment on the dollar *The Financial Times'* Martin Wolf describes a Wile E. Coyote moment in more gentle terms: 'In financial markets, the future is now. If holders of the dollar conclude it is no longer a secure store of value they will dump both the currency and assets dependent on its future value.'[30]

Over the coming years, with the world's baby boomer generation reaching retirement age, American and other politicians will be challenged by constituencies with very different demands. Commerce and industry may encourage a severe fall in the dollar to boost exports, reduce the burden of foreign debts and boost income from foreign investments. But for those expecting their future social security entitlements to provide a reasonable standard of living when they retire a severely devalued dollar will be a disaster.

Exchange Rates

Until the post war Bretton Woods agreements broke down the US could have devalued by changing the parity of the dollar to gold. Instead of an ounce of gold being worth $35, the price pegged in 1934, the parity could have been changed to $50, $100 or whatever was considered the right level to re-align the gold price to inflation since 1934. It wouldn't have been a simple 'let's do it and be done' transaction. The IMF and its members would have been involved. Some bitter infighting on who would bear the devaluation loss on existing dollar claims would surely have followed. However, severing links between the dollar and gold was also not a simple transaction and, to compensate for inflation over the years between 1934 and 1971, the gold price could and should have been increased. Discussing the subject in 1962 the Nobel Laureate economist Milton Friedman wrote 'while the legally fixed price of gold has remained $35 (since 1934) prices of other goods have doubled or tripled. Hence $35 is now less than what the free market price should be.' Friedman's explanation on why the gold price had not been increased had nothing to do with complications affecting trading partners. He reasoned that the gold price would have been raised from time to time in the same way that wheat prices had been raised except for the accident that both Soviet Russia and apartheid South Africa were the two countries with which the US had the least political sympathy and, as the world's major producers of gold, they had the most to gain from a price increase. Looking back on what would have been possible before the breakdown of the post World War II Bretton Woods system is interesting but we have to review current mechanisms for restoring balances and take a view on when by owning gold we can compensate for uncertainties in the monetary system.

Following Milton Friedman's monetarist theories the mechanism for resolving imbalances now is 'freely floating currency exchange rates determined in the market by private transactions without governmental intervention'.[31] With floating currency rates we expect market forces will adjust disparities in currency values and trade imbalances. When Milton Friedman proposed leaving it to market forces 'to provide a prompt, effective, and automatic response to changes in conditions affecting international trade' he was explicit on preserving currency stability. 'Being in favour of exchange rates' he wrote 'does not mean being in favour of unstable exchange rates. The ultimate objective is a world in which exchange rates, while free to vary, are, in fact, highly stable because basic economic policies are stable. Instability of exchange rates is a symptom of instability in the underlying economic structure.'[32] As the dollar has already been falling for five years we can't say adjustments have been prompt nor can we say leaving everything to open markets has been stable.

US Sovereign Debt Credit Standing

Within a month of George Bush being re-elected President in 2004 investors started to question the unquestionable – the US Government's triple-A bond rating. The world's benchmark credit rating agencies, Standard & Poors, Moodys and Fitch had not questioned the US triple-A rating when on 13 December 2004 a small independent agency, Egan Jones Ratings, sounded a warning. Acknowledging that the probability of default remained low, they suggested that US bonds should be downgraded to a double-A rating as the US was allowing its currency to depreciate. Bill Gross, who runs America's largest bond fund, commented 'to suggest that the US is a triple-A credit would be to suggest that it can pay its bills over a long period of time in a stable currency. That is no longer true.' Bill Gross's comments were the last I saw published on Egan Jones's warning at the time.

In January 2008 Moody's Investors Service warned that the US 'triple-A' government bond rating could come under pressure in the long term if its Medicare and Social Security programs are not reformed. The report was not a rating action and the analyst noted that the US sub prime mortgage crisis was not affecting the nation's credit rating. However, the housing downturn and sub prime crisis could result in 'a period of slower growth in coming quarters, although further interest rate cuts by the Federal Reserve could help to maintain positive growth'. Moody's cited a stable outlook and the nation's large and diverse economy and moderate level of debt as support for its current 'AAA' bond ratings.

However the economist Jagadeesh Gokhale, quoted extensively in the following chapter on The Economic Consequences of 9/11 and George W. Bush, has a different view.[33] He and other economists interested in generational accounting have long been cautioning policymakers that the US government's entitlement programs 'are excessively profligate' with spending commitments 'so starkly out of line with available resources that they threaten to unravel the U.S. economy' and, even though there is near unanimity among budget analysts that there is an urgent need for restructuring entitlement programs, 'lawmakers in Congress remain deadlocked on the best course of action'.

Gokhale describes Moody's warning as coming late and being badly worded. 'Indeed' he notes 'it may suggest to policymakers that they need not worry about introducing entitlement reforms for another decade' and fails to recognise that the costs of undertaking corrective action are 'spiralling out of control right now'. Gokhale warns that:

Social Security and Medicare Administrations have estimated those programs' total financial imbalances at a staggering $90 trillion. Interest on that implicit debt at the government's interest rate of 3 percent implies currently accruing costs of $2.7 trillion per year – *more than 10 times larger than today's federal budget deficits.*

That means, by waiting for a decade we would forgo an opportunity to save more than $30 trillion – and adjustments to entitlement programs thereafter would have to be larger and more draconian. Our budget problems are not getting easier to resolve, they are getting harder – today – something that Moody's warning ignores.

Rather than sounding trite warnings on the basis of future deficits and prospective policies, Moody's should base its ratings of government debt on the government's fiscal imbalance.

George Soros on the Demise of the Dollar Standard

The billionaire hedge fund manager and investor George Soros has legendary credentials with currencies. His better known achievements include having famously made over $1 billion profit on a bet against the British Pound in 1992 when its value was being artificially propped up by the inept Prime Minister John Major's Government.

In January 2008 George Soros published comments on 'the end of an era of credit expansion based on the dollar as the international reserve currency' marking 'the culmination of a super-boom that has lasted for more than 60 years' – i.e. from the end of World War II. Over the years 'globalisation allowed the US to suck up the savings of the rest of the world and consume more than it produced' and whenever the US credit expansion ran into trouble the financial authorities injected liquidity or found other ways to stimulate the economy. Soros argues that '[c]redit expansion must now be followed by a period of contraction' and 'the ability of the financial authorities to stimulate the economy is constrained by the unwillingness of the rest of the world to accumulate additional dollar reserves'.[34]

Conclusion

There is no wishing away the dangers associated with the US current account deficit. They include a weak dollar and a transfer of wealth from the US to oil exporters and emerging economies, rising import prices resulting in higher inflation, rising interest payment burdens and the chance of a Wile E. Coyote moment.

Is the dollar again America's currency and everyone else's problem? It will become everyone's problem with no exceptions if the US 'Triple A' sovereign debt rating is reviewed; if unfunded entitlement commitments are classified as debts instead of implicit liabilities; or if for any other reason the rest of the world is unwilling to accumulate additional dollar reserves.

6

The Economic Consequences of 9/11 and George W. Bush

For how long will Asians go on lending for Americans to go on spending?

Fire Ready Aim

The purpose of this study is to delve into factors that led to America's financial crisis – not with a view to heaping blame on George Bush, but with a view to understanding the crisis better and seeking ways to protect ourselves from the fallout. George W. Bush was inaugurated as President of the United States on 21 January 2001 less than seven months before 9/11. On 11 September, two days after the attacks, he announced a global war on terrorism. Within days he ordered an invasion of Afghanistan to overthrow the Taliban regime, destroy Al Qaeda and capture Osama bin Laden. In March 2003 he ordered the invasion of Iraq asserting that Saddam Hussein had control of weapons of mass destruction and war was necessary for the protection of US interests. The invasion became the hallmark of his presidency and has since dominated his and the nation's political and economic agenda. It's obvious now that it was misconceived. If national resources were directed in other directions the alarming deterioration in the financial condition of the US may not have occurred.

Middle East expert Thomas Friedman, who had previously supported an invasion of Iraq as a legitimate action to preserve the credibility of the UN, destroy Saddam's tyranny 'and replace it with a decent regime that could drive reform in the Arab/Muslim world' attended a press conference hosted by President Bush on 5 March 2003. Bush had already deployed 200 000 battle ready troops in the Gulf poised to invade Iraq but was unable to secure an unambiguous United Nations Security Council resolution authorising the invasion. The war he was launching would be under the Security Council Resolution 1440 of 8 November 2002 demanding that Saddam come clean on his weapons of mass destruction 'or face serious consequences'.[1] A few days after the press conference Friedman titled his regular *New York Times* column 'Fire Ready Aim' and wrote:[2]

> I went to President Bush's White House news conference on Thursday to see how he was wrestling with the momentous issue of Iraq. One line he uttered captured all the things that are troubling me about his approach. It was when he said: 'When it comes to our security, we really don't need anybody's permission.' The first thing that bothered me was the phrase, 'When it comes to our security . . .Fact: The invasion of Iraq today is not vital to American security. Saddam Hussein has neither the intention nor the capability to threaten America, and is easily deterrable if he did. This is not a war of necessity. That was Afghanistan . . .And that brings us to the second phrase: 'We really don't need anybody's permission.' . . . for a war of choice in Iraq, we need the world's permission – because of what it would take to rebuild Iraq. Mr. Bush talks only about why it's right to dismantle the bad Iraq, not what it will take to rebuild a decent Iraq – a distant land, the size of California, divided like Yugoslavia. I believe we can help build a decent Iraq, but not alone. If we're alone, it will turn into a U.S. occupation and make us the target for everyone's frustration . . .Mr. Bush growls that the world is demanding that America play 'Captain, May I' when it comes to Iraq – and he's not going to ask anybody's permission. But with Iraq, the relevant question is not 'Captain, May I?' It's 'Captain, Can I?' – can I do it right without allies?
>
>   No.

Friedman, a brilliant journalist and astute commentator, could of course have been wrong. Most commentators have a political bias and there are generally two sides to an issue. But in this case there is no doubt that Bush was flying in the face of credible independent warnings from sources ranging from international partners to respected American institutions. One very clear warning accessible to us to review came from the respected American Academy of Arts and Science in a study *War with Iraq: Costs, Consequences, and Alternatives* published in February 2002. The study addressed the military, economic and political consequences of invading Iraq and the costs of the invasion that had not been recognised by the Bush administration.[3] A section of the report written by the Nobel Laureate Economist William D. Nordhaus reviewed the economic consequences of the war and shouldn't have been ignored. With the benefit of hindsight we can see now that since the invasion Americans, and by association their allies, have been living in an economic fool's paradise. 'The major benefits of a war' Nordhaus noted in the American Academy study:

> . . . are reckoned to be disarming of Iraq of its weapons of mass destruction and removing a leadership that is unrelentingly hostile to the United States. But what of the costs? Even asking such a question may be thought a sign of insufficient resolve at best and appeasement at worst. However, while cost estimates are often ignored when war is debated, most people recognise that the costs in dollars, and especially in blood, are acceptable only as long as they are low. If the casualty estimates mount to thousands, if oil prices skyrocket, if a war pushes the economy into recession or requires a large tax increase, and if the United States becomes a pariah in the world because of callous attacks on civilian populations, then decision makers in the White House and the Congress might not post so expeditiously to battle.

Nordhaus's conclusions on costs were compelling: 'Given the salience of cost' he wrote 'it is surprising that there have been no systematic public analyses of the economics of a military conflict in Iraq.' He accepted that estimates of war costs are virtually certain to be wrong 'for the fog of war extends far beyond the battlefield to include forecasts of political reactions and economic consequences. However, as Keynes said, it is better to be vaguely right than precisely wrong.' Examples he cites of previous war cost miscalculations include Lincoln's Secretary of the Treasury's estimate that the direct cost of the war to the North would be $240 million, amounting at the time to 7% of annual GDP. The eventual cost was $3200 million. About fifteen times the estimate. The costs of the Vietnam War were also grossly underestimated. The original budget projection in 1996 was for $10 billion. The war dragged on until 1973. The direct cost was in the range $110 to $150 billion. Indirect costs including inflation, economic instability, and civil unrest contributed to the growing disenchantment with authority and government in the United States.

Nordhaus estimated costs of the war with Iraq in favourable and unfavourable scenarios. In the best-case scenario he estimated the war could cost $99 billion over the next decade. In a worst-case scenario it could cost in excess of $1.9 trillion over the same period. The latter figure was nearly 10 times the comparable 'worst case' estimate offered by the administration and, as we will see, is likely to correspond with the final costs of the war. Analysing the few publicly available studies of the cost of war with Iraq Nordhaus identified post invasion costs that had been ignored by the Bush administration including: prolonged occupation and peacekeeping which could cost between $75 and $500 billion; funds needed for reconstruction that could reach $105 billion; and humanitarian assistance that would cost a minimum of $10 billion. A macroeconomic impact (cheaper oil) over the next decade could result in a gain of $17 billion in the best-case scenario or a loss of nearly $400 billion following a disruption of oil markets or a resulting recession – as was the case in previous Middle East wars. 'The economic ripples of a war with Iraq' he concluded 'are likely to spread beyond the direct budgetary costs, with the prospect of raising the cost of imported petroleum, slowing productivity growth, and possibly triggering a recession.' He concluded significantly: 'The dangers of tipping into recession are real,' particularly given that the US economy was growing very slowly in the fall of 2002. He also addressed the question of who will be asked to pay the price for military action with Iraq. 'If the war is undertaken without UN sanction or broad international support, the U.S. could be forced to pay the lion's share of the costs' – again as indeed it has been.

The only public estimate of cost accessible to Nordhaus came from an interview conducted for the *Wall Street Journal* with Larry Lindsey, the economist in residence at the West Wing. The *Journal* wrote that Lindsey estimated the upper band cost at $100 billion to $200 billion adding Hussein's ouster could actually ease the oil problem by increasing supplies. 'When there is a regime change in Iraq – you could add three million to five million barrels of production to world supply each day. The successful prosecution of the war would be good for the economy.' A *Journal* editorial supported Lindsey's upbeat assessment and concluded 'the best way to keep oil prices in check is a short, successful war on Iraq that begins sooner rather than later'. In response an OMB Director commented that Lindsey's estimates were 'very very high'.

In fact, as we all know now, Larry Lindsey was wrong about oil production. Iraq was already producing close to its sustainable level. And he was way out on costs.

By October 2007 the Congressional Research Service reported $600 billion had been allocated to the wars in Iraq and Afghanistan and the war on terrorism.[4] Ongoing costs were running at $9 billion a month, of which $7 billion related to Iraq. Costs were also projected for the period 2008 to 2018 on two scenarios. The first scenario was on the basis of a reduction of troops engaged from about 200000 to 30000 by 2010 and then remaining constant till 2017. The associated cost forecast was an additional $570 billion. In the second scenario, the number of personnel deployed to Iraq and other locations associated with the war on terrorism would decline from an average of about 200000 in fiscal year 2008 to 75000 by the start of fiscal year 2013 and then remain at that level through 2017. The forecast for this scenario would total $1.05 trillion over the 2008–2017 period.

The CBO testimony refers to a study by Nobel Laureate Economist Joseph Stiglitz and Harvard Professor Linda Bilmes that concluded the costs of the wars will run to between $2 and $3 trillion.[5] In their analysis Stiglitz and Bilmes put a monetary value on factors not included in official calculations. These include the reduction in wounded veterans' quality of life; the macroeconomic effects of diverting to federal expenditures from civil projects such as the building or maintaining of roads and bridges; the additional effects on the US economy resulting from rising oil prices which they largely attribute to the war's disruption of Iraqi oil exports. They also include costs for longer periods than the Department of Defence. The extent to which their analysis is correct may be in contention. But they are credible commentators and support a conclusion that post 9/11 war costs will in any event exceed $2 trillion.

War Costs without Any Sacrifice by Americans

Iraq war costs have been funded though unspecified external borrowings without any sacrifice by Americans. Paying for wars tends to be associated with the politics of the war. In the last two world wars Patriotic Bonds were sold to engage those not serving in the armed forces with the war effort. Sacrifice was seen as a duty and privilege while fellow Americans were fighting and risking life and limb abroad. But the Bush administration made no calls on Americans to make any sacrifices of any kind for the Iraq invasion. Three obvious reasons come to mind why they didn't. First, post 9/11 economic and monetary policy was framed to stimulate consumer spending, reflate the economy, and head off a recession. 70% of the US GDP comes from consumer spending. Money was being directed into consumers' pockets and not away from them. Second, the invasion of Iraq was not a war of necessity. It was a war of choice, and a deeply unpopular one at that. Calls on the public for funding would have fallen on deaf ears. Third, Americans were unlikely to support the neo cons, who in fact were running the country.

Constitutionally American Vice Presidents are more than figureheads. If the President dies they automatically become President. But in their day to day duties they tend to be sidelined. America's first Vice President John Adams even spoke of 'the most insignificant office that ever the invention of man contrived'. However neither George Bush nor Dick Cheney had an insignificant role in mind for the Vice President. Cheney's influence was apparent as Bush's first cabinet was formed and offices in his administration were filled with fellow neo conservatives. Leading appointees included Donald Rumsfeld, Paul Wolfowitz, John Bolton, Richard Perel and Scooter Libby. All close Cheney associates. All neo cons identified as supporters of the Project for a New American Century launched in 1997.

Déjà Vu Vietnam?

We saw in the previous chapter the extent to which Vietnam War costs, America's deficit spending and domestic inflation contributed to the financial crisis of the 1970s and subsequent social disruption. Comments from Robert McNamara, the US Defense Secretary during the Vietnam War in his autobiography, *In Retrospect*, illustrates how profound the disruptions that follow military misadventures can be. McNamara wrote: 'By the time the United States finally left South Vietnam, . . . our economy had been damaged by years of heavy and improperly financed war spending; and the political unity of our society had been shattered, not to be restored for decades.'

In *The Price of Liberty – Paying for America's Wars* Robert Hormats, a Vice Chairman of Goldman Sachs International, is scathing in his criticism of George W. Bush's fiscal arrogance and writes:

> Of late, the precedents and experiences of past generations have been cast aside. The 9/11 attacks were seen by many legislators as a licence to spend more money on non security programs, and Americans have not been called on to make sacrifices. Tax cuts and spending increases on politically popular but security irrelevant domestic programs have been enacted as if there were no expensive defence programs to be funded. Hard choices were not necessary, most thinking went, because the cost of the war as a portion of the nation's GDP was modest in historic terms and, in any case, growth would shrink the deficit. Using rosy assumptions, advocates of the 2001 and 2003 tax cuts wanted to make them permanent whilst at the same time arguing that the war on terrorism would last for decades – with little acknowledgement that the costs of prosecuting it would last for decades as well.

Hormats' comments on funding the Vietnam War have particular resonance. He notes the Vietnam War was not going well in 1968 when dramatic increases in troop levels were required. At the same time Lyndon B. Johnson's Great Society Agenda required funding. The nation's budget deficit was growing rapidly. Yet Johnson held off asking Congress to increase taxes to avoid a confrontation over funding both his domestic agenda and the war.[6] In remarks that could be repeated almost verbatim on funding for Iraq Hormats writes: 'Far from asking the nation to sacrifice during the early stages of escalation, Johnson reassured Americans that no major tax or spending changes were necessary, calmly asserting that the conflict in Vietnam would not divert resources from Medicare, Medicaid, Head Start, and other domestic programmes.'

Liquidity

George W. Bush will be blamed for the political and economic costs of the Iraq debacle and the surge in US debts on his watch. But it will be a mistake to expect that when a new President is elected he or she will start with a clean sheet. 9/11 changed the course of history. In his book *Jihad – The Trail of Political Islam* Gilles Kepel described 9/11 as '. . . a seismic event with incalculable consequences (that) exposed the fragility of the United States' empire, exploded the myth of its invincibility, and called into question all the certainties and beliefs that had ensured the triumph of American civilisation in the twentieth century'. Whoever was in office as President at the time would have responded decisively.

Kepel made astute observations but he didn't factor in the formidable strength at the time of America's financial resources and its banking system. The economic consequences of 9/11 could have been disastrous were it not for the US Treasury and the Fed's financial muscle and ability to respond instantly with as many tens of billions of dollars as were necessary. Roger Ferguson, a former Vice Chairman of the Federal Reserve, emphasised the importance of liquidity in a speech 'September 11th, The Federal Reserve and the Financial System':[7]

> Liquidity, as you know, serves as the oil lubricating the engine of capitalism to keep it from burning itself out. The efficiency of our financial system at maintaining adequate liquidity is often taken for granted. But on September 11, it could not be taken for granted. The bottlenecks in the pipeline became so severe that the Federal Reserve stepped in to ensure that the financial system remained adequately liquid. In other words, our massive provision of reserves made sure that the engine of finance did not run out of oil and seize up.

Fed Chairman Alan Greenspan was abroad on 9/11 and, as Vice Chairman, Ferguson was responsible for the instant decisions. He spoke of sitting in his office in Washington watching the television with horror as the second plane crashed into the World Trade Center and, a little later, saw thick smoke billow above the trees in the direction of the Pentagon. As events were unfolding, he recounted:

One could easily envision the risks that confronted the United States – and especially the risks to which the Federal Reserve, as the nation's central bank, would have to respond. It was clear that the loss of so many key resources at the core of the financial capital of the United States would strain markets. If allowed to mount, those strains could prompt a chain reaction drying up liquidity, which, unchecked, could lead to real economic activity seizing up. The shocks to the financial system and the economy that were possible could have been disastrous to the confidence of businesses and households in our country and, to a significant degree, the rest of the world.

The Fed lost no time in organising a response that emphasised key objectives. First they had to provide sufficient liquidity through as many means as possible to maintain stability and public confidence and they did. On 12 September alone lending to banks through the discount window totalled about $46 billion, more than two hundred times the daily average for the previous month. Ferguson ended his speech: 'we in the United States are very fortunate to have created, through the efforts of private industry, at times pushed by regulators, the most robust, most efficient financial system in the world'. That was almost seven years ago. It's questionable whether we can take for granted that after the excesses of the last seven years the US financial system as a whole can still be called the most efficient system in the world.

Tax Cuts, Deficits and Debts

The following is an extract from Governor George W. Bush's 2000 'American Dream' GOP Party Platform:

> Over a five year period, as surpluses continue to grow, we will return half a trillion dollars to the taxpayers who really own it, without touching the Social Security surplus. That's what we mean by our Lock-Box: The Social Security surplus is off-limits, off budget, and will not be touched. We will not stop there, for we are also determined to protect Medicare and to pay down the national debt. Reducing that debt is both a sound policy goal and a moral imperative. Our families and most states are required to balance their budgets; it is reasonable to assume the federal government should do the same. Therefore, we reaffirm our support for a constitutional amendment to require a balanced budget.

Read Governor George W. Bush's pre 2000 election 'American Dream' GOP Party Platform now and, however many headlines about yawning deficits and soaring debts your eyes have skated across, it's hard not to be struck by the extent to which the financial condition of the US has deteriorated since he has been in office as President. He may have been over-optimistic when he was campaigning for election to hold out the promise of half a trillion dollars coming back to taxpayers within five years. But he wasn't being cavalier. His political opponents shared his optimism. But in the forthcoming 2008 Presidential elections no candidate will be talking seriously about budget surpluses or returning money to taxpayers. Instead they will be facing the mirror image of the financial situation seen in 2000. In contrast to the prospect of funds flowing from the state back to taxpayers they should be addressing the prospect of higher taxes and instead of budget surpluses they will be addressing budget deficits.

The US federal budget deficit and the US current account deficit are two of the world's most important economic statistics, if not the most important. The US is the world's largest debtor. Its debts are increasing. International financial stability depends not only on whether the US will be able to service its credit and pay its debts but also on whether its creditors will continue to believe it can. At the time of writing, in spite of the dramatic increases in the US national debt and the dollar's steep fall, creditors haven't lost faith and haven't started dumping the dollar yet. But, with no guarantees that they won't start dumping, issues involving debts and deficits are going to be in the spotlight. The new administration that takes office in January 2009 will have to face up to economic realities that affect Americans and the rest of the world and, because of the attention focused on Iraq and the war on terrorism, have escaped the scrutiny and attention they warranted.

Has the deterioration in the US economy since 2000 been so severe that the dollar is in danger of becoming unstable or even risky as it was in 1970 when Richard Nixon's Treasury Secretary John Connally told European central bankers 'the dollar is our currency and your problem'? At the time creditor nations were still entitled to demand settlement of dollar claims in gold. After Richard Nixon closed the gold window on 12 August 1971 those who had demanded gold sustained no losses while those who didn't sustained severe losses.

Governor George Bush promised tax cuts in his year 2000 Presidential election campaign. His party platform read: 'Budget surpluses are the result of over-taxation of the American people. The weak link in the chain of prosperity is the tax system. It not only burdens the American people; it threatens to slow, and perhaps to reverse, the economic expansion.' By the time he took office in January 2001 the US economy was slowing down. By April 2001 the Nasdaq Stock Exchange bubble was starting to pop. By mid-2001 he introduced the first of three tax cuts covering about $1.4 trillion prior to 2008 and a further $850 billion in an emergency fiscal stimulus measure introduced in January 2008.

To forestall a recession after 9/11 President George Bush adopted a strategy of going for growth and, in a sense, wearing blinkers to avoid distractions. The platform for growth was monetary reflation following the well trodden route with America spending and Asia lending. Fed Chairman Alan Greenspan took a similar line and introduced a series of interest rate cuts that brought the Fed funds rate down to 1% and kept it there for over two years. George Bush and Alan Greenspan can take credit for kick-starting the US economy and for orchestrating a global monetary reflation. As other countries followed their lead and reflated their economies global economic growth also revived. Boosted by monetary steroids the recession that started in 2001 became a global boom. By 2006 the IMF could forecast sustained global growth of over 4.5% – not quite the 5.4% peak of the early 1970s, but a great platform for economic and social development across the planet.

However as we have seen in the previous chapter the font for global liquidity was again the US current account deficit funded by foreign suppliers. The following chart illustrates the rising US Gross Federal Debt from 1940 to 2007:

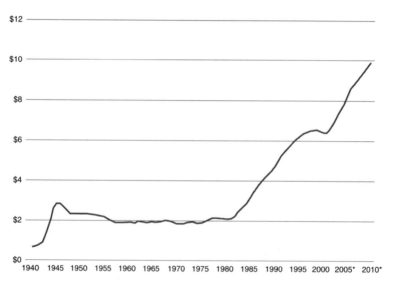

Chart 6.1 Gross US federal debt in $ trillions (2005).

The US national debt will have more than doubled between 2001, the year George Bush first took office as President, and 2008, the year he will leave office. The debt soared from $5.7 trillion in 2001 to over $9 trillion in September 2007. Effective 29 September 2001 Congress increased the debt ceiling from $8.965

trillion to $9.815 trillion. Compare this with the eight years before George Bush took office. Over that period the national debt only grew by $1.5 trillion. And it was being paid down.

Since 2005 the US money supply has increased from $10 trillion to $13 trillion. Although the US Federal Reserve discontinued reporting M3 in March 2006, several sources have reconstructed the data and determined that the US money supply is now growing at an unprecedented annualised rate of 16%.[8] Money supply growth globally has also surged reaching 42% in Russia, 21% in India, 18% in China and 12% in the UK.[9]

'Implicit Debt' on Entitlement Commitments

The $9 trillion US national debt is only part of the nation's financial obligations and not the largest part. An additional $46 trillion of 'implicit debt' on entitlement commitments is not shown as a liability in the US national accounts. $20 trillion of the implicit debts comes from legislation passed during George Bush's presidency. The high levels of US debt and surging global growth in money supply are part of the backdrop to what the economist Dr Marc Faber calls the first synchronised global economic boom in the history of capitalism. He identifies the origins of the boom as:

1 Expansionary US monetary policies;
2 A growing US trade deficit; and
3 A Chinese import and export boom lifting commodity prices and supporting the economies of resource producers.

The consequences of the boom have been rising commodity prices, asset price inflation shifting into consumer price increases, rising wealth inequality and significantly a shift in growth, wealth and the balance of financial power away from the US.

A complete study of the global economic boom is a subject beyond the scope of this book. As investors we need to narrow our sights and concentrate on the current debt crisis being experienced after a period of exceptional monetary and economic growth. In this chapter we examine the main conditions that will support an interest in gold as an alternative investment and focus on three headline developments:

1 The US housing bubble, the sub prime mortgage crisis, the shadow banking crisis and other unintended consequences of the reflationary policies of the Bush administration;

2 Elephants in the room that have been ignored: unfunded social security and healthcare commitments.

Bush's Ownership Society: Dismantling the Barriers to Home Ownership and the Real Estate Bubble

The following is an extract from Governor George W. Bush's 'American Dream' GOP Party Platform – 2001:

> Home ownership is central to the American dream, and Republicans want to make it more accessible for everyone. That starts with access to capital for entrepreneurs and access to credit for consumers. Our proposals for helping millions of low-income families move from renting to owning are detailed elsewhere in this platform as major elements in Governor Bush's program for a New Prosperity. For those families, and for all other potential homebuyers, low interest rates make mortgages affordable and open up more housing opportunities than any government program.[10]

From the start of his electoral campaign in 2000 George Bush crusaded for an ownership society with home ownership as the cornerstone. The following quote from a Fact Sheet published on the White House web site is typical of many on the same theme:[11]

President Bush's Policies Promoting the Ownership Society

Expanding Homeownership

The President believes that homeownership is the cornerstone of America's vibrant communities and benefits individual families by building stability and long-term financial security. In June 2002, President Bush issued *America's Homeownership Challenge* to the real estate and mortgage finance industries to encourage them to join the effort to close the gap that exists between the homeownership rates of minorities and non-minorities. The President also announced the goal of increasing the number of minority homeowners by at least 5.5 million families before the end of the decade. Under his leadership, the overall U.S. homeownership rate in the second quarter of 2004 was at an all time high of 69.2 percent. Minority homeownership set a new record of 51 percent in the second quarter, up 0.2 percentage points from the first quarter and up 2.1 percentage points from a year ago. President Bush's initiative to **dismantle the barriers to homeownership** includes:

American Dream Downpayment Initiative, which provides down payment assistance to approximately 40,000 low-income families;

Affordable Housing. The President has proposed the Single-Family Affordable Housing Tax Credit, which would increase the supply of affordable homes;

Helping Families Help Themselves. The President has proposed increasing support for the Self-Help Homeownership Opportunities Program; and

Simplifying Homebuying and Increasing Education. The President and HUD want to empower homebuyers by simplifying the home buying process so consumers can better understand and benefit from cost savings. The President also wants to expand financial education efforts so that families can understand what they need to do to become homeowners.

We know from the sub prime mortgage credit crisis that roiled global financial markets in 2007 the extent to which barriers to home ownership in the US were dismantled. During the boom years anyone who had a pulse could get a loan. The housing boom was fuelled by ample liquidity, cheap money, loans to buyers who weren't creditworthy, 'exotic' mortgages with zero deposits and adjustable rate mortgages granted with minimal interest rates for teaser periods that allowed the principal debt to grow before interest rates were reset at higher levels. Initially the flood of money into housing stimulated consumer spending. Now that the housing bubble has popped millions of homeowners find themselves unable to service their mortgage debts and we haven't seen the worst of the sub prime mortgage debt fiasco yet.

House prices in the UK were even more inflated than in the US and, if the pound sterling was still the world's principal reserve currency as it was until 1918 when World War I broke out, the focus of this book would be on Britain and the pound instead of the US and the dollar But we focus on the US for these reasons:

1 The dollar is the world's principal global reserve asset and the US is the world largest importer, debtor and borrower;
2 The US is the world's largest economy and the American consumer contributes over 70% of US GDP;
3 The so called sub prime mortgage crisis is an American phenomenon;
4 The 'financialisation' of the US economy is a new paradigm with uncertain outcomes;
5 Extensive borrowings by US consumers against the rising values of their homes fuelled the housing boom and bubble.

Borrowings Using the House as an ATM

In a 13 August 2007 study *Wall Street and Main Street are Joined at the Hip* Northern Trust's Director of Economic Research, Paul Kasriel, raises the question: 'For what purpose might home owners have been borrowing against the equity in their houses?' Kasriel found that from 1929 through 2006, there were only 13 years in which US households incurred deficits – i.e., spent more in total than they earned after taxes. Two of these household-deficit years occurred during the Great Depression of the 1930s, three occurred shortly after the end of World War II and one occurred in 1955. The remaining seven household-deficit years occurred in 1999 and 2001 through 2006. There are three noteworthy points associated with the current levels of borrowings:

1 It was unprecedented for households to run deficits in six out of seven years;
2 The magnitude of the 2004, 2005 and 2006 household deficits was unprecedented, and;
3 The household deficits starting in 1999 occurred in a period when asset prices showed extraordinary increases.

The following chart from the report illustrates the pattern of US household surpluses and savings since 1929:

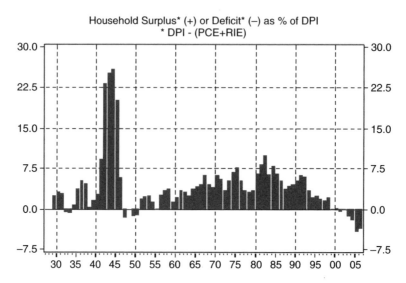

Chart 6.2 Household surplus or deficit.
(Reproduced by permission of the Brookings Institution)

Two further charts prepared by Kasriel illustrate:

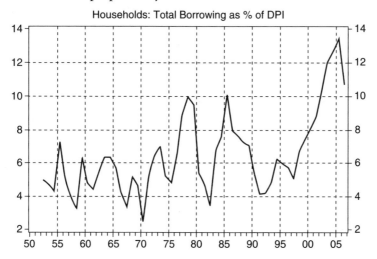

Chart 6.3 US household borrowings as % of disposable personal income.
(Reproduced by permission of the Brookings Institution)

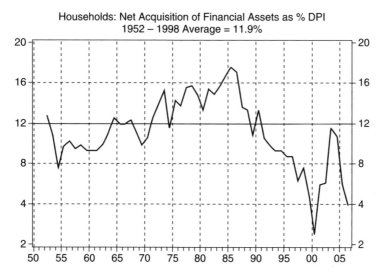

Chart 6.4 Kasriel households net disposal of financial assets.
(Reproduced by permission of the Brookings Institution)

1 Unprecedented levels of borrowings have boosted household disposable income.
2 Notwithstanding their record levels of borrowings against their properties householders have been disposing of financial assets and not acquiring them.
3 Borrowings have been used to subsidise living costs.

What happens now that the easy money that was accessible for homeowners to borrow against the equity of their homes has dried up? Investment banks were key players in the business of packaging mortgage debts into collateralised debt obligations and selling them globally to other banks and investment funds seeking a higher yield than conventional debt products. The debt obligations were oversold on the back of credit agency ratings that it now appears were suspect. Wall Street has a reputation for putting lipstick on a pig. It's nothing new. It's happened before and the regulators allowed it to happen again. With the policy of the Bush administration that home ownership had to be expanded and consumer spending had to keep growing, the banking establishment snatched the opportunity to fuel the gravy train. Could this have happened under an administration that was focused on what was happening on its doorstep instead of what was happening in Iraq? I doubt it. There is nothing new about the perils of uncontrolled financial innovation and Ponzi schemes. The excesses of the house price boom were surely obvious when prices were soaring.

In a paper published in April 2007 by the Levy Institute, *Cracks in the Foundations of Growth*,[12] this comment on financial innovation puts abuses in perspective:

> The financial and banking industries have undergone waves of innovation since consumer credit became widely available early in the 20th century. These waves have been spurred partly by the profit motive and the need to outwit the regulators, and partly by the innate human tendencies of greed, herd behaviour, and over optimism. Hyman P. Minsky's financial fragility theory showed how the economy is subject to one crisis after another, as 'Ponzi' and 'speculative' finance repeatedly burgeon until there is an inevitable and disastrous bust. The Minskyan view holds that the increasing availability of credit and the proliferation of new financial products represents the unsustainable upward phase of a potentially unstable cycle.

Budgets, Social Security and Unfunded Entitlement Commitments

> We might hope to see the finances of the Union as clear and intelligible as a merchant's books, so that every member of Congress and every man of any mind in the Union should be able to comprehend them, to investigate abuses, and consequently to control them.
>
> President Thomas Jefferson to Treasury Secretary Albert Gallatin, 1802

Professor L.J. Kotlikoff of Boston University has been engaged in work on generational accounting since the 1990s. The following comments, with his views on accounting for future entitlement commitments, give useful insight into interpreting national budget deficits:

> The simple fact is that the deficit is not a well-defined economic concept. The current measure of the deficit, or any measure, is based on arbitrary choices of how to label government receipts and payments. The government can conduct any real economic policy and simultaneously report any size deficit or surplus it wants just through its choice of words. If the government labels receipts as taxes and payments as expenditures, it will report one number for the deficit. If it labels receipts as loans and payments as return of principal and interest, it will report a very different number.

A budget should be a straightforward accounting forecast reflecting a positive or negative result that speaks for itself. However in social democracies national budgets are complex almost by definition. One area of complexity comes from changed conditions that affect tax revenues or expenses, including defence, likely to necessitate policy changes. Another comes from governments assuming obligations for social security and healthcare insurance over extended time frames. We may think Kotlikoff goes too far when he says a government can report any size of deficit or surplus it wants to through its choice of words but, when we review how President Bush funded the invasion of Iraq and Afghanistan, we will see that Kotlikoff has been on the right track. The wars have been funded by general borrowings from trading partners, particularly China. There is no way the present generation can pay for them. If it's left to politicians their children and grand-children will inherit the tab.

Budgets aren't in the exclusive domain of politicians and, in the United States, the Congressional Budget Office (CBO) serves as an unbiased analyst and commentator on budget forecasts and performance. When the US President's annual budget proposals are made the CBO reports on the outlook, examines revenue and spending levels for the next ten years and produces its own budget 'baseline' projection that serves as the neutral benchmark against which members of Congress can measure the effects of any legislation proposed. It's important to note that the CBO budget baseline projection is prepared following rules that require it to assume something very unlikely to happen – that is current spending and revenue laws will continue without change. The CBO baseline is thus not a prediction of future outcomes. Predictions in the US are made by the President in January of every calendar year for the fiscal year commencing in October.

President Bill Clinton's budget proposals for the fiscal year 2000 were optimistic and looked straightforward – as can be seen from the following graphic
that accompanied his message to Congress:

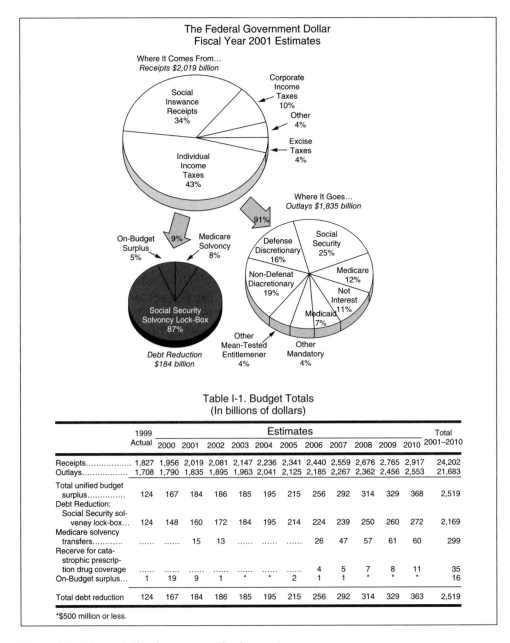

Table I-1. Budget Totals
(In billions of dollars)

	1999 Actual	Estimates 2000	2001	2002	2003	2004	2005	2006	2007	2008	2009	2010	Total 2001–2010
Receipts	1,827	1,956	2,019	2,081	2,147	2,236	2,341	2,440	2,559	2,676	2,765	2,917	24,202
Outlays	1,708	1,790	1,835	1,895	1,963	2,041	2,125	2,185	2,267	2,362	2,456	2,553	21,683
Total unified budget surplus	124	167	184	186	185	195	215	256	292	314	329	368	2,519
Debt Reduction: Social Security solveney lock-box	124	148	160	172	184	195	214	224	239	250	260	272	2,169
Medicare solvency transfers	......	......	15	13	......	......	......	26	47	57	61	60	299
Reserve for catastrophic prescription drug coverage	......	......	......	......	......	......	......	4	5	7	8	11	35
On-Budget surplus	1	19	9	1	*	*	2	1	1	*	*	*	16
Total debt reduction	124	167	184	186	185	195	215	256	292	314	329	363	2,519

*$500 million or less.

Chart 6.5 Clinton's fiscal year 2001 budget estimates.

The proposals included a forecast for a revenue surplus and matching debt reduction for the year of $184 billion and a matching $2.5 trillion surplus and debt reduction over a 10-year period. It was well known that social security and healthcare arrangements had to be revised and he ended his presentation for the year 2000 with this proviso: 'The great and immediate challenge before us is to save Social Security. It is time to move forward now. We have already started the hard work of seeking to build consensus for Social Security's problems. Let us finish the job before the year ends.' Social security wasn't 'saved' as he hoped it would be by 2001. His next budget message, again upbeat, ended with this note: 'To be prepared for the retirement of the baby boom generation, my budget also provides a framework to extend the life of the Social Security and Medicare trust funds, while modernizing Medicare with a needed prescription drug benefit.' However social security wasn't 'saved' by Bill Clinton during his Presidency and the Bush administration inherited the problem.

President Bush and Social Security Reform

President Bush was in office as President in 2001 and he submitted his first budget proposal. As events played out it was his only budget proposal as a peacetime President. His plan proposed retiring $1 trillion of debt over the following four years and included this direct warning on the need to reform social security: 'Finally, this new approach begins to confront great challenges from which government has too long flinched. Social Security as it now exists will provide future beneficiaries with the equivalent of a dismal two percent real rate of return on their investment, *yet the system is headed for insolvency*.' (my emphasis)

Results for the US fiscal year didn't match the forecasts. Tax revenue expectations were dependent on the Nasdaq Stock Exchange bubble staying afloat. But after the stock exchange bubble popped in 2000 tax revenues fell dramatically as the growth surge of the previous years stalled.

Whatever good intentions George Bush had for reforming social security his agenda was hijacked by 9/11 and the invasion of Iraq. At the time of writing in his two terms of office not only has he achieved nothing with social security reform but the Medicaid bill he approved can't be funded.

Robert Hormats observed in *The Price of Liberty – Paying for America's Wars* that five years after the 9/11 attacks neither the President or Congress had come to grips with finding a formula where they would have the funds to successfully prosecute the war on terrorism, meet the growing costs of retirement and healthcare benefits and ensure that the nation's finances retain the confidence of domestic and foreign investors. Instead, Hormats writes, they have been 'maintaining a fiscal policy that in the next decade will result in massive deficits, declining budget flexibility, and further dependence on foreign capital. It is often said that 9/11 "changed everything." In the area of fiscal policy, however, it changed nothing. The country is pursuing a pre-9/11 fiscal policy in the post-9/11 world.'[13]

Bottom Line: Federal US Fiscal Policy Remains Unsustainable

The CBO publish detailed monthly reviews and a substantial annual summer update on treasury performance and prospects. The following chart reflecting uncertainty of budget deficit or surpluses comes from the summer update published in August 2007:[14]

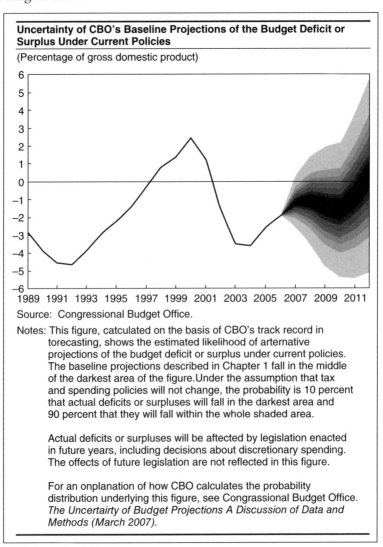

Uncertainty of CBO's Baseline Projections of the Budget Deficit or Surplus Under Current Policies

(Percentage of gross domestic product)

Source: Congressional Budget Office.

Notes: This figure, catculated on the basis of CBO's track record in torecasting, shows the estimated likelihood of arternative projections of the budget deficit or surplus under current policies. The baseline projections described in Chapter 1 fall in the middle of the darkest area of the figure. Under the assumption that tax and spending policies will not change, the probability is 10 percent that actual deficits or surpluses will fall in the darkest area and 90 percent that they will fall within the whole shaded area.

Actual deficits or surpluses will be affected by legislation enacted in future years, including decisions about discretionary spending. The offects of future legislation are not reflected in this figure.

For an onplanation of how CBO calculates the probability distribution underlying this figure, see Congrassional Budget Office. *The Uncertairty of Budget Projections A Discussion of Data and Methods (March 2007).*

Chart 6.6 CBO uncertain baseline projections.

US budget surpluses came to an end in 2001, deficits have since accrued and, as we can see from the above chart, the reference to 'uncertainty' is truly appropriate. The CBO's comment on the long term budget outlook included this information:

> Despite some improvement in the short-term budget picture, the nation faces substantial fiscal challenges over the long term. . . . Over the past four decades, per-beneficiary costs under Medicare and Medicaid have increased about 2.5 percentage points faster per year than has per capita GDP. . . . Even if revenues follow the path projected under current law and rise to about 24 percent of GDP. . . . substantial reductions in the projected growth of spending, a sizable increase in taxes as a percentage of the economy, or some combination of changes in policies for spending and revenues is likely to be necessary to achieve fiscal stability in the coming decades. Such policy changes would certainly have some effect on the economy, but those effects would probably be less than the costs of allowing deficits to grow to unsustainable levels.

The Bottom Line: Federal Fiscal Policy is Unsustainable

The unsustainability conclusion is echoed in reports from David Walker, the US Comptroller General and head of the US Government Accountability Office (GAO). In his April 2007 report Walker reiterated a message he has been delivering for some time: 'Bottom Line: Federal Fiscal Policy Remains Unsustainable . . . The fiscal gap is too large for us to grow our way out of the problem. It would require decades of double-digit real economic growth, but the U.S. has not had a single year of double-digit real economic growth since World War II.'[15]

Walker reports that 'GAO's current long-term simulations reflect ever-larger deficits resulting in a federal debt burden that ultimately spirals out of control.' Of particular concern is the $20 trillion by which liability for unfunded entitlement commitments grew in the five years from 2000 to 2005. In the following table he quantifies the so called 'fiscal gap' – the amount of spending reduction

Table 6.1 Fiscal gap 2007–2081

	Fiscal Gap		Change Required to Close Gap		
	Trillions of 2007 Dollars	Share of GDP	Percentage Increase in Revenue	Percentage Increase in Individual Income Taxes	Percentage Decrease in Non-Interest Spending
Baseline	$27.2	3.7%	19.9%	44.0%	20.3%
Alternative	$54.5	7.4%	40.0%	88.1%	40.7%

Source: GAO analysis.

or tax increases needed to keep debt as a share of gross domestic product (GDP) at or below today's ratio on two different scenarios.

To restore fiscal balance on the extended baseline scenario a 44% tax increase or 20.3% reduction in non interest spending, or a combination of the two, will be necessary. Assuming any politician would even dream of campaigning for that outcome and, by some magical event was elected to office, imagine the financial repercussions and social distress that would follow an attempt to implement such draconian policies. The result would surely be either an episode of hyperinflation with similar consequences to the hyperinflation in the Weimar republic in the 1920s or an episode of deflation with similar consequences to the Great Depression of the 1930s. The 88% 'alternative' tax increase or the 40% decrease in non interest spending is even more unthinkable. To avoid such disastrous outcomes Walker calls for urgent action. The longer solutions are delayed the worse the crisis is going to be. Is Walker scaremongering or is the pending crisis on the scale he forecasts?

A Brookings Institution report with the spicy title 'Still Crazy After All These Years: Understanding the Budget Outlook' confirms Walker's conclusions. The title is spicy but the authors are authoritative figures.[16]

The Brookings report makes three policy assumptions that the CBO can't make for their baseline because, as mentioned above, the CBO's brief is to assume that existing laws continue – an unrealistic assumption when a pattern of extending tax relief is expected. Therefore the Brookings study assumes:

1 all temporary tax provisions will be extended;
2 exemptions to AMT liability and the use of personal non refundable credits against the AMT will be extended; and
3 discretionary spending will grow at the same rate as the popluation.

They also index the AMT exemption, brackets and phase outs for inflation starting 2008, estimate the number of troops deployed in relation to the war on terrorism will be reduced to 75 000 by 2013 and take issue with the misleading financial picture reflected when retirement trust funds on hand are bundled into a unified federal budget.

To give a realistic picture the Brookings study extends the budget horizon to capture time periods in which the cash flows for entitlement programmes turn negative. From this information they project a range of outcomes based on different assumptions and time frames. The following chart extracted from data in the Brookings study reflects a $10.9 trillion deficit over ten years. It is their worst-case scenario for the time frame but, over a 'permanent horizon', the shortfalls rise to as much as $98 trillion.

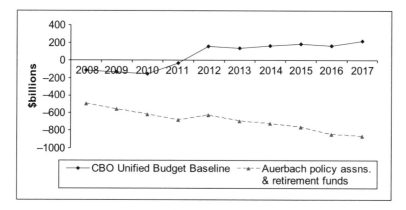

Chart 6.7 US federal budget deficit projections reflecting both CBO baseline and Brookings/Auerbach forecast.

The Realities of Implicit Debt and Generational Accounting

Both Professor Auerbach, the lead contributor to the Brookings report, and Professor Kotlokoff are authorities in the field of generational accounting. There wasn't much comment on generational accounting outside academia and interested economists until a few years ago. Following research on the subject published in 2003 in an article intended for lay readers, the economic historian Professor Niall Ferguson and Professor Kotlikoff explained:

> Economists regard the commitment to pay pension and medical benefits to current and future elderly as part of the government's 'implicit' liabilities. But these liabilities are no less real than the obligation to pay back the principal plus the interest on government bonds. Politically speaking, it may be easier to default on explicit debt than to stop paying Social Security and Medicare benefits. While no one can say for sure which liability the government would renege on first, one thing is clear: the implicit liabilities dwarf the explicit ones. Indeed, their size is so large as to render the U.S. government effectively bankrupt.[17]

Ferguson and Kotlikoff were referring to a paper by Jagadeesh Gokhale, a senior economist at the Federal Reserve Bank of Cleveland and Professor Kent Smetters, a former Deputy Assistant Secretary of Economic Policy at the US Treasury. In the report they asked the following question: 'Suppose the government could, today, get its hands on all the revenue it can expect to collect in the future, but had to use it, today, to pay off all its future expenditure commitments, including debt service. Would the present value (the discounted value today) of the future revenues cover the present value of the future expenditures?' The answer was a definite no. According to their calculations, the shortfall amounts to $45 trillion. To put that figure into perspective, it is twelve times larger than the current official debt and roughly four times the size of the country's annual output.

The Gokhale and Smetters study that brought the debate on appropriate accounting for social insurance obligations into the popular media was introduced with these explanations:

> As the share of retirees in the nation's population balloons and human life spans continue to lengthen, Social Security and Medicare transfers will increasingly dominate total federal outlays. Traditional annual cash-flow budget measures may have been sufficient when *Congress could directly allocate almost all budgetary resources via the annual appropriations process. During this century, however, federal spending will be determined mostly by factors outside of short-term legislative control.*[18]

An update on *Fiscal and Generational Imbalances* published by Gokhale and Smetters at the end of 2005 highlighted yet further explosive growth of US fiscal imbalances and radical increases in taxation that will be needed to fund them. They reported that US fiscal imbalance has grown from around $44 trillion dollars as of fiscal year end 2002 to about $63 trillion, mostly following the recent adoption of the prescription drug bill (Medicare, Part D). Further they reported:

1 The imbalance also grows by more than $1.5 trillion (in inflation adjusted terms) each year that action is not taken to reduce it. This imbalance now equals about 8 percent of all future GDP;
2 The imbalance could, in theory, be eliminated by more than doubling the employer-employee payroll tax from 15.3 percent of wages to over 32 percent immediately and forever – or massive cuts in government spending would be required to achieve fiscal balance;
3 The total federal fiscal imbalance now equals 77.8 percent of non-Social Security and non-Medicare outlays.[19]

The problems of meaningful accounting for national social insurance obligations and the demographic consequences of the baby boomer generation reaching retirement age are not confined to the United States. In 2005 Standard & Poors published a study on the long range prospects for all OECD countries with social insurance obligations. Tweaking John Maynard Keynes's comment that 'in the long run we are all dead' Standard & Poors aptly titled their report 'In the long run we are all debt'.[20] The report warned that unless adequate provisions are made for unfunded entitlement commitments all the countries in the survey are at risk of losing their 'Triple A' credit ratings at the very time when they will need to borrow to meet entitlement commitments.

In the run up to the 2000 Presidential elections candidates expected a budget surplus of $5 trillion over the next ten years. Now credible commentators expect a deficit of almost $7 trillion for the next ten years. Two factors stand out among the many that have contributed to changed expectations The first is that earlier budgets complied with accounting standards that failed to properly reflect social insurance and healthcare obligations. The second is that in 2000 the United States was at peace and now it is at war. It wasn't only George Bush who promised budget surpluses in the run up to the 2000 Presidential elections. His opponent Al Gore made the same promises.

A chapter in Alan Greenspan's book *The Age of Turbulence* is titled: The World Retires But Can It Afford To? The following extracts from his typically lengthy discourse on the subject are revealing:[20]

'A simple test for any retirement system is whether it can assure the availability of promised real resources to retirees without overly burdening the working-age population. By that measure America may be on a collission course with reality;' and '. . . by almost any measure, the additional savings required to take care of the surge in retirees is sufficiently large to raise serious questions about whether the federal government will be able to meet the retirement commitments already made.'

Greenspan ends his discussion with this conclusion 'I've posed a question in the title of this chapter "The World Retires But Can It Afford To?" The answer is it will find ways. The World has no choice. Demography is destiny.'

No doubt Greenspan is right. Even raising the age for retirement by a year or two will make a big difference in funding liabilities. Benefits have been cut in the past and may be cut again. Taxes can also be increased. Compromises will have to be made. But the baby boomers who funded their social security and healthcare benefits via taxes paid will be a powerful constituency to budge. The collision course with reality Greenspan mentions is not going to be easily resolved in the US or elsewhere. Governments have unfunded social insurance obligations that dwarf other national liabilities. With the retirement of the baby boomer generation starting in 2008 there will be no hiding the entitlements in the fog of war as has been the case over the last few years.

Why We Should Consider Gold

The crucial questions we have to address are for how long we can rely on borrowings from China and other trading partners to lend money and fund our financial shortfalls and for how long can we go on expecting the next generation to pick up the tab for unfunded social insurance and entitlement commitments and what has all this got to do with gold? The answer is nothing and everything. Nothing because the gold standard isn't going to come back. Everything because the phenomenon of America spending while the rest of the world lends will come to an abrupt end if either:

1 America's creditors realise that the dollar is again America's currency and everyone else's problem – and they may have already realised it; or
2 The tax burden on US consumers is increased beyond thresholds they can fund to close the fiscal gap – or tax revenues are reduced to keep US consumers solvent as President Bush and Fed Chairman Bernanke now advocate.

Absent an unexpected crisis or a candidate with oddball policies being elected as President in 2008 America's creditors will probably wait for a new administration to take office in January 2009 before they take any damaging actions. If the message from the new administration is that they have a credible plan to close the fiscal gap it won't be in any creditor's interest to rock the boat – particularly as America's creditors are its trading partners. But any credible plan to close the fiscal gap is going to involve tax increases and that leaves a circle to square. The American consumer is already stretched. Without earning more they won't be able to pay more tax. Faced with this situation the prescient Marc Faber has for years forecast that the Fed will have no option other than to print more money.

I have never subscribed to the view that Alan Greenspan was an oracle, as some still think he is, and I even wrote in January 2001 questioning the sustainability of the so-called Goldilocks economy and his expansionary monetary policies that contributed to America's legacy of debt. But I respect his insight into the workings of the global economy and financial markets. In an interview with *Newsweek* magazine in September 2007, a few days after the publication of his book, he gave this frank and I believe correct analysis on the prospects for inflation. I have emphasised some key points in the extract:

> . . . at some point in the next few years, unless contained, inflation will return to a higher long-term rate. . . . 4.5 percent per year. The 4.5 percent inflation rate, on average, for the half century following the abandonment of the gold standard is not necessarily the norm for the future. Nonetheless, it is probably not a bad first approximation of what we will face.
>
> **An inflation rate of 4 to 5 percent is not to be taken lightly – no one will be happy to see his or her saved dollars lose half their purchasing power in fifteen years or so. And while it is true that such a rate has not proved economically destabilizing in the past, an inflation projection in that range assumes a generally benign impact of retirement**

**of the baby boomers, at least through the year 2030.Today's relative
fiscal quiescence masks a pending tsunami. . . .** Over time, unless this is
addressed, it could add massively to the demand for economic resources and
heighten inflationary pressures. Thus, without a change of policy, a higher rate
of inflation can be anticipated in the United States.

**Yet to keep the inflation rate down to a gold standard level of under
1 percent, or even a less draconian 1 to 2 percent range, the Fed, given
my scenario, would have to constrain monetary expansion so drastically
that it could temporarily drive up interest rates into the double-digit
range not seen since the days of Paul Volcker. . . . My fear is that as
Washington strives to make good on the implicit promises made in
the social contract that characterizes contemporary America, CPI
inflation rates by 2030 will be some 4 percent or higher.**

As I was researching this chapter a friend phoned me to ask my opinion on
the run on the Northern Rock Bank in the United Kingdom in September 2007
that led to them having to seek emergency funding from the Bank of England. I
quipped that I never expected I would be lucky enough to be writing a book
about gold at the time of a run on a bank. A few days later I read the Greenspan
interview in *Newsweek*. His comment that 'an inflation rate of 4 to 5 percent is
not to be taken lightly' makes a convincing case for owning gold. Greenspan
warned that people will see their saved dollars lose half their purchasing power
in fifteen years or so if inflation runs at 4% to 5%.

When there are serious expectations for high inflation and other serious
tensions to be resolved gold as stateless money that keeps its value even in the
worst of times makes sense as an asset to hold. This can be seen from the performance of the gold price particularly over the last three years against every
major world currency. By January 2008 it had increased 101% in US dollars,
93% in British pounds, 82% in euros, 93% in Swiss francs, 111% in Japanese
yen and 78% in Russian roubles. In the face of the credit crisis that developed
from mid-2007 central banks made it clear that they intend to provide liquidity
in unlimited amounts to maintain bank solvency and avert a systemic financial
crisis. The inflationary consequences of this policy are obvious. What isn't certain
at this stage is that central bankers and policy makers will be able to avert a global
financial crisis.

For How Long Will Asians go on Lending for Americans to go on Spending?

The view I have taken on this question has been that it's in everyone's interests
to stay with the status quo until a new administration takes office in the US in

January 2009. However I never expected that the US would initiate another fiscal stimulus package that will increase the Federal Deficit by a further $180 billion and until more is known about the economic policies of the candidates in the forthcoming US Presidential elections serious conclusions can not be reached.

One fact we know is that the 1930s depression only ended after a massive increase in liquidity and a major dollar devaluation so that the credit creation process could start again. With the potential for enormous currency losses for America's creditors there must be questions on whether the so-called Bretton Woods II pattern of America spending and Asia lending will remain on track. In the current economic climate, however, gold's stateless money franchise is a valuable and trusted hedge against currency risks and other uncertainties.

7

The End of Cheap Oil, 'Chindia' and Other Tipping Points to Instability

Will alternative energy come to the rescue?

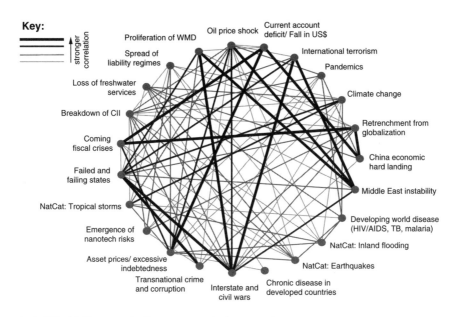

The Correlation Matrix

Chart 7.1 World Economic Forum correlation matrix.

World Economic Forum Annual Risks Review

The World Economic Forum publishes and monitors an annual global risks report with five risk categories. We concentrate on economic risks where owning gold can be motivated as a financial hedge or as risk insurance. Other global mishaps, particularly in relation to international conflict, could easily tilt the economic balance from stability to instability and encourage owning gold as catastrophe insurance.

The following are the global risks as listed by the WEF in 2007:[1]

Economic

- Oil price shock/energy supply interruptions
- US current account deficit/fall in US$
- Chinese economic hard landing
- Fiscal crises caused by demographic shift
- Blow up in asset prices/excessive indebtedness

Environmental

- Climate change
- Loss of freshwater services
- Natural catastrophe: Tropical storms
- Natural catastrophe: Earthquakes
- Natural catastrophe: Inland flooding

Geopolitical

- International terrorism
- Proliferation of weapons of mass destruction (WMD)
- Interstate and civil wars
- Failed and failing states
- Transnational crime and corruption
- Retrenchment from globalisation
- Middle East instability

Societal

- Pandemics
- Infectious diseases in the developing world
- Chronic disease in the developed world
- Liability regimes

Technological

- Breakdown of critical information infrastructure (CII)
- Emergence of risks associated with Nanotechnology

Graphics follow illustrating the likelihood and severity of potential crises. Economic risks are among the most likely to be experienced and the most severe in relation to cost. A retrenchment from globalisation or an asset price collapse could result in losses of more than $1 trillion.[2]

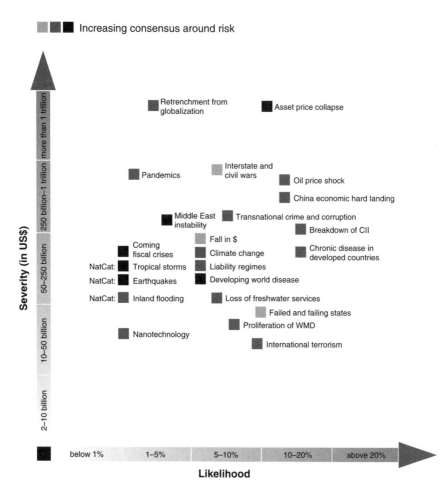

Chart 7.2 World Economic Forum Economic Loss.
Chart Courtesy of World Economic Forum

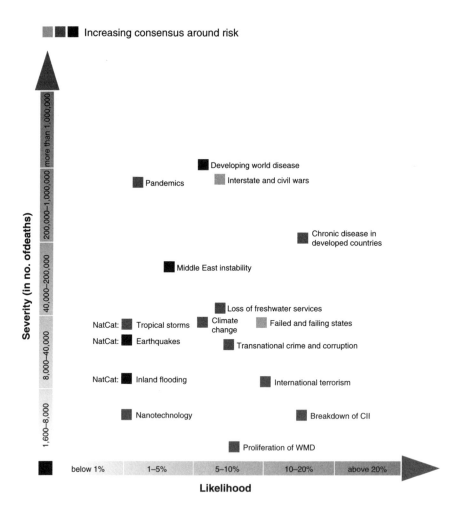

Chart 7.3 World Economic Forum Severity by Number of Deaths.
Chart Courtesy of World Economic Forum

Risks to stable disequilibrium

Before looking at risks and consequences it will be useful to review the concept
of stable disequilibrium introduced into the economists' lexicon in 2003 by analysts with Pimco, the world's largest bond fund.[3] The phrase describes the 'Asia
lends America spends' debtor and creditor relationship between the US and its

mainly Asian exporter suppliers. Pimco Managing Director Paul McCulley recently explained stable disequilibrium as a consequence of post 9/11 reflationary policies, or, put another way, the post 9/11 anti deflationary policies that boosted economic growth and, in the process, triggered 'massive imbalances in the global economy'. He commented in 2006 that any easing of reflationary policies would make the disequilibrium *less stable* and the question of imbalances more troublesome.[4]

The international investing strategist and economist David Roche heads the 'International Strategy' Consultancy and refers to 'a stable state of economic disequilibrium caused by historic serendipidity'. This state, he says, is temporary and will end. And, 'as it does, many assets will see their prices tumble'. Roche's analysis presented as 'The New Monetarism' is reviewed later in this chapter.

The message for us is that conditions could deteriorate rapidly if the global economic equilibrium becomes unstable. We need to prepare for that contingency and review potential tipping points to instability.

The End of the Days of Cheap Oil

Matthew Simmons on oil prospects

'Oil is still cheap and over the 20th century, with a few exceptions, it was almost free' according to Matthew Simmons, a prominent Houston based investment banker serving the energy industry. He has undertaken extensive research into the fuzzy informatiuon available on Saudi Arabia's oil reserves and published his findings in a book *Twilight in the Desert – The Coming Saudi Oil Shock and the World Economy*.[5] The book starts with a challenge to the accepted wisdom that Saudi Arabia has the productive capacity to solve the world's energy problems and goes on to review the world's oil resources, diminishing capacity to meet supply and demand and prospects for the long term price of oil.

Simmons draws attention to the headline statistics on oil. The world is now using 88 million barrels a day – 1.35 trillion a year. That's almost 100% of production. Between 1900 and 1990 oil use grew to 66 million barrels a day. In the past 17 years oil demand has grown another 22 million barrels a day. Increased mobility drives the growth. The world now has 900 million vehicles and adds 50 million vehicles to the global fleet every year.

On price prospects Simmons finds it impossible 'to assemble precise data on all the components that will ultimately drive the long-term price of oil'. But two key factors will support strong prices:

1 Billions of people in emerging economies who in the past either had no access to oil, or used very little, are now adopting the lifestyles of more

affluent nations and are starting to drive up their use of oil by orders of magnitude.

2 As oil production peaks and then decreases the scarcity factor will force prices to far higher levels.

Reviewing where oil prices are going in the future, from the perspective of an investment banker, Simmons is critical of pricing that doesn't compensate for reserve depletion. To refine his approach he poses this question: if a brand new oil system were to be created with every aspect of the long chain of activities being built from scratch, and every stake holder demanding a minimum 10% after tax return, what would the price of oil be today? He expects it would exceed $100 and might be as high as $200 but, without proper knowledge on the replacement costs of assets over the next twenty years, calls his estimates random guesses and warns even $200 per barrel could be too low. Simmons is a frequent keynote speaker at conventional and alternative energy conferences and symposiums. His contributions are accessible on the Internet.[6]

The following information from a recent presentation illustrates sustained demand growth for oil since the beginning of the twentieth century

1900: Oil use was primarily for lighting and baseline	
1920 oil demand:	1,523,000 bbls/day
1950 oil demand:	10,418,000 bbls/day
1980 oil demand:	59,316,000 bbls/day
2000 oil demand:	76.5 million bbls/day
2006 oil demand:	84.5 million bbls/day
1920–2006	4.8% average compound annual growth

Source: DeGolyer & McNaughton & Matthew Simmons.[7]

By 2030 world oil demand is expected to exceed 130 million barrels a day.

Conclusions from the International Energy Association 2007 Outlook

A single statistic from the comprehensive 650 page report on future global energy supply and demand published by the International Energy Agency (IEA) in November 2007 illustrates the gigantic scale of China's future oil requirements: 'The increase in China's energy demand between 2002 and 2005 was equivalent to Japan's current annual energy use.'[8] All the information in the report points to sustained demand and tight supply conditions for oil over the next twenty-five years. The following items bring home the message:

1 China will become the world's largest energy consumer, ahead of the US, shortly after 2010.

2 In the IEA reference scenario, where governments adhere to present policies, by 2030 the world's energy needs will be more than 50% higher than today. Developing countries will account for 74% of the demand growth with China alone accounting for 45%.

3 About $22 trillion, equivalent to almost half of world gross product in 2006, will have to be invested in infrastructure to meet global energy demand over the next twenty-five years.

4 Unless major new discoveries of oil resources are made or new technologies are developed the price of oil is likely to remain high. If OPEC countries are able to increase their contribution from 42% to 52% of world demand the IEA suggested demand could be met with oil priced at $60. However they acknowledged that neither an abrupt increase in oil prices nor a 'supply side crunch' could be ruled out. The Executive Director of the IEA Nobuo Tanaka commented in January 2007, when oil traded at $100, that oil markets were becoming increasingly 'fragile' as a result of low spare capacity and consumer inventories and warned that there was a risk of prices moving even higher.

We have seen from analysis by Matthew Simmons it's unlikely that OPEC will have the resources to meet projected increases in world demand. His conclusions on Saudi Arabia's production potential are:

1 Saudi Arabia will struggle to attain small production growth;

2 There is a real risk that Saudi Arabian oil could soon start to decline;

3 When it is clear that Saudi Arabia's supply has peaked the world's supply too will have peaked.

Only a few years ago analysts were still forecasting $30 oil. A little later it was $35 and then $40 and $50. Oil has since surged to above $100 driven by surging demand. It will continue to surge, particularly in India and China, where growing economies will bring more cars, trucks and factories that all burn oil and gas.

The scenario forecast by Simmons is that global demand will exceed supply and oil shortages, already commonplace in China and other fast developing economies, will become more widespread making shortages the biggest risk we are facing. When shortages start the likely reaction is for users to hoard. Hoarding will start a 'run on the petroleum bank'. The problem will then morph into a nightmare.

A Finance-based Economy with Excessive Debt

Bill Gross, the founder and chief executive of Pimco, can take liberties with style in his analysis that most commentators can't. His monthly *Investment Outlook* published on Pimco's web site in July 2003 titled 'Happiness Running' was written at the end of an ocean cruise with Pimco colleagues.[9] While still on the cruise he came to conclusions on secular prospects for the US economy and promptly wrote them on three small memo pages provided by the 'Crystal Harmony' cruise liner. His notes came with this introduction: 'Thoughts, even investment ideas, tend to come easier in such an environment and so I reproduce for you near verbatim, a short, three-page memo to myself summarising analysis on investment strategy that may be applicable over the next several years.

Note 1 read:

> (1) In contrast with prior decades we live in a financed based economy with excessive debt. Accelerating short term interest rates a la 1978–91 are not possible – must use all means including 'ceilings' to keep costs of financings low.

Note 2 read:

> (2) Rentiers (debt holders) must be *reflated* away – so while capping their returns via 'ceilings,' *inflation erodes the purchasing power* of their principal (3) must depreciate value of currency (dollar.)

Note 3 dealt with his strategies for future bond investing and highlighted TIPS – Treasury Inflation Protected Securities.

At the end of his notes Bill Gross included these remarks:

> I hesitate to elaborate in much detail. There's a certain simplicity to these notes – they may not tell it all, and they may in fact be proved wrong, but they sort of lay it out there rather succinctly and certainly quickly. Let me just add that the referenced 'reflation' in a 'financed based economy' may take years to engineer. As our May Secular Forum suggested, there are substantial structural impediments – 'wet logs' – that will make it difficult for reflation to catch fire. Strong cyclical economic recoveries may be a thing of the past until high global debt levels are diluted via reflation, and the negative competitive influence of China and India is lessened via currency revaluation. These and other wet logs may prevent a 'quick start' to government's inflationary efforts.

The old fashioned word for lenders – 'rentiers' – isn't used much anymore. It comes from the French word *rente* meaning yearly income. A rentier lives off income from renting property or income from lending money. In the 1930s John Maynard Keynes believed that rentiers' contributions to the efficiency of capital had fallen to the point that 'the euthanasia of rentiers' was in sight. 'Euthanasia of the rentiers' is an unforgettable phrase – particularly if you happen to be a rentier! The last time I saw the word used was in Bill Gross's comment – one of the most useful pieces of research I have read over the last few years. The phrase 'a financed based economy with excessive debt' had implications for us all five years ago and it still has now.[10]

It's taken a long time for rentiers generally to respond to the risks of holding dollar fixed income securities but there are signs of discontent now. A report from the US Treasury on capital flows for August 2007 came with this note:[11]

Net foreign purchases of long-term securities were minus $69.3 billion.

- Net foreign purchases of long-term U.S. securities were minus $34.9 billion. Of this, net purchases by foreign official institutions were minus $24.2 billion, and net purchases by private foreign investors were minus $10.6 billion.
- U.S. residents purchased a net $34.5 billion of long-term foreign securities

Net foreign acquisition of long-term securities, taking into account adjustments, is estimated to have been minus $85.5 billion.

Foreign holdings of dollar-denominated short-term U.S. securities, including Treasury bills, and other custody liabilities increased $33.9 billion. Foreign holdings of Treasury bills increased $21.0 billion.

Banks' own net dollar-denominated liabilities to foreign residents decreased $111.4 billion.

Monthly net TIC flows were minus $163.0 billion. Of this, net foreign private flows were minus $141.9 billion, and net foreign official flows were minus $21.1 billion.

A month of negative inflow of funds into the US Treasury doesn't spell a crisis. But, if Americans and foreigners lose their appetite for owning dollars and dollar related securities, a tip from stable disequilibrium to instability will be inevitable.

To keep abreast of current developments a useful resource is Professor Brad Setser's running commentary published on his open access RGE Monitor blog.[12] This was his comment on the August capital flows mentioned above:

. . . (it) certainly doesn't provide any support for the popular argument that the US remained a safe haven – despite all the sub prime turmoil – in times of stress. Foreign demand for US bonds – and particularly corporate bonds – disappeared. American demand for foreign bonds and equities didn't. . . .The flow of funds are insufficient to sustain the current equilibrium and there is no way to spin that kind of outflow as a positive.

Misleading inflation measures

In spite of the shock from crude oil prices trading above $90 official inflation statistics in the US, the UK, Europe and Japan still report inflation as running a little above 2%. However inflation is a general rise in the level of prices and we make a mistake thinking of it as synonymous with any consumer price index, particularly if it excludes energy and food price rises. There have been times when excluding food and energy from core inflation reports made sense on the grounds that higher prices were temporary and would correct in reasonably short time frames. But that's almost certainly no longer the case with food and is certainly not the case with oil. Not only is the oil price high on entrenched supply and demand fundamentals but it will rise dramatically in the event of any adverse geopolitical developments in the Middle East.

Through 2007 rising food costs globally have also resulted in the world facing an unprecedented period of food price inflation. Expanded biofuels industry, climate change and the growing prosperity of nations such as India and China are driving up the costs of farm commodities including wheat, corn, milk and oils. In this context rising prices are structural rather than cyclical and, with the strong upswing in the economic fortunes of China and India this decade there is a very large opportunity for food price inflation.[13]

We don't have to think of crude oil prices over $100 to take a view on whether oil price rises are a temporary disruption. Unless the world experiences a deep recession we only have to recognise it's unlikely that oil will fall as low as $50 again where it was at the end of 2006. At the time of writing it is over $95. Rising oil prices increase the costs of growing and marketing food everywhere in the world. Competition for agricultural resources for use in biofuels stock and for food has also led to rising food costs. Faced with this situation China has already limited the production of ethanol from corn and other food crops in certain areas. Biofuels are proving more costly to produce than was expected.

Research in the US reported in May 2007 revealed a proprietary food commodities index with a dozen agricultural raw materials used by food companies including wheat, barley, milk, cocoa and edible oils, was on track to reflect inflation of 21% – the biggest increase since the index started almost a decade ago.[14]

Inflation statistics are bound to be at best a guide. Consumer and retail price indexes do not need to be perfect to be useful tools for policy makers as long as they are carefully prepared, consistent and their limitations are recognised. The UK Office of National Statistics acknowledge that inflation is not a one size fits all outcome and even includes a personal inflation calculator as a web-based tool 'that allows users to calculate an inflation rate based on their personal expenditure patterns, rather than the averages used in published statistics. It does this by weighting together price indices from the RPI to arrive at a personal inflation rate.'[15]

John Williams, the publisher of an online report 'Shadow Statistics' recalculates inflation reports and other statistics ignoring modifications to the formulae that were introduced in the 1990s that he claims flatter the published statistics. In his opinion the modifications introduced distortions and on his calculations inflation reported by the Fed should be between 5% and 6%. The details of the adjustment Williams makes are fully explained on his web site.[16]

Challenges to $ hegemony

Emerging markets, including the Middle East region, accounted for 30% of the global economy in 2007 and, on revised IMF estimates, are now the world's largest economic bloc. They are also the largest driver of global economic growth and accounted for 47% of growth in 2007. That is more than the US 12% and Developed Europe 28% combined. Further, Morgan Stanley economists suggest 'this is a permanent shift in global economic leadership [leading to] current re-allocation of portfolios towards Emerging Market assets'.

The flow of funds to emerging markets raises the question whether the decline in the US dollar could become disorderly if foreigners lose their appetite for US Treasuries and equities. A worst-case scenario for the US economic outlook would involve a simultaneous weakening of the US dollar and rising US bond yields. That's not happening yet but it can't be ruled out as a prospect.

China may diversify away from dollars

There was loose talk by November 2007 that China intended investing in stronger currencies than the dollar and it planned to diversify its $1.43 trillion foreign exchange reserves. A vice chairman of the National People's Congress, Xu Jian, a vice director of China's central bank, went as far as to say 'The world's currency structure has changed; the dollar is losing its status as the world currency.'[17] Chinese investors were also reported as having reduced holdings of US Treasuries by 5% to $400 billion in the five months to the end of August. In September the Chinese Government was reported as having set up an agency to seek higher returns on currency reserves. Many countries, including China, have established Sovereign Wealth Funds that together already have capital of over $2.5 trillion. It's likely that dollar reserves will in future be invested through these funds more profitably than in the past when the preferred investment was US Treasury securities. Both Sovereign Wealth Funds and concerns over declining foreign investors' appetites for dollars are explored later in this chapter and in the following chapter on Global Economic Rebalancing. The Goldwatcher website also includes headline information on these funds.

The liquidity freeze and shadow banking

Early in 2007 markets were awash with excess liquidity. Within a few months the credit crisis erupted and credit dried up. The catalysts for the changes were the defaults associated with the complex marketing of sub prime mortgage securities packaged with various other mortgage claims and securities and leveraged layers of derivatives. In the packaging process Wall Street and the world's most respected credit rating agencies appear to have put lipstick on a pig. Packages of securitised debt that included high default risks were rated Triple A. Over the next few years it will become clear how it happened these dubious securities were given the same credit rating as US Treasury securities. All that is known at the time of writing is:

1 The credit rating agencies have been vigorously downgrading their ratings on billions of dollars of securities marketed all over the world and credit markets for collateralised debt obligations have frozen; and

2 The securitisation of the debts was accomplieshed in what has been called a 'shadow banking' system comprising special off balance sheet investment vehicles (SIVs), various derivatives and other financial instruments created to trade outside the regulatory framework that monitors and controls banking and financial instutions.

In October 2007 Pimco Managing Director Paul McCulley published a comment on Shadow Banking titled 'A Reverse Minsky Journey' where he addressed the causes and effects of the 2007 credit squeeze. The reader seeking an in depth understanding of the anatomy of the credit squeeze meticulously explained by McCulley and supported by commentary from John Maynard Kenes and Hyman Minsky will find it rewarding to read McCulley's article accessible on the Pimco website – as well as other articles cited by him. The following are tightly abbreviated headline comments from points he made:[18]

1 Seen from the perspective of behavioural economics liquidity is not a pool of money but rather a *state of mind* and in 'loosely regulated banking and capital markets liquidity is about borrowers' and lenders' collective appetite for risk'. McCulley identifies his approach with a function of what Keynes described seventy years ago as 'the willingness of investors to underwrite risk and uncertainty with borrowed money and the willingness of savers to lend money to investors who want to underwrite risk and uncertainty with borrowed money'.

2 McCulley goes on to discuss the background to mortgage finance during the house price boom and the marketing of mortgage backed securities that

led to the credit squeeze in 2007. At the centre of the phenomena was the shadow banking system he describes as 'the whole alphabet soup of non-bank leveraged intermediaries acting in the irrational belief that there would be ever rising home prices and that lenders would have unlimited access to money at low market interest rates'.

3 The 2007 mortgage backed securities crisis was triggered by soaring defaults on sub prime mortgages followed by a de facto run on the shadow banking system by holders of the securities after high levels of default were experienced. As a result the market for the assets collapsed and the credit crisis spread by contagion from mortgage backed securities to financing all other risk assets.

4 The economist Hyman Minsky contributed analysis on stability itself being unstable because people are inclined to take excessive risks when conditions are stable. Now, after the liquidity freeze, McCulley expects a 'reverse Minsky situation' to develop with stability being restored after Ponzi elements are destroyed, speculative debt elements are severely disciplined and sound units make a comeback. However, again quoting Keynes, McCulley warns: '[f]or whilst the weakening of credit is sufficient to bring about a collapse, its strengthening, though a necessary condition of recovery, is not a sufficient condition.'

Securitising junk loans

An October 2007 *Fortune* article 'Junk Mortgages Under the Microscope' revealed the process and alarming consequences of securitising debt underpinned by obligations from buyers unable to service their obligations.[19] In the article Fortune's senior editor explored the extent of what he calls junk debt home loans, usually more politely referred to as money owing by sub prime borrowers. He estimated there were about $1.5 trillion of these loans and losses experienced would be in the range of $200 billion.

Fortune took as an example of how the junk loans had been marketed an off balance sheet vehicle of the investment bankers Goldman Sachs 'GSAMP Trust 2006-S3 (the GSAMP Trust) – a $494 million drop in the junk-mortgage bucket'. According to *Fortune* 'Goldman peddled the securities in late April 2006. In a matter of months the mathematical models used to assemble and market this issue – and the models that Moody's and S&P used to rate it – proved to be horribly flawed. That's because the models were based on recent performances of junk-mortgage borrowers, who hadn't defaulted much until last year thanks to the housing bubble.'

The securities held in the GSAMP Trust included risky second mortgage loans that were granted while the housing bubble was soaring without proper, or any, credit checks. The next sequence was for these loans to be packaged with other loans, or to use the trade word 'securitised' and marketed as investments with higher expected yields than other fixed income securities. 'Less than 18 months after the issue was floated' *Fortune* reported 'a sixth of the borrowers had already defaulted on their loans. Investors who paid face value for these securities, seeking slightly more interest than they would get on equivalent bonds, suffered heavy losses. Their securities have either experienced defaults or been downgraded by credit rating agencies and accordingly devalued.'

Over half the loans were no-documentation or low-documentation. Even if they were thought to be 'owner-occupied' loans, considered less risky than loans to speculators, there was no verification that this was the case. There was also no verification of earnings or employment. People were buying houses without any risk of their own capital if they had any. If house prices went up they made a profit. If they went down they walked away. It was, according to *Fortune* 'go go finance, very 21st century'.

The *Fortune* article explains how the GSAMP securities, one of almost 1000 similar packages, came to be marketed to banks and other investors even though some of the loans in the GSAMP package 'looked like financial toxic waste'. According to *Fortune* 68% of the issue, or $336 million, was rated AAA, as secure as US Treasury Bonds, by Standard & Poors and Moodys. Another $123 million, 25% of the issue, was rated investment grade, at levels from AA to BBB. Only 7% were not rated investment grade. In the same way that a chicken producer gets a better return by selling the parts of the bird separately Wall Street secured better returns by selling tranches, or slices, of the packages separately. Mortgage debts need to be managed. Securities are simpler to deal with. With GSAMP Goldman divided the $494 million of second mortgages into 13 separate tranches. The top tranches were the most secure and yielded the lowest interest rates. Intermediate tranches yielded higher interest rates. Non investment grade tranches yielded the highest interest rates. Buyers of the securities relied on the ratings assigned by the rating agencies Standard & Poors and Moodys. 90% of GASMP was rated investment grade despite the fact that the issue was 'backed by second mortgages of dubious quality on homes in which the borrowers (most of whose income and financial assertions weren't vetted by anyone) had less than 1% equity and on which GSAMP couldn't even effectively foreclose because they only owned a second charge on the property.

It's worth noting that Goldman Sachs, in spite of losing billions of dollars on GSAMP and other securitised obligations they packaged, nevertheless made billions of dollars more on the collapse in the price of junk-mortgage securities by betting that the value of junk-mortgage securities would plummet.

The new monetarism and the liquidity factory

David Roche and his colleague Bob McKee at Independent Strategy have been analysing surging global liquidity and warning of its consequences for several years. They illustrate the imbalance between conventional money and securitised debt and derivatives as the inverted pyramid illustrated below. In their book *The New Monetarism* they explain the theory.[20,21] The global liquidity surge that ran until mid-2007 wouldn't have been possible without derivatives developed for market participants to leverage their holdings.

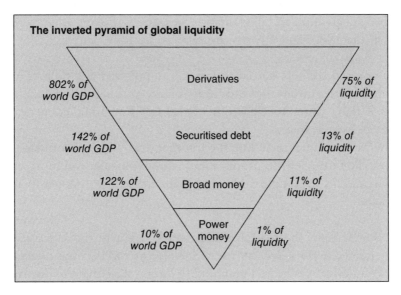

The inverted pyramid of global liquidity

802% of world GDP	Derivatives	75% of liquidity
142% of world GDP	Securitised debt	13% of liquidity
122% of world GDP	Broad money	11% of liquidity
10% of world GDP	Power money	1% of liquidity

Chart 7.4 New monetarism inverted pyramid.
(Courtesy Independent Strategy)

Roche argues that in the past all bubbles have been caused by underpriced capital. The only differences with this credit cycle are that there has been more liquidity than both real assets and real economic activity and the liquidity was not controlled by central banks. They have warned 'the party won't last forever: asset bubbles can collapse under their own weight or when the cost of capital rises'. Now, with global liquidity tightening the cost of capital is heading back towards its long term mean. . . . 'That's a recipe for asset price contraction. Demand for dollar assets has been boosted most. So any loss of confidence in the dollar as a means of international payment or store of value will heap downward pressure on asset markets when they deflate.'[22]

Roche explains money as a 'constantly changing animal' that is not the same from one cycle to the next. With the explosion of liquidity enabled by cheap money post 9/11 derivative finance grew to eight times world GDP and three times the value of the underlying assets to which they related as illustrated in the inverted pyramid above. From the tiny quantity of central bank power money at the bottom of the triangle the liquidity pyramid grew like wildfire. Liquidity creation inflated all asset markets. Between 1990 and 2005 liquidity expanded by 300% and securitised debt grew 200%. But GDP only grew by 80%. So the liquidity to buy assets expanded twice as fast as the money supply.

How did this distorted monetary arrangement come about? Roche explains it was to an extent a product of two decades of disinflation combined with new technology, globalisation and liberalisation of markets. Lower price increases year after year in the 1980s and 1990s were enabled by four factors:

1 Sane central bankers started to target low inflation as a policy.
2 Globalisation empowered producers of cheap things like China and India to sell their wares to rich folk in the US and other countries as trade barriers were lowered.
3 New Technologies including the Internet shattered the mould for corporations, allowing them to produce and market globally and more efficiently.
4 Governments freed up markets and limited their own budget spending and deficits.

Now Roche finds the stage has been reached where the US consumer has overspent and the performance of the US economy has become sluggish. In the same way that derivatives geared up liquidity during the surge the unwinding will be geared up and liquidity will be drained rapidly.

Before filling in the dots between an overhang of derivatives related to an abundance of cheap money and future economic prospects we need more clues. An interview that the stock picker and financial commentator Jon Markman conducted with a derivatives expert Satyajit Das furnished useful information linking the worlds of new monetarism and shadow banking with the US subprime mortgage crisis.[23] Das is a poacher turned gamekeeper. He was a derivatives professional and is now a writer exposing risks and vulnerabilities associated with derivatives.

Das explains linkages between sub prime mortgages and the shadow banking system in the context of a 'global liquidity factory'. He suggests we should stop thinking about mortgages as a way for people to finance houses. We should think of them instead *as a way for lenders to generate cash flow and create collateral during an era of flat interest rate curve*. And, although sub prime US loans seem like 'small change' in the context of the multi-trillion dollar debt market, these high yield instruments were an important part of the machine he calls 'The Global Liquidity Factory'. Indeed, sub prime mortgages were invented so that hedge funds would have high yield debt to buy and, in the same way that a little petrol powers a truck with the right combination of engine, spark plugs, transmission etc. 'sub prime loans became the fuel that supported derivative securities many times their size'.

By recognising the leverage potential for sub prime loans via their high nominal interest rate we can follow Das's explanation of how come 'a single dollar of real capital came to support $20 to $30 of loans and how global derivates in 2007 totalled an amount in the order of $500 trillion – almost ten times global domestic product of $50 trillion'. The message is that the danger of leverage will amplify outcomes on the way down in the same way it did on the way up. Let's see how the leverage worked on the way up, why it has had such a dramatic effect on credit markets on the way down and why it could lead to an epic bear market.

We can start to trace leverage on the way up with some insight into the way mortgages have been funded. It was no longer only banks or specialist lenders like building societies who granted the mortgage loans, owned the debt over its duration and eventually received payment. Thanks to the availability of derivatives loans were 'originated' by banks and other intermediaries who 'warehoused' them on their balance sheet for a brief time and then 'distributed' them to investors. The distribution process involved repackaging the loans into derivatives known as CDOs – collateralised debt obligations rated by credit agencies. Buyers of the CDOs were insurance companies, pension funds and hedge funds all over the world, including institutions who themselves had access to low interest borrowings they could use to acquire more of the high yielding mortgage-backed CDOs. What emerged was a pattern of borrowed money using more borrowed money to buy more securities with more borrowed money that nominally yielded a better return than the borrowed money and, with the backing of strong credit agency ratings, the CDOs were continuously used as collateral for more borrowing. Thus, according to Das, 'The liquidity factory was self perpetuating and seemingly unstoppable . . . and the triple borrowed assets were then in turn increasingly used as collateral for commercial paper . . . purchased by supposedly low-risk money market funds.' The CDOs also contributed to the strength of equity markets via 'structured finance for private equity takeovers, leveraged buyouts and corporate stock buy backs'.

So much for the way up. Now for the way down. Das sees a gigantic liquidity bubble unwinding – 'a process that can take a long, long time' particularly as the entire new risk-transfer model and its associate leverage is being rejected. David Roche, on the other hand, thinks asset price contraction 'could be a long, slow process; or it could be drastic and fatal like the sinking of Titanic'.

Dollar Falls as a Tipping Point

The chart below illustrates the dollar's almost 30% fall since 2002 against a weighted average of the foreign exchange value of the US dollar with the currencies of a broad group of major trading partners including the Euro Area, Canada, Japan, Mexico, China, United Kingdom, Taiwan, Korea, Singapore, Hong Kong, Malaysia, Brazil, Switzerland, Thailand, Philippines, Australia, Indonesia, India, Israel, Saudi Arabia, Russia, Sweden, Argentina, Venezuela, Chile and Colombia.

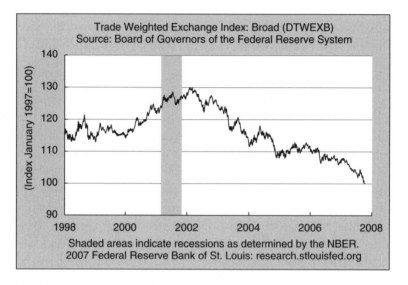

Chart 7.5 US Dollar 1998 to 2008.

Source: Board of Governors of the Federal Reserve System, Federal Reserve Bank of St Louis[24]

Will falls in the dollar be the lever that tips the global economy from stability to instability – or will further falls in the dollar help correct global imbalances by supporting US exports and curbing imports? There are of course different opinions on the subject. The potentially benign outcome for a weak dollar was well outlined by Harvard Professor Martin Feldstein in a comment published in the *Financial Times* in October 2007. He took a refreshingly realistic look at the dollar and raised the question whether and for how long foreign governments, the largest purchasers of dollar debt, would be willing to keep adding to their dollar holdings 'knowing that they will eventually incur losses as the dollar falls' and, even if foreign governments continue to support the dollar, whether private investors will not drive it down as they shift from dollars to euros or other currencies.

Feldstein's blunt message was that it's time for the US to abandon its strong dollar slogan and for everyone to recognise that the dollar has to fall further. A more competitive dollar he argued will raise US exports and reduce the risk of a recession – and that's in everyone's interests. He acknowledged 'a dollar decline by itself puts upwards pressure on the US inflation rate' but went on to argue, unconvincingly, that 'the overall inflation rate need not rise if the Federal Reserve sticks to its goal of price stability. Instead, relative increases in the prices of tradable goods would be offset by lower inflation in other goods and services.'

Acceptance that the dollar is on the skids is not the kind of myopic analysis that leads to the Wile E. Coyote moments and plunges as identified by Paul Krugman and discussed in Chapter 5. In the concluding paragraph of his article Feldstein sets out the essential responses from trading partners that could cushion the global effects of a falling dollar:

> Markets must look beyond the slogan that a strong dollar is good for America to recognise that a more competitive dollar will help sustain US growth and is necessary to correct America's trade deficit. Governments of our trading partners must recognise that the dollar's decline will weaken demand in their economies and should use fiscal and regulatory measures to maintain their growth and employment. With appropriate policies, the dollar's decline will correct the imbalances that threaten the global economy without higher inflation in the US or decreased growth in the rest of the world.

America's circa $800 billion current account deficit is being financed by capital from the rest of the world. Whether the funding can be explained as a benign effect of a global savings glut as Bernanke claims, or a product of reckless spending as other commentators allege, the deficit can't go on rising forever. Even at its present level it will necessitate the US borrowing over $800 billion a year with compound interest accruing. How will the imbalance between the US and its creditors be resolved when the creditors know the dollar has further to fall and they are going to bear the brunt of the loss?

Marginal improvements in the US monthly trade balance have encouraged some commentators to say that the trend has changed and imbalances are being resolved. The most recent US international trade report at the time of writing reflected a monthly deficit for the month of August 2007 of $57.6 billion, about $1.5 billion less than the previous month as illustrated in the following chart:[25]

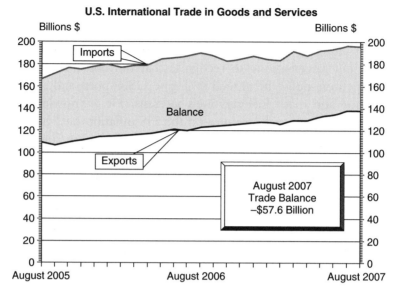

Chart 7.6 US international trade balance.
Source: US Census Bureau

Consequences of an unstable dollar

For meaningful changes in the US adverse trade balance the current pace of narrowing may not be enough and, in any event, there will be other consequences to consider. Creditors will sustain unacceptable levels of capital losses as the dollar falls and, by paying considerably more for oil and other imports, the US will import inflation. To compensate for currency losses creditors funding the deficit will seek higher interest rates on their loans – or invest their money in assets other than US bonds. And, if the dollar continues to fall, countries that still peg their currencies to the dollar will seek to protect themselves from importing inflation. Middle Eastern states, including Saudi Arabia, the United Arab Emirates, Bahrain, Qatar and Oman still have their currency exchange rates pegged to the dollar and are under increasing pressure to abandon the dollar peg. It inevitably results in them holding large dollar reserves and, as a result, over the years these countries have provided considerable indirect support for the dollar. But they find they are bound to follow the Fed's lead when it cuts interest rates and, in current economic conditions, cutting rates again could stimulate their already booming economies further and cause domestic inflation. However if they abandon their US dollar peg to secure more independent management of their monetary policies, stability of the dollar will be seriously undermined and the dollar's role as the world's dominant reserve asset would be compromised.

House price inflation: boom to bust

As the value of homes in the US is now centre stage in the securitised debt crisis let's explore whether there was a bubble in US house prices generally. Real estate is usually a safe investment but time and again it has been subject to as much speculation as dot com shares were in the late 1990s. In his classic book *Manias, Panics and Crashes* Charles Kindelberger traces the history of bubbles over the centuries. Referring to a nineteenth century Chicago real estate bubble he includes this trite quote from an 1890 *Chicago Tribune* article commenting on a real estate bubble inflated by 'men who bought property at prices they knew perfectly well were all fictitious, but who were willing to pay such prices simply because they knew that some still greater fool could be depended on to take the property off their hands and leave them with a profit'[26].

There was an element of knowing prices were fictitious and 'waiting for a greater fool' behind recent house price surges in the US and elsewhere. Speculators in the US 'flipping condos' caught the headlines even though they were only a small part of the mania. For over a decade low interest rates and easy access to credit, not only for creditworthy buyers but for all buyers, gave an extra boost to house price rises. And a surge of funds outside the control of central bankers described by Paul McCulley as shadow banking, by David Roche as the new monetarism and by Satyajit Das as the liquidity factory fuelled the furnace.

Research in depth on US house prices and, to a certain extent UK house prices, has been conducted by the American economist Robert Shiller, a prominent academic, authoritative commentator on real estate and financial markets and a prominent financial writer. He is also associated with a benchmark index of house prices in the United States known as the Standard & Poors' Case Shiller Index.

In his research Shiller describes a speculative bubble as 'a feedback mechanism, operating "through public observation of price increases and public expectations of future price increases, with contagion working through word of mouth and media comment." '[27] He concludes that the boom in house prices in the US since the late 1990s was a classic speculative bubble, 'driven largely by extravagant expectations for future price increases'. And from analysis experienced in past cycles he has warned of the possibility of declines in home prices of as much as 50%, with declines extending over many years in areas that have seen large increases.

Shiller describes all asset price bubbles as a 'social epidemic where certain public conceptions and ideas lead to emotional speculative interest in the markets and, therefore, to price increases'. The process keeps repeating itself again and again and prices keep rising for a while. But the feedback cannot go on forever and, when prices stop increasing, the public loses interest in the investment and the bubble bursts.

The following are Shiller's key conclusions on the house price bubble:

1 The surge in US house prices cannot be explained by fundamentals such as rents or construction costs. Labour costs were static and rents went up only 4% over the last decade.[28]
2 Though it is not impossible that prices could stabilise, or even rise, home prices generally follow long price trends and steady and substantial real home price declines are expected extending over years.
3 The house price boom was spurred by what he describes as a 'social epidemic' that encourages a view of housing as an important investing opportunity.
4 The sub prime mortgage market, virtually non existent before the mid-1990s, rose to account for 29% of all new mortgages by 2005 and burgeoned to approximately $375 billion a year. At the same time denial rates on mortgage applications plunged and new loans went disproportionately to lower income borrowers and racial and ethnic minorities.
5 The magnitude of the boom was unprecedented. Its implications and possible reversal over coming years will be a serious challenge for policy makers.

Looking ahead Shiller notes that in the US, residential investment as a percentage of GDP has had a prominent peak before almost every recession since 1950 with a lead time varying from months to years. The ends of recessions have in the past been accompanied by sharp upturns in residential investment within months of the end of the recession.

Central banks and asset bubbles

Should central bankers have been more responsive to bubbles than they were over the last decade? Kindelberger's view is that 'most central bankers choose price stability as the main target of monetary policy, whether it be wholesale prices, the consumer price index or the gross domestic product deflator is not a critical issue'. But he notes 'if the explosion of a bubble in stocks or real estate can affect bank solvency in general there is a basis for saying that central bankers should keep an eye on asset prices too'.

Paul de Grauwe, Professor of Economics at the University of Leuven in the Netherlands, contends, I think correctly, that there are lessons to be learned from the current credit crisis on the responsibilities of central bankers.[29] In an article contributed to the *Financial Times* in November 2007 he challenges the policy followed by Greenspan and Bernanke of ignoring bubbles. According to him central banks must prick bubbles and, because they ignored the housing bubble, they must accept some responsibility for the credit market rout that followed. His line of reasoning is:

The credit crisis has unveiled the fallacy of this hands-off view. If the banking system were insulated from the asset markets, the view that monetary policies should not be influenced by what happens in asset markets would make sense. Asset bubbles and crashes would affect only the non-banking sector and a central bank is not in the business of insuring private portfolios. The problem that we have seen in the recent crisis is that the banking sectors were not insulated from movements in the asset markets. Banks were heavily implicated both in the development of the bubble in the housing markets and its subsequent crash.

Central banks, as lenders of last resort, were forced to provide liquidity following the credit crisis because they were the only institutions capable of doing so. Therefore, de Grauwe argues 'when asset prices experience a bubble it should be a matter of concern for the central bank because the bubble will be followed by a crash, and that is when the balance sheet of the central bank will be affected'. Without using the phrase 'shadow banking' he makes the point that over recent years a significant 'part of liquidity and credit creation was generated outside the banking system with hedge funds and special conduits borrowing short and lending long and creating liquidity and bubbles on a massive scale'. He exposes the fallacy of the argument that a bubble can never be recognised ex ante:

One had to be blind not to see the bubble in the US housing market, or the internet bubble. This is the case for most asset bubbles in history. It has been argued that even if central banks can detect bubbles, they are pretty much powerless to stop them. This argument is unconvincing. It is not inherently more difficult to stop asset bubbles than it is to stop inflation. . . . The fashionable inflation-targeting view is a minimalist view of the responsibilities of a central bank. The central bank cannot avoid taking more responsibilities beyond inflation targeting. These include the prevention of bubbles and the supervision of all institutions that are in the business of creating credit and liquidity.

Will the unwinding of the sub prime mortgage crisis be the tipping point that tips the global economy from stable disequilibrium to instability? It certainly could and will if foreigners lose faith in the ability of the Fed and other central banks to efficiently regulate shadow banking and derivative financing operations.

Before leaving the subject it's worth mentioning that Das points the finger of blame for the sub prime mortgage crisis in three directions:

1 'Regulators who stood by as US Banks developed ingenious but dangerous ways of shifting trillions of dollars off their balance sheets into the hands of unsophisticated foreign investors.'
2 Hedge fund and pension managers who gorged on high yield debt instruments they didn't understand.
3 Financial engineers who built towers of securitised debt with mathematical models that were fundamentally flawed.

The only comment that I add is to repeat Paul Krugman's remark quoted at the end of Chapter 5 of *The $ Standard and the Deficit Without Tears* on prospects for a Wile E. Coyote moment and a dollar plunge: '[i]t's not going to be fun.' America's creditors are likely to stop being myopic, seek the best returns for their funds and, on present indications those returns won't come from fixed income securities at low rates of interest in dollars. Better returns will be sought by aggressive investing through their Sovereign Wealth Funds.

Sovereign Wealth Funds

All aspects of allegedly open capitalist societies, anxieties by politicians with protectionist leanings, xenophobia by elements of society and intentions of creditor countries in relation to their financial muscle will be in issue as the shift occurs from the US 'deficit without tears' and post Bretton Woods II arrangements to optimal returns on money via Sovereign Wealth Funds. The outcome could be benign and stable. But Sovereign Wealth Funds could also usher in conflict and instability. In the following chapter we discuss the subject further.

By way of introduction an abbreviated extract of the Testimony of US Under Secretary for International Affairs David H. McCormick before the Senate Committee on Banking, Housing, and Urban Affairs on 14 October 2007 on the subject follows:[30]

> . . . This is a timely hearing on a very important topic. At Treasury, we have been increasingly focused on sovereign wealth funds for more than a year now. I am pleased to be able to share with the Committee some of our views.
>
> **History and Context**
>
> First, some history: sovereign wealth funds are not new. The oldest of these funds date back to the 1950s in Kuwait and Kiribati. Over the next four decades, their numbers slowly grew. Three of the largest and most respected funds – the Abu Dhabi Investment Authority, Singapore's Government Investment Corporation, and Norway's Government Pension Fund-Global – were founded in 1976, 1981, and 1990, respectively. By the year 2000, there were about 20 sovereign wealth funds worldwide managing total assets of several hundred billion dollars.
>
> Today, what is new is the rapid increase in both the number and size of sovereign wealth funds. Twenty new funds have been created since 2000, more than half of these since 2005, which brings the total number to nearly 40 funds that now manage total assets in a range of $1.9–2.9 trillion. Private sector analysts have projected that sovereign wealth fund assets could grow to $10–15 trillion by 2015. Two trends have contributed to this ongoing growth. The first is sustained high commodity prices. The second is the accumulation of official

reserves and the transfers from official reserves to investment funds in non-commodity exporters. It should be noted, that within this group of countries, foreign exchange reserves are now sufficient by all standard metrics of reserve adequacy. For these non-commodity exporters, more flexible exchange rates are often necessary, and Treasury actively pushes for increased flexibility.

So what are sovereign wealth funds? At the Department of the Treasury, we have defined them as government investment vehicles funded by foreign exchange assets, which manage those assets separately from official reserves. Sovereign wealth funds generally fall into two categories based on the source of the foreign exchange assets:

In contrast to traditional reserves, which are typically invested for liquidity and safety, sovereign wealth funds seek a higher rate of return and may be invested in a wider range of asset classes. Sovereign wealth fund managers have a higher risk tolerance than their counterparts managing official reserve. They emphasize expected returns over liquidity and their investments can take the form of stakes in U.S. companies, as has been witnessed in recent months with increased regularity.

However, sovereign wealth fund assets are currently fairly concentrated. By some market estimates, a handful of funds account for the majority of total sovereign wealth fund assets. Roughly two-thirds of sovereign wealth fund assets are commodity fund assets ($1.3–1.9 trillion), while the remaining one-third are non-commodity funds transferred from official reserves ($0.6–1.0 trillion).

To get a better perspective of the relative importance of sovereign wealth funds it is useful to consider how they measure up against private pools of global capital. Total sovereign wealth fund assets of $1.9–2.9 trillion may be small relative to a $190 trillion stock of global financial assets or the roughly $53 trillion managed by private institutional investors. But sovereign wealth fund assets are currently larger than the total assets under management by either hedge funds or private equity funds, and are set to grow at a much faster pace.

In sum, sovereign wealth funds represent a large and rapidly growing stock of government-controlled assets, invested more aggressively than traditional reserves. Attention to sovereign wealth funds is inevitable given that their rise clearly has implications for the international financial system. Sovereign wealth funds bring benefits to the system, but also raise potential concerns.

Benefits

A useful starting point when discussing the benefits of sovereign wealth funds is to stress that the United States remains committed to open investment. On May 10, President Bush publicly reaffirmed in his open economies statement the U.S. commitment to advancing open economies at home and abroad, including through open investment and trade. Lower trade and investment barriers benefit not only the United States, but also the global economy as a whole. The depth, liquidity and efficiency of our capital markets should continue to make the United States the most attractive country in the world in which to invest.

Foreign investment in the United States, including from sovereign wealth funds, strengthens our economy, improves productivity, creates good jobs, and spurs healthy competition. In 2006, there was a net increase of $1.9 trillion in foreign-owned assets in the United States. Foreign direct investment (FDI) is particularly beneficial to our economy. FDI supports nearly 10 million U.S. jobs directly or indirectly, 13% of R&D spending in the U.S., 19% of U.S. exports and pays 30% higher compensation than the U.S. average.

As many observers have pointed out, sovereign wealth funds have the potential to promote financial stability. They are, in principle, long term, stable investors that provide significant capital to the system. They are typically not highly leveraged and cannot be forced by capital requirements or investor withdrawals to liquidate positions rapidly. Sovereign wealth funds, as public sector entities, should have an interest in and a responsibility for financial market stability.

Potential Concerns

Yet, sovereign wealth funds also raise potential concerns. Primary among them is a risk that sovereign wealth funds could provoke a new wave of investment protectionism, which would be very harmful to the global economy. Protectionist sentiment could be partially based on a lack of information and understanding of sovereign wealth funds, in part due to a general lack of transparency and clear communication on the part of the funds themselves. Concerns about the cross-border activities of state-owned enterprises may also at times be misdirected at sovereign wealth funds as a group. Better information and understanding on both sides of the investment relationship is needed.

Second, transactions involving investment by sovereign wealth funds, as with other types of foreign investment, may raise legitimate national security concerns. The new Foreign Investment and National Security Act (FINSA) authored by the Chairman and Ranking members of this committee and signed into law by President Bush last summer, implemented through the Committee on Foreign Investment in the United States (CFIUS), ensures robust reviews of investment transactions, based on the consideration of genuine national security concerns, and requires heightened scrutiny of foreign government-controlled investments. CFIUS is able to review investments from sovereign wealth funds just as it would other foreign government-controlled investments, and it has and will continue to exercise this authority to ensure national security.

As we take our work forward on sovereign wealth funds, Treasury is also considering, non-national security issues related to potential distortions from a larger role of foreign governments in markets. For example, through inefficient allocation of capital, perceived unfair competition with private firms, or the pursuit of broader strategic rather than strictly economic return-oriented investments, sovereign wealth funds could potentially distort markets. Clearly both sovereign wealth funds and the countries in which they invest will be best served if investment decisions are made solely on commercial grounds.

Finally, sovereign wealth funds may raise concerns related to financial stability. Sovereign wealth funds can represent large, concentrated, and often non-transparent positions in certain markets and asset classes. Actual shifts in their asset allocations could cause market volatility. In fact, even perceived shifts or rumors can cause volatility as the market reacts to what it perceives sovereign wealth funds to be doing.

Will Alternative Energy Come to the Rescue?

The 2008 World Economic Forum global risks report of focuses on issues shaping the global risk landscape including systemic and financial risk, food security and the role of energy. Food security is seen as the emerging risk of the 21st century. Prices of many staple foods had already reached record levels in 2007 and have since then continued to rise. Economic growth in emerging markets, the cost and availability of sufficient food to feed the world and the cost of energy are interlocked. Predictions for the global population are 9 billion by 2050 – almost a third more than the population is now. As emerging economies advance, they consume more protein-rich foods that require more grain to produce. Annual per capita consumption of meat in China has grown from 10 kilograms in 1950 to 40 kilograms now. Global arable farmland per head of population has declined. Yet crops are being allocated to biofuels to reduce carbon emissions and dependence on imported energy.

On the consequences of climate change and the scope for alternative energy I am not unbiased and have commentated on the subject. My position is that though climate change is not proven absolutely there is weighty evidence it is occurring. We all make decisions on major everyday issues relying on far flimsier evidence. Use of fossil fuels may in time be significantly replaced by eco-friendly renewable resources. But we are deluding ourselves if we expect quick results.

Ten years ago oil was being almost given away at $10. Perceptions on future supply and demand relationships were so flawed that *The Economist* published a cover feature headlined *Drowning in Oil* with the message that oil was heading for $5 where it would stay for a long time. Now The McKinsey Global Institute report that between 2007 and 2020 the oil exporting nations of the Gulf Cooperation council will earn about $10 trillion. That is more than triple their earnings from 1963 through 2006.[31] High energy costs are a menacing tipping point to instability. The balance of global economic power is slipping away from the US and other western consuming economies. Conservation could improve the economic balance but unfortunately it is not being taken seriously. Discussions on this subject will be continued on www.thegoldwatcher.com.

8

Globalisation & Global Economic Rebalancing

Can the IMF avoid global financial meltdown?

Introduction: Skating on Thin Ice

In April 2005 former Fed Chairman Paul Volcker published an op-ed piece in the *Washington Post* titled 'An Economy on Thin Ice'.[1] He wrote about high US economic growth rates being supported by growth in China and India and his concerns that 'under the placid surface, there are disturbing trends: huge imbalances, disequilibria, risks – call them what you will' and commented that Americans were spending 'as if there is no tomorrow, buying houses at rising prices and the nation consuming and investing about 6% more than they were producing'. Pointing to vulnerability in the system he commented:

> What holds it all together is a massive and growing flow of capital from abroad, running to more than $2 billion every working day, and growing. There is no sense of strain. As a nation we don't consciously borrow or beg. We aren't even offering attractive interest rates, nor do we have to offer our creditors protection against the risk of a declining dollar . . . More recently, we've become more dependent on foreign central banks, particularly in China and Japan and elsewhere in East Asia . . . for the most part, the central banks of the emerging world have been willing to hold more and more dollars, which are, after all, the closest thing the world has to a truly international currency.

However Volcker warned 'The difficulty is that this seemingly comfortable pattern can't go on indefinitely. The United States is absorbing about 80 percent of the net flow of international capital.' He argued that a time will come when central banks and private institutions will 'have their fill of dollars' and concluded:

> So I think we are skating on increasingly thin ice. On the present trajectory, the deficits and imbalances will increase. At some point, the sense of confidence in capital markets that today so benignly supports the flow of funds to the United States and the growing world economy could fade. Then some event, or combination of events, could come along to disturb markets, with damaging volatility in both exchange markets and interest rates. We had a taste of that in the stagflation of the 1970s – a volatile and depressed dollar, inflationary pressures, a sudden increase in interest rates and a couple of big recessions.

Too wise to forecast dates Volcker wrote 'I don't know whether change will come with a bang or a whimper, whether sooner or later.' Change almost came with a whisper at an OPEC meeting in November 2007. A contentious proposal by Venezuela and Iran related to concerns that dollar weakness was damaging oil producers' economies was being discussed and voted down. But an accidental broadcast of a private discussion made comments by the Saudi foreign minister public. In the comments he warned that if OPEC even mentioned discussions concerning dollar weakness in their final statement, or just indicated 'that we have charged finance ministers with studying this issue . . . would mean a decision taken by OPEC would have the opposite effect and the media would pick up on this point, . . . *and then perhaps we would find that the dollar had collapsed*, instead of us having done something in the interest of our countries'.[2] However the message for us is clear. Once OPEC is discussing the possibility of not pricing oil in dollars the risk of a dollar plunge gets too close for comfort. And the case for investors having gold on our agendas becomes compelling.

In May 2003 Richard Duncan, author of *The Dollar Crisis,* discussed in Chapter 4, contributed an op-ed commentary for the *Asia Times* with his warning of dangers associated with the dollar crisis.[3] Duncan defines the primary characteristic of the Dollar Standard as having allowed 'the United States to finance extraordinarily large current account deficits by selling debt instruments to its trading partners instead of paying for its imports with gold as would have been required under the Bretton Woods System or The Gold Standard'. He argues that the Dollar Standard enabled the age of globalisation 'by allowing the rest of the world to sell their products to the United States on credit'. With more rapid economic growth in the developing world than would have occurred benefits to the US included 'downward pressure on consumer prices and, therefore, interest rates in the United States as cheap manufactured goods made with very low-cost labour' were imported by the US 'in rapidly increasing amounts'. He points to 'undesirable and potentially disastrous consequences' of the dollar standard:

. . . as countries which built up large stockpiles of international reserves through current account or financial account surpluses have experienced severe economic overheating and hyper-inflation in asset prices . . . (and) . . . flaws in the current international monetary system have also resulted in economic overheating and hyper-inflation in asset prices in the United States as that country's trading partners have reinvested their dollar surpluses (i.e. their reserve assets) in dollar-denominated assets. Their acquisitions of stocks, corporate bonds, and US agency debt have helped fuel the stock market bubble, facilitated the extraordinary misallocation of corporate capital, and helped drive US property prices to unsustainable levels.

Duncan's key conclusion relates to 'overinvestment on a grand scale across almost every industry worldwide'. His warnings go back a few years and there have been times when it appeared he was on the wrong tracks. However, in relation to developments in 2007, his commentary has the support of the collapse of the house price bubble, the sub prime mortgage associated credit crisis and widespread concerns on the subject of global imbalances and associated economic disequilibrium. We may have reached the stage now where global financial instability threatens the wave of globalisation experienced over the last few decades.

Financial Imbalances and Global Economic Meltdown

The global imbalances between the US, the world's biggest creditor, spender and borrower and its mainly Asian suppliers have concerned policy makers for years. US borrowings in excess of $800 billion a year to fund its trade imbalance and China's foreign exchange reserves surging above $1 trillion have been recognised as critical issues affecting the global economy and the stable disequilibrium between the US and its creditors. In the US the imbalances have fuelled protectionist sentiment based on the notion that China, in particular, has been depressing the value of its currency in order to secure competitive advantage. In September 2006, prodded by the US, the IMF advanced plans for proactive surveillance of currency management among its members that led to consultations on global imbalances with the countries concerned.

Harvard Economics Professor Kenneth Rogoff's opinions on macro economic issues are widely sought and respected and, as he has served as an economic advisor to the IMF, his comments on issues concerning the IMF carry additional weight. In September 2006, ahead of IMF and World Bank meetings, he published an article with the dramatic title 'Can the IMF avert a global meltdown?'[4] His message was that the US had been borrowing excessively and while a smooth resolution to the crisis was not out of the question 'if policymakers continue to sit on their hands, it is not hard to imagine a sharp global slowdown or even a devastating financial crisis' with the danger of a precipitous currency realignment 'that would likely set off a massive dollar depreciation and possibly much worse'.

The following are other points he raised:

1 The scale of the US's foreign borrowings and the extent to which they were absorbing the lion's share of the world's savings were without historical precedent. Would the IMF be able to coax the US and China to diffuse the risks posed by their massive trade imbalances?
2 A solution to global imbalances will require engagement by the US, China, Japan, Europe, Saudi Arabia and the other major oil exporters, now the world's biggest source of new capital, who will all have to take steps to alleviate the risk of a crisis.
3 If world leaders fail to cooperate with the IMF in finding solutions to a pending imbalances crisis 'they will be blamed for not seeing an impending catastrophe that was staring them in the face'.

Was Rogoff right to warn of global financial meltdown? I was surprised when I first read his extreme title. The US was having no difficulty borrowing funds at low interest rates to fund its deficits. China's economy was achieving double digit growth. US Treasury Secretary Henry Paulson had established a framework for strategic policy discussions with China. And, though politicians in the US were beating the protectionist drum, their case wasn't compelling. With US unemployment at 4.5% common sense would surely prevail and protectionism was unlikely to move beyond rhetoric, particularly as it was known what had to be done to rebalance the global economy: less dependence on the US consumer and more domestic economic growth in China and other emerging economies.

Rogoff's dire warnings of catastrophe and financial meltdown were surely intended more as a wake up call to world leaders than as a general warning of an imminent crisis. Either way his comments must be taken seriously. In an October 2004 paper *The Unsustainable US Current Account Position Revisited* compiled with Professor Maurice Obstfeld, Rogoff and his co-author concluded that 'whereas the dollar's decline may be benign as in the 1980s we argue that the current conjecture more closely parallels the early 1970s when the Bretton Woods system collapsed'.[5] Only a few months after Rogoff's September 2006 'meltdown' article the US housing bubble started deflating and in its wake the sub prime mortgage crisis that froze credit markets followed.

In October 2007, when the dollar had already fallen appreciably Rogoff contributed a further article titled 'High Noon at the IMF' again ahead of IMF and World Bank meetings.[6] In this comment he raised recent adverse developments including:

1 The global housing bubble starting to deflate and money markets, especially in Europe, being 'traumatised by the festering global credit crunch record-high food and energy prices, combined with sharply rising wages in China leading to inflation in the rest of the world and the US productivity boom decelerating'.

2 The world wanting to know what, if anything, IMF officials plan to do if the dollar continues to sink and what China is planning to do with its $1.4 reserves.

3 Whether the pressure on the euro and the Canadian dollar in the wake of the dollar's fall could be relieved.

4 And, as the IMF had 'asserted the right to take action if countries engage in sustained one-way currency intervention' whether the new IMF Managing Director Dominique Strauss-Kahn, taking office at the end of October 2007, would be able to act quickly enough to avert a crisis.

Rogoff's most recent contribution on the subject, *Dog Days for the Super Dollar,* was published in December 2007.[7] This thoughtful contribution addressed the 'exorbitant privilege' accorded the dollar that rankled the French when President Charles de Gaulle called for a restoration of the gold standard in 1965 and the US was able to 'flood the world with dollar currency and debt without ever seeming to pay a price in terms of higher inflation or interest rates'.

Rogoff raised the question whether the US's super power status would be affected if the dollar lost its super currency status and suggested it might not, but the US would 'certainly find global hegemony a lot more expensive if the dollar falls off its perch'. Until now 'America's financial supremacy has certainly eased the burden of being a superpower'. But following the sub prime crisis and falls in the value of the dollar 'America's exorbitant privilege now looks a bit shaky'. He argued that inertia was on the side of the US. It took decades and two world wars before the British £ lost its super currency status and as yet there is no obvious successor to the dollar. But '[u]nless the US gets its act together soon, it may find the value of its super-currency franchise much diminished'. The message for us must surely be that the value of gold's stateless money franchise will, at the same time, be enhanced.

Protectionism, Mercantilism and Mutual Interest

Issues associated with currency exchange rates include the claims by US politicians promoting a protectionist agenda that China was engaged in 'blatant currency manipulation' and mercantilism. Mercantilism, they claim, starts with a grossly undervalued currency that works in the same way as a tariff on US exports that also forces other Asian nations to engage in currency manipulation to remain competitive. The protectionist lobby also claim that mercantilism by China extends to a range of export subsidies and tax preferences inconsistent with the rules of the World Trade Organization and they accuse China of counterfeiting branded products, intellectual property piracy and allowing production with lax health and safety provisions to gain cost advantages for their exporters.

However the core competitive concern with China relates to the exchange rate of its currency. There is a widespread belief in the US that China's currency is undervalued making US imports from China artificially cheap and exports to China artificially expensive. To level the playing field they seek an upward revaluation of the renmimbi. However, the question of undervaluation is contentious, as is the question whether the US would gain or lose if China stopped intervening in currency markets to prevent its currency appreciating further.

Harvard Professor Jeffrey Frankel is among those who have warned that if China took America's advice and stopped intervening in currency markets politicians could come to rue the day they called for such action as:

> . . . the result could well be an abrupt upward movement in US interest rates when the Chinese authorities stopped intervening in the market by buying dollar securities. The same could be the result if the Chinese authorities were to switch the composition of their reserves away from the dollar, perhaps in line with the ongoing shift in the currency composition of their reference basket away from the dollar.[8]

Frankel supported IMF actions to achieve multilateral cooperation on currency relationships and global imbalances and commented:

> Agreeing on such multilateral cooperation will not be easy. Both sides will be reluctant to make the necessary concessions. The United States is not likely to give up easily on the politically attractive idea that China bears some responsibility for its trade deficit, represented numerically by the bilateral deficit . . . China for its part is not likely to give up easily on the idea that it has the sovereign right to move as slowly on currency reform as it deems in its interest. But both sides also have something important to lose if the issue is not settled. China's leaders run the danger of losing free access to a very large and important export market. The US leaders run the risk of the political momentum behind the scapegoat strategy backfiring, in the form of either self-inflicted protectionist legislation or a hard landing for the dollar and US securities in global financial markets. The RMB/dollar rate and associated imbalances is a better subject for multilateral surveillance and international cooperation than any subject to come along in many years, and it is more likely to be amenable to progress in the forum of the

IMF than anywhere else. If nothing else, this process might help delay and deflect protectionist fervour in the US Congress.

IMF Engagement on Global Economic Imbalances

There is no question that the IMF is the organisation responsible for global currency issues, including imbalances. This is clear from its Articles of Agreement that define its role as:[9]

(i)   To promote international monetary cooperation through a permanent institution which provides the machinery for consultation and collaboration on international monetary problems.

(ii) To facilitate the expansion and balanced growth of international trade, and to contribute thereby to the promotion and maintenance of high levels of employment and real income and to the development of the productive resources of all members as primary objectives of economic policy.

(iii) To promote exchange stability, to maintain orderly exchange arrangements among members, and to avoid competitive exchange depreciation.

(iv) To give confidence to members by making the general resources of the Fund temporarily available to them under adequate safeguards, thus providing them with opportunity to correct maladjustments in their balance of payments without resorting to measures destructive of national or international prosperity.

(v)   In accordance with the above, to shorten the duration and lessen the degree of disequilibrium in the international balances of payments of members.

Between September 2006 and March 2007 the IMF conducted a programme of multilateral consultations on global imbalances with China, the Euro Area, Japan, Saudi Arabia and the United States. Brief early reports on the consultations gave the impression successful discussions had taken place with positive outcomes. But a lengthy and comprehensive IMF Staff Report on the Multilateral Consultation Between September 2006 and March 2007 on Global Imbalances with China, the Euro Area, Japan, Saudi Arabia, and the United States reveals a less unambiguous picture.[10] I use this report for information on the consultations and refer to all functionaries and different departments of the IMF as 'the IMF' whether the reference is to Directors, staff or committees. The consultations started with discussions between IMF staff and representatives of each individual country.

Then meetings followed attended by senior officials from each country and the IMF staff team chaired by an IMF Director.

The following comments drawn from information in the Staff Report give a more complete picture of the IMF's approach. At the end of some paragraphs I have added my comments in italics.

Extracts from Headline Comments from IMF Staff Report on Financial Imbalances

The IMF called for sustained actions to implement an agreed policy strategy to underpin an orderly unwinding of global imbalances at the same time as maintaining strong global economic growth. The strategy involved steps to boost national saving in the United States, including fiscal consolidation; further progress on growth-enhancing reforms in Europe; further structural reforms, including fiscal consolidation, in Japan; reforms to boost domestic demand in emerging Asia, together with greater exchange rate flexibility in a number of surplus countries; and increased spending consistent with absorptive capacity and macro economic stability in oil producing countries.

According to the IMF Staff Report the multilateral discussions were against the backdrop of a benign global environment. Global growth remained strong, with IMF growth forecasts revised upwards in 2006 in both the Spring and Fall World Economic Outlooks. Downside risks to the outlook, which were seen to be significant at the outset, diminished subsequently, reflecting falling oil prices, limited spill overs from the US housing market, and generally benign financial conditions. *All the benign conditions mentioned have since deteriorated severely and continue to deteriorate.*

Again, according to the IMF Report, while imbalances were still widening at the time the consultations started, they have since shown some signs of stabilising, albeit at high levels. In particular, the US non-oil trade deficit narrowed by ¼ % of GDP in 2006 facilitated by some rebalancing of domestic demand – particularly stronger demand growth in Europe and Saudi Arabia and weaker demand growth in the United States – and the lagged effects of past dollar depreciation. Falling crude oil prices also helped reduce imbalances between August 2006 and January 2007, but with prices rebounding since then, the effect has been largely reversed. *High oil prices in 2007 are bound to increase imbalances again. It was naïve to forecast falling oil prices when it was well known that demand was surging and production capacity was not.*

The IMF reported that the US current account deficit continued to be relatively easily financed, partly reflecting the size and innovativeness of US financial markets for bonds and structured products. Reflecting a search for higher returns, foreign purchases of corporate and agency bonds had increased in recent years, offsetting a decline in purchases of US Treasuries. *This conclusion must be an embarrassment to the IMF staff. US innovation with structured financial products led to the credit crisis and, after US creditors heard on the best authority, the IMF, that the dollar had to go on sinking, sustained demand for fixed income US securities can not be counted on.*

The most brash observation made by the IMF staff was that 'despite large external borrowings, the U.S. net international investment position as a share of GDP has remained broadly unchanged since 2001, reflecting valuation gains from U.S. dollar depreciation and – especially in 2005 and 2006 – from domestic returns on overseas equity holdings'. *It must have offended foreign creditors losing capital as the dollar sinks to be reminded that US investors, smart enough not to own dollars, were profiting from falls in the value of the dollar.*

The $ as America's Currency and Everyone Else's Problem Again?

The IMF Staff Report is a lengthy document with repeated references to the benefits of cooperation, the general good, all participants agreeing the consultations were a good idea etc. The report reads as if it was intended for review by senior management and the authors would be asked 'did you get all the boxes ticked?' Typically the report states:

> The participants reiterated their support for the IMF strategy to reduce imbalances through policies that were in each individual countries' own interest as well as desirable from a multilateral perspective, and indicated that their policy plans are consistent with it.

Surely it is most unlikely that any participant agreed to only doing things in their interests if they were also desirable from a multilateral perspective. They were not a cartel.

If you read between the lines, it's not clear that the consultations achieved what they were intended to. My interpretation of the report and the consultations and is that the IMF were in a sense attempting a mission impossible. They were leading discussions with representatives of countries the US owes trillions of dollars on the dollar being their problem and on what they should do about a dollar plunge. Consider if you or I were representing our countries at the consultations. We would probably have said all the polite things expected of us about the general good etc. But we would have concentrated on making plans in the best interests of our countries. I wouldn't tell you or anyone else the plan I devised to limit my country's losses and wouldn't expect you to tell me your plan. We would also have felt let down when, after buying dollar fixed income securities thinking they were the world's premier risk free asset, we learned that we had backed a sure loser. And we would have expected the IMF to explain why the dollar *has to* sink further at the same time as US Treasury Secretary Paulson repeats his mantra that a strong dollar is in America's interests and does nothing to ensure the dollar stops falling.

But the IMF staff certainly did a thorough job with their consultations. I think they convinced everyone that dollar fixed income securities were not worth owning at prevailing low interest rates, or maybe at all.

Scenarios Outlined by the IMF

As background for the consultations the IMF staff presented three scenarios for an unwinding of global imbalances:

(i)   a purely market-led adjustment scenario, with no additional policy action in any of the major economies;

(ii) a disruptive adjustment scenario, characterised by a worldwide decline in demand for US assets and rising protectionist pressure; and

(iii) a strengthened policies scenario, assuming – along the lines of the IMF Strategy – fiscal consolidation in the United States; greater exchange rate flexibility in emerging Asia; growth-enhancing structural reforms in the Euro Area and Japan; and additional spending by oil exporters. According to the Staff Report the scenarios highlighted that the imbalances will eventually correct and implementation of the IMF strategy 'would help ensure that this adjustment takes place in an orderly fashion, consistent with maintaining robust global growth' with rebalancing of demand accompanied by changes in exchange rates.

Scenario 1: A market-led adjustment?
This scenario assumed that:

> imbalances adjust through gradual changes in private sector saving behaviour and portfolio preferences, with no additional policy action in any of the major economies. As the various shocks that drive the current constellation of imbalances unwind, the world economy gradually adjusts . . . generating a steady improvement in the US current account deficit to about 4 percent of GDP by 2015, with U.S. net foreign liabilities rising substantially over time.

However there were conditions attaching to this scenario from which it appears that it was not a market-led scenario at all. The viability of the scenario depended on two assumptions. The first was that foreigners will accommodate a further 'very substantial build up' in US foreign liabilities, ultimately to about 85% of GDP 'without demanding a large risk premium notwithstanding continued foreign exchange losses'. On its own this assumption makes this scenario a creditor financed scenario and not a market-led adjustment. The second assumption was that protectionist pressures will be held in check. Surely, however, such an assumption can't be made as politicians in democracies wouldn't and couldn't make such a commitment without the engagement of lawmakers.

Scenario 2: A disruptive adjustment

> This scenario relates to a dollar plunge. It assumes a rise in protectionist pressures, 'accompanied by a worldwide decline in demand for U.S. assets including an abandonment of pegs in emerging Asia . . . an abrupt contraction in economic activity in the United States, accompanied by a large real depreciation of the U.S. dollar and a sharp correction in the U.S. trade balance.'

This scenario plays out as a sharp slowdown in economic growth with Emerging Asia experiencing the sharpest real exchange rate appreciation. Implications for global growth and stability are negative but the US current account goes into balance by 2010.

Scenario 3: A strengthened policies scenario

The strengthened policies scenario outlines the advantages of the IMF joint strategy proposals:

- *Greater exchange rate flexibility in emerging Asia.* It is assumed that exchange rates in emerging Asia become more flexible, accompanied by a rise in domestic consumption, and, over the longer term, a boost to productivity growth, driven for countries such as China by financial sector reforms. The resulting real exchange rate appreciation occurs through nominal exchange rate flexibility, rather than inflation, and is more rapid than in the baseline. Correspondingly, the current account surplus is reduced more sharply.
- *Fiscal consolidation in the United States.* We assume a substantial reduction in the U.S. budget deficit over the medium term (some of which is already under way) that becomes fully credible to investors after a period of 2 years. The adjustment, consisting of a combination of tax increases and expenditure cuts, leads to a broadly balanced budget excluding social security by 2012-18 and results in a more than 30 percent reduction in the government debt-to-GDP ratio over the longer term. . . .

U.S. net foreign liabilities fall by about 9 percent of GDP relative to baseline after 5 years and considerably more than that thereafter . . . Current account surpluses in the rest of the world are correspondingly reduced, and medium-term growth benefits everywhere from lower world interest rates.

- *Structural reforms in the euro area and Japan.* It is assumed that the degree of competition in product and labour markets in Europe and Japan gradually increases, eliminating about two thirds of the gap with the level prevailing in the United States over a 10-year period. These policies are assumed to become increasingly credible over time, inducing households and firms in this region to invest relatively more in their home economies . . .

The IMF Staff Report is presented with numerous tables and charts reflecting a range of outcomes based on different assumptions. However information in the report is too conditional to draw any firm conclusions. The authors of the report acknowledge that their strategy depends on 'smooth and gradual adjustments in portfolio preferences that cannot be taken for granted e.g. in the face of a sharp adjustment in risk appetite' and if 'risks are exacerbated in the current environment by the strength of protectionist sentiments which could intensify if imbalances remain high or if global growth were to slow'.

Outcome of the IMF Consultations

There is no tangible evidence that the IMF consultations on global financial imbalances have been successful. It could even be cogently argued that the disruptive adjustment scenario is playing out now in currency markets. There was also a setback for the multilateral consultations when the IMF Managing Director Rodrigo de Rato resigned on 30 July 2007. He developed the strategy of consulting on financial imbalances and identified himself with the outcome. Dominique Strauss-Kahn, his successor, only took office on 31 October 2007 and any new leader of a major organisation, coming from outside the organisation, needs time to cement his relationships with key participants. Further it was unlikely that any substantive agreements involving long term US policy could be cemented until a new administration takes office in 2009.

The commitments made by participants in the IMF consultations on financial imbalances can be accessed on http://www.imf.org/external/np/pp/2007/eng/062907.pdf. IMF progress reports and other developments will be monitored on www.thegoldwatcher.com.

We can gain a better understanding of the positions of China and the US from commentary outside the consultations. China's position is explained in the following article and America's position is outlined in a speech by Treasury Secretary Paulson presented at the 2007 China–US Relations Conference. The article and the text of the speech follow.

China's Approach to Growth, Reform and Stability

Hu Xiaolian, a Deputy Governor of the People's Bank of China and the Administrator of the State Administration of Foreign Exchange contributed an article on China's rapid economic development to the September 2007 issue of *Finance and Development*, an IMF quarterly publication.[11] He described China's policy as being 'based on long term goals that aim for stability' and discussed industrialisation drawing hundreds of millions of peasants to the cities seeking employment and China at the same time integrating rapidly with the rest of the world. Hundreds of thousands of enterprises, many established in association with foreigners, now manufacture a range of items for export across the globe.

With the rapid industrialisation achieved China's 1.3 billion population achieved an average annual GDP growth rate of 9% over the past three decades and China has become an important engine of world economic growth. Global economic growth in 2006 was 3.9% in 2006 and China contributed 0.5 percentage points to the growth. In China living standards improved and as many as 400 million Chinese have shaken off the shackles of poverty. Hu Xiaolian explained:

> Because of China's industrialization, urbanization, and globalization the rest of the world is naturally paying considerable attention to how China grapples with the challenges of ensuring sustained and steady development and of dealing with issues such as unemployment, an expanding income gap, the imbalance between investment and consumption, environmental protection, and social security.

A development policy was drawn up by the Chinese adapting lessons from elsewhere to their own circumstances and the country constantly monitors the progress of development.

Sustainable Development as China's Priority

China's GDP grew at an annual rate of 9.8% during the period 2001 to 2006. 56 million new jobs were created in urban areas. On average, urban residents' income grew at 10%, fiscal revenues increased at 18%, and net per capita income of rural residents increased at 6%. The government increased spending on agriculture, education, health care, and social security.

Through its pursuit of currency stability, its monetary policy objective, China's central bank has supported the economic development goal. Over the past year, when faced with an overly rapid expansion of investment and credit, the central bank took measures to tighten credit conditions. Since 2006 it has raised the reserve requirement ratio on nine occasions, the benchmark lending rate on five occasions, and the benchmark deposit rate on four occasions. Overexpansion of credit growth and any effects of withdrawal of liquidity have been moderated by frequent fine-tuning of monetary policy.

China's Current Account Surplus

Addressing the reasons for the increase in China's current account surplus Hu Xiaolian pointed to several factors. One factor, ignored by the West, is that 'the domestic national saving rate is high because of China's inadequate social security network, as well as insufficient medical care, education, and housing systems'. Other factors that have contributed to growth are the rapid increase in fixed capital investment over the past few years and the consequent expansion of manufacturing capacities that have contributed to the incentive for enterprises to increase their exports while domestic demand remained sluggish and:

> as a result of China's opening to the rest of the world, foreign direct investment has been pouring into the country for many years, turning China, in many respects, into an important processing export base for multinational corporations. In 2006, the volume of exports and imports by foreign-funded enterprises accounted for 58.9 percent of China's total foreign trade and 51.4 percent of the trade surplus. In addition, the economic structure of leading advanced countries, characterized by a chronic low saving rate, high growth, high consumption, and high indebtedness, has also driven demand for Chinese exports. These factors are mainly long term and structural; they need to be addressed gradually by deepening reforms and implementing structural adjustment.

Hu also detailed steps taken by the China central bank to moderate future reserve growth:

> First, *the positive role of financial activities in promoting consumption has been further enhanced* through efforts to develop consumer credit, improve access to financing, and provide more financial products. Consumer credit recorded an average annual growth of 28 percent during 2001–06.
>
> Second, *the reform of the renmimbi (RMB) exchange rate regime has moved ahead in a proactive, controllable, and gradual way to increase the role of the market in establishing the RMB exchange rate*. On July 21, 2005, China moved to a managed floating exchange rate regime based on market supply and demand with reference to a

basket of currencies. Over the past two years, the RMB had appreciated by 9.4 percent against the U.S. dollar, and the real effective exchange rate of the RMB had appreciated by 6.3 percent, according to the Bank for International Settlements.

A number of reforms have been initiated to give the market a bigger role in determining the RMB exchange rate. These measures include introducing a market-maker system and over-the-counter transactions in the interbank foreign exchange market; increasing the variety of foreign exchange products by introducing forward and swap transactions; and widening the daily floating band of the RMB against the U.S. dollar in the interbank spot foreign exchange market from 0.3 percent to 0.5 percent.

Third, *reform of the foreign exchange management system has been accelerated with a view to gradually promoting RMB convertibility under the capital account.* Steps have been taken to facilitate the holding and use of foreign exchange by enterprises and individuals. A system of qualified institutional investors has been established, and efforts have been made to liberalize domestic financial and capital markets in an orderly way. Various means have been explored to facilitate capital outflows, and enterprises have been encouraged to invest abroad. The monitoring of cross-border capital flows has been strengthened to pave the way for further opening up.

Approach Emphasizes Stability

With an emphasis on stability, China has adopted an orderly and gradual approach to implementing economic policy. Improving the infrastructure of the market-based system entails strengthening the banking system, improving the legal and regulatory framework, accounting standards, professional expertise, and institutional capacity.

Plans have also been advanced for a market-based interest rate structure including liberalisation of interest rates in the money and bond markets followed by gradual liberalisation of interest rates on loans and deposits. Gradual reforms have 'helped safeguard the stability of the financial system and helped create a favorable environment for advancing and deepening financial sector reform'.

US Treasury Secretary Paulson's Approach to Cooperation with China

US Treasury Secretary Paulson has a long and informed relationship with China and leads the dialogue between the two countries. The following is from the text of his statement at the 2007 China–US Relations Conference:[12]

China's re-emergence on the global stage is one of the most consequential geopolitical events of recent times. China's global influence is expanding. . . . There is hardly an issue – from trade, to national security, to climate change – or a place – from North Korea to Iran to Sudan – where American and Chinese interests do not increasingly overlap. Because China is now integrated into the global economy, what happens in China's economy affects the entire international community. The U.S.–China relationship has become central not only to each nation's interests, but also to the maintenance of a stable, secure and prosperous global system – which benefits the world.

My focus at Treasury is on the U.S.–China economic relationship, which is a core element of our overall bilateral ties. Yet, the tectonic plates of the U.S.–China economic relationship are shifting. This demands new visions from our leaders and new mechanisms from our governments.

First, U.S.–China economic interdependence is deepening. We need each other more and on a broader number of economic and economically consequential issues. Over the past five years, U.S. exports to China have grown at five times the pace of U.S. exports to the rest of the world, and China has become our fourth largest export market.

Exports to China benefit American businesses by providing new market opportunities for American products and services. Imports from China continue to benefit the American economy and the American consumer by providing an increased diversity of products at lower prices. Imports from China also raise challenges, as I will discuss in a moment. Just as competition from trade with China pushes our industries to stay on the cutting edge, competition will also speed China's development as a more market-oriented and balanced economy.

Moreover, the United States and China are shaping, and being shaped by, global energy and environmental trends, which have strong economic consequences. Our countries are the world's largest energy consumers and the largest emitters of greenhouse gases. What happens with China's environment impacts all nations; air and water know no boundaries.

These trends create challenges that can not be resolved by the United States or China alone. They certainly can not be solved without China at the table.

Second, whereas trade and investment were once largely a source of stability in bilateral relations, they are now increasingly also a source of tension. Such tensions are straining our domestic consensus on the benefits of economic engagement.

America's large corporations – the longtime proponents of bilateral engagement – as well as America's smaller businesses – who are finding new markets in China – increasingly are concerned about the openness of China's economy, and Chinese counterfeiting of trademarks and pirating of intellectual property. Some American workers believe the field of competition is uneven and unfair. Also, American consumers have very real concerns about the safety of food and product imports from China.

These anxieties manifest themselves in several ways, which leads me to the third dynamic confronting us: the rise of economic nationalism and protectionism in both our nations. These sentiments may constrain leaders from adopting policies that are in the long-term interests of the citizens and economies of the United States and China. Such views also obscure each nation's ability to assess the other's long-term intentions.

In responding to globalization, policymakers in both countries must resist the impulse to discard the hard-fought and long-term gains of open economies by pursuing short-term and misguided policy responses. I am committed to working to maintain an open trade and investment climate in America and to working to open markets in China to greater competition from American goods and services.

These three emerging dynamics to our economic relationship – deepening interdependence, a strained policy consensus, and the rise of economic protectionism – are mutual and require cooperative solutions.

These dynamics informed the creation of the Strategic Economic Dialogue (SED) by President Bush and President Hu Jintao in 2006. They envisioned a forum to allow both governments to communicate at the highest levels and with one voice on issues of long-term and strategic importance to ensure bilateral economic stability and prosperity.

By definition, this is a complex relationship and managing complexity is daunting. It begins with speaking to the right people – at the right time – on the right issues – and in the right way.

The Strategic Economic Dialogue – as a new and leading institution in U.S.–China relations – has created these useful channels among policymakers in Washington and Beijing. Through this framework we have advanced the U.S.–China economic relationship by establishing new habits of bilateral cooperation and re-setting the foundation for stable and prosperous economic interactions.

We have embraced a broad agenda that covers cross-cutting economic and economically consequential issues, including regulatory transparency, energy conservation, environmental protection, food and product safety, as well as the important economic issues of exchange rate policy, market access, financial sector liberalization, and macroeconomic policy.

Our approach engages multiple and diverse government officials in both countries to facilitate more inclusive interactions. It breaks down classic bureaucratic stove-pipes that hinder effective communication and impede results. At the same time, we have continual, high-level interactions to set priorities and ensure their full implementation. I talk regularly on the phone with my counterpart Vice Premier Wu Yi, and our staffs are in constant contact.

That said – process is not result. . . .

The pace of China's growth has clearly been remarkable, but it carries both opportunity and risk.

I liken it to some of America's fastest growing entrepreneurial companies, who see sales rise exponentially in a short time and then must earnestly work to build the infrastructure to sustain those sales. This is the challenge that China's leaders now face – to make the jump in strategy and policy needed for an economy that is no longer in the first stages of growth.

A major risk China faces is that its government won't act quickly enough to take the policy steps necessary to deal with the economic and social imbalances created by its growth model. Without strong policy underpinnings and implementation, China's economic performance becomes unsustainable. We are encouraging key reforms that will help China manage the blistering pace of its economic growth; these include financial market liberalization and a plan for rebalancing growth. China has proven to the world that it can grow fast, but can it grow differently and, ultimately, grow smarter?

Bold structural policies are needed to shift China's growth away from heavy industry, high energy use, and dependence on exports – towards greater reliance on domestic demand, greater production of services, and greater provision of material well-being to China's population.

As I have said before, this will be much easier, and the prospects for achieving sustained, balanced growth in China and in the world economy much greater, if the Chinese increase the pace of RMB appreciation in the short term and implement a fully market-determined currency in the medium term. Currency appreciation to date has not slowed the Chinese economy.

Accelerating the rate of appreciation and introduction of flexibility will help China deal with the imbalances that have grown in the economy and make monetary policy much more effective in responding to inflation.

We must also recognize that currency is not the only driver of China's economic imbalances. Even more fundamental and important are internal structural issues, such as why Chinese households save so much and consume so little. Rebalancing China's growth is necessary for China to grow without generating large external imbalances.

A key to China's success here will be its willingness to accelerate the pace of its market-based economic reforms. Going beyond its WTO commitments, resisting protectionist sentiment, and opening up its economy to greater international competition for goods and services will help rebalance the Chinese economy and spread prosperity more broadly among the Chinese people.

These reforms are – and will continue to be – resisted by increasingly influential Chinese businesses. In my judgment, the greatest risk to China's long-term economic security is that protectionists prevail, and Chinese reforms proceed too slowly.

And finally, we are also encouraging China to act responsibly as a global economic power. China is influencing capital and resource markets all over the world; its economic influence is being felt from Chicago, to Sao Paolo, to Kinshasa.

We welcome China into key international financial institutions and are giving China a greater voice in them as well. Increased participation will allow

China to advance its interests in those institutions, but it is also important that Beijing recognize the responsibilities of greater participation.

China has become a major source of foreign aid for many of the poorest countries. We look forward to working with China to assure that foreign aid and lending practices promote sustainable development.

This new era in U.S.–China economic relations requires new and dynamic ways of doing business. We are meeting these challenges through the creation of the political space and the institutional capacity for long-term stability in our bilateral economic relations.

While dialogue and negotiations are important, they are far from sufficient to ensure that we keep the bilateral relationship future-oriented and on an even keel. The SED is both long-term and strategic, but tangible progress in the form of signposts and benchmarks is critically important to demonstrating that we are making progress in achieving our long-term objectives.

I believe that we are making progress and we are able to point to steps that are enhancing and transforming our economic relationship in mutually beneficial ways. Three brief examples illustrate my point: civil aviation, energy and the environment, and financial services.

In May, we announced a new air services agreement that will make it easier, cheaper, and more convenient to fly people and to ship goods across the Pacific. Not only will this agreement stimulate an estimated $5 billion in new business over the next several years, the new routes will double passenger traffic by 2012 and allow full air cargo services by 2011. Perhaps as early as April 2008, there will be the first non-stop flight between Atlanta and Shanghai, the first from America's southeast for a U.S. airline.

The benefits of the civil aviation accord are many, including more commerce, greater cultural exchanges, and enhanced understanding.

We have also collaborated with China on a series of policies to help promote energy conservation and environmental protection. Those specific agreements foster demand for the development and deployment of clean and efficient, next-generation energy technology. This, in turn, will create a future in which two of the largest economies in the world become examples of bilateral cooperation towards sustainable development.

The SED has made consistent strides to further develop China's capital markets. As a result of our deliberations, the New York Stock Exchange and NASDAQ will open offices in China. China has also removed a barrier to the entry of new foreign securities firms, and will expand the scope of business open to foreign-invested securities firms.

These actions do not only expand the opportunities for international financial services firms. By allowing greater financial flows, they will help China move more quickly to a fully market-determined exchange rate. Competitive and efficient capital markets are also key to balanced, sustainable and higher quality economic growth – a critical Chinese goal over the next two decades.

In addition to the areas of positive cooperation, our enhanced dialogue means we must confront problems frankly and honestly – and often rapidly. Recent and repeated reports of tainted food and product imports are causing fear and uncertainty in American consumers and harming the 'Made in China' brand here in the United States.

The effectiveness with which China manages these safety issues will have long-term implications for U.S.–China trade relations, the integration of China into the global trading system, and the sustainability of China's economic growth trajectory. We are actively working together to enhance the safety of products coming from China and to protect the American consumer. We also need to make sure that policymakers in both countries are focused on science-based safety decisions, not protectionism or retaliation. . . .

The economic and geopolitical landscape of the 21st century will be greatly influenced by the way in which the United States and China work together. That emerging future requires a distinct vision and effective mechanisms to achieve it. The SED has allowed both the United States and China to begin to write the next chapter of our strategic economic relationship.

Can the IMF Avoid Global Financial Meltdown?

Given the shared economic and geopolitical interests between the US and China is there a danger of global financial meltdown because of China's exposure to the weak US dollar? Arguably neither party can afford a breakdown of their association. But China can't acquiesce in an arrangement where the estimated $500 billion plus it owns of dollars and dollar-based securities are going to be paid in a devalued currency with reduced purchasing power. As China has no developed social security and pensions network the 'savings glut' Bernanke speaks glibly about includes money saved by Chinese people for their retirement. While there is a good chance that no precipitous actions will be taken by any of America's creditors until after the 2008 US Presidential elections we should keep in mind Paul Volcker's warning that the US economy has been skating on thin ice and, 'at some point of time, central banks and private institutions will have had their fill of dollars'.

My reading of the IMF consultations is that what they definitely achieved was to convince China and America's other creditors that the worst thing they can do with their money will be to leave it invested in low interest rate US Treasury securities – knowing that the dollar will continue falling. This realisation has, in my opinion, encouraged the rapid growth of the Sovereign Wealth Funds structured to invest national monetary reserves in the most rewarding situations. Sovereign Wealth Funds already control over $2 trillion and are expected to control over $10 trillion within five years. With such financial firepower they are set to become game changers in global financial markets. In the following chapter I argue that they will invest in gold, if indeed they have not already invested, and are a swing factor affecting demand for gold that could drive the gold price to considerably higher levels than markets currently expect.

Can the IMF avoid global financial meltdown? Possibly – but not via their consultations. However the IMF have now started a dialogue on Sovereign Wealth Funds and, if they can agree a working relationship between these funds and members of the IMF they will have succeeded in establishing a framework for this new investing paradigm to work for the benefit of all parties instead of being a disruptive force.

On 16 November 2007 the IMF convened the first annual roundtable of Sovereign Asset and Reserve Managers from 28 countries. Global reserve holdings are currently around US$6 trillion compared to less than US$2 trillion a decade ago and participants discussed options that countries are considering. The IMF Managing Director Dominique Strauss-Kahn, who addressed the opening session of the conference, noted that 'a process is underway to define a role for the Fund (the IMF) on the issue of how Sovereign Wealth Funds (SWFs) can be managed in ways that are consistent with global financial stability'. He also stressed that some form of agreement on best practices for the operations of SWFs would help maintain an open global financial system, and discourage recipient countries from imposing unilateral restrictions on capital flows.

The policy proposals outlined by participants in the IMF consultations on financial imbalances were intended to take the sting out of global financial imbalances. The proposals are included in the Fact Book reference to this chapter for information and monitoring in future.

9

Gold Prices: Inflation, Deflation, Booms and Busts

Do trees grow to Heaven?

'Most, probably, of our decisions to do something positive, the full consequences of which will be drawn out over many days to come, can only be taken as the result of *animal spirits* – a spontaneous urge to action rather than inaction, and not the outcome of a weighted average of quantitative benefits multiplied by quantitative probabilities . . . *it is our innate urge to activity that makes the wheel go around.*'

John Maynard Keynes: *The General Theory of Employment, Interest & Money,* 1934

Introduction: A Crisis of Confidence

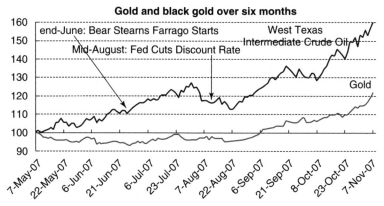

Chart 9.1 Gold and oil prices, May to November 2007.
Chart courtesy of Lombard Street Research

2007 was a wild year for currencies, commodities and investors. In only six months from May to November the dollar price of oil was up 60%, gold was up 20% and the trade weighted US$ fell by about 10%. Such extreme price movements were surely enough to inspire punters' 'animal spirits' to take a fresh interest in gold. The legendary get rich quick prospect. But, if we look at changes in the economic fundamentals over the year, can we identify effects likely to continue to influence the value of gold, the dollar and other currencies in future? I believe we can. Since I started monitoring it on a daily basis in September 2001 prospects for gold haven't looked better and prospects for the dollar and with it other fiat currencies haven't looked more ominous.

In Chapter 7, The End of Cheap Oil, 'Chindia' and Other Tipping Points to Instability, we canvassed a range of risks threatening the stable disequilibrium of the global economy. They include the US housing bubble deflating, the sub prime mortgage crisis imploding, the rapid unfurling of the global 'shadow banking' enterprise, rising oil prices, the falling value of the dollar, loss of economic leadership by the West to emerging markets, the festering insurgencies and unresolved invasions of Iraq and Afghanistan, instability in Pakistan, signs of a loss of appetite for fixed income dollar-based securities by America's creditors and the advent of Sovereign Wealth Funds.

In spite of the challenges to the strength and hegemony of the dollar prospects for global economic growth were exceptionally strong until mid-2007. A July 2007 *Fortune* Magazine article on 'The Greatest Boom Ever' illustrates the speed with which the economic pendulum can swing from optimism to anxiety. US Treasury Secretary Paulson was quoted in the article saying 'This is far and away the strongest global economy I've seen in my business lifetime.' However in the same article he also gave this warning on risk:

> We haven't had a global financial shock since 1998. I believe that these large and dramatic increases in private pools of capital [hedge funds and private equity] and in the credit derivatives markets since then have helped manage and disperse risk and make the economy more efficient. When we do have one (a global financial shock) – and it's when, not if; that's not me being negative, it's just that we're not going to defy economic gravity – we'll be seeing for the first time how some of these instruments perform under stress.

Credit markets froze when Paulson's instruments came under stress within weeks of the July 2007 *Fortune* article. It wasn't long before the Fed, the Bank of England and other central banks, as lenders of last resort, had to oblige with first tens and later billions of dollars to prevent systemic damage in their areas of responsibility. The 'increases in private pools of capital [hedge funds and private equity] and in the credit derivatives markets' that Paulson calls 'instruments' together make up the financial intermediaries other commentators call 'shadow banking'. They have been exposed as a debt enabled complex of leveraged securities and derivatives that mushroomed outside the control of central bankers and financial regulators.[1] Pimco's Paul McCulley defines shadow banking as 'the whole alphabet soup of non-bank levered intermediaries'. Pimco's Bill Gross refers to another of McCulley's shadow banking analogies 'where credit is composed on a keyboard as opposed to a printing press'. Bill Gross also refers to 'financialization of the U.S. economy beginning with the de linking of the dollar from gold and the deregulation of banking and interest rates'.[2]

Granted neither a conventional nor a shadow banking crisis, a house price boom and bust, a weak dollar or reckless marketing of securities with high default risks will inevitably change the way the world works. But loss of confidence will. And, through 2007, in many quarters confidence has been lost in the stability of the dollar, the integrity of the US financial system and even the cohesion of the global economy. In mid-2007 reported losses from the so called sub prime mortgage crisis amounting to a few billion dollars were enough to cause credit markets to freeze up. Within a few months associated losses incurred by Goldman Sachs, Citibank and Merrill Lynch, three of the world's most highly regarded financial empires, brought the tally to above $20 billion. In a recent report Goldman Sachs' Chief Economist Jan Hatzius indicated losses from sub prime exposure would be far greater than had been assumed and could be as high as $400 billion. The impact on the economy will be more severe if banks and other lenders are forced to reduce lending by as much as $2 trillion. Hatzius estimated this corresponds with 7% of total debt owed by the US non financial sector and 'the drag on economic activity could be substantial'. How does a $400 billion loss in the credit markets translate into $2 trillion of economic damage?

A *Business Week* article on Jan Hatzius's report explains:

> The answer is debt, or leverage. Banks, hedge funds, and private equity firms often borrow $10 or more for each $1 of equity they use in a transaction, according to estimates by the New York Federal Reserve. When the investments pan out, the use of debt boosts their return. When the investments go south, the use of debt exacerbates the loss and often leads lenders to be more conservative in the future.

A knock on effect of the credit crisis and steep falls in the value of the dollar is that China, and other trading partners funding the US trade deficit have good

reason to be anxious about their dollar holdings. Recycling dollar claims into US
Treasury securities can make sense in the context of a long term trading relationship where creditors access large markets and accept a secure debt obligation in
return for granting credit. But the 'America spends and Asia lends' formula can't
make sense for exporters while the dollar sinks in value and while the US banking
establishment faces a 'tsunami of red ink'.[3] And, as support for the dollar wanes,
can the disequilibrium between the US and its creditors remain stable or are we
bound to face a Wile E. Coyote moment and a dollar plunge?

Information Resources Including the LBMA
Annual Gold Price Forecasts

In the following chapters (11–13) Frank Holmes deals with the historical relationships between gold, oil prices and dollar weakness, mean reversion and the other
key factors he takes into account when deciding whether gold prices are reasonable or not. The reader will also have access to the most recent London Bullion
Market Association's annual analysts' survey of gold and other precious metals
price forecasts for the current year supported by reasons for each analyst's conclusions. While analysts have different views, together their price forecasts define a
track of reasonable expectations.[4]

Selected analysts' comments from 2007 follow:

Ross Norman
TheBullionDesk.com, London
_ Gold
Range: $840–$1,250
Average: $976

> Following the stonking 30% rise in 2007, we remain manifestly bullish for gold
> prices and forecast that the market is set for another bumper year in 2008. Many
> of the factors that have taken us to record highs are likely to remain in play, but
> more so: specifically, accelerating investment demand of gold ETFs, safe-haven
> buying on ongoing concerns about the stability of the economy – but perhaps
> most importantly, rising inflation.

> Geopolitical tension may ease with the departure of Bush from the White House,
> and indeed the dollar may have seen the largest part of its decline, which could
> mitigate things. However, with mine supply remaining static, central bank sales
> comparatively limited, and the demand side fundamentals looking positive, we

believe further significant gains are afoot with jewellery demand providing a welcome drag on runaway prices.

Davis, David
Credit Suisse Standard Securities
Johannesburg
_ Gold
Range: $760–$1,110
Average: $950

Upward pressure on the gold price is likely being driven by the US economic environment, rising oil and commodity prices and a change in the dynamics surrounding supply and demand. These combined factors have resulted in a weakening of the US dollar, which in turn has driven gold higher. The economic environment in the US was recently jolted by subprime mortgage losses, the tightening of the credit market and the lowering of interest rates. Higher oil prices will likely result in inflationary pressures, which in turn will put upward pressure on gold.

Turning to supply-and-demand fundamentals, over the longer term, our studies indicate that global gold production (primary supply) will begin to decline as the diminishing number of new reserves fails to compensate for dying mines. The decline in production will likely be accelerated should the gold mining industry continue to incur significant year-on-year inflation rates which are not offset by similar or significantly higher gold price increases.

We believe central bank sales will likely wither going forward, and the banks could become net buyers. Producer de-hedging has accelerated in recent years. In particular, we expect that AngloGold Ashanti could enter the de-hedging market, contributing an additional 3 to 3.5 Moz during 2008. We also believe investment demand (ETFs) will continue to berobust during 2008. Volatile and higher gold prices coupled with the expected economic slowdown in the US and Europe could, however, stem jewellery demand in these areas, but demand from China and India will likely remain positive.

Geopolitical tensions, which generally lead to higher gold prices and price volatility, have heightened with the political turmoil in Pakistan after the assassination of Benazir Bhutto and the crossborder operations of Turkish troops to hunt down Kurdish separatists in Iraq. Tensions are also ever-present between the US and Iran and the US and North Korea. Given this longer-term scenario, we believe the supply-demand imbalance going forward will begin to accelerate at an ever-increasing pace into a net deficit, which in turn will likely put significant upward pressure on the gold price.

Jeffrey Christian
CPM Group, New York
_ Gold
Range: $770–$1,060
Average: $850

> Political, economic, and financial market concerns will cause investors to
> continue buying historically high volumes of physical gold. In December 2006
> we said 2007 would be a year of great volatility across markets. It was. We
> expect 2008 to see even greater volatility, in currency markets, equity markets,
> and precious metals prices. Mine production will rise, as will scrap recovery.
> Central banks will continue to sell gold, but the key factor directing gold prices
> will be investment demand, as it always is.

Accessible Information

Every week Frank Holmes's US funds group publish an investor alert reviewing,
analysing and interpreting current economic and market developments, risks and
opportunities.[5] Every day the *Financial Times*'s authoritative commentators analyse
current developments and the consequences of events being played out on the
world economic stage, as do commentators writing for the *Wall Street Journal* and
other newspapers with finance pages. The Webliography at the end of this book
includes a carefully selected list of links to accessible information on the range of
subjects affecting gold.

A few decades ago many of us regarded macroeconomics as a subject strictly
for professionals. But that's no longer the case. Information is generally accessible
to us now to support investing decisions.

Investors interested in gold mining companies will find they lack the knowledge and information resources that specialist funds command. But they will find
they can easily access research that monitors the performance of gold fund
managers.

Though we all now have access to useful current information that affects our
interests we also have experience of being swamped with information we don't
need or can't use. My approach to keeping well informed is to focus a wide angle
lens on the gold mining industry, supply and demand for gold, factors affecting
the dollar and other fiat currencies, global macroeconomic and geopolitical issues.
The focus covers the spectrum of information I might need and I have routines
for filtering out information I don't use.

Let's very briefly review some of the ground covered in the previous chapters.
Our starting point was gold's stateless money franchise. To gain a better understanding of why gold is valuable as stateless money we have looked at the gold

mining industry, rising production costs miners are experiencing, supply and demand for gold as a quasi currency (stateless money) and as a commodity used mainly in the jewellery manufacturing industry, the rise and fall of the gold standard, the dollar standard and the deficit without tears that has endured even though the US is now the world's biggest debtor and borrower. We have examined the former Chairman of the Dallas Federal Reserve Bank Robert McTeer's candid description of the dollar standard as being rather like a poker game where you never have to cash in your chips and Professor McKinnon's theory about dollar securities being the world's premier risk free security and not at all like a poker game. We have analysed the post 9/11 global monetary reflation, the economic consequences of George W. Bush and 9/11 including the costs of the war on terrorism, the Iraq and Afghanistan wars, the US housing bubble, and the sub prime mortgage credit crunch. We have addressed the financial imbalances between the US and the rest of the world, found the global economy in a state of stable disequilibrium and reviewed tipping points to instability including rising energy and food prices and the overwhelming importance of the Chindia growth dynamic. We have reviewed global economic rebalancing and IMF initiatives directed at advancing global cooperation to achieve orderly reduction of imbalances. We have exposed the shadow banking mushrooms that grew like fungi in the woods screened from public view by bankers using off balance sheet manipulations and have commented on the emergence and potential of Sovereign Wealth Funds owned by countries with surging current account surpluses seeking optimal returns for their foreign reserves.

Drawing the Threads Together

You may not agree with the way I draw the threads together but this is how I approach prospects for gold and the dollar. Firstly I distinguish between a pre 9/11 world and a post 9/11 world. America was being harassed by Osama bin Laden and other extremists in the pre 9/11 world but was not at war. In the post 9/11 world America is engaged in wars more unsuccessful and more costly in current dollar terms than Vietnam financed with borrowings from trading partners. Wars are inflationary, war debts are often repaid with an inflated currency and currencies of countries at war tend to be weak.

I believe that post 9/11 President Bush, Fed Chairman Alan Greenspan and the world's central bankers and policy makers did the right thing when they orchestrated global monetary reflation. But they went too far. The liquidity and easy credit spigots were left too wide open for too long. A flood of cheap money unleashed asset price inflation and resulted in bubbles with serious consequences for economic stability.

Looking ahead I expect policy makers will find themselves obliged to walk a tightrope between consumer price inflation and asset price deflation. They are likely to recognise deflation as the greater of the two evils and inflation as the lesser. If that's the case, unless a frightful event like another war or a major bank failure changes the course of history, central bankers and politicians are likely to encourage another reflationary rescue and follow a 'muddle through'[6] policy agenda until a new President takes office in the White House in January 2009 and his or her administration get to grips with challenges. That's unlikely to be before mid-2009. But there are two situations that may not wait patiently for resolution until then. The first is America's creditors seeking better returns for their funds than low interest fixed income US$ Treasury securities. The second is the menacing negative equity *crisis* developing for homeowners in the US who overpaid for properties they couldn't afford to buy. They will be unable to service their mortgage obligations and unable to sell their homes at prices to clear their mortgage debt. It will be a *crisis* because negative equity on a large scale will have economic, social and political consequences that restrict the choices open to US policy makers. If housing bubbles deflate in other countries, including the United Kingdom, similar challenges will be faced.

Prospects for Gold

The World Gold's Council's report on sales for the third quarter of 2007 reflected significantly increased demand for gold as an investment. The report was introduced with this comment:

> A surge in investor interest on top of robust jewellery demand made Q3 2007 a further quarter of strong demand for gold. Total identifiable demand reached a new record in dollar terms at $20.7bn, up 30% on a year earlier; in tonnage terms the rise was 19%. Jewellery demand rose by 6% in tonnage terms over Q3 2006 and by 16% in dollar terms. However, identifiable investment demand was nearly double year-earlier levels in tonnage terms due to a record inflow into Exchange Traded Funds and similar products. The rise in dollar terms was 115%.[7]

Demand for gold has been growing steadily over the years but mined gold reached a peak of 2600 tonnes in 2001 and has since declined to under 2500 tonnes. For 2008 only 2400 tonnes are expected. In Chapter 3 on gold supply and demand we identified jewellery as stable grass roots demand and identified two swing factors that affect price. Central bank sales and investor interest. We know central banks are now committed to a quota sales agreement – and in any event would be unwise to sell gold in current turbulent economic conditions and know investor interest has been at an all time high.

Sovereign Wealth Funds could become a third swing factor affecting demand for gold – and the most potent factor. We still know little about these funds except that they will command trillions of dollars and be a boon to the asset management industry. A Bloomberg report quotes Morgan Stanley economist Stephen Jen's estimates that foreign currency assets held by nation states – minus central banks' official reserves – will swell from about $2.5 trillion now to $12 trillion by 2015. Merrill Lynch forecast they will be funded with $7.9 trillion by 2011, compared with $1.9 trillion at present. Standard Chartered Plc forecast the funds will have $13.4 trillion in assets within a decade, a six fold increase from the current level of $2.2 trillion. A gigantic sum of money will be channelled into global assets through Sovereign Wealth Funds.[8] A page on The Goldwatcher blog will be devoted to recording and commenting on developments with Sovereign Wealth Funds.

Many knowledgeable commentators have expected that as a way of reducing their over exposure to dollars Asian central banks would increase their holdings of gold. But that hasn't happened and probably hasn't been practical as central banks usually disclose any changes in their gold reserves to the IMF. Consider this situation. If, for example, China were to announce they had increased its gold reserves by even a few billion dollars the announcement would drive the gold price up dramatically. The situation would be like the OPEC meeting quoted in the chapter on Tipping Points when the Saudi Energy Minister was overheard saying that if the press ever heard OPEC were concerned about a dollar fall they would experience the fall *instantly*. But, unlike central banks, Sovereign Wealth Funds don't have to tell anyone what they are doing with their funds. They may already be buying gold ETFs. And, whether or not that's the case, we know they are as free to buy gold via ETFs as anonymously as you or me. That is why I suggest there are now three swing factors affecting the price of gold. Investors, central banks and Sovereign Wealth Funds. Over the four years that they have existed gold ETFs have built up a holding of 700 tonnes of gold worth $19 billion. Sovereign Wealth Funds have already been capitalised with about $2.5 trillion. If they were to hold $25 billion, 1% of their current assets in gold, the supply demand equation for gold would change radically.

There may also be a fourth swing factor affecting demand. The retail investor. If the gold mining industry and the World Gold Council launch a marketing campaign aimed at the public for coins and small gold bars in the current economic climate they may be very successful.

The Reflationary Rescue

Investment bank analysis is now generally supportive of gold price prospects. Citigroup's global investment research team forecast that economic challenges will lead to another round of monetary reflation and have published reports on *Gold: Riding the Reflationary Rescue*. The reports home in on the multi currency euro, yen and dollar gold price rally as a crucial 'credibility test' passed by gold. The following points headline gold price prospects as outlined in the reports:

1 A mix of 'macro/monetary/and supply/demand drivers' support a favourable case for the gold price. Gold will be a 'prime beneficiary of the "Re-Flationary Rescue"' that they expect will generally be positive for hard assets and raw materials.
2 After gold traded above its 28-year high of $730 per ounce in October 2007 it entered a new investment-driven phase and reasserted its safe haven status; and
3 Supply and demand fundamentals remain strong. Jewellery industry with fabrication demand in dollar terms was up significantly year over year, led by India up 91%, China 32% and the Middle East 22%.

An 'Anti Risk Strategy'

Jeremy Grantham, the widely respected value investor and co-founder of the money managers 'GMO', has a committed view on economic outcomes over the next five years. After the global credit crisis erupted in mid-2007 he spelled out the opportunity for a major 'anti-risk bet'. A bet he calls 'the real McCoy'. His take on the disruptions in credit markets was that it was like 'watching a very slow motion train wreck' and his reasoning followed this line: 'The overstretched, overleveraged global financial bubble will now certainly deflate. Within five years at least one major bank (broadly defined) will fail, half the hedge funds and a substantial percentage of the private equity firms in existence now will simply cease to exist.' Grantham acknowledges 'anti risk' is 'a diffused and complicated opportunity'. The best way to play it, he advises, is 'to create a basket of a dozen or more different anti-risk bets, for to speak the truth none of us can know how this unprecedented risk bubble with its new levels of leverage and new instruments will precisely deflate'.[9]

I can't say whether Jeremy Grantham would agree that gold, if bought at a reasonable price, is an ideal anti-risk holding. But as far back as early 2006 Marc Faber published a commentary titled *Why the Fed has no other alternative but to print money*.[10] 'When debts are as large as they are now,' he wrote 'deflating prices and especially deflating asset prices would wreak havoc in the economic system.' As Marc Faber expects the Fed will print money excessively he regards gold and other precious metals as essential investor protection. To illustrate his argument he presents two charts. The first illustrates debt in the US at over 331% of GDP and the second illustrates low US 10-year interest rates only a few points above 4% – a rate of return inadequate to compensate the holder for the risks of inflation and currency depreciation.

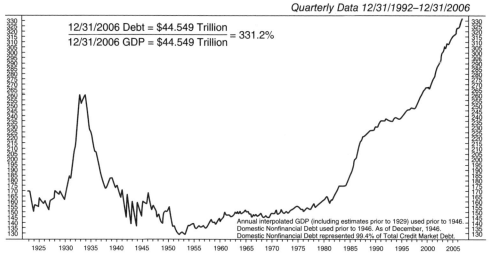

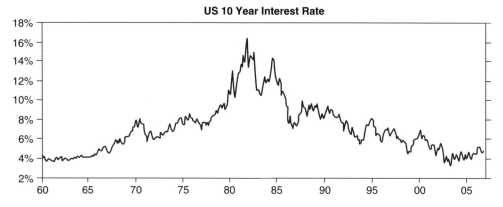

Chart 9.2 Total US credit market debt 1925 to 2006 as % of GDP and US ten year interest rate 1960 to 2006.
Chart courtesy of Marc Faber

Faber explains that it isn't enough to look at monetary growth alone to get a picture of inflationary pressures. Credit growth must also be factored in. At the time of his study commercial and industrial loans were growing at an annualised rate of over 18%, real estate loans were growing at a rate of over 16% and asset-backed security issuance was growing at 21%. In other words US credit was growing more than four times faster than GDP growth – 'not exactly the sign of a sound and well balanced economy'. He concluded the exceptional rise in home prices being experienced at the time was a product of the rapid expansion of credit.

Monetary and credit growth may have slowed down since 2006 but Marc Faber's observation on deflating asset prices 'wreaking havoc' in the US economic system and leading to massive defaults and bankruptcies certainly rings true now. Keep in mind also that loose monetary policies will lead to further dollar weakness and, with oil prices surging, fighting inflation won't go off the Fed's agenda. How will the Fed cope with walking a tightrope between inflation and deflation?

Ben Bernanke makes no secret of his opinions on the causes of the great depression and his commitment to fend off deflation at all costs. If he sees any danger of deflation, including asset price deflation and the house price bubble deflating, he is likely to provide liquidity as necessary even if it has the effect of driving down the value of the dollar. Marc Faber's conclusion on gold prices is that if the dollar is debased by excessive money printing it won't mean much if gold is worth $1000, $5000 or $10000 an ounce. The test will be the relative purchasing power of the dollar and of gold. In this context gold surely qualifies as anti-risk investment.

Messages from History

Will the performance of gold over the coming years correspond with previous responses to financial market developments and world events? At the time of writing the gold price was over $800; the dollar had fallen to an all time low against the euro; the oil price was above $95; the extent of the losses that will be experienced as a result of the sub prime mortgage and shadow banking crises were still unknown and signs were appearing that Asian investors were losing their appetite for dollars. Middle East instability remained menacing and President Musharraf had declared martial law in Pakistan, a nuclear state. Against the background of bad news the gold price had spiked to a twenty-eight year high of $840.

Pundits had been calling for the gold price to reach $850, the level it spiked to in 1980. That's equivalent to about $1900 in 2007 money.[11] However a price spike and a price average over a longer period are very different situations. A spike by definition is a short term phenomenon. Spikes often occur in currency and commodity markets when short sellers are active and, contrary to their expectations, prices go up instead of down. The short sellers then find themselves forced to cover their positions at market prices regardless what it costs. Prices often also spike when speculation is rife or when rumours spread of a serious mishap. The Citigroup analysis mentioned above recognised the possibility of the gold price spiking to $1000 and even more. But the year average gold price they forecast at the time for both 2008 and 2009 was $750.

Price Overshoots

Major price overshoots have also been experienced in currency and commodity markets when short term speculators seeking high returns, or investors over anxious for safety, drive a currency's value to unsustainable levels. Then, impressed by the price rises trend chasers start buying and push the overvaluation to a height and duration orthodox economists can't explain. At this stage it's not unusual for highly intelligent economists, puzzled with the extent and duration of the 'over-valuation', to advance theories about why *things are different this time* and why the overvaluation is sustainable after all. This encourages market bulls to believe the extraordinary returns of the past will continue into the future and they start to buy and chase the price even further above economic fundamentals. The final stage of the overshoot is when the supply of trend chasers and other buyers comes to an end and a market crash that resembles the collapse of a Ponzi scheme follows. In Jeremy Grantham's words 'The workings of competitive capitalism are, in the end, an irresistible force and that is why everything always trends to normal and every very different bubble has always burst.'

What's Different this Time?

In 1980 when the gold price spiked to an $850 peak reported inflation was in the double digits. Now, on reported figures it's still between 2% and 3%. Market enthusiasm for gold in 1980 was inspired by rumours that Ronald Reagan was going to bring back the gold standard and gold would go to $1000. While no such rumours drive the gold price now gold supply and demand factors are more positive than they were in 1980. Another factor in favour of gold now is that in 1980 sentiment was negative to South Africa and Russia, the world's two main suppliers of gold at the time. South Africa because of Apartheid and Russia because of the Cold War and a rise in the gold price would have benefited both countries as the main suppliers at the time of the world's gold. There is no longer antipathy to either country and there are now also many other supplying countries.

But surely the two most potent demand drivers now are Exchange Traded Funds and surging economic growth in China, India, other developing economies and the gushing wealth in Middle East and other oil exporting countries.

Gold Price Suppression

Serious and combatant gold activists associated with GATA, The Gold Anti Trust Association, have over many years challenged the transparency of central bank gold derivatives transactions and accused central banks, including the Fed, of suppressing the gold price.[12] Any evidence of impropriety on these lines could lead to a surge in prices with central banks having to cover short positions in hostile markets. I have only two comments to make on the subject. The first is that I am sceptical of conspiracy theories because of the number of people who would have to be involved at different levels of government and private enterprise in the conspiracy. The second is that the conspiracy argument is not compelling. The basis of their case is that more gold has been sold into the market that has been mined or accounted for in reductions of known gold holdings. Therefore, they argue, central banks must have made gold available to the market via derivatives trades. There are, however, two reasons why that may not be the case. The first is that calculations on the world's stock of gold are really only estimates. The second is that, even assuming all production statistics over the last century used in the calculations are accurate, it is well known that mines sustain continuous thefts of production and, over a century, the seepage can account for a lot of gold that never appeared in production records.

A One Way Risk to Prices

Morgan Stanley's chief currency economist Stephen Jen makes a strong case that since the anchor of the gold standard was abandoned 'the price level has had only one direction. Up. Deflation is virtually ruled out in our paper currency system and risks to prices are almost entirely on the upside. This is because central banks are averse to deflation, and they usually don't correct for upside one-off surprises for inflation.' Marc Faber says much the same thing. Jen has further conclusions following a study of almost two centuries of consumer price data for the US, the UK and Germany:

1 Low inflation usually doesn't last. Since 1820, periods of exceptionally low inflation have usually been followed by periods of high inflation. Episodes of high inflation occur typically, but not exclusively, around military conflicts.

2 Inflation has gone global. It has become more synchronised across countries over time, probably reflecting increasing globalisation.

Papering Over the Cracks

Among Alan Greenspan's contributions to the direction of the US economy was his almost unqualified support for financial derivatives. At a meeting of the Futures Industry Association in March 1999 Greenspan said:

> By far the most significant event of finance during the past decade has been the extraordinary development and expansion of financial derivatives .. As we approach the twenty-first century, both banks and non-banks will continually reassess whether their own risk management practices have kept pace with their own evolving activities and with changes in financial market dynamics and readjust accordingly. Should they succeed I am quite confident that market participants will continue to increase their reliance on derivatives to unbundle risks and thereby enhance the process of wealth creation.

Greenspan may have been right that reliance on derivatives to 'unbundle risks and enhance the process of wealth creation' could be constructive. But what about derivatives as they were employed in the shadow banking enterprise? For months after credit markets froze in July 2007 we learned in instalments about a derivatives industry that was designed to evade regulation, create dubious profit opportunities and, as Masters of the Universe, make their own laws. The first revelation of this syndrome was when it was exposed that collateralised mortgage and other debt obligations were being valued according to theoretical models and not to market prices. The next revelation was that leading banks were using off balance sheet investment structures on a grand scale to leverage assets beyond what would be permissible if the assets were normally accounted for. The third alarming revelation was that debt packages were being marketed with Triple A credit ratings that included non performing debt. The fourth revelation was that junk securities had been peddled throughout the world. Between January and the end of 2007 barely a day went by without another revelation that pointed to both systematic abuse of derivatives by leading financial institutions, potential for systemic risk within the banking system and disclosure of further multi-billion dollar losses. Developments in the deleveraging of finances by investment banks, hedge funds and other institutions and bailouts by central banks will be monitored on The Goldwatcher blog. At the time of writing no one in the world knows how much money will be lost as the shadow banking enterprise collapses or how long it will take before credit markets are restored to normal. It may be years before reliable estimates of losses can be made. All we know now is that central banks in the developed world had to be blind not to see what was happening before and are now papering over the cracks and making vast sums of money available to try and prevent a global financial breakdown.

With inflation rising the world's central banks are now lowering their interest rates. Northern Trust's Paul Kasriel has summed up the consequences of these actions in a single sentence: 'So, while fiat currencies float along in tandem as their supplies increase in tandem, all of them are likely to sink in value relative to the *genuine reserve currency* – gold.'

It's surely a case that gold's stateless money franchise has come into its own again.

Do Trees Grow to Heaven?

The case for gold price rises is strong. But so are the prospects for a recession and tight money. Loose money fuelled the boom in asset prices. Tight money would deflate price excesses. Another factor that will keep gold prices down to earth is *the miracle of compound interest* that investors in gold forego. A serious investor holding gold over a period will factor in loss of interest and holding costs when buying. Six years ago when gold was under $300 and cheap loss of interest may not have been a factor. The upside was far greater than the downside. But it's an important consideration now.

Gold bulls had the right message in 2007. But have the dollar and the financial system allied to the hegemony of the United States had their day? Or can the mess be cleaned up? I have commented on economic developments since March 2007 on The Goldwatcher blog – www.thegoldwatcher.com – and will continue to raise these questions. Equity markets weren't shocked by a belated April 2008 IMF report revealing a global credit crisis, an estimated $1 trillion loss exposure by banks, funds and financial intermediaries and global growth on the skids. Perhaps the market response was yes, things are worse than expected, but the IMF and the Fed are on the case now. The crisis is on the mend. In a pool of global financial assets of almost $170 trillion a $1 trillion loss isn't going to break the bank. The reality, alas, is different. The global economy is in choppy uncharted waters. There are no landmarks. Only hazard warnings.

Persistent inflation erodes the value of paper money. Hyperinflation destroys it. There's no textbook definition of hyperinflation. Inflation doesn't have to reach the absurd levels seen in Zimbabwe to qualify as hyperinflation. In our economies, when house prices were rising 50–100 % over a few years it's arguable that we experienced house price hyperinflation. When the price of crude oil doubled and doubled again within a few years it's arguable we experienced energy hyperinflation. With prices for some staple foods rising by 20–30 % it's arguable we are experiencing food price hyperinflation. And, if that argument is flawed, we are in any event experiencing serious inflation. Robert Mundell, in an article on gold at $10,000 quoted in Chapter 4, argued that inflation in the low double digits would push the price of an ounce of gold to the $5000 to $10,000 range within a generation and democracy wouldn't survive galloping inflation. That challenge was averted in the 1980s when the Fed, global central banks and policy makers tamed inflation. But in the 21st century they may have lost the plot again.

To bolster tax revenues in countries over-dependent on service industries it suited the US and UK political establishments to encourage all profit opportunities – particularly profits booked by the *innovative* financial services industry. In the process bubbles were allowed to inflate. Spurred by artificially cheap money house prices ran wild. The over-leveraged activities of the shadow banking establishment were left under-regulated. In the heyday of his fame, only a few years ago, former Fed Chairman Alan Greenspan declared that monetary authorities could neither recognise a bubble inflating nor do anything about it. Instead of encouraging the orgy surely it was the responsibility of governments to prick bubbles. Without reassurance on future policy commitments the chances of a systemic solvency crisis, resembling in some ways the crisis experienced in the 1930s, can't be ignored – and we still don't know who the next US President will be, who will be in the administration and what mandate they will have from the electorate. But we know that in the past daunting challenges have been overcome in countries with strong economies, resolve and committed leadership. Even the soaring oil price could be brought back to earth by energy conservation or rationing. In 2007 and early 2008 seismic economic developments spurred gold price rises that were predictable, dramatic and probably sustainable. Gold bugs are now urging investors to bet the ranch on gold. On my analysis that would be foolhardy. Frank Holmes also advocates moderation in the following chapters (11–13).

10

Investing Choices
What gold?

Bullion, Coins, Shares in Funds and Mining Companies

Having decided you want to own gold and are comfortable with the price you must decide whether to own physical gold bars (bullion), gold bars via shares in Gold Exchange Traded Funds (ETFs), gold coins, jewellery, shares in funds that invest in gold mining companies or gold mining companies. You also have to decide how much gold to own. Frank Holmes advises a strategy of moderation and an allocation of not more than 10% of a portfolio in gold. He has been quoted as saying that if you had made that allocation and kept topping up your exposure during the dot com bubble, when gold was cheap and out of fashion, you would have done exceptionally well with your investment.

When gold is bought as insurance against catastrophe and absolute worst-case situations it makes sense to keep it in your possession. Systemic failure in the banking system may be a remote possibility but is a risk that can't be ignored. For that eventuality gold held by a bank on your behalf would not be as instantly accessible as gold in your personal possession. However physical possession involves storage and insurance charges if the gold is in a safe deposit facility and insurance charges even if it is held in your own personal safe.

Gold Bullion and Coins

The world's professional gold market is conducted in London by the London Bullion Market Association (LBMA). The Association trades in 400 oz (approximately 12 kg) 'good delivery' bars .9999 Fine Gold currently worth over $300 000 each.[1] The serial numbered gold bars seldom leave the security of their vaults. The professional market is extremely competitively priced but inaccessible to the retail investor. However smaller certified gold bars are sold by bullion merchants in a vast range of sizes.

Gold Coins and Bullion Bars

The Fact Book contains information on certification and measurements of the purity of gold either as a percentage or by carat weight. The same grading applies to coins and to gold bars but the cost of buying bullion or bullion coins can vary. Prices are set by the current gold price to which the dealer adds a premium. Because the gold price is public you will always know the extent of the premium you are paying. Coins are available in denominations as low as a quarter of an ounce and bars are available with as little as a single gram of gold. Comment in the Fact Book from Lawrence Chard, a leading gold coin dealer, addresses premiums attaching to different levels of overall purchase, the size of the coin and supply and demand.

It's important to buy bullion coins priced on their gold content and sold without a numismatic premium. The Kruger Rand was introduced in the 1960s at a time when South Africa was unpopular and it traded at the lowest premium of any gold coin. Though South Africa is now a favoured nation the coin still generally attracts the lowest premium. Typical premiums being charged for gold coins range from as low as 5% over gold content to over 30%. Smaller coins attract the higher premiums. Premiums increased across the board in 2007 as demand for gold coins increased.

Advice from a Coin Dealer

Lawrence Chard, the Managing Director of Tax Free Gold, has provided the following advice for readers on gold coins and bars:

General

Gold coins and gold bullion bars are a good way for small investors to buy and invest in physical gold, but what is the best, and are there any pitfalls? There is a lot of advice and opinion available, some of it conflicting or confusing. We use our 40+ years of experience to give you a simple guide, and importantly we give you the reasoning behind our recommendations.

Investment Gold

Many countries allow free import of, and untaxed trade in legal tender gold coins, with some restrictions. Others include gold bars.

In the EU, since January 1st 2000, all legal tender gold coins mined since 1800, of at least 90% gold content, have been classed as investment gold, and are exempt from VAT. Gold bars of recognised weight with a minimum fineness of 99.5% are also classed as investment gold.

Our Basic Advice

- **Timing**
  Try to time your buying sensibly. Most small investors tend to buy only when the underlying gold price is rising strongly, by which time it is often too late. The price of most investments, whether commodities, shares, stocks, or bonds, oscillates. It often makes sense to wait for a lull or dip in the market, or buy on a downtrend. To some people this sounds counter intuitive, but think about the old adage 'buy cheap and sell dear'.

- **Premiums**
  Buy at the lowest premium, within reason, By premium, we mean the percentage over the intrinsic spot bullion value. Most dealers or brokers will offer better rates for larger quantities. Different sizes of coins and bars will also carry different premiums. Very small coins and bars cost more, pro rata, to make, and therefore usually cost an unrealistically high premium.

- **Our Top Three**
  For most of the time, our choice of investment would be, in order:

1 **British Gold Sovereigns**
  Buy only if you are buying say 50 or 100 coins at a time, when the premium is only slightly higher than Krugerrands. If you buy small quantities, you may be paying a 'collectable' or 'retail' premium. We speak to investors who only want Krugerrands because they do not want to pay the slight extra collectability premium for sovereigns. This can be false economy, because the actual extra is very slight, whereas the potential resale value is actually much higher, and they are often easier to sell. They can generally be bought at a lower premium than their near equivalent quarter ounce Kruger Rand. Another slightly illogical reason some people avoid buying sovereigns is mental laziness; they cannot be bothered, or don't know how to calculate the gold content of a sovereign, and its intrinsic gold content. True it does need a slight extra effort, but we feel this effort is more than worthwhile.

  Profits from investments in sovereigns (as sterling) are also exempt from Capital Gains Tax in the UK.

2 **Krugerrands**

The archetypal modern one ounce bullion coin. They are issued at a low ex-mint premium. The South African Mint sell them at only 3% plus shipping and insurance, subject to minimum quantities, but only to major banks and bullion dealers. There are now numerous other competitor coins, but Krugerrands have been around longer, and millions were sold in the period from 1967 to 1980, and this pool of secondary market gold helps to keep the premium low on Krugers. In 1980, fractional size Krugerrands were introduced, but these tend to cost a higher premium, and for this reason we would not normally recommend them.

3 **Gold Bars**

'Small' gold bars include anything under the 400 ounce London Good Delivery bars, and range from 1 gram to 1 kilogram. Yes, a kilogram bar costing over £10,000 ($20,000) is classed as a small bar, size is relative! Very small bars, under about 20 grams tend to be too expensive, while larger 'small' bars such as kilo bars can be harder to dispose of. Gold bars can often be bought at a premium similar to, or slightly lower than, equivalent gold coins, but may be slightly harder to sell, and bring a correspondingly lower price. It is mainly for this reason that we only list bars in third place on our list.

- **Remain Flexible**

Market conditions change, and the 'best buys' may change with them. Follow advice intelligently not dogmatically. If, for example, you are offered fractional Krugerrands at the same premium as one ounce ones, then buy them instead. You should be able to sell them at a higher premium when they are wanted. As another example, our company now offers a slightly better rate (lower premium) when selling 'our choice' of one ounce gold coins compared with Krugerrands. The reason for this is that we sometimes get sold quantities of other one ounce coins, leaving our stocks unbalanced, and being able to deliver other coins instead helps us, so we pass on the benefit to our customers. You also get a coin which would normally cost more, for a lower price.

- **Real Traditional Coins versus Modern Bullion Coins**

Before the Kruger Rand was invented in 1967, there were many different gold coins on the market. These included British gold sovereigns, French 20 francs, Swiss 20 francs, Belgian 20 francs, Netherlands 10 guilders (10 florins), German 20 marks, American 20 dollar double eagles, Mexican 50 pesos, Austrian 1 and 4 ducats, 20 francs, 10 francs, Italian 20 lire. Before the Kruger Rand was introduced, many of these coins may have been trading at a relatively high premium, and the Kruger Rand at its low issue premium, coupled with effective marketing, soon became very popular. This had the side effect of lowering the premiums on older coins. Certainly the premium on sovereigns used to be over 40%, and is now very close to that on Krugerrands.

Most of these older, traditional, real coins can be bought at very similar premiums, sometimes slightly more, sometimes less, than Krugerrands. It is worth paying a small extra premium for collectibility, as it will probably give you an enhanced return when the time comes to sell.

- **Regional & National Issues**

As a UK based business our advice is aimed primarily at British investors, but we have always dealt worldwide, and the advent of the internet has increased the international reach of our business, and we try to reflect this in our advice. Investors outside the UK may find that there is a local gold coin which is more readily available, or is in good demand. Swiss investors may prefer to buy Vreneli (Swiss 20 francs), Americans may prefer one ounce modern gold eagles or older $20 double eagles.

- **Tax, Duty, Imports**

There can be other country specific factors, such as sales tax, or import duties, or embargoes on certain items. Canada and Australia charge import tax on gold coins which are less than .9999 pure. This is possibly a protectionist measure designed to encourage their citizens to buy their own local product, but it still remains an important consideration.

Many countries, if not most, now have a low or zero tax rate on 'investment gold', including the EU. Some countries do not. We cannot be expected to have expert knowledge about tax and import regimes in every country of the world. If you wish to import gold coins or bars, you should find out your own relevant national import particulars for yourself.

- **Timing**

Apart from timing your purchase relative to short term price movements, it is important to try to see the 'big picture'. There are many financial analysts who are paid to spend their entire working life doing this, and they do not always get it right. Individuals can read many opinions from many different sources. It may seem slightly amateurish to use 'gut feeling', but this is what the vast majority of people will be doing, so by using it, you may be tuning in quite accurately to market sentiment, and hopefully keeping ahead of it.

If you feel strongly that it's time to buy something, have the courage of your own convictions, and get in before everybody else gets round to it. Similar advice also applies to selling.

We try to avoid being goldbugs, and try to take a balanced view of the market, present and future. At current gold levels, even though they are now close to the all-time highs of 1980, we feel gold prices are much more likely to rise than fall. Many pundits expect gold to hit new highs of $900; $1,000; $1,700; and higher. We have even seen arguments for gold reaching $8,500 per ounce or more. While we think some of these higher prices are over-optimistic, we thought the same thing about gold hitting $100 per ounce back in the 1960s when it was still only valued at $35 per ounce!

- **Selling & Posting**

One other reason for avoiding gold bars, particularly larger ones, is that if you wish to post them to a buyer, you may not be able to get sufficient postal insurance. In the UK, the maximum cover for 'Special Delivery' is £2,500 per packet, so it is easily possible to split a batch of 100 sovereigns or Kruger Rand into multiple packages, splitting a one kilo bar is a little more difficult!

- **Small Change**

  There is some value to be attached to owning smaller sized coins or bars, as long as you only pay a relatively small premium for buying them. If you have ever tried to pay for an espresso coffee with a €500 banknote, you will understand why.

- **Proof Coins, New Issues, Higher Premiums**

  In general, avoid buying newly issued coins, including proof collections and sets. These are usually sold at quite high premiums over the value of their metal content, typically double or more. In most cases, they can be bought in the secondary market much more cheaply a few years later.

  On the other hand, when gold bullion prices rise, the premium on recent proof coin sets can be squeezed downwards to the point where they are as cheap to buy as bullion coins, in which case they can be an excellent buy. It's also a way of hedging your gold investment. If gold continues to rise, so does the intrinsic value of your proof coin set, while if gold prices drop back, your set is likely to retain its value, in effect a 'heads you win, tails you don't lose' situation.

- **Other Advice**

  We are often approached by potential investors who have read advice elsewhere. Sometimes the advice is good, often it is not. Some Canadian websites, for example, extol the virtues of buying Canadian Maple Leaves. The usual reasons cited are the fact that they are 'fine' gold (actually .999 or .9999 or even .99999 fine). There is no intrinsic advantage in buying 'fine' gold over 22 carat (.916) gold coins. Our guess is this advice is given because it's what the dealer wants to sell you. There are lots of dealers who give 'loaded' advice. There is also quite a lot of 'amateur advice'. Again some of this is good and sound, but some is unsound and rooted in ignorance.

Silver doesn't enjoy the same VAT exemption as gold; nor does gold jewellery. In the United Kingdom gold coins and bullion also qualify as investments for Self Invested Personal Investing Schemes (SIPPS) that enjoy substantial tax benefits. However similar benefits are enjoyed for investments in all Exchange Traded Funds whether they are for gold or other commodities. As a result owning gold for SIPPS plans can be accomplished economically by owning shares in an Exchange Traded Fund. There has been talk of a SIPPS scheme for owning physical gold that will be run on a similar cost basis to owning gold in an ETF but so far it hasn't happened.

When buying gold bullion or coins, unless your bank deals in coins, as banks in Europe often do and banks in India have started doing, you will be buying from an unregulated trader. However there are well established vendors of bullion and coins and, subject to the normal care taken with any major purchase, you will have little difficulty verifying the reliability of your supplier. Start by enquiring how long they have been in business and don't be shy to ask for references. If they are reputable they will be pleased to furnish them and if they don't – caveat emptor!

You can buy gold bars from a bullion merchant in a range of sizes starting with a few ounces either at their premises or on line. The gold price is fixed twice a day in the morning and afternoon and merchants make their profits from the margin between buying and selling prices plus their trading premiums. The following web site sponsored by leading companies in the Gold Mining Industry is a complete and reliable information resource on all gold bars produced: www.goldbars.worldwide.com.

Further names of on line vendors of coins and gold bars are listed in the Webliography (www.thegoldwatcher.com).

The web site of the Internet coin vendor www.taxfreecoins.co.uk contains extensive information on available gold bullion coins with current price indications and general information on grades and quality. Content prepared by them is included in the Fact Book for information.

The Bullion Vault www.thebullionvault.co.uk arranges purchase and sale of remotely stored gold and offers an economic dealing, storage and insurance service. The gold is held in secure vaults outside the banking system. The Bullion Vault service includes an Internet trading platform quoting up to the minute prices with instant execution at a price inclusive of all costs.

Exchange Traded Funds

The most convenient and economic way to own gold is through owning a share in a Gold Exchange Traded Fund. The investment enjoys all the protection that comes when dealing with a regulated financial entity, is liquid and economic. Gold Bullion Securities, traded on the London Stock Exchange, charges a management fee of 0.4% a year and the buy–sell price spread quoted on its web site is about 0.33%. Buying and selling the share and the ETF is subject to normal charges for dealing in shares which, with on line brokers, is very low.

Headline information on ETFs and a listing of Funds is maintained on www.thegoldwatcher.com.

Futures Contracts and Increased Risk Reward Exposure with all Derivatives

Dealing in a derivative affords the opportunity to leverage a trade with greater upside potential if the gold price rises but involves greater downside risks if the price falls. It's outside the context of this book to explore gold derivatives. Useful information on market activity can be obtained from the Commitment of Traders Report published by the US Commodity Futures Trading Commission. The following web site includes the report and a guide to interpreting it: http://www.cftc.gov/marketreports/commitmentsoftraders/cot_about.html.

Further information on accessing and interpreting information from gold market activity is included in the Webliography (www.thegoldwatcher.com).

Gold Mining Shares and Gold Funds

Frank Holmes describes physical gold as a value investment and gold mining shares as a growth investment. Gold mining shares and gold funds investing in mining shares leverage upside potential in bull markets but also face increased downside risk in bear markets. When an investment is made in a managed fund the investor is backing a strategy and a manager. Before investing you need to know the fund's strategy and management's track record. Your independent financial advisor will have ready access to fund activity and performance. You can also research funds in the sector and their performance from resources in financial newspapers including the *Financial Times*, the *Wall Street Journal* and the range of specialist investing publications available in different parts of the world. *Morningstar* www.morningstar.com analyse all investment funds.

Investing in Gold Mining Shares and Gold Funds

In the following chapters Frank Holmes gives an insight into the strategies, disciplines, analysis, monitoring, risks and rewards associated with investing in gold mining shares. Warren Buffett's sage and well known advice to investors is to buy shares only in businesses you understand. If you are thinking of investing in gold mining shares it's worth taking that advice on board. Without the knowledge of the industry, the geology and the mining regions it's not possible to make the informed decisions specialist fund managers make. It's different when it comes to selecting and monitoring a fund. Here we have the advantage of the transparency that comes with fund management and the support of services monitoring fund performance. Eagle Wing Research, a boutique information provider, are one of the services that report on US Gold Funds. They monitor 22 leading US Gold Funds – part of their information is free and part is subscription. The subscription service includes data on the investment characteristics of each fund and their regular reports cover:

- fund objectives with comments and information;
- fund investment policies;
- expense ratios and loads;
- size of assets in fund;
- portfolio turnover ratios;
- stocks and ADRs found in most portfolios;
- recent and long term changes in net asset values;
- gold fund beta and relative position indicator;
- special brokerage arrangements.

Timing and Strategies

Investing and speculation are defined by motivation, timing and strategies and information in this book is intended for investors. Traders and speculators require an additional body of information on technical analysis and market timing.

Contrarian investors have in the past been the most successful with gold. Marc Faber's advice to Bill Gates to sell his Microsoft shares at the height of the Nasdaq bubble and buy gold must be the classic example of a contrarian call that, with the benefit of hindsight, was obvious. The only reason I mention this again is as a reminder that it's not a good enough reason to buy gold because the price is rising. There will be times when a runaway price is a good reason not to buy.

Gold will always have the drawback of being a sterile investment. There is no dividend and no interest payment and it costs money to keep. If gold is bought as a hedge against inflation, currency or market risks both the upside and downside price potential need to be considered when the investment is made and kept in mind while the investment is being held. The simplest way to escape the sterile trap is to invest in gold mining shares and gold funds with a track record of profitability.

Taxation

Investing in a gold fund in the US is more tax efficient than investing in an ETF. Gold ETFs are taxed at 28%, the same rate as collectibles such as gold coins. But long-term capital gains taken on stocks are only taxed at 15%. Before investing in gold you need to check the taxation implications in the country where you live. Investing in gold through a SIPPS Pension in the UK can secure the benefit of a tax refund from the Inland Revenue and you should be aware of any regional tax provisions that operate in your favour or against you.

'How to' Resources for Trading and Monitoring

More information is published on gold daily than on any other asset, currency or commodity except perhaps oil. The quarterly performance of the gold mining industry is extensively reported on by the World Gold Council and analysed by Virtual Metals and Goldfields Mining Services. Virtual Metals' analysis is of equal standard to other fee-based research and is currently accessible free on their web site.[2] Extracts from their report to the end of the third quarter of 2007 with their forecast for 2008 are included in the Fact Book for information.

Investing through a broker with experience in gold or commodities will be useful when an asset allocation to gold is made. If you can't arrange access to an informed broker you can spread your risk by investing in a few funds with proven track records.

When it comes to keeping informed on macroeconomics, names in the Webliography will link you with sources of reliable and informed comment. Access to information and the knack of using it well are of course not the same thing. We all know, or should know, our strengths and limitations and committing money to gold as an investor is not a trivial decision. If you don't feel sufficiently well informed or comfortable about investing in gold don't act without first accessing professional advice.

Eagle Wing Research on Gold Funds

Larry Martin who compiles the Eagle Wing research prefaces his guide with a caution that the information they receive should not excuse any investor from contacting the fund or a broker to receive an individual prospectus prior to investing. 'Funds' he writes 'want your business and most will respond within days. Slow response is an indication of a fund you may not want to deal with.'

He that states the purpose of his 'Guide' is:

> . . . to provide information and is not to promote gold as an investment. There are times to own gold and there are times not to own gold. My personal favorite method of investing in gold is with gold funds, and this 'Guide' is but a result of my private research over the past sixteen years.

For more serious investors Eagle Wing's subscription service provides comprehensive data including management objectives. A page on gold fund performance accessible on http://www.eaglewing.com is freely available to all investors.

Sample reports that follow cover monthly percentage change in net asset value; relative position of the funds; relative fund volatility; and stocks often held in fund portfolios.

Sample 1 – Eagle Wing Report on US Gold Funds
Monthly percentage change in net asset value (nav)
November 30, 2007

fn		Fund	1mo	3mos	12mos	2yrs	3yrs
24	GLD	StrtTrks Gold Shrs ETF	-1.7	16.2	20.1	57.5	71.4
25	SLV	iShrs Silver Trust ETF	-3.2	15.9	-0.5		
7	SGGDX	First Eagle Gold A .	-5.9	25.2	20.9	60.5	76.2
1	ASA	ASA Ltd.	-6.3	25.5	19.1	57.2	78.9
26	HUI	Amex Gold Bugs Index .	-6.6	24.1	14.3	66.9	71.4
22	VGPMX	Vanguard Prec Metals .	-7.4	16.0	29.9	85.8	147.1
2	FGLDX	AIM Gold & Pr Mtls Inv	-7.9	22.2	18.2	73.4	94.8
23	GDX	Mkt V Gold Miners ETF.	-8.4	23.1	10.4		
6	FSAGX	Fidelity Select Gold .	-8.7	27.5	21.4	69.8	109.2
8	FKRCX	Franklin Gold & PrMt A	-8.9	25.4	23.1	85.4	118.7
27	XAU	Phlx Gold/Silver Index	-9.1	21.5	14.6	49.3	60.3
16	RYPMX	Rydex Prec Metals .	-9.5	19.9	13.1	58.0	60.0
5	EKWBX	Evergreen Prec Mtls B.	-9.6	25.2	17.3	85.5	106.3
12	OCMGX	OCM Gold .	-9.6	23.4	15.3	83.4	91.2
18	USERX	US Global Gold Shares.	-9.7	27.1	8.9	92.9	114.8
3	BGEIX	Amer Cent Global Gold.	-9.8	25.1	9.1	62.9	72.5
4	SGDAX	DWS Gold & Prec Mtls A	-10.4	25.1	17.3	72.2	75.0
20	USAGX	USAA Precious Metals .	-10.5	23.6	21.0	101.5	131.8
9	GOLDX	GAMCO Gold AAA .	-10.6	25.4	19.4	78.8	99.8
21	INIVX	Van Eck Intl Inv GoldA	-11.4	25.0	20.1	88.5	109.2
17	TGLDX	Tocqueville Gold .	-11.4	16.9	10.2	70.3	89.0
13	OPGSX	Oppenheimer Gold A .	-11.6	21.8	27.0	107.5	134.1
11	MIDSX	Midas Fund .	-12.4	26.9	25.2	113.0	150.5
19	UNWPX	US Global World Pr Mns	-13.6	22.7	13.7	99.7	122.8
15	INPMX	Riversource Prec MtlsA	-13.8	12.3	7.4	68.5	77.3
14	PMPIX	Profund Prec Mtls Ultr	-14.7	30.0	17.2	51.4	57.4

Sample 2 – Eagle Wing Report on US Gold Funds
Relative Position Indicator
November 30, 2007

This number gives the relative position of a fund nav between its 52 week high and low. Its high is represented by +100 and its low by -100.

fn		Fund	pos	Net asset value	
				10/31/07	11/30/07
24	GLD	StrtTrks Gold Shrs ETF	86.4	78.62	77.32
7	SGGDX	First Eagle Gold A.	72.7	27.28	25.66
22	VGPMX	Vanguard Prec Metals.	63.7	39.66	36.71
26	HUI	Amex Gold Bugs Index.	61.6	435.08	406.21
4	SGDAX	DWS Gold & Prec Mtls A	59.1	28.08	25.16
6	FSAGX	Fidelity Select Gold.	56.8	47.58	43.43

Sample 2 – (Continued)

fn		Fund	pos	Net asset value	
				10/31/07	11/30/07
25	SLV	iShrs Silver Trust ETF	56.8	143.60	139.00
8	FKRCX	Franklin Gold & PrMt A	55.3	44.05	40.11
12	OCMGX	OCM Gold.	52.6	23.77	21.49
23	GDX	Mkt V Gold Miners ETF.	52.5	50.60	46.36
2	FGLDX	AIM Gold & Pr Mtls Inv	52.4	8.08	7.44
1	ASA	ASA Ltd.	52.2	80.30	73.25
9	GOLDX	GAMCO Gold AAA.	51.7	34.61	30.93
5	EKWBX	Evergreen Prec Mtls B.	51.2	73.40	66.38
20	USAGX	USAA Precious Metals.	50.7	38.37	34.36
21	INIVX	Van Eck Intl Inv GoldA	50.0	22.20	19.68
27	XAU	Phlx Gold/Silver Index	49.7	188.10	171.07
3	BGEIX	Amer Cent Global Gold.	43.8	24.71	22.28
18	USERX	US Global Gold Shares.	42.7	20.25	18.28
17	TGLDX	Tocqueville Gold.	41.2	64.39	57.05
16	RYPMX	Rydex Prec Metals.	40.0	73.75	66.75
14	PMPIX	Profund Prec Mtls Ultr	39.3	60.72	51.80
19	UNWPX	US Global World Pr Mns	38.3	37.03	31.98
11	MIDSX	Midas Fund.	34.7	6.35	5.56
15	INPMX	Riversource Prec MtlsA	33.1	18.22	15.71

Sample 3 – Eagle Wing Report on US Gold Funds
Relative Fund Volatility Indicator
November 30, 2007

This number measures the relative movement of a fund's nav over 52 weeks as compared to the gold fund group average, 1.0. A fund with the higher number is more volatile, meaning its net asset value changes quicker with each movement in gold.

fn		Fund	beta
14	PMPIX	Profund Prec Mtls Ultr	1.52
11	MIDSX	Midas Fund.	1.16
13	OPGSX	Oppenheimer Gold A.	1.13
9	GOLDX	GAMCO Gold AAA.	1.09
21	INIVX	Van Eck Intl Inv GoldA	1.09
27	XAU	Phlx Gold/Silver Index	1.06
8	FKRCX	Franklin Gold & PrMt A	1.06
20	USAGX	USAA Precious Metals.	1.05
4	SGDAX	DWS Gold & Prec Mtls A	1.05
5	EKWBX	Evergreen Prec Mtls B.	1.03
23	GDX	Mkt V Gold Miners ETF.	1.03
3	BGEIX	Amer Cent Global Gold.	1.02
19	UNWPX	US Global World Pr Mns	1.00

Sample 3 – (Continued)

fn		Fund	beta
26	HUI	Amex Gold Bugs Index.	1.00
6	FSAGX	Fidelity Select Gold.	0.99
22	VGPMX	Vanguard Prec Metals.	0.97
18	USERX	US Global Gold Shares.	0.97
1	ASA	ASA Ltd.	0.94
12	OCMGX	OCM Gold.	0.94
16	RYPMX	Rydex Prec Metals.	0.87
2	FGLDX	AIM Gold & Pr Mtls Inv	0.87
17	TGLDX	Tocqueville Gold.	0.86
15	INPMX	Riversource Prec MtlsA	0.83
7	SGGDX	First Eagle Gold A.	0.79
25	SLV	iShrs Silver Trust ETF	0.63
24	GLD	StrtTrks Gold Shrs ETF	0.60

Sample 4 – Eagle Wing Report on US Gold Funds
Common Stocks Often Held in Fund Portfolios
November 30, 2007

Major	Gold Stocks	symbol	exch	10/31/07	11/30/07
1	Agnico-Eagle Mines	AEM	N	56.89	48.12
2	Anglo American	AAUK	NASD	34.95	33.69
3	Anglogold Ltd	AU	N	46.45	48.77
4	Apex Silver	SIL	N	20.50	17.05
5	Apollo Gold	AGT	A	.49	.48
6	Barrick Gold	ABX	N	44.13	40.51
7	Buenaventure	BVN	N	57.41	55.83
8	Couer d'Alene	CDE	N	3.95	4.17
9	Crystallex Inter	KRY	A	3.14	2.31
10	Freeport-McMoran Cop	FCX	N	117.68	98.93
11	Gabriel Resources	GBU.TO	TOR	2.55	1.35
12	Goldcorp	GG	N	35.13	32.41
13	Golden Star Res	GSS	A	3.60	3.02
14	Gold Fields Ltd	GFI	N	18.07	16.45
15	Harmony Gold	HMY	N	11.20	10.44
16	Hecla Mining	HL	N	9.62	11.73
17	IAMGold	IAG	N	8.77	8.57
18	Ivanhoe Mines	IVN	N	13.74	11.26
19	Kinross Gold	KGC	N	19.68	17.35
20	Lihir Gold Ltd	LIHR	NASD	40.07	33.54
21	Meridian Gold	MDG	N	40.96	35.81
22	Miramar Mining	MNG	A	6.79	6.29
23	Nevsun Resources	NSU.TO	TOR	2.15	1.97

Sample 4 – (Continued)

Major	Gold Stocks	symbol	exch	10/31/07	11/30/07
24	Newmont Mining	NEM	N	50.90	49.69
25	Northgate Exploration	NXG	A	3.44	3.05
26	Novagold Resources	NG	A	18.80	9.83
27	Pan American Silver	PAAS	NASD	33.13	31.80
28	Randgold Resources	GOLD	NASD	35.94	35.18
29	Rio Tinto	RTP	N	375.00	467.48
30	Royal Gold	RGLD	NASD	35.34	28.72
31	Silver Standard Res	SSRI	NASD	42.46	36.25
32	Silver Wheaton	SLW	N	16.87	14.97
33	Stillwater Mining	SWC	N	11.13	9.70
34	Yamana Gold	AUY	A	15.02	12.86
	ADRs	**symbol**	**exch**		
1	AngloPlatinum	AGPPY	NASD	166.50	144.75
2	Durban Deep	DROOY	NASD	8.79	8.14
3	Impala Platinum	IMPUY	NASD	36.95	34.30
4	Newcrest	NCMGY	NASD	30.80	29.30
5	Randgold Exploration	RANGY	NASD	2.86	2.80

PART TWO

GOLD INVESTING STRATEGIES

Frank Holmes

11

Inside U.S. Global Investors

As an investor, one of the most difficult things to do is to develop an investment strategy to guide your actions and then impose the discipline needed to resist temptation and adhere to that strategy. With information being so fluid and so many choices available in an ever-shifting marketplace, it's easy to say you will follow a certain strategy as an investor and then take actions that run counter to that strategy.

It's no different for investment professionals whose job is to deliver the best returns for their clients.

My company, U.S. Global Investors, is an investment manager in the natural resources sector, with a special reputation for expertise in gold equities. Our funds have earned a number of mutual fund awards over the year for their performance. I'm the chief investment officer for our two gold funds, as well as our other 11 mutual funds and our offshore clients serving international investors. Since few were willing to talk about emerging markets and natural resources at the beginning of this secular bull market, I have become a media commentator on trends in the natural resources and gold-mining industry and in 2006 I was named the Mining Fund Manager of the Year by the British magazine *Mining Journal*, one of the leading publications in the field.

U.S. Global Investors was founded in the late 1960s and in the early 1970s, we started the first no-load gold fund in the United States. That fund is now known as the Gold and Precious Metals Fund (ticker USERX), and it focuses on unhedged 'senior producers' – multinational gold-mining companies with proven resources and strong production and cash flow. Our World Precious Minerals Fund (ticker UNWPX) also invests in senior gold producers, but its more diversified portfolio includes intermediate and junior gold companies – those with smaller levels of production or merely promising prospects – for added growth potential. Together the two funds had more than $1 billion in assets under management as of 31 December 2008. We also hold gold investments in several of our other funds.

Our funds invest in physical gold only through small positions in exchange-traded funds. We prefer to own pieces of the mines themselves. To our way of thinking, bullion is for value investors and mining stocks are for growth investors. We are growth investors.

Table 11.1 Gold equity volatility compared to Internet and Biotech.

Standard Deviation (as of 9/30/07) based on 5-Year Data			
	Weekly	Monthly	Quarterly
AMEX Gold BUGS Index (HUI)	4.80%	9.49%	14.83%
Dow Jones Composite Internet Index (DJINET)	3.89%	7.55%	13.50%
NASDAQ Biotechnology Index (NBI)	3.04%	5.95%	10.66%

This chapter will give you a look under the hood to see how the engine works at U.S. Global Investors. Many investors have had bad experience with asset classes with higher-than-average volatility, such as gold stocks, so we work to educate on how to better manage volatility and understand the value drivers for picking good gold stocks. I find it interesting that gold has retained for many investors a negative stature as an asset class, particularly in light of the fact that its volatility is comparable to that of Internet or biotech stocks.

Being familiar with our inner workings will also help you better understand the next two chapters, where we discuss in greater depth the nuts and bolts you should keep in mind as an investor and our outlook for the gold-mining industry going forward.

Our Golden Rule: Moderation

Despite resistance from Wall Street and many in the media, gold and other hard assets are gaining acceptance as a permanent asset class. One strong indicator of that rising respectability is that US pension funds, known for their conservative investing style, are directing more of their assets to hard assets.

In early 2008 the California Public Employees Retirement System (CalPERS), the largest pension fund in the United States and a trendsetter among its peers, voted to increase its stake in natural resource-related investments to as much as $7.2 billion by 2010 to take advantage of long-term market opportunities.

We put a lot of messages into the marketplace, but the one we stress most when it comes to gold is moderation. Don't try to get rich with gold because the corresponding risk is simply too high. Gold is a volatile asset whose daily price action can be far more dramatic than blue-chip stocks and many other asset classes. Evidence of that volatility was seen in the spring of 2006, when the price of gold peaked around $725 per ounce in May and within a few weeks it had tumbled more than 20%.

Volatility is not necessarily a bad thing – many short term traders make a nice living from gold's many mood swings. These swings often tie back to the emotional components of investing that comprise behavioural finance, as well as the intermarket relationships of gold to oil and the dollar. Gold speculators – be they long or short – thrive when fear or greed is in the air, which at the extreme tends to signal market highs and lows.

As part of our counsel of moderation to manage volatility, we advocate that investors limit their exposure to gold as an asset class to 10% of their portfolio, and that they rebalance each year to keep that level of exposure. Within that 10% investment, we advise no more than 5% in bullion and no more than 5% in gold equities in the form of stocks or funds. Even when gold was soaring in late 2007 and early 2008 and investors were being beckoned to pile in to take advantage of the momentum, we never changed our position.

We arrived at these limits based on the results of several research works going back a few decades, and we also view it in the context of a well-reasoned portfolio management strategy. A few years back Roger Gibson, a financial planner and author, wrote a book called *Asset Allocation: Balancing Financial Risk* that makes a well-reasoned case for dividing one's portfolio into four parts – domestic stocks, international stocks, fixed-income investments and hard assets – and then rebalancing each year to maintain the desired level of exposure to each asset class.

We find a lot of merit in the Gibson approach, given the market's long term tendencies toward mean reversion – what goes up comes down and what goes down comes up, with the result being a long term average that an investor can use to help determine if an investment is overvalued, fairly valued or undervalued. We view mean reversion as a key principle that investors should build into their thought processes so they are prepared to take advantage of market rotation.

Gold stocks as a whole were among the worst performers in the late 1990s before rising to be the best sector in 2001 and 2002. They also did well in 2003 before falling off again the following year, and then they bounced back to near the top in 2005 and 2006. Those who purchased gold and gold stocks to rebalance their gold holdings when the sector was down would have realised more profits in the rally that began after Fed chairman Alan Greenspan labelled the technology boom 'irrational exuberance', and they would have been in a position to use those profits to rebalance other portfolio allocations that may have lost value. We'll discuss mean reversion in greater detail in the next chapter.

How We Work

The investment team at U.S. Global holds its many meetings in the 'strategy room' of our headquarters building in San Antonio, Texas. The room is similar to those functional spaces found throughout corporate America, but with one unusual feature: two of its walls are floor-to-ceiling dry-erase boards.

I've covered almost every square inch of the boards in multicolored ink, most of it to stress investment process: valuation formulas, fund allocation checklists and various flow charts that the dozen portfolio managers, analysts and traders apply in their daily work.

But scrawled among the practical tips are snippets of wisdom and inspiration from some of my favorite thinkers, some of it going back hundreds of years. Ben Franklin reminds the team that 'you may delay but time will not' and nineteenth century economist Vilfredo Pareto offers his so-called '80-20 rule': applied to a portfolio manager, 80% of his total returns will come from 20% of his investments. Japanese academic Ikujiro Nonaka informs them that there are two types of knowledge, explicit and tacit, and the interplay between them leads to new knowledge.

And written in several places, underscoring its importance, is a quote from Michael Mauboussin, chief strategist at mutual fund giant Legg Mason: 'What separates good from great investors is not knowledge or raw smarts, but patterns of behavior.' What he means is that investors seeking superior returns should focus their attention more on developing consistency in their investment habits and processes (behaviour) than on their desired results (maximum profits).

Mauboussin is a thought leader in the developing field of behavioural finance, which taps into economics, psychology and other social sciences to try to figure out why people make suboptimal decisions about their money. Modern economic theory is built on the assumption that market participants coolly analyse any given situation to arrive at a rational decision in pursuit of a beneficial outcome. But it's been shown that most people don't work that way. They are often influenced by fear, greed, despair, overconfidence and other emotions when making their financial decisions.

There's a growing list of cognitive biases that apply to investing, and I'll mention a few of the most common ones faced by both individual and professional investors. The 'disposition effect' is the tendency of investors to sell their best performers too soon and hang onto their laggards too long. The 'sunk-costs effect' is the tendency to place greater value on an existing investment than on a future opportunity, which can lead to throwing good money after bad to salvage the existing investment if it falls in value. 'Herd behavior', also called the 'bandwagon effect', is the tendency of many investors to copy the buy or sell actions of the crowd because they see safety in numbers. 'Outcome bias' is the tendency to judge an investment decision by how it turns out rather than by the quality of the thinking used to arrive at the decision. And akin to outcome bias is the 'self-affirmation bias', in which an investor credits positive outcomes to his own savvy and negative results to bad luck or other external forces.

In all of these situations and many more, the investor is operating with impaired judgment and exptoses himself to a suboptimal outcome. Everyone has behavioural biases that influence his financial decision-making – the trick is recognising those biases and adjusting for them to improve (though not guarantee) one's chances for success.

We are active money managers at US Global, and the members of the investment team are expected to follow specific patterns of behaviour. We use both fundamental and statistical models to manage our investment decisions in our effort to drain away the emotional distractions. We use a variety of seasonal and multi-year cycles to help manage expectations, game theory to determine probabilities and relative valuation based on the drivers of the return-on-capital model that we'll spell out in greater detail in the next chapter.

Our processes have helped us build a number of award-winning funds over the years, so it may surprise you to learn that we never have the goal of being a No. 1 fund. Such a lofty goal would create all kinds of pressure that would complicate our decision-making – for instance, we might take on too much risk that could ultimately hurt our funds and their shareholders. Having a top-ranked fund involves a fair bit of luck, so we like to think of ourselves as having built a sleek boat and trained the crew well before the wind hit our sail.

We strive to keep all of our funds in the top half of their peer group on a consistent basis. Due to sector rotation and mean reversion, that's a more ambitious goal than it might seem at first glance. If a fund remains at the 51st percentile or better consistently for a three year period, it most likely will outperform 80% of all funds. I like to compare it to school grading by saying that 'investing is the only place where three Cs gets you an A'. Aiming for top half is the best way to balance long term risk and return.

To build tacit knowledge, we travel extensively to emerging market countries and remote regions to see what we own or might be buying. If we're visiting a mine on a tour with a very bright mining engineer and an extraordinary geologist, they're both going to be really technical in their questioning. We can handle the financial end, and we're going to learn the technical risks and opportunities from the engineer and the geological risks from the geologist. Oftentimes that kind of travel can be rough, be it on rickety Russian helicopters or along the treacherous roads of Latin America or central Africa. You get a tent in place of a five-star hotel and swarms of mosquitoes instead of air conditioning, but that's what good money managers in the mining sector do to get an edge.

Our natural resources analysts gain explicit knowledge by attending many investor conferences, along with continuing education courses at the Colorado School of Mines to learn better how to value mineral deposits. Usually we are the only investment company at these classes, which use 'Monte Carlo simulations' and other complex modelling techniques. Over the course of the year, dozens of high-level executives from mining companies around the world find their way to San Antonio to visit us to present new opportunities or provide updates on existing projects.

The team has collective patterns of behaviour to follow, and for that the members spend a couple of hours of each day in the strategy room I described to you earlier. As a group, each with different knowledge and analytical strengths, they distil vast quantities of information to find the important bits that they can act on as investors.

These meetings are held regardless of our rigorous travel schedules and market urgencies because consistent expectations lead to consistent behaviour, which is critical when trying to create a high-performing team. I deeply believe in the philosophy of the late football coach Vince Lombardi when it comes to teamwork and time management. He has a lot of quotes on the subject, but one of my favourites is 'Practice does not make perfect. Only perfect practice makes perfect.'

Mondays are devoted to macro concepts, the big picture factors driving the world's economy. The team starts the week at 7.30 a.m. by gathering around the conference table to discuss the 10 sectors of the S&P 500. Those sectors are divided up among our analysts, who present recaps on the key drivers and how each performed in the previous week, the previous month and the previous quarter. We also try to spot any political and economic factors, as well as intermarket relationships, that could affect those sectors during the current week or any trends that could affect the investing landscape over the longer term.

I've found that many book-smart analysts have difficulty integrating macro trends with stock picking. Macro analysis is often called 'top-down analysis' and fundamental stock picking is called 'bottom-up analysis'. To help these bright young analysts, I created this structure to get them to look past the names in their portfolio. This is a broad-thinking discipline that can be used by anyone.

We spend more time sorting through the market noise for the valuable bits of news or intelligence that might not be so noticeable. Examples of this might be signs of a consumption slowdown in key markets or proposed law changes that might affect mining companies. Part of the reason we travel so much is to get a first-hand look at economic conditions around the world. We like to see, for example, how busy the gold merchants in Shanghai are, and if consumer prices are showing signs of inflationary pressures. We also like to visit gold mines to talk to field engineers and see for ourselves how efficiently they operate.

We're also looking to academia to help us make better choices. In early 2007 U.S. Global committed $200 000 to a four-year partnership with the business school at the University of Texas in San Antonio to develop quantitative investment research and analysis. The students and professors taking part in the programme will create complex mathematical models to determine investment valuations, which are the basis of rational buying and selling decisions. The researchers will have the opportunity to publish their work, and U.S. Global will have access to the results for use in our investment processes. We see this as a good way to leverage intellectual capital to support our team's goals and help our financial community shape new talent.

Like any other investor, the timeliness and the quality of the information we get and the timeliness and quality of our decisions based on that information is the key variable in determining how well we perform in the marketplace. As a team of professional money managers, we strive to have a competitive advantage over most individual investors and financial planners. Like our competitors, we have Bloomberg terminals and receive research reports from a wide range of market analysts, and we have the training and manpower to develop a sophisticated matrix of models to improve our chances of making good choices.

We look at markets as 'complex adaptive systems', meaning they comprise many interrelated components and they have the tendency to change in response to internal and external influences. With this awareness, our investment team is structured as a complex adaptive system to be able to discern changes in our investment sectors and then quickly adapt its thinking models and strategies to keep pace with those changes.

Tuesday through Friday is dedicated to stock-picking. Each morning around that same long conference table we go over the specifics of individual companies. Analysts pore over the stacks of company and industry reports that come in each week in search of undervalued stocks or to build a case for why we might want to buy something for or sell something in the funds.

These discussions tend to focus on both fundamental and technical attributes of the stocks in question, and the only criterion for expressing an opinion is that the analyst be able to back up his views with relevant facts. At lunch Monday through Thursday, each day we drill down deeper into one of the S&P 500 sectors on a rotating basis and on Fridays we review the week for commodities and currencies and their interplay.

On Friday afternoons, after the markets have closed for the weekend, we start preparing for the coming week. Portfolio managers compile a 'SWOT' analysis that records the key strengths (S) and weaknesses (W) of the sector for the last week, last month and last quarter along with the most significant opportunities

(O) and threats (T) for the coming week, month and quarter. It is a process of sorting and prioritising facts, so if the portfolio manager believes the strengths are more sustainable than the weaknesses, it would suggest that opportunities should flourish in the coming months. This discipline is similar to that of sports teams, where coaches and players analyse their last game as a way to prepare their strategy for the next one.

This analysis forms the heart of our free Investor Alert, an electronic newsletter sent weekly to more than 25 000 subscribers. It also readies the team for that Monday morning macro meeting, when this intensive process begins all over again.

Week in and week out, this is how we watch game film, gain critical knowledge and improve our performance. As Vince Lombardi said, 'Perfection is not attainable, but if we chase perfection, we can catch excellence.'

12

Investing in Gold Equities

As we said in the previous chapter, bullion is for value investors and gold stocks are for growth investors. This chapter will focus on what to look for when you are researching gold equities with an eye toward investing.

The world of gold stocks is vast and varied, and it can be organised in a number of ways.

Gold producers can loosely be grouped as major producing companies, intermediates and juniors. At the high end of that continuum are the handful of industry giants who operate around the world. Their annual production is measured in millions of ounces and their revenue each year is well into the billions of dollars. At the other end are the many highly speculative startups that have little more than a name, an idea and a chunk of workable land. Some of the juniormost juniors don't even have the land.

There are gold companies whose production comes mostly from politically stable countries like the United States, Canada, Australia and South Africa, and there are companies with the bulk of their assets in more volatile nations.

There are gold companies whose production is pretty much limited to gold, and there are companies whose gold mines also include vast quantities of silver, copper and other valuable metals that provide a more diverse revenue stream.

A gold stock investor should have a good working knowledge of each of these different groupings before plunking down any money. That will allow him to better assess investment opportunities and gauge his appetite for risk.

Sometimes market conditions for gold will be strong, other times they'll be weak and then there will be times when they just go sideways for months or even years at a time.

Regardless of market trends, there are fundamental factors that you should always consider as an investor.

What's Driving Gold?

For our two gold funds, the weekly SWOT analysis (strengths, weaknesses, opportunities and threats) pays particularly close attention to the key drivers affecting gold. There are several, and the relative importance of each can shift depending on market conditions, as you can see below on our 'What's Driving Gold' chart.

This chart has long been one of our most popular publications because it captures the major global influences on gold prices on a single page. It's just as relevant for gold stock investors as for bullion, given their direct price relationship. It's important for investors to grasp that investing is not a linear process. We have created a more complex matrix of the many drivers that can influence gold volatility.

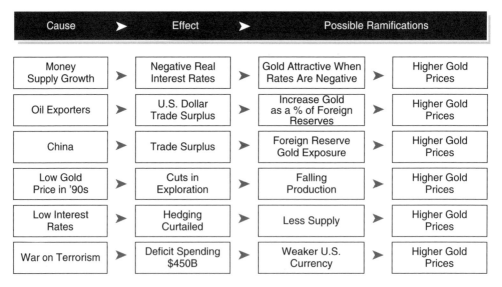

Cause	>	Effect	>	Possible Ramifications	
Money Supply Growth	>	Negative Real Interest Rates	>	Gold Attractive When Rates Are Negative	> Higher Gold Prices
Oil Exporters	>	U.S. Dollar Trade Surplus	>	Increase Gold as a % of Foreign Reserves	> Higher Gold Prices
China	>	Trade Surplus	>	Foreign Reserve Gold Exposure	> Higher Gold Prices
Low Gold Price in '90s	>	Cuts in Exploration	>	Falling Production	> Higher Gold Prices
Low Interest Rates	>	Hedging Curtailed	>	Less Supply	> Higher Gold Prices
War on Terrorism	>	Deficit Spending $450B	>	Weaker U.S. Currency	> Higher Gold Prices

Chart 12.1 Key factors driving gold price.

Let me give you a brief overview of each of the causes, effects and possible ramifications. Some of these factors have been presented already in this book, and others will be discussed at greater length in this chapter.

Growth in world money supply. Easy credit policies by central banks can create scenarios in which too much money chases too few goods, which tends to create inflationary pressures. When inflation is a worry, investors turn to gold as a hedge.

In early 1980, when gold spiked up to its historic high of $850 an ounce, the US was enduring double-digit inflation, largely due to high oil prices. There is also concern about negative real interest rates, which occur when the rate of inflation exceeds interest rates. When this happens, purchasing power is eroded and confidence in paper currency falls. Gold, as a hard asset, has and will always have an intrinsic value that paper money doesn't have. A famous quote by Ayn Rand in her novel *Atlas Shrugged* sums up this value: 'When you accept money in payment for your effort, you do so only on the conviction that you will exchange it for the product of the effort of others. It is not the moochers or the looters who give value to money. Not an ocean of tears nor all the guns in the world can transform those pieces of paper in your wallet into the bread you will need to survive tomorrow. Those pieces of paper, which should have been gold, are a token of honor – your claim upon the energy of the men who produce.'

Oil Exporters. One of the most powerful historical interrelationships is between gold and oil. Oil exporting countries took in about $970 billion for their output in 2006, according to Federal Reserve Bank of New York. That's more than triple their oil revenue in 2002. The World Bank estimates trade surpluses of $550 billion for these countries in 2006, roughly eight times higher than in 2002. The US dollar is the primary currency used in the oil trade, so exporters are accumulating vast quantities of dollars. They use much of that surplus to buy US government debt or toxic AAA-rated paper based on BBB-rated paper, such as sub prime debt. They are also spending an increasing amount on gold. Over a five-year period, the positive correlation between gold and oil is valid about 90% of the time.

China. China continues to have record annual trade surpluses with the West, particularly the United States. Some of the surplus is invested in low-yielding US government debt, prompting a call by Chinese economists that Beijing increase its reserves of gold, which stood at 600 tonnes in 2006. Rising incomes in China have also stimulated demand for gold jewellery. The Shanghai gold exchange and new policies that allow citizens to freely buy gold have also boosted demand in China. Per capita gold consumption in China is low by Asian standards, but given its population of 1.3 billion, even modest rises could have a huge impact on prices. It's important to recognise that jewellery is the most significant demand driver for gold, and that demand is predominantly rooted in China and India, where gold-giving holidays are a tradition and where people like to wear their wealth. Gold markups in these countries are much lower than in the West. Whenever we get a spike in gold prices, demand from China, India and the Middle East drops dramatically. Prices then fall back and find a new base, and then the demand starts to pick up again for jewellery and investment.

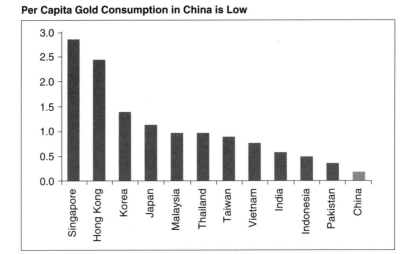

Chart 12.2 China's gold consumption per capita is low.

Low Gold Prices in the '90s. Low gold prices in the late 1990s did not create a lot of incentives for companies to develop their reserves or to spend money hunting for new deposits. It's important to recognise that it's not easy for gold producers to find massive deposits these days – just like with oil companies, the low-hanging fruit has been harvested. And even if a huge find were located, it is not unheard of for ten years to pass before a company obtains all of the required government permits and to build the infrastructure to get that gold to market. This arduous path to production creates many opportunities for delays and disappointments.

Low Interest Rates. When real interest rates are low, especially when the real interest rates are negative (inflation exceeds interest rates), many investors move away from declining paper assets and towards hard assets like gold. In this scenario, which occurred between 2001 and 2006, there is a reduced incentive for hedging, so gold is removed from the market. This can shrink short term supply at the same time that demand is increasing, creating a market imbalance that can drive prices higher.

War on Terrorism. Since the 9/11 attacks in New York and Washington, the United States has spent billions of dollars on the global war on terror. An estimate in 2006 pegged that amount at $200 million per day. The official federal deficit in 2006 was about $300 billion and in 2007, it was another $161 billion,with much of those shortfalls attributable to military operations in Iraq and Afghanistan. These large deficits have undermined the dollar's strength, with many overseas investors turning instead to gold as an alternative reserve asset. There tends to be an inverse relationship between gold price and the value of the dollar. On top of that, legislation like the USA Patriot Act, Sarbanes-Oxley Act and money laundering laws all contribute to negative sentiment about the United States that further weakens the dollar.

The Investing Universe

The gold equity universe can be divided into three broad geographic groups in descending order by market capitalisation: the North American stocks, the South African stocks and the Australian stocks. The Toronto Stock Exchange in Canada has by far the most mining stocks listed, including gold miners, and it has represented the vast majority of all financings for mining companies. Other primary exchanges for these companies are New York, Vancouver, Johannesburg, London and Sydney.

Each of those stock exchanges includes a range of gold companies: major producers, mid-level producers, small producers and non-producers. There are many hundreds of publicly traded gold companies in existence, but there are only a few dozen producers of any significance.

The major producers – those with production exceeding one million ounces per year – were always a small club and industry consolidation has made their ranks even smaller. At the end of 2006, they numbered a dozen, though further shrinkage is almost inevitable. These are the companies that should be thought of as the blue-chip large-caps of the gold world.

Table 12.1 Major gold producers.

Company (domicile)	2006 production in ounces
Barrick Gold (Canada)	8.6 million
Newmont Mining (US)	5.9 million
AngloGold Ashanti (South Africa)	5.6 million
Gold Fields (South Africa)	4.1 million
Harmony Gold (South Africa)	2.3 million
Goldcorp (Canada)	1.7 million
Freeport McMoRan Copper & Gold (US)	1.6 million
Zijin Mining (China)	1.6 million
Kinross Gold (Canada)	1.5 million
Newcrest Mining (Australia)	1.5 million
Buenaventura (US)	1.5 million
OJSC Polyus Gold (Russia)	1.2 million
Rio Tinto (UK)	1.0 million

Source: World Gold Analyst

It's worth pointing out that Freeport McMoRan and Rio Tinto are primarily copper companies that also produce sizeable amounts of gold from what are known as 'copper-gold porphyry' deposits.

That was a real benefit in 2006 and 2007, when both gold and copper prices were at multi-year highs and the companies had two strong revenue streams. Being diversified can also act as a hedge to provide some cushion for the company if the price of one of the metals is weak. And on the other side of the ledger, since both metals come out of the same hole, the relative cost of production can be lower compared to competitors.

The lowest cost producer in the gold industry in 2006 was Agnico-Eagle Mines, a Toronto-based company whose property in Quebec yields mostly gold but also marketable quantities of silver, copper and zinc. Revenue from the three by-product metals in 2006 more than covered the cash cost to produce the gold – in essence, the gold was free.

In 2006 there were roughly the same number of intermediate producers – those with production between 250 000 ounces and one million ounces – as there were major producers. Consolidation, however, also stands to reduce the head count in the near future.

Some of the better known names in this category include South Africa's DRDGold (550 000 ounces in 2006); Canada's IAMGold (640 000 ounces), Centerra Gold (585 000 ounces) and Yamana Gold (310 000 ounces); Australia's Lihir Gold (650 000 ounces); and the UK's Randgold Resources (450 000 ounces).

One step further down are the small producers, with the best-known names including US-based Coeur d'Alene Mines (116 000 ounces), which is primarily a silver producer. These companies typically operate only a single gold-producing property, so on a risk basis they don't have diversity of production in the event that a mine slows down or shuts down for whatever reason.

For non-producing companies, they can be split into three categories: the ones with known gold in the ground that is in the process of being developed or on a timeline for development; those with a discovery whose extent and feasibility of producing are still uncertain; and those that have a drill rig and a lot of hopes and dreams.

All of these scenarios fall into the speculative realm, so extra care must be taken as an investor. It's true that a fortune can be made by investing in penny-stock gold companies that make a big discovery. But those 'base-loaded home runs' are very rare indeed. History has proven that the vast majority of gold companies will never be gold producers – a lack of success as an explorer will likely cause these stocks to collapse, so mining promoters often 'roll back' the stock and refinance for a new high risk exploration play.

Back in 1990, Pierre Lassonde wrote an excellent volume simply called *The Gold Book* that was full of useful facts and figures for a gold investor during that

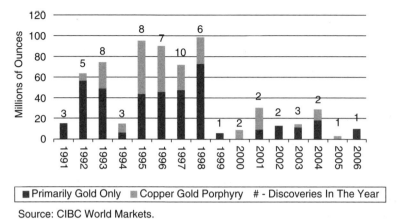

Chart 12.3 Large discoveries (>3 million ounces) are on the decline.

time, Lassonde and Seymour Schulich built Franco-Nevada Mining Corp., the most successful gold royalty company. He later became CEO of Newmont Mining following its merger with Franco-Nevada, and by the time he retired in 2007, Newmont was the world's No 2 producer.

The Gold Book is a collector's item now, even though much of the information in it is long out of date – for instance, many of the big producing companies he talks about no longer exist due to mergers and the ways to invest in gold have broadened. But a few sections of the book remain as relevant today as when originally written. One of those sections is Pierre's six colourful, common-sense rules for buying into a gold exploration company. I will offer some thoughts in parentheses for some of these rules.

1 Never bet more than you can afford to lose

'In a game played with 52 cards, you have 16 face cards. So each time you're given a card, you have a one in four chance of getting a face card. . . . It's estimated that less than one in a hundred junior companies finds gold, while no more than one in two hundred finds gold worth mining. To be absolutely sure of winning this game, you would have to hold at least two hundred stocks in your portfolio . . .

'Most investors end up with 10 to 15 stocks, making their odds of winning one in 20. It's better than a lottery but worse than a good poker game. . . . Before you invest in a penny stock, remember the definition of a good promotion: "In the beginning the promoter has the vision and the public has the money. In the end, the promoter has the money and the public has the vision". It's irreverent but it does cover two key questions every investor should ask: Who is the promoter and what is the vision?'

(What is the promoter's track record for creating wealth for investors? Who are the Michael Jordans and the Tiger Woods of the industry?)

2 Know what you are buying

'If you are interested in a stock, read the company's latest annual report, its latest information circular, and if it's an American company, its latest 10-K or 10-Q (earnings reports) . . . While you're at it, ask for corporate profiles of the top people as well as other corporate material. In most cases you'll be surprised at how much information you will receive.'

3 Know the people behind the promotion

'Promoters are a unique breed of people who share a common ability to create and share a vision. Some of them can do it with an almost evangelical fervor. . . . As an investor you should ignore the eccentricities of the individual promoter and look for honesty. Avoid anyone involved in bankruptcy proceedings, justice department filings, fraud charges, tax evasions and any other legal problem. Look carefully at the promoter's track record. Success attracts success, especially in the mining industry. . . . The best plays are often in companies where a combination of strong promotional and excellent technical skills is at the helm.'

4 Don't overpay

'When it comes to paying for your stock, don't pay any more than double what the promoter paid if it's a new promotion. . . . If the promoter's average cost for each share is 35 cents, don't pay more than 70 cents. Once the stock hits $1 he'll start selling his stock and by $1.50 he'll be gone.'

(This is a cynical yet realistic portrayal of the 1960s through the 1990s. Promoters today, however, need to have a solid reputation to be able to raise capital – the industry has been quick to identify bad deals in this tougher regulatory environment. That said, these stricter standards still cannot change the fact that the odds of making a significant discovery are very slim.)

5 Don't be greedy

'Investors in junior exploration companies should try to get their money back as soon as possible and let their profits ride intelligently. . . . Speculating on penny stocks is risky but if you always get your ante back you can keep playing. If you see in the insider trading reports issued by the stock exchanges that the promoter is bailing out, follow him. . . . There might come a time when one of the stocks you own becomes outrageously overpriced. But no matter how good the story, sell before reality reasserts itself.

6 Don't hang onto your losers

'The great majority of investors tend to hang onto stocks they bought at lofty prices, even though those stocks have slipped to pennies a share. Get rid of them. . . . The only reason many speculative juniors drift in the market at 15 or 20 cents a share is because of thousands of investors hanging on in vain hope. Don't fall in love with your stocks. Try to spot your mistakes early and be ruthless. . . . You may occasionally miss a rebound, but you'll never end up holding bundles of worthless certificates.'

Gold Stock Funds

Another way to invest in gold equities is to buy shares in funds that invest in gold mining stocks.

These funds come in many shapes and sizes. Some have sales fees while others don't. Some are built to closely track gold stock indexes and others apply their own skill and research to set their composition and allocation. Some limit themselves to gold producers, while others have a mix of producers and exploration companies. Some only own gold mining companies, some focus on gold and other precious metals and some include gold as a part of a broader mining fund.

At the beginning of 2008 there were about four dozen distinct precious metals mutual funds available in the United States, and these funds covered a range regarding the number of stocks in their portfolio, their company concentrations (the percentage of the fund made up by top ten holdings), the average market capitalisation of the companies in their portfolio and how much of the equity concentration was in gold.

While there is always risk attached to gold investing, there are a number of advantages to buying a gold mutual fund as opposed to trying to build a gold stock portfolio. This is especially the case for investors who don't have the time or desire to spend evenings and weekends navigating company websites and poring over company reports and financial filings.

The most obvious appeal of a gold fund is that, because it is made up of a number of company stocks, it is a more diversified investment than what most people could create on their own. Picking the right individual stock could yield a big win, but it also exposes the investor to risks that could be unique to that specific company. Buying into a gold fund provides protection from that risk and at the same time provides exposure to the broader gold mining industry. And with the minimum initial investment of many funds being $5000 or even less, that diversification comes at a relatively low price.

Individual gold mining companies face a long list of risks. There are geological risks (resource depletion, less gold than expected, mine collapse), political risks (change in government policies, seizure of assets, local opposition to operations) and environmental risks (regulatory violations). For investors, there is also the risk that a company's management may make an acquisition that reduces the value of its shares.

One option is to buy a gold fund that links to an index, of which there are many around the world. These indices are in most cases weighted by market capitalisation, meaning larger companies make up a greater share of the index than smaller ones.

The FTSE Gold Mines Index series includes a global index as well as regional indices for Europe, the Middle East and Africa; Asia and the Pacific; and the Americas. The FTSE indices are made up of all gold mining companies that have sustainable production of 300 000 ounces per year and which derive at least 75 % of their revenue from gold mining.

The best known indices in the United States are the American Stock Exchange's Gold Bugs Index (HUI) and the Philadelphia Stock Exchange's Gold and Silver Index (XAU). Both of these market-cap-weighted indices are made up of the stocks of gold-producing companies, with a few silver producers among the 16 members of the XAU. The HUI is composed of 15 companies, of which 11 were also part of the XAU in mid-2007, though in different percentages. There's also the Amex Gold Miners Index (GDM), which debuted in 2004. It comprises about three dozen gold and silver producers on a market-cap-weighted basis.

In Canada, the S&P/TSX Global Gold Index comprises the world's largest gold miners, weighted by market cap, that trade on the Toronto, New York or Nasdaq stock exchanges. There are also gold indices associated with the Australian and Johannesburg stock exchanges.

Another advantage of a gold fund is professional management. Earlier in this section we spoke about the time needed to stay informed about what's going on in the gold mining industry, but what about all of the time needed to learn about the many complexities of gold and gold stock companies so all of those research reports and financial statements make sense?

Gold fund managers are paid to eat, sleep and breathe the industry. Many of them have a background in geology or engineering that they couple with their skills as financial analysts. They attend investment conferences and have access to many sources of sophisticated research, and some of them even visit mines, which

I think is important. On top of that, in many cases they also have access to the high level management of the companies in their portfolio. The good ones know the right questions to ask, and when the answers are less than satisfying, they have the knowledge and experience to follow up effectively.

Professional fund managers, given their knowledge and connections, can also have an advantage in discovering opportunities sooner than the typical individual investor. The ability to get in early on promising projects creates more potential upside if the project is a success.

Leveraging gold

Gold mining stocks are riskier than physical gold, since a mining company's share could theoretically plummet to zero in the case of bankruptcy (though this rarely occurs). It's also true that investing in gold stocks is an indirect bet that physical gold prices will climb. When bullion prices rise, gold stocks can create higher returns for investors than if they were buying gold by the ounce. The primary reason is leverage – rising gold prices increase revenue and earnings for gold companies, and higher earnings tend to drive up their share prices.

Here's a simple example to illustrate leverage. Let's say today the price of gold is $500 per ounce and XYZ Gold Co. is an unhedged producer with cash costs of $300 per ounce. That means XYZ can sell its gold for $200 per ounce above its production costs. Now let's say a year from today, gold is selling for $600 an ounce. An investor in bullion would see a profit of 20% ($100 gold price increase divided by $500 starting price). But assuming no change in production expenses, XYZ Gold Co. can now sell its gold for $300 above its costs. That's a 50% profit growth for XYZ's shareholders ($100 gold price increase divided by $200 original per ounce profit).

The impact of leverage is also the reason why the US Global gold funds steer clear of companies that hedge their production. Because hedging locks in a future price, the company loses the upside created by rising gold prices. Going back to our example, if XYZ Gold Co. hedged half of its output at $525 per ounce, the profit on that share of production would increase only 12.5% when the gold price climbs to $600 ($25 hedge premium divided by $200 original per ounce profit). The hedge reduces XYZ's overall profit growth to 31.3% in our example – higher than the return for the bullion owner, but considerably less than the 50% seen in the unhedged scenario.

Of course, these illustrations can also work in reverse. Leverage would amplify losses for a gold stock investor compared to a bullion investor when gold prices are declining, and an unhedged producer could endure greater losses than a hedged producer during a price drop.

Call and put options on gold stocks can also be used for leverage, as can gold company warrants, which provides a right (but not an obligation) to buy the underlying stock at a specific strike price in the future.

Warrants are commonly used securities in the mining industry that offer leverage without borrowing. In a rising market, they can help an investor's risk-adjusted performance, measured as alpha. In a falling market, they can fall faster and hurt performance. As a defensive measure, we have increased our cash levels after big price runs, which de-leverages these warrants and at the same time allows us to create a portfolio with exposure to the best investment ideas.

Warrants differ from options and LEAPs (long term equity anticipation securities) in that they are issued by a company, often in connection with an initial public offering or a private financing. They also tend to have a much longer life than options or LEAPs. Where options often expire within a few months and LEAPs after a year or two, warrants are commonly issued for up to five years.

Many mining company warrants are exchange-traded, and they can be attractive for medium term or long term strategies. The key investment factors for warrants are (1) the underlying fundamentals of the stock and (2) the time remaining on the warrant.

Warrants can be divided into two groupings: 'in the money' and 'out of the money'. Those that are in the money have appreciated above the strike price. In-the-money warrants attract a broader community of investors, so their liquidity expands.

Here's an example of how leverage works with a warrant. Say XYZ Gold Co.'s common stock sells for $10 per share in July 2008 and the company has a class of free-trading warrants that are trading at $3 per warrant with a strike price of $12 and an expiration date in 2012.

A purchase of 1000 common shares of XYZ Gold would cost $10000, while it would cost only $3000 to buy 1000 XYZ Gold warrants. The warrants give the buyer control over the same number of common shares but for $7000 less in initial investment.

Now let's say by July 2010 that XYZ Gold's common stock has appreciated to $24 per share. In this case each warrant would be worth at least $12 ($24 share price minus $12 strike price). The 1000 warrants purchased two years earlier would be worth $12000, making for a 300% return on the initial investment of $3000.

Of course, it's also possible that the share price of XYZ Gold could be below the strike price when the warrant expires. In this case, the warrant would expire 'out of the money' and thus would be worthless. If the buyer in the example above held the 1000 warrants to expiry, it would result in a $3000 loss. This illustrates why the time component is so important when investing in warrants.

The use of five-year warrants by mining companies has grown dramatically. When the US Global Investors' gold funds are approached to participate in new financings, we often ask for warrants as an additional benefit for our fund shareholders to offset the elevated risks of new mining ventures, particularly those in emerging countries. A good source of research and other information about these securities is a newsletter called Precious Metals Warrants, which is available online.

The Return on Capital Model

When considering an investment in a gold mining company, it is important to look at the company's return on capital as a measurement of how much value the company is creating for its shareholders.

There's a basic mathematical formula to determine return on capital, also called return on invested capital: net operating income after taxes divided by amount of invested capital (both shareholder equity and debt). The result is typically conveyed as a percentage, and the higher the percentage the better.

Taking the calculations one step further, one can compare the company's return on capital to its cost of capital, which in simple terms is a weighted sum of the interest rate on its borrowed capital and the opportunity cost of its equity capital.

If the gold mining company's return on capital is greater than its cost of capital, the company is creating value for its shareholders. The more the return on capital exceeds the cost of capital, the more value the company is creating and the higher the valuation it should support. If the return on capital is less than the cost of capital, the company is destroying value for its shareholders.

We have found that there are always a lot of gold projects in development in which the only way they can expect to see a high return on capital is if the price of gold is very high and the mining company has used hedging to bring risky, low-margin projects into production. We find those projects too speculative and instead focus on those companies whose projects have the best chance for sustainably high returns on capital.

For mining companies, we see three basic drivers for increasing profitability and thus sustaining a high return on capital: growth in production per share, growth in reserves per share and growth in cash flow per share.

These drivers should come as no surprise. To improve profitability now and in the future, a gold mining company has to assure investors that it is increasing the number of ounces it owns in the ground to ensure future viability, that it is increasing its output of gold and thus its current revenue, and that it's controlling its costs so more of that rising revenue falls to the bottom line.

During this secular bull market for commodities, we have focused on the companies generating the highest return on capital and those that have the potential to do so over the next 12 months, and we've enjoyed success by overweighting polymetallic producers like Freeport-McMoRan (gold and copper) and Agnico-Eagle (gold, copper and zinc). For exploration and developing companies, we have applied the optionality concept to value reserves in the ground and have invested in those companies that offer the highest potential for return with rising commodity prices.

We like to rank companies from best to worst in reserves per share, from best to worst in production per share, and from best to worst in cash flow per share. Then we try to focus on the companies with the lowest valuations in those three metrics because we're looking for the most upside potential.

Generally speaking, growth in production is important because the more gold the company produces, the greater its revenue. But increasing production doesn't necessarily mean increasing profits for the company's investors, so there are questions on the cost side that have to be addressed.

How much can the company increase its project's production with existing infrastructure and workforce? Even a small increase in production efficiency can boost the company's return on capital. If additional capital expenditure is required, how much must be spent? If a significant investment in construction, equipment and workforce is needed to boost production, it stands to make the company less appealing on a return on capital basis.

Another question is whether the company's ore body can support a production increase at an attractive per ounce cost. Say a company's current production yields an average of six grams of gold per tonne of rock. It wants to expand production, but the best it can extract from the new source is three grams of gold per tonne of rock. Assuming the same cost structure for both ore bodies, the new production would be twice as expensive as the original when measuring it in grams per tonne of rock and thus could have a big impact on the company's return on capital, not to mention its earnings and share price.

Quality is also an issue when measuring growth in reserves, which is the amount of gold a company has in the ground. Are the new reserves estimated at three grams per tonne of rock or 10 grams per tonne? The answer could mean a huge difference in a company's cost structure.

And are we talking about a 'reserve' whose extent has been delineated by a thorough drilling and rating programme, or is it a 'resource' whose extent is less well-known and thus far more speculative? If it's a reserve, is it a 'proven' reserve or a 'probable' reserve? Investors should pay close attention to the wording used in gold company reports and press releases to keep from reaching errant conclusions about a project's merits.

For a company not yet in production, the ability to increase the size of its reserves is important, and on a per share basis it is critical to achieve superior relative performance. The more gold the company has, the easier it will be for that company to get the financing necessary to become a producer. Rising reserves also improve a junior company's chances of finding a partner or being bought out at a premium by a competitor.

We take into account the quality of reserves. A million-ounce gold reserve that is only worth producing when the price of gold is $500 per ounce counts for less than a same-size reserve that is economical at $400 gold.

Gold mining companies are valued on a discounted cash flow basis, and two of the key factors in that equation are production and reserves. A company with organic growth in its reserves – that is, new discoveries – can be rewarded with a huge premium in its stock.

A gold company's cash flow per share becomes an important measure once it is in production, and for exploration companies, its stock price can reflect the expectation of what the cash flow per share will be when the company begins producing.

Companies in the royalty business – that is, those that buy the royalty revenue from metals production – have historically generated the highest returns on capital and free cash flow. Companies that extract two metals from the same rock, such as copper-gold porphyry deposits, have also been able to generate consistently higher free cash flows than single-metal miners.

Cash flow is also impacted from the cost side, as was the case in 2007 for many gold producers facing escalating expenses that have not been offset by a corresponding increase in the price of gold.

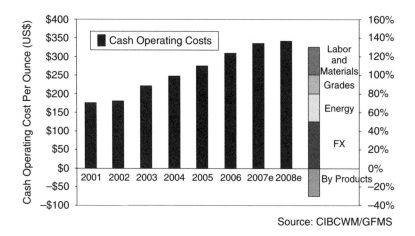

Source: CIBCWM/GFMS

Chart 12.4 The rise in costs has been a big disappointment.

Large-scale gold production is a complex and costly process that involves digging, transporting, crushing and chemically treating massive quantities of rock even to get small amounts of the shiny yellow metal. The scale is almost mind-boggling: a commercially viable deposit could contain just a tiny fraction of an ounce of gold for every tonne of mined rock.

With oil averaging more than $70 per barrel in 2007, rising energy costs have been the single biggest component of margin compression for gold mining com-panies. A mine is a huge consumer of diesel fuel to run the shovels and the dump trucks hauling ore to the mill for processing, while natural gas, coal and electricity can also be used in abundance.

Investors looking at gold companies with new projects should ask whether those projects are near power and water, two critical requirements for a mine. Relative proximity to infrastructure can have a huge impact on the cash flow multiple. Many mining companies have started building their own sources of power because rising energy prices are compressing the profit margins for gold.

Cash flow per share can also be influenced by changes in tax rates or royalty regimes.

There has been tens of billions of dollars worth of merger and acquisition activity in recent years in the mining sector. The base metal companies have been consolidating to get scale and to broaden the range of metals they produce as a way to diversify. For the gold miners, there have been more than 20 major trans-actions in the past couple of years, and most of them have been done to get reserves and resource replacement, not to diversify or get scale.

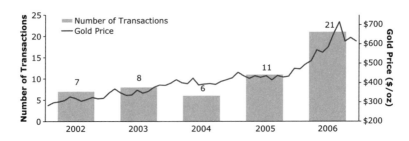

Chart 12.5 Gold mergers and acquisitions are a key trend.

The Five Ms

How tough is it to pick a winning gold stock?

A few decades ago, when there were many more gold exploration companies than exist now, I remember seeing a fascinating piece of research from prominent geologist Robert Sibthorpe that found that only one in 2000 companies would ever find a million ounces of gold, and that only a third of those successful explorers would ever get their deposit into production.

So now you know – Mother Nature is heavily stacked against investors in gold exploration companies. Of course, the odds are also heavily stacked against people who visit casinos, but that too is a flourishing industry and for the same reason – the potential for huge payoffs.

Gold stock investors can, however, improve their odds by learning how to assess the fundamentals of these exploration companies. A good tool for this job is what I call 'The Five Ms'.

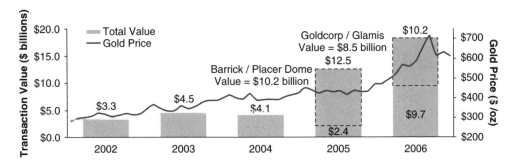

Chart 12.6 Rising value of precious metals mergers.

By using the Five Ms, an individual investor can build a simple but powerful model to initially sort through the many hundreds of upstart gold companies to find better opportunities. The information needed for a Five Ms analysis is not hard to find on company websites or in regulatory filings, press releases and gold industry publications.

As a professional money manager, before we buy we strive to operate like a jet pilot routinely going through his checklist prior to takeoff. This helps us ask the important questions during our analysis so we can compare stocks using consistent metrics.

And while most of our discussion will centre on junior companies, the Five Ms can also be used when considering investments in intermediate and senior gold producers.

1 Market cap

Market capitalisation is, of course, the number of shares outstanding multiplied by the stock price. If it's a junior gold company and there are 10 million shares outstanding at $1, the company is valued at $10 million. The question any money manager or investor should ask is, 'Is this company really worth $10 million?'

One way to address that question is to look at the company's gold assets in the ground. If it has a million ounces of gold reserves, the investor asks 'What does the market pay for an ounce of gold as a reserve?'

Let's say the market pays $25 per ounce of gold in the ground – in that case, the company should be valued at $25 million (one million ounces in reserve at $25 per ounce). If the company's market cap is only $10 million, as illustrated above, it may look undervalued. Conversely, if the company's market cap is $50 million, it may appear to be overvalued unless it is within a year of going into production.

If the company has cash but no reserves, an investor should resist paying more than two times cash per share.

The market cap analysis changes when it comes to larger gold companies. In those cases, an investor can measure their market cap against their production level, their reserve assets, their geographic location and other metrics to establish relative valuation. There are industry averages that can help an investor determine whether a company is overvalued or undervalued compared to its peer group.

It's important to recognise that quantitative research has shown that one of the key factors for being a good stock picker, be it gold or any other sector, is to buy those companies that are most undervalued relative to their peers. The reason, as Warren Buffett puts it, is that the 'margin of safety' is much greater.

There's a great expression in the mining industry: 'It takes a man to make a mine, but not to find one.' The best an investor can hope to do is to improve the probabilities with geophysics but it really comes down to luck to have a deposit that is sufficiently sized to get the financing to bring into production.

2 Management

When we look at management, we look at two things: What is their explicit knowledge and what is their tacit knowledge?

Explicit knowledge relates to their educational background and training. Are they engineers? Are they geologists? MBAs? Lawyers? Then I overlap that with tacit knowledge. How much industry experience do they have? Do they really have hands-on knowledge? What is their industry knowledge of the brokerage business and mutual fund business? Who are their relationships?

The ability to raise capital and to communicate are very, very important for shareholder evaluation. Research has shown that the gold companies that have the highest price-to-book ratio also have the highest number of retail shareholders and generally they have higher valuations than their peers.

A good executive team is one with great communications skills and one that appreciates both retail and institutional investors, and the smartest executives focus on the return-on-capital model. When I talk with these managers, I'll ask about their knowledge of the capital markets. This is important because quite often the heads of junior companies are geologists or engineers who may know the rocks but they have no relationships in the brokerage business. The idea of capital information and capital valuation comes from relationships and confidence, and many of these technical types have little interest in the capital markets.

This lack of relationships impedes their ability to generate market support and earn the confidence of institutional brokers. Even their access to newsletter writers, who are a key source of information, is very limited until they have a proven track record.

I've seen cases where a gold company has great assets but it isn't recognised in the public arena because its leaders don't have the correct relationships or communication skills. Potential investors just don't let anyone come in the door and say 'Hey, I have a good idea – buy my idea!' It takes relationship nurturing to build trust and the ability to communicate the opportunities and risks.

I find some of the most successful company builders in the gold-mining industry are what I call the 'financial engineers' – people who have the relationships and understand the capital markets and how to generate returns, and who may have some technical training and know how to hire the best geological and engineering teams. We tend to have more confidence investing in them.

Pierre Lassonde, the former Newmont CEO discussed earlier in this chapter, is a classic example of a 'financial engineer'. He was trained as an engineer but later worked as a money manager and built a tremendous network of relationships. Back in the 1980s he teamed up with Seymour Schulich, now one of the most prominent financiers in Canada, to form Franco-Nevada Mining Corp. to buy gold royalty companies because they had the highest returns on capital. For every $10 000 invested with them, the investor made $1 million over a 15-year period.

3 Money

When you are looking at a gold exploration company, you have to have the same mindset and business model that a venture capitalist would use. These companies spend substantial amounts over several years with no cash flow, which creates inherent risks if there are delays in building the mine. As a potential investor, you have to try to determine this burn rate and whether the company will have to come back to the capital markets for additional financing.

This is important because if the company doesn't make a discovery after spending its first couple of million dollars and it needs more money to continue, the stock will fall. Everyone will suspect 'there's no goods' and they will sell the stock down. This is not the Internet boom of the late 1990s, where a startup company's status derived from how fast it burned through its investors' money. The gold equities market is efficient at judging reserves per share, so if the exploration company doesn't come up with the results necessary to get an evaluation, investors quickly lose confidence.

When we're looking at a junior company, first we try to determine how much cash it has. If it has $25 million and it's spending $5 million a month, it will have no cash in five months. What value is it going to deliver in that time? As an exploration company, it has to deliver reserves per share – in other words, to have a chance at another round of financing, it has to discover enough gold to be able to convince the capital markets that it is an attractive investment on a per share basis.

The math is simple: exploration reserves are valued at approximately one third of the value of a producing mine's reserves. If the industry averages $150 per ounce for a producing company, a junior explorer's reserves will be valued at roughly $50 per ounce. So if the junior company doesn't find gold for less than $50 per ounce, it will run out of cash and its stock will fall.

There is an old rule when it comes to exploration companies: never pay more than two times cash per share if there are no assets in the ground. For comparison's sake, at the top of the technology boom, startup companies were trading at 10 to 20 times cash per share. I've seen similar ratios for mining exploration companies when investors get so feverishly excited about the sector. That is a clear sign of a bubble. When junior exploration companies with no reserves go from two times their cash per share to five times, that is normal market behaviour. But when they go to 10 times, watch out!

4 Minerals

The highest price-to-earnings multiples in the mining world belong to gold mining companies. Gold companies also have the highest industry valuations based on other metrics, including price to cash flow, price to enterprise value and price to reserves per share.

We've found that companies operating mines that produce gold and a significant amount of another metal, typically copper, tend to have lower valuations than pure gold companies or companies whose production is nearly all gold. Continuing down the scale, pure copper companies tend to have even lower valuations.

Why is this important? At the top of a gold price cycle, copper/gold deposits end up rising to the same multiples as pure gold companies. That's because the market's focus is on the gold component of overall production.

So when it comes to picking stocks in anticipation of an upward price move for gold, the investor's margin of safety is increased by selecting companies with both gold and copper production. That's because those companies are cheaper to buy on a discounted cash-flow basis, and when the gold price starts running, the market treats these companies like pure gold companies.

When the gold run-up is at its pinnacle, all of these gold and gold-copper companies historically trade at 35× cash flow per share. An investor who buys a gold-copper stock at 10× cash flow per share stands to see much larger gains than an investor who buys a pure gold producer at 15× cash flow per share.

Another way to generate alpha from copper-gold producers is from the copper itself. This is particularly true when copper prices are strong, as we've seen in recent years. In 2007, Freeport McMoRan, a gold-copper company, saw returns on invested capital of 50%, while Newmont Mining, a pure gold producer, was less than 10%. The gold price has to be greater than $1000 for Newmont to have returns on capital comparable to that of Freeport McMoRan. The difference is the mineral – in this case, copper.

Agnico Eagle is another good example. As we said earlier in this chapter, its zinc and copper byproducts essentially drove down the cash cost of gold production to zero. The company's cash flow absolutely exploded when the zinc prices went through the roof, and this made the stock perform spectacularly well.

Investors should also keep in mind the concept of 'high grading' by gold mining companies during times of low prices and the potential ramifications when prices improve.

When a company engages in high grading, it focuses on mining its best quality ore to get the most gold from every tonne of rock. This can be important to the company's viability during lean times because it generates needed cash to keep the mine operating while reducing per ounce production costs.

But there is a potential negative for investors. Depending on how long low gold prices prevail, a gold company that resorts to high grading as a survival measure may deplete or even exhaust its best ore. When prices improve, it may face higher cash costs than its peers because its remaining ore yields less gold per tonne of rock. Higher cash costs mean narrower margins and lower profits per ounce, which can affect that company's stock price.

5 Mine lifecycle

The development and operation of a gold mine is marked by obstacles that have to be overcome, and those obstacles exert a strong influence on share price behaviour.

In the exploration and development phase, the price of a gold stock often follows a course that ends up looking like a double-humped camel. First there's euphoria over exploration results that are better than expected. The stock price rises as investors race to buy shares, thinking they're going to get rich, like it's a lottery ticket.

Then reality sets in – this gold discovery is still years away from being an actual producing mine. First the company has to do a pre-feasibility study, and if things still look good, there's the feasibility study. Millions of dollars have to be raised in the capital markets, all of the permits have to be secured, heavy equipment has to be bought and transported to the mine site, sources of water and electricity have to be found, and so on.

At this point, there's a huge correction in the stock price because only a tiny percentage of gold discoveries actually become mines. We've looked at hundreds of projects over several decades, in gold and other minerals, and have found that the share price tends to fall to the square root of its peak. If the initial excitement drives the share price from $1 to $9, it wouldn't be a surprise for the onset of reality to bring shares back down to around $3, the square root of $9. At this point, 80% or more of those early shareholders have gotten out of the stock.

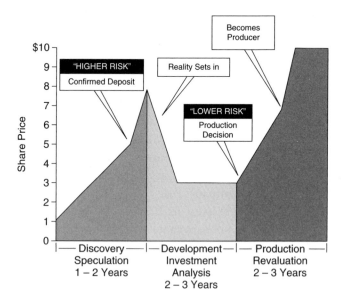

Chart 12.7 Hypothetical life cycle of a mining share.
(Source: Pierre Lassonde, *The Gold Book*)

This same pattern is also seen in other industries, such as biotechnology. A company makes a breakthrough discovery in genetic research or a promising new cancer drug and its stock skyrockets. Then reality sets in – the company faces years of additional research and testing and uncertainty that in the end the treatment will pass muster with federal regulators. The share price retreats sharply as a result.

Back to the gold mine, assuming the company continues down the path to development, its share price drifts sideways until around six months before the first ounce of gold is expected to be produced. At this point, most of the uncertainty about the project coming to fruition is gone and the company is on the verge of generating income after years of being a money pit. The stock begins a strong new leg up when a more sophisticated set of shareholders – oftentimes institutional investors – come into the market. Eventually the price drops off and then levels as the speculative money moves on to the next hot opportunity and the company transitions from explorer to producer.

A classic example of such a 'camel-back' can be seen in the chart below for Goldcorp in the 1990s as it developed its first project, the ultra-rich Red Lake Mine in northern Canada.

Goldcorp was reorganised in early 1994 as a result of a merger and its newly issued stock traded under $3 until early 1995, when it announced a significant discovery at Red Lake in an area that was previously thought to not have any commercial potential. This news excited investors, and Goldcorp's share price more than tripled by early 1996.

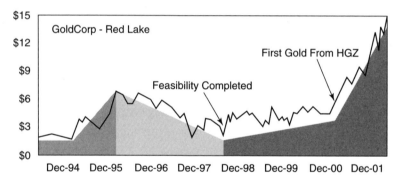

Chart 12.8 Goldcorp shares after Red Lake discovery.

Then came further exploration, permitting and feasibility studies, and you can see the stock price fall from its first peak back to the $3 level during this period due to project uncertainty. When a key feasibility study is finished in late 1998, the price trend for Goldcorp shares slowly starts back up again as confidence grows that the mine will come into production.

Shares then take off to new heights in early 2001 when the first gold is produced from Red Lake's high grade zone (HGZ), one of the world's richest gold concentrations ever found at more than two ounces of gold per tonne of rock.

This mine lifecycle doesn't stop with the early production. To remain an attractive investment relative to its peers, the company must adhere to the return-on-capital model by increasing its production, increasing its reserves and increasing its cash flow.

We strongly believe in using cycles to better manage risks and expectations, and we see this as a way for others to manage their emotions when it comes to investing. Knowing where a company is on the mine lifecycle can be a tremendous asset to an investor in gold equities who seeks to minimise risk and optimise performance. It's one more tool the investor can use to try to manage volatility and his own market expectations.

Managing Volatility

We've said it several times already, and it's worth saying it again – gold stocks are prone to volatile price swings that can be much greater in intensity and frequency than other equity sectors.

So how do you manage that volatility? As professional money managers, we spend a lot of time talking about volatility, among ourselves and to our fund shareholders. We've published a two-part research piece titled 'Anticipate Before You Participate' that emphasises the importance of being ever mindful of volatility. We'll cover some of that territory here as we apply it to our gold equity funds.

In the previous chapter we offered some steps you can take to manage risk in your gold investments.

The first and most important step is to address volatility as 'moderation' – limit your exposure to the asset class. Our unwavering suggestion is to have no more than 10% of your portfolio invested in gold, with a maximum allocation of 5% in bullion and 5% in gold equities. You should also rebalance your portfolio at least annually to keep your desired level of diversification.

Neither of these steps will guarantee profits or protection from losses in a declining market, but they could improve your odds of success as an investor.

It's key that investors appreciate standard deviation and the power of mean reversion to understand the cyclical patterns of volatility over different time lines.

Standard deviation

Standard deviation, also known by its Greek letter 'sigma', is a valuable statistical tool for gauging a fund's volatility, as it measures how much the fund's returns vary from their mean, or average, over a given period of time.

For most funds, returns will be within one standard deviation, or one sigma, of their mean 68% of the time and within two standard deviations (two sigma) of the mean 95% of the time. Returns fall within three sigma 99% of the time.

You can see this basic concept in the bell-shaped curve below, which we use as a simple illustration – a real sigma curve would likely be slightly distorted to the right or left of centre.

The straight line down from the highest point on the curve is the mean (average) return over the specified time period. The area in dark grey is one sigma above and below the mean. By adding the area in medium grey, you have gone out two sigma on either side of the mean. The light grey segments expand the shaded area to three sigma.

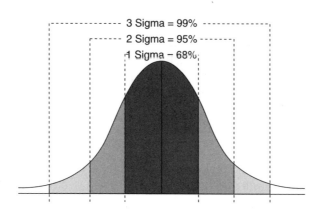

Chart 12.9 Standard deviation (sigma) measures degree of variance from average.

As an investor, sigma can help you understand the level of volatility to expect from a particular investment. That knowledge allows you to manage your risk and it keeps you from getting overly excited when your investment's ups and downs fall within its normal range. It can also help you identify when to buy or sell a stock or a fund.

Let's look at the Gold and Precious Metals Fund, one of U.S. Global Investors' most volatile funds, as an example of how to use sigma.

For the five years ending December 31, 2007, that fund has had a weekly sigma of 4.60%. That means if you marked each weekly return for the last five years on a graph, you could expect 68% of those marks to be within 4.60% above or below the average (mean) return. 95% of those marks would predictably fall within 9.20% above or below the mean return because that's two sigma.

Standard Deviation (as of 12/31/07) based on 5-Year Data

	5-day	20-day	60-day
Gold and Precious Metals Fund (USERX)	4.60%	9.24%	15.88%
World Precious Minerals Fund (UNWPX)	4.60%	9.63%	16.57%
Global Resources Fund (PSPFX)	3.49%	7.26%	11.82%
Eastern European Fund (EUROX)	3.57%	6.88%	10.53%
China Region Opportunity Fund (USCOX)	3.13%	6.44%	11.36%
Holmes Growth Fund (ACBGX)	2.31%	4.14%	6.20%
All-American Equity Fund (GBTFX)	2.34%	4.45%	6.46%
Global Megatrends Fund (MEGAX)	1.76%	3.19%	5.42%
AMEX Gold Bugs Index (HUI)	4.74%	9.16%	15.01%
S&P 500 Index	1.67%	2.93%	4.81%

Chart 12.10 Standard deviation for U.S. Global funds and key indexes as of 12-31-07, based on 5-year data.

A gain of 4% in a week might sound exceptional for an investment, but for the Gold and Precious Metals Fund, that level of return falls within the range of normal over the past five years. Likewise, a weekly drop of 4% can sound scary, but if you know the sigma for the Gold and Precious Metals Fund, you know that too is within its normal movement.

But because different funds have different sigmas, not all price movements mean the same thing. For instance, looking at our monthly table for standard deviations, you can see that one sigma for the World Precious Minerals Fund is plus or minus 9.63%. You can also see on the charts that the standard deviations for our gold-oriented funds align closely with the Amex Gold Bugs Index (HUI), one of the two main indexes for US gold equities.

You can also see in the table above how sigma for the HUI compares to the broader equity market as represented by the Standard & Poor's 500 Index, and how that ratio changes with time. The weekly and monthly volatility of the gold index is more than three times that of the S&P 500. A monthly swing of 8.5% for HUI is well within its normal range, but for the S&P that would be nearly a three-sigma event – something that statistically would be expected to occur once every 100 months, or roughly every eight years. When you look at the quarterly sigma for the indexes, you might expect them to be triple that of the monthly sigma, but in reality they are both less than twice the monthly figure because the longer time period mitigates the short term emotional moves.

When it comes to managing sigma, I think we look at different factors than does the average active money manager. We like to raise our cash levels or invest our cash, depending on which way the market is going, because we have observed that investors often come in at the wrong time and we want to try to protect the cash as much as possible.

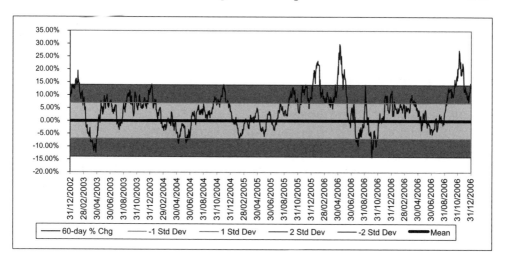

Chart 12.11 Applying standard deviation to gold price fluctuations.

On the chart above, you can see the price movements of gold (expressed in sigma) over the past five years. The mean price over the period is marked by the black line, and the jagged ups and downs depict the deviations from that mean over rolling periods of 60 trading days. The light grey bands represent one sigma movement from the mean, while the darker bands denote one to two sigma above or below the mean price.

When we see the gold price approach or exceed two sigma above the long term mean, our models call for raising our cash levels because statistically speaking the odds overwhelmingly favour a price decline. Conversely, when the price dips close to or beyond two sigma below the mean, the odds favour a recovery so our models tell us to invest our cash. This is nothing more than following the statistical signposts in an attempt to buy low and sell high.

In the spring of 2006, you can see on the chart that the gold price was more than three sigma above the mean. This meant that the odds of a correction were statistically greater than 99%, so we raised the cash level in our gold funds to nearly 40%. In mid-May came one of the most abrupt corrections ever, with gold falling about 20% in 20 trading days.

Mean reversion

Mean reversion is a theory rooted in mathematics that, when applied to investing, holds that prices tend to move back toward their mean (average) over the long term. This is the basis for the common investment strategy of buying an undervalued stock or asset class in the expectation that in time it will rise to its 'true' value, or selling an overvalued commodity in the expectation that it will drop back down to its long term average.

It's important to realise that the mean value can climb, stay flat or fall with the passage of time, so a price that would have been well above the mean 25 years ago may actually be below the mean today.

It's also important to keep in mind that inflection points – when a price peaks or bottoms out and starts moving back toward the mean – are not on a fixed schedule of occurrence, nor is it assured that any singular reversion will actually reach the long term mean before changing direction again. Mean reversion theory does not provide any guarantees of price direction – rather it helps manage expectations by defining a long term trend (the mean) and offering probabilities that any given price might be a candidate for reversion based on past behaviour.

The chart below is what we call 'the periodic table' because it looks like the periodic table of the earth's elements used in chemistry. The name is also suitable because it depicts the periodic rotation of the various asset classes in terms of their relative returns. That rotation is another useful visual in explaining mean reversion.

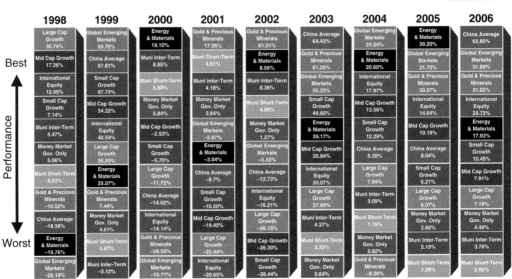

Chart 12.12 Sector performance rotates year to year.

Let's look specifically at gold and precious minerals. From 1998 to 2000, that sector twice had negative returns and each year it was among the worst performers among the 11 categories that cover our key investment sectors. The dollar was strong back then, and the fact that gold and other resources are priced in dollars contributed to their relative weakness. The Internet boom was firing up for much of that time, so small-cap and mid-cap growth stocks did well until the bust in 2000, when the fixed income sector bobbed to the top.

Then from 2001 through 2003, as markets struggled in the wake of the high-tech implosion, gold equities outperformed all of the other sectors by a wide margin. Growth stocks tumbled to the bottom for a couple of years before the S&P 500 posted a strong recovery in 2003.

After three years at or near the top, gold stocks plummeted in 2004 and were the worst performers before they bounced back with strength in 2005 and 2006.

Correlation

When deciding when to buy or sell a gold mining stock, an investor should keep in mind a number of correlations that can help with that decision. There are both positive and negative correlations, and they function independently of what's going on within the company itself.

The most reliable correlation for gold stocks is the price of gold itself. When the price of bullion is rising, gold mining companies tend to see increased revenue and profits, and thus they are viewed as being more valuable. The correlation works the other way as well – a falling bullion price usually drags down the gold mining stocks due to revenue and profit worries. Over any short period, that correlation can weaken but in the longer term, it is very strong.

There are other correlations that relate to gold and gold stocks. We'll discuss some of the most prominent and how we use them to help us with investment decisions.

We're not going to provide an exhaustive analysis of these complex correlations. Individual investors shouldn't get too caught up in the details, but they should know about them in general so they can better manage their expectations.

Gold and oil

There is a very strong positive correlation between oil and gold over the long term, meaning the price of each tends to move in the same direction.

A key reason is that when the price of oil is strong, the major oil-exporting countries see much greater inflows of foreign currency, and they often diversify those foreign reserves by investing a portion of it in gold. This action increases gold demand and thus price.

Measuring on a scale of 0 (no correlation) to 1 (perfect correlation), the five-year correlation for oil to gold is about 0.9, or 90%. Over a three-year period, the correlation is about 0.8. Short-term volatility for either gold or oil can weaken that correlation for a while, but sooner or later it tends to revert to its mean.

As investors, we do risk management analysis that looks at the short term correlation and the long term correlation to try to predict the price for gold now and in the future. One of the important questions we ask in that analysis is 'Where do you think the price of oil is going?'

If we see factors that indicate a strong upward movement in oil's price, we ask ourselves whether we think that the increase is just a supply blip caused by a temporary factor or if it represents a fundamental shift in supply or demand patterns that is sustainable in the longer term.

Based on that answer, we form probabilistic models that set a price range for oil over a certain period that we would express as, say, $20 to the upside from the current price and $10 to the downside over the next year.

From the parameters of that model we construct a separate model for bullion that also uses an upside-downside price range, and based on that we look at the relative attractiveness of gold stocks during the same period.

Over the last four decades or so, there has been an average 15:1 ratio between the prices of gold and oil – that is, one ounce of gold would be able to purchase 15 barrels of oil.

In the late 1990s, that ratio went to about 30:1 when gold was around $300 per ounce and oil was at $10 per barrel. But in early 2008, that ratio had gone the other way to 10:1 – gold was around $900 to $1000 per ounce and oil hovered around $100 per barrel. Since 1970, each time the ratio has been under 10:1 or above 20:1, or one standard deviation lower or higher than the historical average, it has rebounded to the mean or higher within a few years.

At 15:1, if oil remained around $100 a barrel, the price of gold would top $1500 an ounce. Even if oil fell to $80, the historic ratio could make a compelling case for $1200 gold.

Some market pundits point to this ratio as the most important tool for gauging the gold price, but we disagree. These patterns help apply a probability model, and when overlaid with other probability tools like 60-day oscillators and histograms, investors can better understand the price risk of markets, though not the fundamental value risk.

Currency correlations

Because gold is money, it is traded against the dollar, the euro and other currencies in foreign-exchange markets.

When comparing gold to the dollar, we find that 70% of the time, gold and the dollar move in the opposite direction – that is, they have an inverse correlation.

Currency strength also become a consideration when it comes to picking gold stocks in specific countries.

South Africa, the world's largest gold producing nation, provides a good example of the currency factor. South African gold companies there need a weak rand to prosper because their deep underground mines have the highest operating costs in the world. So to get an index-beating return, investors have to either overweight or underweight the South African gold producers, depending on the condition of the rand.

For instance, several years ago, when our Gold and Precious Metals Fund was the top-performing gold fund in the United States, one of the big drivers was that we had a tremendous overweighting in South African gold stocks, which more than doubled that year.

The rand was trading around 14 : 1 to the dollar at that time. Then currencies reversed and the rand started to get strong versus the dollar. Eventually the exchange rate got down to around 7 : 1 – basically the rand doubled in value. Gold bullion went up $100 an ounce, but all of the South African gold stocks fell in value because the appreciation of the rand hurt their profit margins. There was a rotation by investors to North American producers, driven to a large degree by relative currency values. Foreign exchange swings can have a significant impact on cash flow for mining companies.

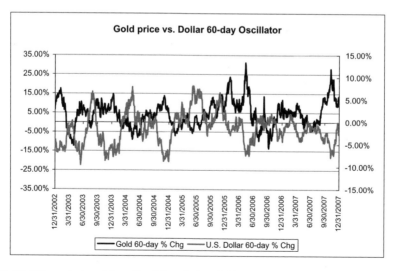

Chart 12.13 The relationship of gold and the dollar.

The chart on page 247 shows how we view the price movements of gold compared to the dollar. In mid-May 2006, the spread between these two currencies was at its most extreme, with gold over $700 and the dollar hitting what were then record lows against the euro.

With gold up more than two standard deviations over 60 trading days and the dollar down sharply, we saw little upside potential for gold and went to nearly 40% cash in our gold funds as a defensive manoeuvre. It proved to be a successful, low-risk decision – over the next 20 trading days, gold fell off by more than 20% in one of the most dramatic corrections ever as the dollar recovered from its depths. This illustrates the power of mean reversion.

The spread between gold and the dollar is what signals caution or opportunity to increase weightings in either currency. We prefer never to gamble 100%, but rather to be gradual and opportunistic. Under normal circumstances it's a gradual process to either invest or disinvest in gold.

Gold Seasonality

On top of all of the other correlations for gold, there's also one that relates to the calendar. Given that the price of gold is the strongest influence on the price of gold equities, this correlation is worth a mention.

On the dark line on the chart measuring the Comex futures contracts on page 249, you can see that the relative strength of gold bottoms out in late August and early September. The lighter line shows the historical pattern over three decades, with the late-summer period also being one of the weakest times of the year.

Gold prices have risen every September since 2000 as investors in Europe and North America wrap up their summer holiday season and a cluster of holidays take place around the world for which gold is bought and given as gifts.

India is the world's largest market by volume for gold jewellery, and jewelers there typically begin stocking up on gold for the fall festival and wedding seasons. Gold, in the form of intricately crafted jewellery, is a traditional gift for Indian brides whose parents want them to have not only something beautiful they can wear, but also an enduring financial asset.

The second largest market for gold jewellery by volume and the largest by retail value is the United States, according to the World Gold Council. The greatest demand is seen late in the year – not only from Christmas shoppers, but also from Indians and other prosperous immigrant communities that have brought their cultural affinity for gold to their new homeland.

In mid-September, Muslims begin their most important holiday season – the month-long observation of Ramadan. Fasting, prayers and introspection are

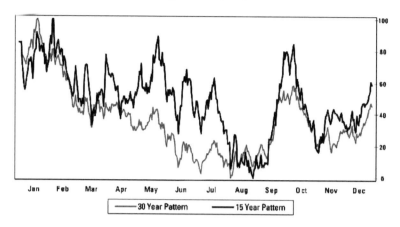

Chart 12.14 Gold's price fluctuations with seasonal demand trends.
(Source: Moore Research Center, Inc.)

stressed during Ramadan, but the end of the solemn holy month is marked by a period of celebration and gift-giving. And in late December comes Eid ul-Adha, a four-day festival of sacrifice that also features the giving of gifts.

Going back to the chart, we can see these demand drivers at work. The 30-year and 15-year trend lines both show a sharp spike in relative strength in the early fall and then another one in the final six weeks of the calendar year.

Based on the long-term record, this time of year may represent a good entry point for those who want to buy gold in advance of a seasonal upswing in demand. Managing expectations by using historical patterns can improve the chances for success but of course it doesn't guarantee against losses.

13

Gold Mining Opportunities and Threats

If there's one thing a gold equity investor can rely on, it's that the price of bullion will have its ups and downs and so will the share prices of the companies that produce it. But after that less than profound bit of wisdom, what are the other factors that an investor should be mindful of as he navigates the world of gold stocks?

In late 2007, U.S. Global Investors co-hosted a webcast with Paul Burton, editor and publisher of the World Gold Analyst and one of the best observers of the global gold sector. The webcast was called 'Gold: Thriving or Surviving?', and it addressed the current state of the industry and what might be in store in the coming years.

The presentation identified five key trends for the gold mining industry that investors should know and consider when thinking about taking positions in companies. Those trends include a geographical shift in gold mining, current and future production, exploration spending, industry consolidation and cost pressures.

These challenges are not always neatly compartmentalised – for instance, it would be difficult if not impossible to entirely separate exploration spending and future production, or rising costs and the ongoing consolidation within the industry. That said, we have tried to frame and analyse each key trend from the viewpoint of a gold equity investor to offer perspective on the opportunities and threats attached to each so the investor can make informed choices and manage expectations.

To help illustrate our points, we have tried to incorporate current examples from the gold industry to take what might otherwise be dry and theoretical information and make it easier to comprehend by applying it to real world situations. It might be too late to get in early on the companies that we mention in our examples, but learning the broader lessons could be beneficial in recognising similar opportunities in the future.

Geographical Shift

Back in the mid-1990s, gold production was dominated by four countries – South Africa, the United States, Australia and Canada. Together these nations accounted for more than half of the world's gold output.

But by 2006, these four major sources of gold saw their share of global production drop to around 36%. South Africa remained the top gold producer, a position it assumed in the early twentieth century, but its output tumbled more than 40% between 1996 and 2006. Canada and the United States fell 37% and 23%, respectively, and Australia slipped about 16%.

Large scale gold production has expanded into other countries, and this shift creates new opportunities for gold equity investors. China's gold output rose from around 160 tonnes in 1996 to nearly 250 tonnes a decade later to replace Australia as the third largest gold producing nation. In 2007 China overtook the United States to become No. 2, and by some estimates it also surpassed South Africa to become the world's top producer.

Peru's relative increase was even more dramatic – it more than tripled during the ten years to roughly 200 tonnes of gold in 2006 after several major mines opened, including South America's largest, the open-pit Yanacocha mine co-owned mostly by Newmont Gold and Compania de Minas Buenaventura, based in Peru. Russia, long known for its large deposits, realised a 30% hike in production. Those two nations are now in the top ten among gold-producing nations.

Other countries have also emerged in recent years, among them Indonesia, Mexico, Argentina and Chile in South America, some of the former Soviet republics and several countries in western Africa.

The emergence of new gold mining territories provides opportunities for junior exploration companies to establish themselves as bona fide gold producers. For individual stock investors and gold funds, this represents a chance to get in early on stocks that could rapidly appreciate in value, either due to takeovers by larger miners or by development of new mines.

Of course, as we discussed in the previous chapter, it's not always easy to identify these companies among the many hundreds of them out drilling cores in the far-flung corners of the world. And if you are savvy or lucky enough to pick a winner, don't forget the double-humped camel chart associated with the lifecycle of a mine – given the years needed to bring a mine into production, there's a good chance that the stock price pop accompanying the discovery will fade back and begin trading sideways until the first production, if it ever gets that far.

When it comes to takeovers, statistics gathered by the Metal Economics Group found that in 2006 companies buying other companies or their projects placed the greatest premium on Latin America, which is considered the most promising gold frontier. Companies seeking to establish a position in Mexico or South America paid an average of $150 per ounce of gold resources, roughly double the price of the same ounce in Australia or Canada and triple that of Africa, Asia or the United States.

China's gold industry includes thousands of small, privately owned mines producing just a few thousand ounces per year, and as a result it is unconsolidated, undercapitalised and inefficient. There are, however, a growing number of world class projects that involve publicly traded foreign operators. These veteran operators are bringing in big budgets, modern equipment and the latest techniques for both exploration and production to make low grade deposits worth developing. China is one of the few places where gold production is accelerating and valuations are relatively inexpensive.

But there are challenges in nations where large scale gold mining is emerging as a new industry. First, there's the question of political stability – many of the fastest growing gold provinces are in African, South American and Asian countries where central governments may be subject to military overthrow, well-armed ethnic opposition in the hinterlands and other hazards to longevity. Will a deal made with today's leadership last long enough to bring a gold project into production?

In addition, the managers of companies working to develop projects in these countries have to find local partners that both understand financial markets and can serve as the developer's eyes, ears and advocate. Relationships with political figures and labour officials need nurturing and bewildering bureaucracies often must be navigated to obtain the necessary permits to operate. In China it has been particularly difficult for foreign companies to successfully make their way through the regulatory system.

A good example of regulatory and partnership risk is Mundoro Mining, a junior Canadian company with a 79% interest in the huge Maoling gold project in north-east China. Mundoro has invested in an extensive drilling programme and feasibility studies at Maoling, which has gold reserves and resources estimated at more than 9 million ounces, but as of the second half of 2007, Mundoro's business licence had expired and its efforts to secure a renewal were coming up empty. On top of that, the company was served written notice by the Liaoning provincial government, its joint venture partner, that it may move to terminate their deal.

Such risks are not exclusive to emerging gold nations – aggressive exploration companies working in new regions can also act against the best interests of their shareholders. In mid-2007, Canadian junior company Southwestern Resources revealed that its Boka gold project in China had significantly less resources than initially reported. The company has taken legal action against its former chief executive and former general manager at Boka, accusing them of fraud and insider trading for allegedly tampering with the project's database to make the deposit appear richer than it actually was.

Gold Production Peak

The following chart shows a decade's worth of gold production that depicts a steady climb to 2001, when gold production hit its all-time peak of nearly 2650 metric tonnes, followed by five erratic years culminating with 2006, when the world's output was 2475 metric tonnes, 6.6% off the peak.

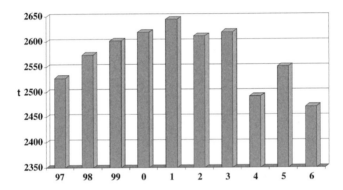

Chart 13.1 Gold production has declined significantly since 2001.
(Source: World Gold Analyst)

There are a number of factors behind this trend line, key among them a lack of exploration in the late 1990s when the price of gold was very low. We have discussed that it takes years to build a new gold mine after an economic deposit is discovered, given the feasibility studies that must be conducted, the rounds of financing and the many permits that must be secured. All of these obstacles contribute to the 'delays and disappointments' that often are encountered when trying to bring a new mine into production.

Back in the late 1990s, there was another variable as well – the Bre-X gold mine scandal. Bre-X Minerals Ltd, a junior Canadian mining company, claimed that it discovered a massive gold deposit in the jungles of Borneo in Indonesia and its stock rocketed up to more than $200 per share. It soon came out during the geological assessment that Bre-X's super-rich discovery was in fact the greatest fraud in mining history. When it became known that Bre-X salted its core samples with gold dust to make the deposit appear larger than it was, the company's stock collapsed and investors – among them several large pension funds – lost $4 billion in equity. This in turn led to a litany of lawsuits and an overhaul of Canada's stock markets that pretty much dried up capital for junior gold companies during this low price period.

The result was that gold exploration, already waning, was cut back even further as venture capital turned its attention to the booming high-tech sector and gold producers focused on their existing projects, oftentimes using high grading of ore deposits to keep their cash costs under control. Between 1997 and 2001 there was no significant exploration and very few new gold deposits were found.

Fast-forwarding to the present, the turmoil leading up to the turn of the millennium leaves us with a dearth of new production coming on line. Some copper-gold projects have been revived and reworked due to high prices for both metals, so it's not totally bleak, but even these projects are few and far between.

The largest companies in the industry are finding it difficult just to maintain current production levels. They are producing about 6 million ounces per quarter, which is the equivalent to two major gold discoveries. They need to keep building reserves and resources and they're not finding that easy because the grass-roots-level projects haven't been there. That is beginning to change, but there is typically a five- to six-year lag in this industry from feasibility study to permitting to construction and finally production.

While some risks were cited in the previous section, good opportunities do exist in China. As of late 2007, about 50 publicly traded companies were active in China's gold and silver industry, and more than 100 projects existed in varying stages of development. Sino Gold probably has one of the higher profiles, given its aggressiveness and its success in developing the Jinfeng project that began production in 2007 at a rate of 180 000 ounces per year. It has a number of other projects and joint ventures in the works as well, and its strong relationships have led to offers to take part in projects around the country. Eldorado Gold has the Tanjianshan project (120 000 ounces per year), and Jinshan Gold Mines Inc. (largely owned by Ivanhoe Mines) was producing from the CSH 217 project in Inner Mongolia that is expected to yield 120 000 ounces per year.

Leyshon Resources, based in Australia, was developing the Zheng Guang mine and its 100 000 ounces of gold and 7000 tonnes of zinc per year. The polymetallic (multi-metal) deposits such as Zheng Guang may be the lowest risk investments, particularly when industrial metal prices are relatively strong, because the operator can create more than one revenue stream from the same pit.

Also let me re-emphasise the 'return on capital' model discussed in the previous chapter. When sorting through gold stocks, focus on companies with increasing production per share, increasing reserves per share and increasing cash flow per share. These measure how solid the underlying valuations are – companies that meet these criteria are attractive to the investor because they demonstrate capital discipline and get results, and they often become takeover candidates.

In recent years the major gold producers have been more risk-averse when it comes to acquiring projects from the exploration companies as the legal environment has changed, costs have climbed and new projects with a clear path to production have diminished. It used to be that the big boys wouldn't hesitate to buy into an initial discovery. Then they started holding off until there was a reserve calculation, and after that they wouldn't move off the sideline until all of the necessary permits were in hand. Nowadays the prudent move might be to wait until it's certain that new mining projects are actually hitting their production targets. This form of risk management by gold producers can raise the cost of the new reserves obtained and thus lower their profitability, but there also tends to be less money lost on gambles that don't work out. For investors in the junior companies, the euphoria of discovery may not show up in the share price for years into the future.

Exploration Spending

Exploration spending in the mining sector has covered a wide range since the mid-1990s, as the accompanying chart indicates. Spending built up in the years leading up to 1997, when about $5 billion went into the hunt for new sources of minerals, including gold. Then came softening prices and the Bre-X scandal and its impact on the junior companies, and spending fell off steadily until it bottomed out in 2002 at less than $2 billion. In the subsequent four years, exploration has charged up again as prices and the reputation of the junior sector recovered and in 2006 it surpassed $7 billion, a record amount. Not all of that spending relates to gold, but gold has followed the industry trend.

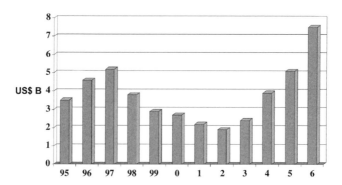

Chart 13.2 Several years of low exploration spending is affecting today's gold supply. (Source: World Gold Analyst)

While this all may look good, there are some caveats that must be considered. One is that the exploration budgets are not adjusted for inflation, so that $7 billion spent in 2006 is not so much different from the $5 billion or so spent a decade earlier.

And on top of that, exploration in the current environment is much costlier than in the late 1990s. Drilling costs have shot up, as have energy expenditures, salaries and environmental compliance costs. It can be very difficult to actually run an exploration project due to a shortage of drilling rigs and related equipment, as well as trained personnel. So while the dollar amounts allocated to exploration may be higher, the impact of each dollar stands to be less.

In addition, gold projects as a percentage of total spending in the mining sector have been falling. Back in the 1990s, gold accounted for as much as 60% of mining exploration, but in 2007 it was down to less than half. More money is being directed towards other resources, including diamonds, uranium, copper and iron ore. And when it comes to gold, much of the spending is on projects already in the advanced stages because of the emphasis on getting those reserves into production to take advantage of current prices. That means a declining share of gold company exploration budgets is going toward the early stage efforts aimed at finding new deposits.

The consolidation of the gold industry has contributed to this significant decline in exploration spending. A couple of examples from the world's biggest companies illustrate this impact.

In the year prior to their 2001 merger, Barrick Gold and Homestake Mining had a combined exploration budget of $149 million, which dropped to $104 million in the subsequent year for a company producing about 6 million ounces of gold per year. For 2007, after more acquisitions that have led Barrick's output to surpass 8 million ounces annually, the company's exploration budget was $170 million, with just half of that directed toward work in 'greenfields', meaning new areas. Newmont Mining also allocated about $170 million to exploration in 2007, but only 20% of that amount was for greenfields work.

Still, whether companies find their own gold or buy another company's discovery, someone has to find the deposit in the first place. This makes clear the paramount importance of exploration efforts as established mines get older and less productive.

It's been said that all of the easy gold has already been found, so that leaves the gold mining industry going further afield to find prospects, just as the oil industry did several decades ago when it ventured to the top edge of Alaska, the North Sea and into the deep Gulf of Mexico, among other places. Of course, working in remote areas lacking roads and other infrastructure is more technically challenging and costs more than similar work closer to the grid. As an investor, you will want to monitor how much a company spends on these pricey projects and what they are getting for results. The less a company spends to discover an ounce of gold, the more accretive that discovery is likely to be to future earnings and future share price if and when it is developed.

But even when a company is successful in its exploration efforts, a changing political and permitting landscape in some countries can create a new set of challenges that must be overcome to get that gold out of the ground. A good example of this is Aurelian Resources' Fruta del Norte, a multi-million-ounce gold-silver prospect in Ecuador. The company announced promising results from test drilling at FDN in July 2007, but a month later Ecuador president Rafael Correa was quoted as saying that he wanted to ban open-pit mines in the country. That news drove Aurelian's stock price down 10% in a day and cast considerable doubt on the company's ability to bring Fruta del Norte into production on a cost-competitive basis.

Scenarios of this nature are all too common, reinforcing the need for investors to keep in mind where they are in the mine lifecycle that we discussed in the previous chapter. In Aurelian's case, optimism from drilling results at FDN and subsequent rounds of financing lifted the stock from 22 cents Canadian per share in April 2006 to a peak of $10 Canadian per share seven months later. That euphoric rise quickly ebbed, with shares falling 30% in just a few weeks before entering a period of volatile trading punctuated by the plunge when the Ecuadorean president spoke of banning surface mines.

In many parts of the world it's not enough to just find the gold – discoveries in these places simply mark the end of a difficult geological journey and the beginning of a political trek strewn with pitfalls that can derail even the most promising project.

Industry Consolidation

There are two ways for gold companies to acquire reserves – by exploration and by acquisition. And the trend in recent years of high prices indicates that it's much quicker to grow bigger by buying the known assets of a rival than by the less certain approach of drilling core samples and filling out permit applications.

In 1996, the ten largest gold-mining companies produced 25% of that year's gold output. In 2006, the top five miners alone – Barrick Gold, Newmont Mining, AngloGold-Ashanti, Gold Fields and Harmony Gold – produced 33% of the new gold and the next five added another 11%.

2006 was a busy year for megadeals, with Barrick and Goldcorp teaming up to buy Placer Dome for $10.4 billion, Goldcorp later taking out Glamis Gold for $9.5 billion and Iamgold acquiring Cambior for $1.2 billion. Altogether the gold mining sector saw more than $25 billion worth of acquisition activity in 2006, more than the previous five years combined. The urge to merge carried over into 2007, with the notable combinations including Kinross Gold's $3 billion purchase of Bema Gold early in the year.

While the pace may have quickened, consolidation has long been a driving force within the gold mining sector. Most junior companies never intend to develop their own mine – their goal from the start, shared by their investors, is to find something of value that will lead to a buyout by a bigger company.

When the gold price is rising, investors can generally count on good assets being bought out at some point by a major producer looking to replace depleted reserves or perhaps a mid-tier company seeking to become a major. For this reason, it is advised that investors in junior companies focus on those with assets that offer solid valuations that will make them attractive to a buyer.

There are a number of recent examples of this flight to growth, among them Goldcorp's buyout of Glamis Gold to take possession of the Penasquito deposit in Mexico and Agnico Eagle's acquisition of Cumberland Resources to get the Meadowbank property in far northern Canada. Companies with good projects stand to be bought at a premium because there is a scarcity of them.

Investors in more senior companies doing the buying should take a different perspective. Consolidation was expected to be a catalyst for higher stock prices for the companies that survived, but given the rising costs facing gold miners, regulatory uncertainties and other factors, many deals have resulted in acquirers overpaying for assets and eventually being forced to write down part of the invest-ment. Most deals are done with optimistic gold prices in mind, so higher gold prices on a sustained basis are necessary to make most acquisitions work. When prices level off or decline, deals made during rosier times don't look as smart.

China's emergence as a major gold producer was accomplished largely without the participation of the senior companies in the West. This could be an area of future consolidation assuming the junior companies at work in China start making sizeable discoveries.

Rising Operating Costs

While gold mining companies are getting much more for their production than a decade ago, they are also paying a lot more to get the gold out of the ground.

As we discussed earlier, operating costs have been rising at a rapid pace in recent years. As you can see in the accompanying table, the average cash cost of production has risen from roughly $170 per ounce at year-end 2001 to more than $250 per ounce at the end of 2004 and on to around $300 per ounce two years later.

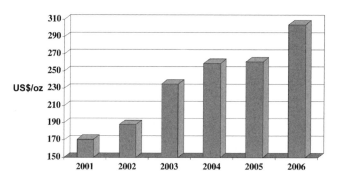

Chart 13.3 Cash costs to produce gold have risen sharply.

The price of fuel for mine equipment has gone up substantially, as have the costs for utilities, labour, mine construction materials (cement, industrial metals, lumber and the like), and chemicals for gold separation. On top of that, the high grading of ore from the years of low prices means many miners have to move and process more rock to get the same ounce of gold, which compounds their cost pressures.

In 2006, the cash cost per ounce climbed about 20% but the price of gold rose by 24%, so miners were able to maintain their margins, though not without some squeeze.

The rapid rise in operating costs has stripped the leverage away from gold equities, and that's a key reason why the mining stocks underperformed bullion through most of 2007.

The escalating cost structure for gold miners showed signs of levelling off in the first half of 2007, which would have boosted profitability of gold miners. But that trend reversed itself in the second half and the cost climb resumed. Late in the year the average cash cost was pushing $400 per ounce. The major producers are having the most difficult time controlling costs, so they would be the ones who would likely benefit most from a revaluation of gold stocks. According to World Gold Analyst, in mid-2007 the emerging producers were being valued at roughly $90 per ounce of gold in the ground, the majors at $100 per ounce and the intermediate producers – the most likely targets of acquisition – were valued at about $180 per ounce in the ground. The inability of the majors to keep a lid on their costs is a key factor in this lower valuation.

Higher costs also amplify the benefits for the polymetallic mining companies – those that produce gold and copper, or gold and one or more other metals in significant quantity – during times of strong commodity prices. It is likely that the market will continue to place a premium on the multi-metal miners, just as it does the companies with high grade gold projects. Per unit costs for these companies are lower than for their competitors, so their profit potential is greater.

Of course, this premium takes us back to the production and exploration challenges facing the industry. Everyone is looking for these properties, but they are not easy to find. If history is a guide, the best place to find one of these polymetallic deposits is near an existing one, so that is where companies will most likely focus their attention. Doing this would prolong the trend of spending most exploration dollars on brownfields projects, whereas one could argue that the companies' long term viability depends on success in greenfields exploration.

The pursuit and development of large copper-gold porphyry projects will be a dominant theme in the gold mining industry over the next decade, maybe even longer if the emerging-markets-driven demand for copper continues to support high prices for this industrial metal. And when companies find a rich copper-gold-silver deposit, they move quickly to take advantage of market opportunities. A case in point is the Xietongmen project in Tibet, which is governed by China. The Canadian company Continental Minerals discovered the promising mineral resources at Xietongmen in mid-2005, and within about two years it went through several rounds of financing, bought out its Chinese partner in the project and completed a feasibility study that pegged annual production at 190 000 ounces of gold, 1.7 million ounces of silver and 116 million pounds of copper.

Summary

Gold stocks face a number of challenges that historically high gold prices alone cannot remedy. Stock valuations are based on future earnings, and for gold miners, it is not clear how bullion prices will behave going forward or how successful the companies will be in facing their biggest obstacles – controlling their operating costs and replenishing their reserves.

PART THREE
APPENDIX

Fact Book: Gold Statistical Information Tables

(Information courtesy Virtual Metals: www.virtualmetals.co.uk)

World Total Supply and Demand (Tonnes)

	2003	2004	2005	2006	2007e	2008f
Supply						
Mine Supply	2512	2351	2411	2387	2413	2414
Scraps recycling	900	1100	938	1057	991	917
Hedging	196	69	84	40	42	25
Central Bank sales	571	464	616	379	583	495
Total supply	4171	3983	3947	3845	4016	3751
Demand						
Jewellery fabrication	2808	2878	2996	2276	2257	2334
Legal tender coins	85	91	101	102	90	92
Electronics	310	332	357	372	403	416
Other end uses	315	350	393	315	311	313
ETFs	33	125	192	253	241	178
Central bank purchases	39	61	39	132	54	61
Dehedging	529	524	223	482	442	235
Total demand	4119	4382	4304	3912	3796	3628
Residual						
Supply less demand	52	(378)	(357)	(70)	220	123

Total Demand by Region

Total demand by region			(tonnes)			
	2003	2004	2005	2006	2007e	2008f
North America	827	816	844	1036	853	645
Western Europe	777	823	818	739	742	737
Asia	857	887	931	800	794	832
India	698	747	819	516	540	608
Middle East	524	552	631	518	447	456
Latin America	104	131	79	68	67	63
Africa	129	204	36	65	72	105
Australasia	150	147	81	95	192	92
Eastern Europe	53	54	61	76	89	99

Primary Mine Supply

Primary mine supply, 2003–2008f (tonnes)						
	2003	2004	2005	2006	2007e	2008f
South Africa	375.8	343.0	294.8	272.0	260.0	245.0
Ghana	70.0	60.0	66.5	72.0	80.0	75.0
Mali	48.0	40.0	44.2	62.0	64.0	68.0
Tanzania	45.0	48.0	45.5	45.0	42.0	50.0
Guinea	16.5	13.0	13.0	14.0	14.5	15.0
Other Africa	11.9	10.9	15.7	18.6	14.0	15.0
Congo (Dem Rep)	5.0	5.0	5.0	5.0	5.0	6.0
Ethiopia	6.0	6.0	6.0	6.0	6.0	6.0
Sudan	5.0	5.0	5.0	3.5	5.0	5.0
Zimbabwe	12.6	20.0	14.0	11.0	8.7	5.0
Cote d'Ivoire	2.0	0.0	2.0	1.4	2.0	3.0
Total Africa	**597.9**	**550.9**	**511.7**	**510.4**	**501.2**	**493.0**
China	213.0	220.0	224.0	240.0	260.0	260.0
Indonesia	147.0	100.0	142.0	110.9	147.9	125.0
Other Asia	16.7	10.7	10.7	9.2	22.0	30.0
Mongolia	12.0	16.0	18.0	18.0	18.0	20.0
Japan	8.2	8.0	7.5	7.5	7.3	7.0
Philippines	5.8	5.0	6.2	6.0	6.5	7.0
North Korea	5.0	5.0	5.0	5.0	5.0	5.0
Total Asia	**407.7**	**364.7**	**413.4**	**396.6**	**466.7**	**454.0**

Primary mine supply, 2003–2008f (tonnes) (Continued)

	2003	2004	2005	2006	2007e	2008f
Australia	284.0	253.0	264.0	244.0	253.0	250.0
Papua New Guinea	66.0	71.0	68.7	59.0	60.0	65.0
New Zealand	10.0	11.0	11.0	10.0	9.0	10.0
Fiji	3.6	4.0	2.8	1.7	2.8	3.0
Other Australasia	0.0	0.0	0.0	0.0	0.0	0.0
Total Australasia	**363.6**	**339.0**	**346.5**	**314.7**	**324.8**	**328.0**
Russia	158.0	159.0	168.0	165.0	159.0	160.0
Uzbekistan	86.0	90.0	86.0	86.0	88.0	88.0
Kazakhstan	20.0	22.0	22.0	20.0	23.0	21.0
Kyrgyzstan	22.5	22.0	17.0	11.0	15.0	19.0
Other Eastern Europe	10.0	9.0	7.7	4.2	8.0	10.0
Total Eastern Europe	**296.5**	**302.0**	**300.7**	**286.2**	**293.0**	**298.0**
Sweden	5.8	5.7	6.0	5.2	6.8	5.0
Spain	7.0	7.0	5.0	3.0	3.0	2.5
Other Western Europe	11.2	8.9	6.5	6.3	9.3	3.3
Total Western Europe	**24.0**	**21.6**	**17.5**	**14.5**	**19.1**	**10.8**
India	3.3	5.0	3.4	2.5	3.5	4.0
Total Indian sub-continent	**1.4**	**3.3**	**5.0**	**3.4**	**2.5**	**3.5**
Peru	172.6	173.0	207.8	203.6	180.0	185.0
Chile	38.9	39.0	39.6	42.0	48.0	50.0
Brazil	34.0	34.0	35.0	40.0	42.0	42.0
Colombia	46.5	30.0	35.8	37.0	39.0	38.0
Mexico	22.2	24.0	31.6	33.7	35.0	35.0
Other Latin America	1.6	11.0	15.7	22.2	26.0	35.0
Argentina	28.6	27.0	25.0	43.2	38.0	30.0
Venezuela	15.0	15.0	14.0	16.0	16.0	15.0
Bolivia	7.0	0.0	8.9	9.6	10.0	10.0
Ecuador	4.0	0.0	4.0	4.0	4.0	5.0
Guyana	12.0	12.0	8.2	6.4	6.0	5.0
Nicaragua	3.5	5.0	3.4	3.4	3.6	3.7
Honduras	5.0	4.0	4.5	4.5	4.5	3.0
Dominican Republic	0.0	0.0	0.0	0.0	0.0	0.0
Total Latin America	**390.9**	**374.0**	**433.4**	**465.6**	**452.1**	**456.7**
Saudi Arabia	8.8	8.0	8.0	8.0	8.0	8.0
Other Middle East	0.8	1.0	0.0	0.0	0.0	0.0
Total Middle East	**9.6**	**9.0**	**8.0**	**8.0**	**8.0**	**8.0**
USA	280.0	260.0	261.0	260.0	248.0	250.0
Canada	140.6	129.0	118.5	104.0	105.0	110.0
Total North America	**420.6**	**389.0**	**379.5**	**364.0**	**353.0**	**360.0**
World total	**2 511.6**	**2 351.1**	**2 411.2**	**2 367.0**	**2 413.1**	**2 413.7**

Source: Raw Materials Group, Chamber of Mines, South Africa, News Wires

Inflation Adjusted Gold Price

Inflation-adjusted gold price (in 2007 dollars)

	Nominal gold price ($/oz)	US CPI (2007 = 100)	Real gold price (2007 dollars)
1980	612.6	40.1	1,529.4
1981	459.9	44.2	1,040.7
1982	375.6	46.9	801.1
1983	424.1	48.4	876.1
1984	360.3	50.5	713.6
1985	317.2	52.3	606.7
1986	367.7	53.3	690.2
1987	446.5	55.2	808.4
1988	437.0	57.5	760.2
1989	381.4	60.3	633.0
1990	383.5	63.5	603.9
1991	362.2	66.2	547.1
1992	343.7	68.2	504.0
1993	359.8	70.2	512.4
1994	384.1	72.0	533.1
1995	384.2	74.1	518.7
1996	387.7	76.2	508.5
1997	331.2	78.0	424.5
1998	294.2	79.2	371.3
1999	278.6	81.0	344.2
2000	279.1	83.7	333.5
2001	271.1	86.1	315.0
2002	307.2	87.4	351.4
2003	363.3	89.4	406.3
2004	409.2	91.8	445.7
2005	444.4	94.5	470.3
2006	603.8	96.5	625.7
2007	688.0	100.0	688.0

Source: VM Group   *average year to date, CPI October 2007.

Official Sector Purchases and Sales

Official sector purchases, 2003–2008 (tonnes)

	2003	2004	2005	2006	2007e	2008f
Africa	0.0	0.0	0.0	0.0	0.0	0.0
Asia	7.0	3.1	3.7	6.7	4.3	1.0
Australasia	0.0	0.0	0.0	0.0	0.0	0.0

Official sector purchases, 2003–2008 (tonnes) (Continued)

	2003	2004	2005	2006	2007e	2008f
Eastern Europe	3.5	3.4	5.4	25.3	40.3	50.0
Western Europe	0.0	0.0	0.0	0.0	0.1	0.0
Indian sub-continent	0.0	0.0	0.0	0.0	0.0	0.0
Latin America	28.3	54.8	0.0	0.0	1.8	0.0
Middle East	0.0	0.0	30.0	100.0	18.0	10.0
North America	0.0	0.0	0.0	0.0	0.0	0.0
IMF/BIS	0.0	0.0	0.0	0.0	0.0	0.0
Total	**38.8**	**61.3**	**39.1**	**132.0**	**64.4**	**61.0**

Source: IMF, national central banks websites, VM Group

Official sector sales, 2003–2008f (tonnes)

	2003	2004	2005	2006	2007e	2008f
Africa	57.5	0.0	0.0	0.0	1.0	0.0
Asia	19.8	34.0	66.9	11.0	26.3	10.0
Australasia	0.0	0.0	0.0	0.0	0.0	0.0
Eastern Europe	5.1	0.0	0.0	1.2	15.0	0.0
Western Europe	453.7	410.0	529.0	328.3	517.5	475.0
Indian sub-continent	0.0	0.0	0.0	0.0	0.0	0.0
Latin America	0.0	0.0	0.0	6.0	0.0	0.0
Middle East	20.0	20.0	20.0	20.0	0.0	0.0
North America	15.2	0.0	0.0	2.0	0.0	0.0
IMF/BIS	2.0	0.0	7.0	10.0	22.7	10.0
Total	**573.3**	**464.0**	**622.9**	**378.5**	**582.5**	**495.0**

Source: IMF, national central banks websites, VM Group

Gold Usage in Electronics

Gold usage in electronics, 2003–2008f (tonnes)

	2003	2004	2005	2006	2007e	2008f
Japan	118.5	125.0	131.6	135.5	146.3	150.7
South Korea	46.2	55.5	66.6	69.2	74.8	77.0
Singapore	11.9	13.5	15.4	15.6	16.9	17.4
China	1.7	2.5	3.8	5.7	7.4	8.5
Taiwan	3.1	3.3	3.4	3.6	3.9	4.0
Total Asia	**181.4**	**199.8**	**220.8**	**229.6**	**249.2**	**257.6**

Gold usage in electronics, 2003–2008f (tonnes) (Continued)

	2003	2004	2005	2006	2007e	2008f
Australia	0.5	0.5	0.5	0.6	0.6	0.6
Total Australasia	**0.5**	**0.5**	**0.5**	**0.5**	**0.6**	**0.6**
Russia	15.6	16.0	16.5	17.2	18.6	19.1
Total Eastern Europe	**15.6**	**16.0**	**16.5**	**17.2**	**18.6**	**19.1**
Germany	10.8	10.8	10.9	11.3	12.2	12.6
France	8.3	8.9	9.5	9.9	10.6	11.0
Switzerland	8.4	8.9	5.4	9.8	10.6	10.9
UK & Ireland	5.7	5.5	5.4	5.6	6.0	6.2
Other Western Europe	33.1	34.1	35.1	36.6	39.5	40.7
Total Western Europe	**40.4**	**41.5**	**42.6**	**44.3**	**47.9**	**49.3**
India	0.1	0.1	0.1	0.1	0.1	0.1
Total Indian sub-continent	**0.1**	**0.1**	**0.1**	**0.1**	**0.1**	**0.1**
Brazil	1.3	1.4	1.4	1.5	1.6	1.6
Mexico	0.1	0.1	0.1	0.1	0.2	0.2
Total Latin America	**1.5**	**1.5**	**1.5**	**1.6**	**1.7**	**1.8**
Israel	0.1	0.1	0.1	0.1	0.1	0.2
Total Middle East	**0.1**	**0.1**	**0.1**	**0.1**	**0.1**	**0.2**
USA	70.1	72.2	74.4	77.4	83.5	86.0
Canada	0.7	0.7	0.7	0.7	0.8	0.8
Total North America	**70.8**	**72.9**	**75.1**	**78.1**	**84.3**	**86.9**
World total	310.4	332.5	357.3	371.6	402.6	415.5

Source: VM Group

Jewellery Fabrication

Jewellery fabrication, 2003–2008f (tonnes)

	2003	2004	2005	2006	2007e	2008f
South Africa	8.0	9.6	9.6	8.2	7.4	7.5
Morocco	10.0	10.0	10.0	6.0	5.7	5.8
Libya	5.0	5.0	5.0	3.0	3.0	3.0
Algeria	5.0	5.0	5.0	3.0	2.9	2.9
Tunisia	1.0	1.0	1.0	0.6	0.7	0.7
Total Africa	**29.0**	**30.6**	**30.6**	**20.8**	**19.6**	**19.8**
China	230.0	240.0	250.0	260.0	234.0	245.7
Indonesia	100.0	100.0	100.0	60.0	57.0	65.6
Thailand	75.0	75.0	70.0	56.0	53.2	54.8
Taiwan	75.0	70.0	70.0	56.0	53.2	53.2
South Korea	50.0	50.0	52.0	31.2	31.5	33.1
Malaysia	50.0	50.0	55.0	33.0	31.4	31.4
Japan	25.0	25.0	25.0	22.5	21.4	20.4

Jewellery fabrication, 2003–2008f (tonnes) (Continued)

	2003	2004	2005	2006	2007e	2008f
Vietnam	25.0	30.0	34.5	20.7	18.5	19.4
Hong Kong	15.0	17.3	20.0	17.0	15.2	15.9
Afghanistan	10.0	10.0	10.0	8.0	7.9	8.0
Singapore	10.0	10.0	10.0	8.0	7.6	7.7
Cambodia	10.0	10.0	10.0	6.0	5.7	6.6
Other Asia	8.0	9.0	9.0	5.4	5.1	5.8
Total Asia	**683.0**	**696.3**	**715.5**	**583.8**	**555.6**	**582.1**
Australia	5.0	5.0	5.5	4.7	4.3	4.3
Total Australasia	**5.0**	**5.0**	**5.5**	**4.7**	**4.3**	**4.3**
Russia	30.0	30.0	35.0	29.8	26.8	27.0
Uzbekistan	3.0	3.0	3.0	2.6	2.3	2.1
Croatia	0.6	0.7	0.7	0.6	0.5	0.5
Bulgaria	0.3	0.3	0.3	0.3	0.3	0.3
Estonia	0.1	0.2	0.2	0.2	0.2	0.1
Total Eastern Europe	**34.0**	**34.2**	**39.2**	**33.4**	**30.1**	**30.1**
Italy	350.0	330.0	320.0	304.0	297.9	283.7
Turkey	225.7	263.6	283.5	192.7	194.0	203.7
UK & Ireland	50.0	49.0	38.0	32.0	31.4	29.9
Spain	30.0	30.0	30.0	28.5	27.9	26.6
Switzerland	30.0	30.0	30.0	28.5	27.9	26.6
Germany	25.0	22.5	22.5	21.4	20.9	20.0
France	22.0	20.0	22.0	20.9	20.5	19.5
Greece	9.0	10.0	10.0	9.5	9.3	8.9
Portugal	10.0	10.0	10.0	9.5	9.3	8.9
Poland	5.2	5.5	5.5	5.2	5.1	4.9
Other Western Europe	19.9	19.1	19.6	18.6	18.3	17.4
Total Western Europe	**776.8**	**789.7**	**791.1**	**670.8**	**662.6**	**650.0**
India	500.0	532.0	592.5	355.5	373.2	429.2
Pakistan	50.0	50.0	50.0	30.0	31.5	36.2
Bangladesh	20.0	20.0	14.0	8.4	8.8	10.1
Sri Lanka	5.0	5.0	5.0	3.0	2.7	2.7
Total Indian sub-continent	**575.0**	**607.0**	**661.5**	**396.9**	**416.2**	**478.3**
Mexico	30.0	30.0	30.0	25.5	24.2	23.1
Brazil	20.0	20.0	22.0	18.7	17.8	16.9
Dominican Republic	6.0	6.0	6.0	5.1	4.8	4.6
Peru	5.0	5.0	5.0	4.3	4.0	3.8
Chile	5.0	5.0	5.0	4.3	4.0	3.8
Colombia	3.0	3.0	3.0	2.6	2.4	2.3
Bolivia	2.9	3.0	3.0	2.6	2.4	2.3
Venezuela	2.0	2.0	2.0	1.7	1.6	1.5
Ecuador	2.0	2.0	2.0	1.7	1.6	1.5
Argentina	1.5	1.5	1.5	1.3	1.2	1.2
Total Latin America	**77.4**	**77.5**	**79.5**	**67.6**	**64.2**	**61.1**

Jewellery fabrication, 2003–2008f (tonnes)

	2003	2004	2005	2006	2007e	2008f
Saudi Arabia	170.0	180.0	190.0	133.0	139.7	146.6
Egypt	75.0	75.0	85.0	55.3	58.0	60.9
UAE	47.5	50.0	55.0	38.5	40.4	41.2
Iran	35.0	35.0	40.0	34.0	35.7	36.4
Iraq	35.0	30.0	35.0	21.0	22.1	22.5
Kuwait	15.0	15.0	17.5	10.9	11.4	12.0
Israel	14.0	15.0	15.0	12.3	11.7	11.2
Lebanon	9.0	10.0	12.0	6.6	6.9	7.1
Other Middle East	15.6	16.0	16.3	9.3	9.8	10.2
Total Middle East	**416.1**	**426.0**	**465.8**	**320.8**	**335.7**	**348.0**
USA	200.0	200.0	195.0	165.8	157.5	150.0
Canada	12.0	12.0	12.0	11.4	10.8	10.3
Total North America	**212.0**	**212.0**	**207.0**	**177.2**	**168.3**	**160.3**
World total	**2,808.3**	**2,878.2**	**2,995.6**	**2,275.8**	**2,256.6**	**2,334.0**

Source: VM Group

Official Sector Holdings by Region

Official sector by region, 2001–2008 (tonnes)

	2003	2004	2005	2006	2007e	2008f
Africa	420	420	420	420	419	419
Asia	2,356	2,326	2,262	2,257	2,235	2,226
Australasia	80	80	80	80	80	80
Eastern Europe	926	930	935	959	991	1,041
Western Europe	14,461	14,051	13,522	13,194	12,680	12,205
Indian sub-continent	432	432	432	432	432	432
Latin America	516	571	571	565	566	566
Middle East	1,092	1,072	1,082	1,162	1,180	1,190
North America	8,140	8,140	8,140	8,138	8,138	8,138
IMF/BIS	3,411	3,425	3,418	3,408	3,385	3,375
Total	**31,833**	**31,444**	**30,861**	**30,614**	**30,106**	**29,672**

Source: IMF, national central banks websites, VM Group

Jewellery Consumption by Region

Jewellery consumption, 2003–2008f (tonnes)

	2003	2004	2005	2006	2007e	2008f
Morocco	8.8	8.8	8.9	5.4	5.2	5.3
South Africa	5.2	5.9	5.9	5.1	4.8	4.7
Other Africa	13.9	13.7	14.1	8.5	8.5	8.6
Total Africa	**27.9**	**28.4**	**28.9**	**19.0**	**18.4**	**18.6**
China	258.2	265.0	274.2	252.6	240.4	251.1
Indonesia	81.3	82.0	82.8	57.7	53.9	60.0
South Korea	37.5	37.5	39.0	23.4	23.6	24.8
Japan	29.4	28.8	28.8	24.2	23.1	22.7
Afghanistan	26.1	27.0	28.5	19.9	20.5	21.7
Thailand	29.9	29.9	28.3	21.6	20.5	21.4
Taiwan	29.3	27.5	27.3	21.8	20.7	20.8
Vietnam	25.0	30.0	34.5	20.7	18.5	19.4
Malaysia	27.7	27.6	29.1	18.4	17.5	18.0
Singapore	18.9	18.9	19.4	12.9	12.2	12.7
Myanmar	11.7	12.7	12.6	8.0	7.8	8.5
Philippines	11.7	11.7	11.8	7.5	7.1	7.7
Other Asia	15.8	16.1	16.5	10.7	10.1	11.3
Total Asia	**602.2**	**614.4**	**632.9**	**499.3**	**476.9**	**501.3**
Australia	5.0	5.0	5.5	4.7	4.3	4.3
Total Australasia	**5.0**	**5.0**	**5.5**	**4.7**	**4.3**	**4.3**
Russia	30.0	30.0	35.0	29.8	26.8	27.0
Uzbekistan	3.0	3.0	3.0	2.6	2.3	2.1
Croatia	0.6	0.7	0.7	0.6	0.5	0.5
Bulgaria	0.3	0.3	0.3	0.3	0.3	0.3
Estonia	0.1	0.2	0.2	0.2	0.2	0.1
Total Eastern Europe	**34.0**	**34.2**	**39.2**	**33.4**	**30.1**	**30.1**
Turkey	112.1	128.5	137.6	98.9	98.8	103.4
Italy	92.5	87.4	85.1	81.1	79.4	75.8
Switzerland	72.9	72.7	71.7	63.7	61.2	58.6
Germany	59.0	58.5	57.4	50.1	47.9	45.9
UK & Ireland	55.8	54.5	51.2	47.0	45.4	44.5
Spain	39.0	38.9	38.3	36.2	35.4	34.0
France	22.0	20.5	21.8	20.8	20.3	19.6
Portugal	15.9	16.0	15.5	14.5	14.2	13.8
Greece	10.3	10.8	10.8	10.3	10.0	9.8
Austria	9.7	9.1	9.3	8.9	8.7	8.5
Belgium	9.8	9.7	9.3	8.8	8.5	8.4
Netherlands	8.9	8.5	8.1	7.6	7.4	7.1
Poland	7.5	7.6	7.3	6.8	6.7	6.4

Jewellery consumption, 2003–2008f (tonnes) (Continued)

	2003	2004	2005	2006	2007e	2008f
Yugoslavia	3.2	3.0	3.0	2.9	2.8	2.7
Other Europe	21.9	21.2	20.1	18.6	18.3	17.4
Total Western Europe	**540.2**	**546.8**	**546.5**	**476.1**	**464.9**	**455.9**
India	497.4	526.0	576.3	353.2	369.9	419.5
Pakistan	89.2	93.2	100.2	61.4	64.1	72.6
Bangladesh	35.5	36.5	32.9	19.7	20.7	23.8
Sri Lanka	5.0	5.0	5.0	3.0	2.7	2.7
Total Indian sub-continent	**627.1**	**660.7**	**714.5**	**437.3**	**457.4**	**518.6**
Mexico	27.4	27.4	27.4	23.3	22.1	21.0
Brazil	11.0	11.0	12.0	10.2	9.7	9.2
Other Latin America	26.3	26.5	22.6	22.6	21.5	20.5
Total Latin America	**64.7**	**64.8**	**66.0**	**56.1**	**53.3**	**50.7**
Saudi Arabia	143.9	152.3	160.0	116.8	120.1	124.1
Egypt	74.0	76.7	85.8	56.4	58.6	61.5
Iran	49.1	49.7	55.6	44.0	46.1	47.4
Iraq	55.5	54.1	60.3	39.0	40.5	42.0
UAE	36.2	40.4	43.1	31.3	31.1	32.4
Lebanon	31.9	34.3	38.1	24.6	25.6	26.6
Syria	29.6	32.2	34.4	23.4	24.2	25.3
Yemen	29.4	31.3	33.3	22.8	23.7	24.8
Kuwait	25.8	27.7	30.8	20.3	20.8	21.8
Jordan	25.6	27.3	29.0	18.6	19.4	20.2
Israel	1.7	1.8	1.8	1.5	1.5	1.4
Total Middle East	**502.6**	**527.7**	**572.3**	**398.7**	**411.5**	**427.6**
USA	386.7	378.5	372.2	334.5	323.8	311.4
Canada	17.9	17.7	17.7	16.8	15.9	15.5
Total North America	**404.6**	**396.2**	**390.0**	**351.3**	**339.8**	**327.0**
World total	**2,808.3**	**2,878.2**	**2,995.6**	**2,275.8**	**2,256.6**	**2,334.0**

Source: VM Group

Legal Tender Coins (tonnes)

Legal tender coins, 2003–2008f (tonnes)

	2003	2004	2005	2006	2007e	2008f
South Africa	2.2	2.9	3	3	2.7	3.1
Total Africa	**2.2**	**2.9**	**3**	**3**	**2.7**	**3.1**
Japan	0	0	0	0	0	0
Singapore	0	0	0	0	0	0

Legal tender coins, 2003–2008f (tonnes) (Continued)

	2003	2004	2005	2006	2007e	2008f
South Korea	0	0	0	0	0	0
Taiwan	0	0	0	0	0	0
Thailand	0	0	0	0	0	0
Total Asia	**0**	**0**	**0**	**0**	**0**	**0**
Australia	3.4	5.2	6	6	5.5	6.3
Total Australasia	**3.4**	**5.2**	**6**	**6**	**5.5**	**6.3**
Austria	6.5	7	7.5	7.5	6.3	7.2
Belgium	0	0	0	0	0	0
France	0	0	0	0	0	0
Italy	0	0	0	0	0	0
Netherlands	2.5	2.4	2.5	2.5	2.3	2.6
Switzerland	0	0	0	0	0	0
Turkey	45	45	55	50	41.7	47.9
UK & Ireland	2.5	2.4	3	3	2.7	3.1
Yugoslavia	0	0	0	0	0	0
Total Europe	**56.5**	**56.8**	**68**	**63**	**52.9**	**60.9**
Chile	0	0	0	0	0	0
Mexico	0	0	0	0	0	0
Venezuela	0	0	0	0	0	0
Total Latin America	**0**	**0**	**0**	**0**	**0**	**0**
Canada	7.4	8.9	10	12	8	9.2
USA	15.1	16.7	14	18.2	10.5	12.1
Total North America	**22.5**	**25.6**	**24**	**30.2**	**18.5**	**21.3**
World total	**84.6**	**90.5**	**101**	**102.2**	**79.6**	**91.5**

Source: VM Group

Financials: Prices, Volatilities and Lease Rates

Gold prices in various currencies, average, 1994–2007

	S/oz	Euro/oz	Rand/kg	Yen/gr	A$/oz
1994	384.02	324.26	42,409	1,261	527.24
1995	384.18	296.91	43,343	1,162	517.53
1996	387.71	309.91	52,205	1,356	493.66
1997	331.37	293.10	47,377	1,287	444.82
1998	294.17	262.39	50,729	1,238	469.37
1999	278.73	261.45	53,006	1,018	432.90
2000	279.14	302.78	60,106	967	480.54
2001	271.10	302.82	74,496	1,056	524.66
2002	307.20	328.03	101,011	1,243	569.83

Gold prices in various currencies, average, 1994–2007 (Continued)

	S/oz	Euro/oz	Rand/kg	Yen/gr	A$/oz
2003	363.32	321.06	85,026	1,346	558.89
2004	409.17	329.16	84,361	1,422	556.18
2005	444.45	358.28	90,829	1,577	583.45
2006	603.77	480.43	131,490	2,256	801.48
Jan-06	549.86	453.22	107,284	2,040	732.45
Feb-06	555.00	464.84	108,872	2,104	748.98
Mar-06	557.09	463.05	111,832	2,101	767.01
Apr-06	610.65	496.60	119,188	2,292	828.26
May-06	675.39	528.48	136,993	2,425	884.22
Jun-06	596.15	470.65	133,408	2,197	805.93
Jul-06	633.71	499.37	144,107	2,357	842.66
Aug-06	632.59	493.90	140,804	2,357	829.01
Sep-06	598.19	469.92	142,911	2,253	791.81
Oct-06	585.78	464.15	143,601	2,233	776.96
Nov-06	627.83	487.10	145,867	2,367	812.45
Dec-06	629.79	476.66	142,321	2,370	801.89
Jan-07	631.17	486.00	145,481	2,444	806.83
Feb-07	664.75	507.94	152,744	2,573	848.98
Mar-07	654.90	494.31	154,266	2,469	826.17
Apr-07	679.37	502.21	154,376	2,597	819.98
May-07	666.86	493.73	149,995	2,590	808.69
Jun-07	655.49	488.32	150,450	2,584	778.48
Jul-07	665.30	484.90	148,702	2,596	767.82
Aug-07	665.41	488.69	153,807	2,499	802.42
Sep-07	712.65	511.95	162,228	2,636	840.38
Oct-07	754.60	530.15	163,353	2,811	838.76
Nov-07	806.25	549.30	173,674	2,875	901.03

Source: VM Group

Price Volatility

Price volatility, 1994–2007 (%)

	Daily	1 M	3 M	6 M	12 M
1994	6.47	8.12	8.35	9.19	9.89
1995	4.22	5.70	5.74	5.91	6.05
1996	4.44	5.45	5.52	5.66	5.80
1997	7.52	9.80	9.78	9.23	8.81
1998	9.29	12.32	12.80	12.95	12.86

Price volatility, 1994–2007 (%) (Continued)

	Daily	1 M	3 M	6 M	12 M
1999	9.44	13.41	13.87	13.10	12.64
2000	8.57	12.37	13.40	15.94	17.13
2001	8.17	11.41	11.83	11.89	11.75
2002	10.42	12.72	12.78	13.00	13.04
2003	11.53	15.69	16.13	15.79	15.31
2004	11.32	14.05	14.03	14.37	14.77
2005	9.31	11.60	11.39	11.27	12.29
Jan-06	19.03	27.56	20.71	16.71	13.93
Feb-06	13.08	20.20	22.01	18.11	14.72
Mar-06	19.87	19.43	22.54	19.23	15.49
Apr-06	13.52	19.85	19.90	20.12	16.30
May-06	29.17	26.75	22.80	22.21	17.91
Jun-06	20.07	34.84	29.39	26.08	20.64
Jul-06	24.06	26.07	30.81	25.96	21.76
Aug-06	18.04	26.86	29.43	26.63	22.96
Sep-06	16.64	20.59	24.84	26.84	23.55
Oct-06	21.24	23.16	23.52	27.24	24.13
Nov-06	13.17	18.38	21.11	25.54	24.36
Dec-06	12.33	14.56	19.11	22.14	23.92
Jan-07	12.33	17.02	16.60	20.44	23.24
Feb-07	12.48	15.50	15.84	18.55	23.02
Mar-07	14.13	19.31	17.41	18.25	22.94
Apr-07	8.79	10.77	15.61	16.23	22.47
May-07	9.91	12.99	14.70	15.25	20.49
Jun-07	7.51	12.26	12.03	14.93	18.62
Jul-07	7.56	10.82	12.08	13.96	17.15
Aug-07	8.27	11.89	11.59	13.20	16.01
Sep-07	11.34	10.74	11.38	11.73	15.03
Oct-07	12.92	14.04	12.52	12.37	14.14
Nov-07	17.42	17.76	14.51	13.36	14.39

Source: VM Group

Chart Book

Weights, Measures and Conversions

Source: National Mining Association www.nma.org

Gold

- The chemical symbol for gold is Au.
- Gold's atomic number is 79 and its atomic weight is 196.967.
- Gold melts at 1064.43° Centigrade
- The specific gravity of gold is 19.3, meaning gold weighs 19.3 times more than an equal volume of water.

．．．．．．．．．．．．

WEIGHT EQUIVALENTS

1 troy ounce	=	1,097 ordinary ounces
1 troy ounce	=	480 grains
1 troy ounce	=	31.1 grams
1000 troy ounces	=	31.3 kilograms
1 gram	=	.03215 troy ounces
1 kilogram	=	32.15 troy ounces
1 tonne	=	32.150 troy ounces
1 ordinary ounce	=	.9115 troy ounces
1 ordinary pound	=	14.58 troy ounces

．．．．．．．．．．．．

Percent Gold	=	European System	=	Karat System
100%	=	1000 fine	=	24 karat
91.7%	=	917 fine	=	22 karat
75.0%	=	750 fine	=	18 karat
58.5%	=	585 fine	=	14 karat
41.6%	=	416 fine	=	10 karat

I Grain = 64.8 milligrams
4 grains = 1 carat
1 troy ounce = 480 grains
1 troy pound = 12 troy ounces
Source: www.goldcalculator.com

Production & Reserves

Cumulative Production vs World Resources Estimate Basis 100 000 Tonnes World Resource

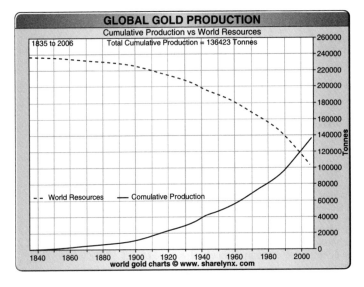

Data for World Resources estimated from information in http://minerals.er.usgs. gov/minerals/pubs/ commodity/ gold/

Regional and Demand

East vs West Gold Demand 1983 to 2007

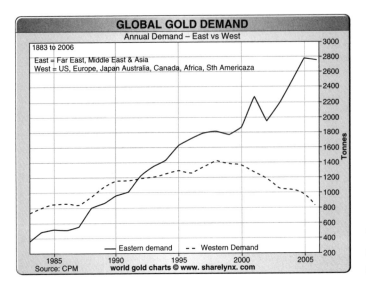

The East likes gold and their spending power is increasing fast

Economics/Purchasing Power

US M3 vs Gold

M3 Calculation based on data from http://research. stlouisfed.org/publications/mt/20060401/cover. pdf

US Money Stock Measures – M1 M2 M3

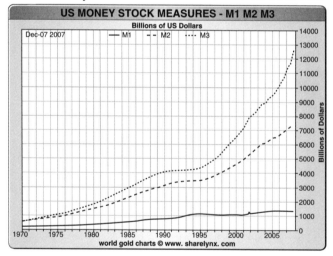

M1: is the sum of legal tender held outside banks, travelers checks, checking accounts (but not demand deposits), minus the amount of money in the Federal Reserve float.

M2: is the sum of: M1, savings deposits including money market accounts from which no checks can be written, small denomination time deposits less than $100 000 and retirement accounts.

M3: M2 plus time deposits above $100 000, eurodollar deposits, dollars held at foreign offices of US banks, and institutional money market funds.

Source: http://www.theshortrun.com/data/Financial/aggregates/msexplain.html

CPI: US $ Purchasing Power 1960 to 2006

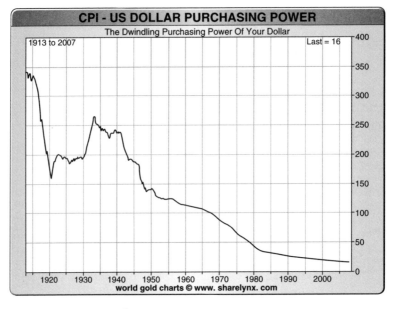

Source: Federal Reserve Board

Euro Gold Price 2000 to 2007

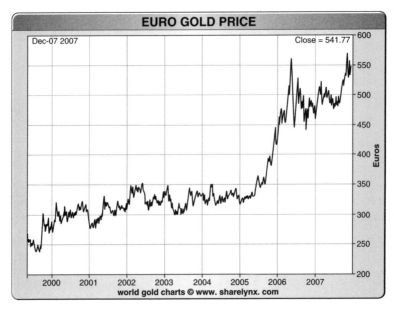

Strong gold price performance against all currencies reinforces its stateless money credentials.

South African Rand Gold Price 1970 to 2007

1970 to 2007 Gold & British Pound, Japanese Yen & Swiss Franc

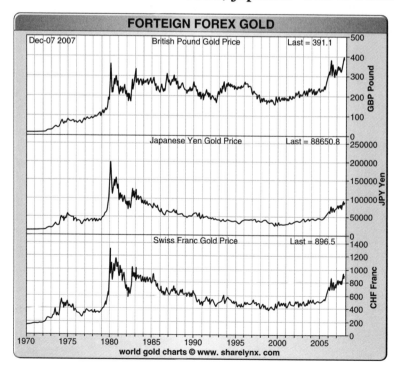

1970 to 2007 Gold & Australian, Canadian & New Zealand Dollars

1970 to 2007 Gold & Chinese Renmimbi, Indian Rupee & South African Rand

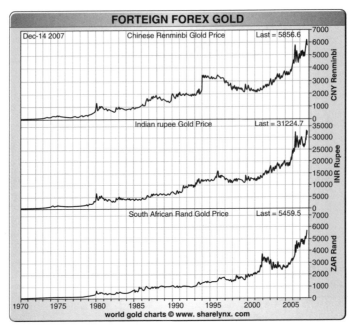

Indices

HUI – Amex Gold Bugs Index 1998–2007

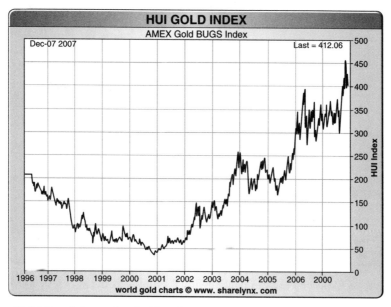

American Gold Bugs' favourite Gold Index

BGMI Weekly Index 1938 to 2007
Barrons Gold Mining Index

Seventy years of history tracking the seven largest gold producers in the United States

PM Mutual Funds Sentiment: 1986 to 2007

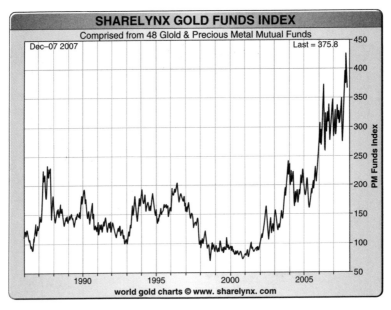

Crafted from 48 Gold or Precious Metal Mutual Funds this index can be a leading indicator for investors.

CRB Index 1946 to 2007

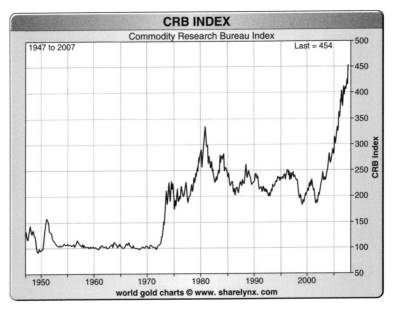

Chart showing similar pattern to the 1970s

200 Years DJIA Index 1800 to 2007

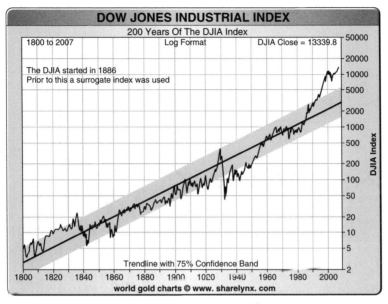

A surrogate index has been used for the period from 1800 through to 1886 when the Dow Jones Industrial Index was introduced.

Comex Gold Stockpiles 1970 to 2007

Increased market activity as reflected by Comex stockpiles

Gold Futures COTs

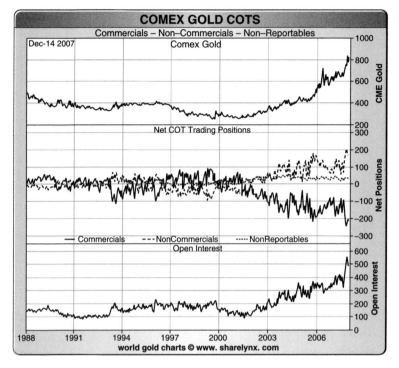

The data for this chart is supplied by the CFTC http://www.cftc.gov/ Important information for all market participants

Gold Lease Rates 1986 to 2007

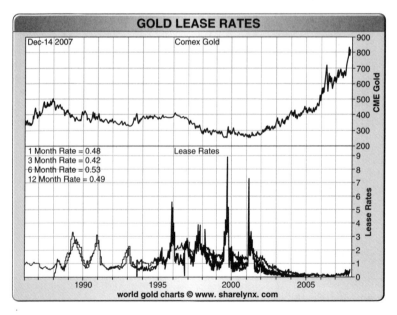

Lease rates spike when supply is tight.

Gold – Average Yearly Percentage Change

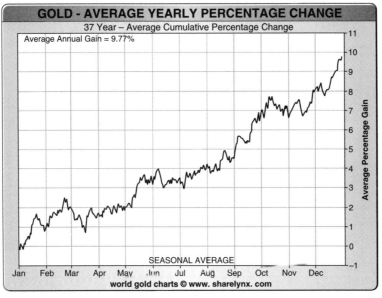

AVERAGE TAKEN OVER 37 YEARS

The chart here shows the average seasonal growth rate of the gold price averaged out over 37 years of data (since 1970).

GC – Comex Gold 1970–2007

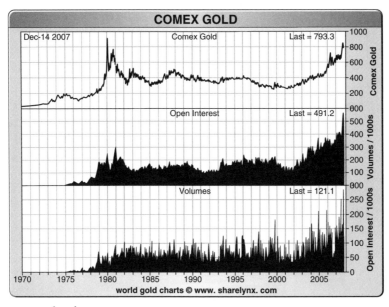

Open interest and volumes seen at extremes

Long Term Gold – Log Format 1725 to 2007

CPI Adjusted Gold Price 1720 to 2007

Gold would have to rise to $2000 in current dollars to be worth the same in purchasing power as it had in 1981 when the price spiked to $850.

Comex Gold – Highs And Lows 1970 to 2007

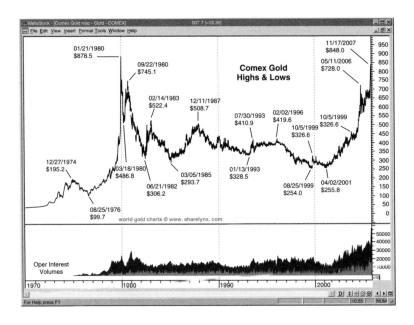

1971 – Nixon demonetizes gold

1974 – US citizens allowed to buy and hold gold bullion and coins for the first time in 40 years

1976 – IMF starts 5 year gold sales program

1980 – Gold peaks at historic high of $850oz January 21st, IMF finishes gold sales program

1985 – US Dollar Index peaked after a 4 year run where the index doubled

1987 – Gold peaks a few months after the 1987 sharemarket crash

1996 – Central Banks start selling large gold holdings

1997 – Central Banks in Asia suffer currency wars and sell gold

1999 – Washington Agreement for Gold Sales signed on September 26th

2001 – Post 9/11 world

Hyperinflationary Gold: DM 1919 to 1923

When money becomes worth less than the paper it is written on

Hyperinflation: Zimbabwe Industrial Average
Index – 2004 to 2007

Hyperinflation: The world's best performing Stock Exchange on index growth in 2007 and the biggest loser of value!

Hyperinflation: Zimbabwe – 2005 to 2007

Current hyperinflation in Zimbabwe

Production

Annual Global Gold Production – 1835 to 2006

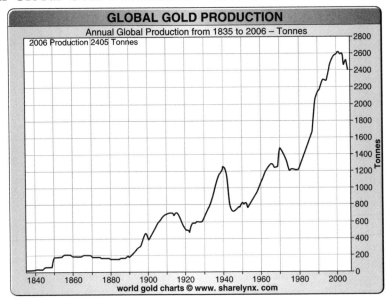

Peak gold – have we turned the corner?

Cumulative Gold Production – 1835 to 2006

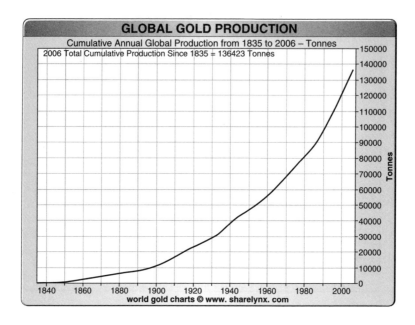

Global Gold Production – 1950 to 2007
Annual Production/Demand/Deficit

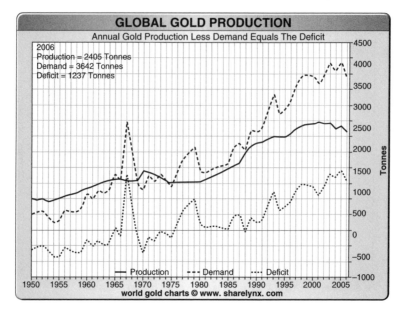

Annual production, demand and supply deficit.

Cumulative Production/Demand/Deficit

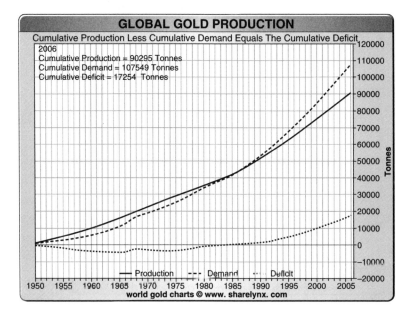

Since 1950 approx 18 000 tonnes has been sold by the official sector to meet the demand deficit.

Ratios

200 Years Dow Gold Ratio – Log Format

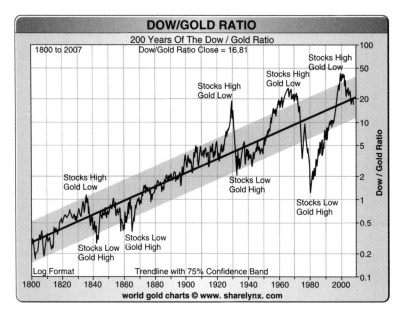

When shares are over priced gold tends to be cheap and vice versa.

200 Year Dow Gold Ratio – Linear Format

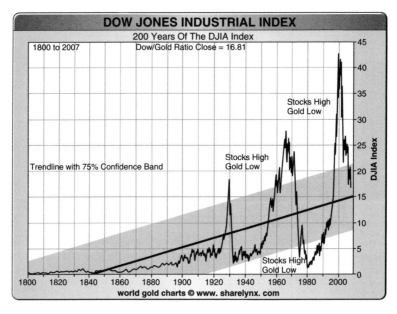

Note the roller coaster rides

Equity Bubbles Defined by Gold CAC40 vs Gold Ratio 1980 to 2007

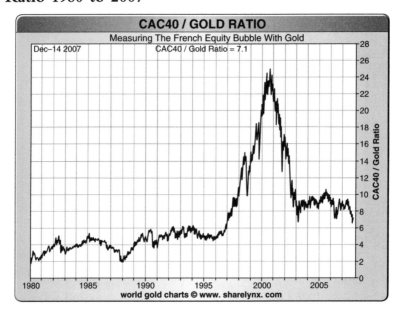

Stock market level doesn't look extreme in relation to gold.

DAX vs Gold Ratio 1980 to 2007

Stock market level not extreme and rising

FTSE vs Gold Ratio 1980 to 2007

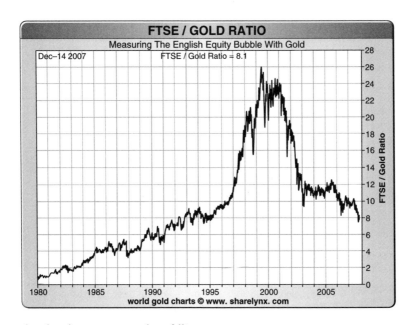

Stock market level not extreme but falling

N225 vs Gold Ratio 1980 to 2007

The Nikkei market topped in 1989 and has been retracing ever since.
Shares no longer appear overvalued in relation to gold.

US Dollar Index vs Spot Gold 1970 to 2007

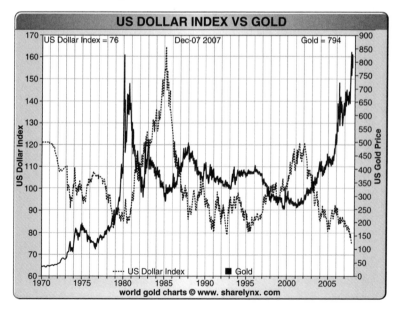

The dollar and gold tend to move in opposite directions.

Reverse Alchemy? Lead vs Gold Ratio 1990 to 2007

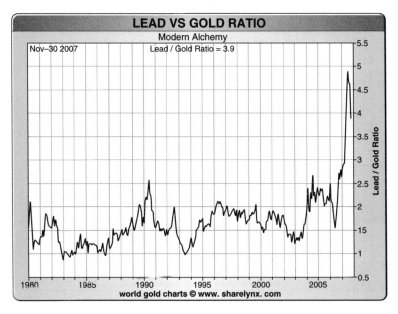

Lead outperformed gold in the recent commodities rally!

Spot Gold vs Crude Oil Ratio 1970 to 2007

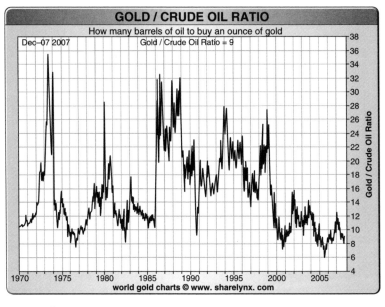

The ratio to watch.

US House Price in Ounces of Gold 1963 to 2007

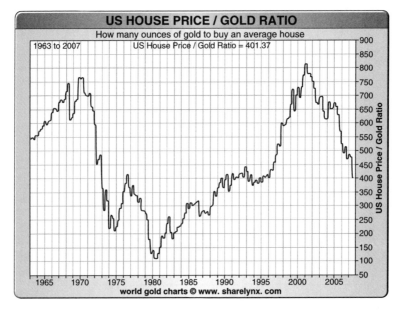

There may not be all that much more to fall.

UK House Price in Ounces of Gold 1953 to 2007

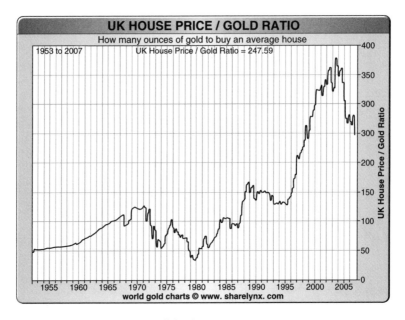

House prices look high – and are still high.

Gold: Chronology

4000 BC Gold mined in the Transylvanian Alps or the mountains in Thrace. People use it in Europe to fashion decorative objects.

3000 BC In what is now southern Iraq gold is used in jewellery including styles still worn currently.

2500 BC As gold becomes a recognized medium of exchange for international trade the vast gold-bearing regions of Nubia contribute to Egypt's wealth and power.

   The Shekel, a coin originally weighing 11.3 grams of gold, becomes a standard unit of measure in the Middle East. It contains a naturally occurring alloy called electrum that was approximately two-thirds gold and one-third silver.

1350 BC Babylonians first to use fire assay to test the purity of gold.

1200 BC Egyptians master the art of beating gold into leaf to extend its use, as well as alloying it with other metals for hardness and colour variations and start casting gold jewellery using techniques still employed.

1091 BC Small squares of gold are legalised in China as a form of money.

560 BC The first coins made purely from gold are minted in Lydia.

344 BC Alexander the Great crosses the Hellespont with 40 000 men, launching one of the most ambitious campaigns in military history. Vast quantities of gold seized from the Persian Empire.

300 BC The pseudo science of alchemy, the quest of turning base metals into gold, starts in Alexandria. Alchemy continues through the dark ages into the Renaissance.

218 BC–202 BC Romans gain access to the gold mining region of Spain and start recovering gold from streams and hard rock mining.

58 BC After a victorious campaign in Gaul, Julius Caesar brings back to Rome enough gold to give 200 coins to each of his soldiers and repay all Rome's debts.

50 BC The Aurius coin first issued by the Romans.

476 The Roman Empire falls.

600–699 Mining resumes in central Europe and France, in areas untouched since the fall of the Roman Empire.

742–814 Charlemagne overruns the Avars and plunders their vast quantities of gold, financing his control over much of western Europe.

1066 Following the Norman Conquest a metallic currency standard is re-established in Great Britain with pounds, shillings, and pence. The pound sterling was based on a pound weight of sterling silver.

1284 Venice introduces the gold Ducat, which became the most popular coin in the world for the next five centuries.

1284 Great Britain issues its first major gold coin, the Florin. It was followed by the Noble, and later by the Angel, Crown and Guinea.

1377 Great Britain adopts a monetary system based on gold and silver.

1511 King Ferdinand of Spain commands explorers, 'Get gold, humanely if you can, but get gold'. Expeditions follow to the newly discovered lands of the Western Hemisphere.

1556 Georgius Agricola publishes *De re Metallica*, explaining the fire assay of gold used during the Middle Ages.

1700 Gold is discovered in Brazil. By 1720 Brazil became the world's largest producer of gold and accounted for nearly two-thirds of mined gold.

1717 Isaac Newton, Master of the British Mint, fixes the price of gold at 84 shillings, 11½ pence per troy ounce. A Royal Commission recommends a recall of all old currency and issuance of new specie with a gold/silver ratio of 16-to-1. By devaluing gold to silver a de facto gold standard was established with a price that lasted for 200 years.

1744 Mining in Russia begins with the discovery of a quartz outcrop in Ekaterinburg.

1787 The first US gold coin is minted.

1792 The Coinage Act places the United States on a bimetallic silver-gold standard, and defines the US dollar as equivalent to 24.75 grains of fine gold and 371.25 grains of fine silver.

1797 Following the outbreak of the Napoleonic Wars the Bank of England suspends convertibility of British currency.

1799 A 17-pound gold nugget is found in North Carolina, the first documented gold discovery in the United States.

1803 The first US gold rush starts after gold is discovered at Little Meadow Creek, North Carolina.

1804–1828 North Carolina starts to supply the gold coined by the US Mint in Philadelphia as currency.

1810 British Bullion Committee confirms gold is itself the measure of all exchangeable value and the scale to which all money prices are referred and bullion is the true regulator of both the value of local currency and the rate of Foreign Exchange.

1816 Great Britain ties the pound to a specified quantity of gold.

1817 Great Britain introduces the gold Sovereign coin valued at one pound sterling.

1844 The Bank of England resumes convertibility of its currency into gold after the Napoleonic Wars end.

1830 The formula for fired-on Glanz (bright) Gold used in Meissen gold-decorated china is discovered.

1837 The weight of gold in the US dollar is lessened to 23.22 grains valuing one fine troy ounce of gold priced at $20.67.

1848 The California gold rush is triggered by discovery of gold at John Marshall's sawmill in Sacramento.

1850 Gold is discovered in New South Wales, Australia.

1859 Gold and silver are discovered in Australia.

1862 The Latin Monetary Union sets denominations of silver and gold coins for France, Italy, Belgium and Switzerland and in 1868 for Greece. The countries agree to accept each other's coinage as full legal tender.

1868 Gold is discovered in South Africa. 40% of all gold ever mined was to come from South Africa.

1873 Following revisions to minting and coinage laws the United States comes onto an unofficial gold standard.

1887 John Steward MacArthur is granted a patent for the cyanidation process for recovering gold from ore. The process resulted in a doubling of world gold output over the next twenty years.

1898 Gold is discovered in Klondike, Alaska triggering a gold rush.

1900 The Gold Standard Act commits the US to maintaining a fixed rate of exchange in relation to other countries on the gold standard.

1903 The Engelhard Corporation discovers an organic medium to print gold on surfaces that becomes the foundation for microcircuit printing technology.

1913 The Federal Reserve Act establishes the US Federal Reserve and specifies that Federal Reserve Notes be backed 40% in gold.

1914–1919 Outbreak of World War I – combatants suspend gold standard. In 1917 the US suspends gold exports.

1919 The UK suspends gold exports without official permission.

1925 Winston Churchill as Chancellor of the Exchequer returns the UK to a gold bullion standard, with currency redeemable for 400-ounce gold bullion bars but with no circulation of gold coins. Convertibility into gold is set at 77 shillings and 19 pence – the pre war parity.

1931 The UK abandons the gold standard.

1933 To alleviate banking panic, President Franklin D. Roosevelt prohibits private holdings of all gold coins, bullion and gold certificates and, to prevent hoarding, criminalises gold ownership by Americans.

1934 The US Gold Reserve Act of 1934 gives the government permanent title to all monetary gold and halts the minting of gold coins and restricts ownership of gold certificates to the Federal Reserve Banks. A limited gold bullion standard is restored with redemption in gold restricted to dollars held by foreign central banks and licensed private users.

Roosevelt devalues the dollar from $20.67 an ounce of gold to $35 an ounce.

1936 Agreement reached between US, UK and France to buy and sell gold between each other in exchange for their own currencies.

1937 Fort Knox vaults open in the US.

1939 September: Outbreak of World War II. London gold market closes.

1942 President Roosevelt issues a Presidential edict closing all US gold mines.

1944 The Bretton Woods agreement, ratified by the US Congress in 1945, establishes a gold exchange standard and two new international organisations, the International Monetary Fund (IMF) and the World Bank. The new standard involves setting par values for currencies in terms of gold and the obligation of member countries to convert foreign official holdings of their currencies into gold at the par values. The dollar continues to be convertible to gold at the $35 parity set in 1934.

1945 December: IMF Articles of Agreement become effective. Par values established for members based on gold value of US dollar on 1 July 1944 (0.888671 grams of fine gold).

Gold backing of Federal Reserve Notes reduced by 25%.

1947 The first transistor assembled at AT&T Bell Laboratories uses gold contacts pressed into a germanium surface.

1954 London gold market, closed during World War II, reopens.

1960 AT&T Bell Laboratories is granted the first patent for the invention of the laser. The device uses gold-coated mirrors to maximise infrared reflection into the lasing crystal.

1961 Americans are forbidden to own gold abroad as well as at home.

The central banks of Belgium, France, Italy, the Netherlands, Switzerland, West Germany, the United Kingdom and the United States form the London Gold Pool and agree to buy and sell at $35.0875 per ounce.

1967 South Africa produces the first Krugerrand. It becomes the world's most widely circulated gold coin.

1968 London Gold Market closes for two weeks after gold demand surges. The Gold Pool announce they will no longer buy and sell gold in the private market. A two-tier pricing system follows: official transactions between monetary authorties are transacted at $35 and other transactions are transacted at a free market price.

The US Mint terminates policy of buying gold from and selling gold to anyone licensed by the US Treasury to hold gold.

The requirement of gold-backing for Federal Reserve Notes ends.

Intel introduces microchips with 1024 transistors interconnected with invisibly small gold circuits.

1970 Bell Telephone Laboratories invent the charge-coupled device used to record the faint light from stars, the device using gold to collect the electrons generated by light. Applications in numerous devices, including home video cameras follow.

1971 On August 15 US President Richard Nixon terminates all gold sales or purchases including conversion of foreign officially held dollars into gold.

Following the Smithsonian Agreement sealed in Washington the US devalues the dollar by raising the official dollar price of gold to $38 per fine troy ounce.

1973 In February the US further devalues the dollar and increases the official dollar price of gold to $42.22 per fine troy ounce.

Widepsread dollar-selling continues and currencies are allowed to 'float' freely, without regard to the price of gold. By June 1973 the market price of gold in London has risen to more than $120 per ounce.

Japan lifts prohibition on imports of gold.

1974 Prohibition against Americans owning gold is lifted on December 31.

1975 The US Treasury holds a series of gold auctions. 754 000 troy ounces are sold in January and another 499 500 in June.

Trading in gold for future delivery begins on New York's Commodity Exchange and on Chicago's International Monetary Market and Board of Trade. The Krugerrand is launched on to the US Market.

1976 The IMF sells one-third of its gold holdings, 25 million troy ounces to IMF members at SDR 35/ounce in proportion to members' shares of quotas on 31 August 1975, and sells 25 million troy ounces at a series of public auctions for the benefit of developing member countries.

1978 The US Treasury sells 15.8 million troy ounces of gold to strengthen the US trade balance.

Amended IMF articles are adopted, abolishing the official IMF price of gold, gold convertibility and maintenance of gold value obligations. Gold is eliminated as a significant instrument in IMF transactions with members; and the IMF is empowered to dispose of its large gold holdings.

The US abolishes the official price of gold.

1978 Interest in gold spurred by weak dollar, recognition of Communist China and developments in Iran.

US Congress passes the American Arts Gold Medallion Act, representing the first official issue of a gold item for sale to individuals since 1934.

Japan lifts ban on gold exports starting a 'gold rush' among investors.

1979 The Canadian 1-ounce Maple Leaf gold coin is introduced.

1980 21 January: gold reaches intra-day historic high of $870 in New York. Closes at year-end at $591.

1981 Treasury Secretary Donald Regan establishes a Gold Commission to review the appropriate policy of the US government concerning the role of gold in domestic and international monetary systems.

1982 Congress passes Olympic Commemorative Coin Act, which includes issuing the first legal tender US gold coin since 1933.

1982 US Gold Commission report recommends no future monetary role for gold, but supports a US gold bullion coin.

New gold deposits discovered in North America and Australia.

Canada introduces the fractional Maple Leaf coins in sizes of 1/4 ounce and 1/10 ounce.

China introduces the Panda gold bullion coin.

1985 Plaza Agreement on currencies. OECD countries agree to cooperate in allowing dollar to fall.

The American Eagle Gold Bullion Coin is introduced by the US Mint. The Treasury resumes purchases of newly mined gold.

Goldcorp Australia issues the Nugget gold bullion coin.

The gold coated discs surpass aluminium and are not subject to oxidative deterioration of the surfaces.

1986 World stock markets suffer sharp reversal in October and volatile investment markets lead to increased gold trading.

The World Gold Council is established to sustain and develop demand for the end uses of gold.

1987 Louvre Accord: OECD countries agree to cooperate for dollar to fall to re-align currency values to lower dollar value.

British Royal Mint introduces the Britannia Gold Bullion Coin.

1988 Large gold purchases made by Japanese government in preparation for the minting of a major commemorative coin honouring the sixtieth anniversary of Emperor Hirohito's reign.

1989 Austria introduces the Philharmoniker bullion coin.

1990 The US becomes the world's second largest gold producing nation.

1992 Treaty on European Union signed at Maastricht provides for qualifying countries to proceed to Economic and Monetary Union and single currency by January 1999. National central banks mutate into European System of Central Banks (ESCB) overseen by the European Central Bank (ECB). The ECB empowered to call for Ecu50bn (Euro 50bn) of gold and foreign reserve assets from participating countries. Reserve management of all ECSB banks, including that of gold holdings, subject to guidelines to be issued by the ECB council.

1992 World Gold Council introduces the Gold Mark as an international identification mark for gold jewellery.

1993 Germany lifts value added tax restrictions on financial gold reviving private demand.

India and Turkey liberalise their gold markets.

1994 Russia establishes a domestic gold market.

1997 US Congress passes Taxpayers Relief Act, allowing US Individual Retirement Account holders to buy gold bullion coins and bars for their accounts of a fineness equal to, or exceeding, 99.5%.

1998 Austria, Belgium, Finland, France, Germany, Ireland, Italy, Luxembourg, Netherlands, Portugal and Spain confirmed as participants in European Monetary Union scheduled to start in January 1999.

The Governing Council of the European Central Bank resolves that 15% of its initial reserves of 39.5bn euro, due to be transferred to it on the first day of 1999, will consist of gold. The Council also agrees that before the end of the year it will adopt an ECB guideline which will subject all operations in foreign reserve assets remaining with the national central banks, including gold, to approval by the ECB.

1999 The Euro European currency is introduced, backed by the ECB holding 15% of its reserves in gold. European Monetary Union starts. The eleven founding members transfer a total of 39.6bn euro of gold and foreign exchange reserves to the European Central Bank. 15% of this is gold.

European Central Bank Agreement on Gold that became known as the Washington Agreement announced following a period when uncoordinated sales of gold destabilised the market and drove the price down. The participating banks hold nearly a quarter of all the gold thought to be above ground (equivalent to around 33 000 tonnes in September 1999). Following the agreement the gold price starts stabilising.

2003 The Shanghai Gold Exchange formally opens for business. At the end of March 2003 rules governing both domestic and international participation in the gold fabrication are relaxed.

2004 The Central Bank *Washington Agreement* renewed for a further five years from 27 September 2004 to 26 September 2009 with an annual limit to sales of 500 tonnes.

Notes

Chapter 1

1 British Bullion Committee report 1810, see Bernstein, *Power of Gold*, p. 211.
2 'Voices of Innovation', *Business Week,* 20 February 2006.
3 Lowenstein, Roger, 2001. *When Genius Failed.* Fourth Estate, Harper Collins.
4 www.wallmart.com.
5 Bernstein, Peter L., 2001. *The Power of Gold – The History of an Obsession.* NewYork: John Wiley & Sons, Inc.
6 Concluding chapter of *Power of Gold.*
7 Waggoner, John. 'How to hedge against two scary scenarios', *USA Today*, 20 June 2005: http://www.usatoday.com/money/perfi/columnist/waggon/2005–06–30-scenarios_x.htm.
8 http://www.ft.com/cms/785d3460-86d6-11dc-a3ff-0000779fdac.html.
9 Silver is also considered a monetary metal. But it is more dominated by industrial demand and tarnishes.
10 Details of warehousing and associated schemes in Chapter 10 and associated section of Webliography.
11 Bernstein, Peter L. 1996. *Against the Gods: The Remarkable Story of Risk.* New York: John Wiley & Sons, Inc., p. 68.
12 *$118 Trillion and Counting: Taking Stock of the World's Capital Markets.* McKinsey Global Institute: www.mckinsey.com/mgi/publications/gcm/.
13 *$118 Trillion and Counting: Taking Stock of the World's Capital Markets*: McKinsey Global Institute: www.mckinsey.com/mgi/publications/gcm/.
14 http://www.columbia.edu/~ram15/grash.html.
15 Kepel, Gilles, 2002. *Jihad: The Trail of Political Islam.* IB Tauris & Co., p. 1
16 Question raised by Harvard Professor Kenneth Rogoff, a former chief adviser to the IMF in an article published in August 2006. www.projectsyndicate.org.
17 http://business.guardian.co.uk/story/,,1663233,00.html.
18 http://www.lbma.org.uk/publications/2007survey.pdf.
19 http://www.lbma.org.uk/publications/2008survey.pdf.
20 Cheuveux is an investment bank in the French Crédit Agricole banking group.
21 www.usfunds.com.
22 *Financial Times,* 17 August 2004.
23 Answer to question at reception after a lecture in the Kannaly Trust Company Distinguished Lecture Programme.

24 Italics my emphasis.

25 Video presentations by David Walker on America's Fiscal Future. http://www.
    mckinsey.com/mgi/pdfs/third_annual_report/CapMarkets_Perspective.pdf;
    http://www.gao.gov/special.pubs/longterm/exposurenew.html. In February 2008
    David Walker resigned as Comptroller General to head the Peter G. Peterson
    Foundation and campaign for fiscal sanity. http://www.thegoldwatcher.com/
    ?s=david+walker

26 Bernanke: http://www.federalreserve.gov/boarddocs/speeches/2005/200503102/
    default.htm.

27 Wolf, Martin. *Will Globalisation Survive?* Third Whitman Lecture. April 2005: http://
    www.petersoninstitute.org/publications/papers/wolf0405.pdf

28 Friedman, Thomas L., 2005. *The World is Flat – A Brief History of the Twenty-first
    Century.* Farar, Strauss & Giroux, p. 407.

29 Rashid, Ahmed, 2001. *Taliban: Islam, Oil and the New Great Game in Central Asia.*
    London: I.B. Tauris & Co. Ltd.

30 Mujahideen means soldiers of Islam.

31 Kepel, Gilles, 2002. *Jihad: The Trail of Political Islam.* London: I.B. Tauris & Co. Ltd.

32 Gates, Robert M., 1996. *From the Shadows. The ultimate insider's story of five Presidents
    and how they won the cold war.* New York: Simon and Schuster Paperbacks, p. 349.

33 Kepel, Gilles, 2002. *Jihad: The Trail of Political Islam.* IB Tauris & Co., p. 147.

34 Abdullah Azzam and the Islamist Revolution. http://www.lib.unb.ca/Texts/JCS/
    Fall03/mcgregor.pdf

35 Crile, George, 2003. *Charlie Wilson's War: The Extraordinary Story of How the Wildest
    Man in Congress and a Rogue CIA Agent Changed the History of Our Times.* New York:
    Grove Press Books.

36 Open Democracy: the war for Muslim minds: an interview with Gilles Kepel: http://
    www.opendemocracy.net/faith-europe_islam/article_2216.jsp.

Chapter 2

1 Bernstein, Peter L., 2001. *The Power of Gold. The History of an Obsession.* New York:
   John Wiley & Sons, Inc.

2 *Brookings Papers on Economic Activity*, Vol. 1982, No. 1, pp. 1–56.

3 Green, Timothy. *Central Bank Gold Reserves – A Historical Perspective since 1845.* World
   Gold Council Research Study No. 23: http://www.gold.org/pub_archive/pdf/Rs23.
   pdf.

4 http://minerals.usgs.gov/minerals/pubs/commodity/gold/gold_mcs07.pdf.

Chapter 3

1 www.usfunds.com.

2 Ferguson, Niall, 2001. *The Cash Nexus: Money & Power in the Modern World 1700–
   2000.* Alan Lane, The Penguin Press.

3 http://www.mineweb.com/mineweb/view/mineweb/en/page34?oid=41767 &sn=Detail.
4 www.gold.org.
5 www.gold.org. Press release, 29 September 1999.
6 http://www.gfms.co.uk/.
7 http://virtualmetals.co.uk.
8 http://www.gata.org.
9 www.thegoldwatcher.com.
10 http://www.robertmundell.net/pdf/The%20International%20Monetary%20System% 20in%20the%2021st%20Century.pdf

Chapter 4

1 Cooper, Richard N., Dornbusch, Rudiger and Hall, Robert E., 'The Gold Standard: Historical Facts and Future Prospects'. *Brookings Papers on Economic Activity*, Vol. 1982, No. 1 (1982), pp. 1–56. doi:10,2307/2534316.
2 http://www.ft.com/cms/s/0/301c112e-bd51–11dc-b7e6–0000779fd2ac.html.
3 http://nobelprize.org/nobel_prizes/economics/laureates/1999/mundell-lecture. html.
4 http://www.measuringworth.com.
5 http://news.bbc.co.uk/onthisday/hi/dates/stories/november/4/newsid_ 3910000/3910627.stm.
6 www.measuringworth.com.
7 http://www.time.com/time/magazine/article/0,9171,950548,00.html.
8 Jastram, Roy, 1977. *The Golden Constant. The English & American Experience, 1560– 1976.* New York: John Wiley & Sons, Inc.
9 http://select.nytimes.com/gst/abstract.html?res=F10A13FE3C5D12718DDDA 00994D8415B8084F1D3.
10 Mundell advised Reagan on tax policy and takes credit for the economic stimulus after Reagan's tax cuts were implemented.
11 Cooper, Richard N. et al. 'The Gold Standard: Historical Facts and Future Prospects'. *Brookings Papers on Economic Activity*, Vol. 1982, No. 1, pp. 156.
12 Gold Standard: http://eh.net/encyclopedia/article/officer.gold.standard. Bimetallic standards: http://eh.net/encyclopedia/article/redish.bimetallism.
13 Bernstein, Peter L., 2000. *The Power of Gold: The History of an Obsession.* New York: John Wiley & Sons, Inc.
14 *Wall Street Journal*: 7 December 2005: Bernanke's Research.
15 http://foreignpolicy.com/story/cms.php?story_id=3272.
16 http://www.millercenter.virginia.edu/scripps/digitalarchive/speeches/spe_1929_ 0304_hoover.
17 http://eh.net/encyclopedia/article/Bierman.Crash.
18 htttp://eh.net/encyclopedia/article/Bierman.Crash.

19 http://www.millercenter.virginia.edu/scripps/digitalarchive/speeches/spe_1933_0304_roosevelt.

20 Friedman, Milton, 1962. *Capitalism & Freedom.* University of Chicago Press, 40th Anniversary Edition, p. 60.

21 Bernstein, Peter L., 2000. *The Power of Gold. The History of an Obsession.* New York: John Wiley & Sons, Inc.

22 Bernstein, Peter L., 2000. *The Power of Gold. The History of an Obsession.* New York: John Wiley & Sons, Inc.

23 http://www.columbia.edu/~ram15/LBE.htm.

24 http://web-xp2a-pws.ntrs.com/popups/popup.html?http://web-xp2a-pws.ntrs.com/content//media/attachment/data/econ_research/0403/document/pc030104.pdf.

25 http://measuringworth.com/calculators/uscompare/.

26 http://www.wtrg.com/prices.htm.

27 Mundell, Robert A. *The International Monetary System in the 21ˢᵗ Century. Could Gold Make a Comeback?* Lecture, March 1997: http://www.robertmundell.net/pdf/The%20International%20Monetary%20System%20in%20the%2021st%20Century.pdf.

28 http://www.econbrowser.com/archives/2008/04/heres_the_basis.html.

29 http://www.imf.org/external/pubs/ft/gfsr/2008/01/index.htm.

30 http://www.lewrockwell.com/rockwell/keynes-default.html.

Chapter 5

1 McKinnon, R.I. (2000) 'The International Dollar Standard and the Sustainability of the U.S. Current Account Deficit'. *Brookings Papers on Economic Activity*, Vol. 2001, No. 1. pp. 227–239.

2 Mundell, R. http://www.robertmundell.net/.

3 International Monetary Fund, International Financial News Summary, Vol. XXIII, No. 50 (December 22–30, 1971), pp. 417–421.

4 Robert Mundell Nobel Prize Speech: http://nobelprize.org/nobel_prizes/economics/laureates/1999/mundell-lecture.pdf.

5 http://www.thegoldwatcher.com

6 Peterson Institute US current account deficit. http://www.petersoninstitute.org/research/topics/hottopic.cfm?HotTopicID=9.

7 Xafa, M, 2007. *Global Imbalances and Fnancial Stability:* http://www.imf.org/external/pubs/ft/wp/2007/wp07111.pdf.

8 McKinnon, R.I. (2000) 'The International Dollar Standard and the Sustainability of the U.S. Current Account Deficit'. *Brookings Papers on Economic Activity* Vol. 2001, No. 1, pp. 227–239.

9 McKinnon, R.I. (2000) 'The International Dollar Standard and the Sustainability of the U.S. Current Account Deficit'. *Brookings Papers on Economic Activity* Vol. 2001, No. 1, pp. 227–239.

10 Duncan, R. (2003 updated 2005). *The Dollar Crisis – Causes, Consequences & Cures.* John Wiley & Sons, Asia. Chapter 1: The Imbalance of Payments.

11 Duncan, R., 2003. *The Dollar Crisis. Causes, Consequences, Cures.* Singapore, John Wiley & Sons (Asia) Pte Ltd., p. 13.

12 http://people.ucsc.edu/~mpd/InternationalFinancialStability_update.pdf.

13 http://people.ucsc.edu/~mpd/InternationalFinancialStability_update.pdf.

14 The words core and centre countries are both used in the analysis and have the same meaning.

15 D, F & G (2003) *An Essay on the Revived Bretton Woods System*: http://www.frbsf.org/economics/conferences/0502/w9971.pdf.

16 IMF working papers express the views of the author and do not necessarily express the views of the IMF. http://www.imf.org/external/pubs/ft/wp/2007/wp07111.pdf. Notes in brackets in the extract are the author's.

17 Bernanke's Global Savings Glut theory is discussed below.

18 www.rgemonitor.com. Access to Roubini's blog is free.

19 http://www.imf.org/external/np/tr/2007/tr070913.htm.

20 Roubini, N. (2005) www.regmonitor.com.

21 Roubini, N. (2007) *The Risk of a U.S. Hard Landing and Implications for the Global Economy and Financial Markets.* IMF: http://www.imf.org/external/np/tr/2007/tr070913.htm. Roubini www.rgemonitor.com. Access to Nouriel Roubini's blog is free.

22 Bernanke, B. *Global Imbalances*, 11 September 2007: http://www.federalreserve.gov/newsevents/speech/bernanke20070911a.htm.

23 Bernanke, Ben S. *The Global Savings Glut and the U.S. Current Account Deficit*, 10 March 2005: http://www.federalreserve.gov/boarddocs/speeches/2005/200503102/.

24 Obstfeld, M. and Rogoff, K. *The Unsustainable US Current Account Revisited*: http://www.nber.org/papers/w10869.

25 elsa.berkeley.edu/~obstfeld/KN_Obstfeld.PDF.

26 http://www.nber.org/papers/w10497.

27 http://www.imf.org/external/pubs/ft/wp/2007/wp07111.pdf.

28 Published on Cabezon Capital Blog.

29 Krugman, P. (2007) *Will There be a Dollar Crisis?*: http://www.econ.princeton.edu/seminars/WEEKLY%20SEMINAR%20SCHEDULE/SPRING_05–06/April_24/Krugman.pdf.

30 http://www.ft.com/cms/s/0/9c0a6592-6b81-11dc-863b-0000779fd2ac.html?nclick_check=1.

31 Friedman, Milton, 1962 *Capitalism and Freedom.* 40th Anniversary paperback edition. University of Chicago Press, p. 59.

32 Friedman, ibid, pp. 67–69.

33 http://www.cato.org/pressroom.php?display=comments&id=806

34 Article published in the *Financial Times*: http://www.georgesoros.com/?q=worst_in_60years. View from the Top audio interview with the *Financial Times*: http://www.ft.com/cms/55569c24-c38d-11dc-b083-0000779fd2ac.html?_i_referralObject=627561916&fromSearch=n.

Chapter 6

1 http://www.un.org/News/Press/docs/2002/SC7564.doc.htm.

2 *New York Times*. 9 March 2003.

3 *War with Iraq: Costs, Consequences, and Alternatives*. American Academy of Arts and Sciences: http://www.amacad.org/publications/monographs/Iraq_Press.pdf.

4 CBO Testimony October 2007: Estimated Costs of US Operations in Iraq etc.: : http://www.cbo.gov/ftpdocs/86xx/doc8690/10–24-CostOfWar_Testimony.pdf.

5 Stiglitz, Joseph E. and Bilmes, Linda J., 2008. *The Three Trillion Dollar War: The True Cost of the Iraq Conflict.*London: Allen Lane, Penguin Books.

6 Hormats, Robert D., 2007. *The Price of Liberty. Paying for America's Wars*. New York: Times Books.

7 http://www.federalreserve.gov/boarddocs/speeches/2003/20030205/default.htm.

8 www.shadowstats.com.

9 http://www.bmsinc.ca/content/view/402/33/.

10 Republican Party Platform: 2000 Presidential Elections.

11 http://www.whitehouse.gov/news/releases/2004/08/20040809-9.html.

12 www.levy.org.

13 *The Price of Liberty*, p. 281.

14 http://www.cbo.gov/ftpdocs/85xx/doc8565/08-23-Update07.pdf.

15 http://www.gao.gov/new.items/d07983r.pdf.

16 'Still Crazy After All These Years: Understanding the Budget Outlook' Brookings Institution April 2007 report: http://www.brookings.edu/views/papers/gale/ 20070427furman.htm. The authors are Alan J. Auerbach, the Robert D. Burch professor of economics and law and director of the Burch Center for Tax Policy and Public Finance at the University of California, Berkeley, and a research associate at the National Bureau of Economic Research; Jason Furman, a senior fellow and director of the Hamilton Project at the Brookings Institution; William G. Gale, the Arjay and Frances Fearing Miller chair in federal economic policy at the Brookings Institution and co-director of the Urban-Brookings Tax Policy Center.

17 Ferguson, Niall and Kotlikoff, Laurence, 2003. 'Going critical: American power and the consequences of fiscal overstretch.' *The National Interest*, Fall 2003. http://findarticles.com/p/articles/mi_m2751/is_73/ai_109220697.

18 Gokhale, Jagadeesh and Smetters, Kent, 2003. *Fiscal and Generational Imbalances: New Budget Measures for New Budget Priorities*. Pamphlet, American Enterprise Institute, Washington D.C. http://irm.wharton.upenn.edu/WP-Fiscal-Smetters.pdf.

19 Gokhale, Jagadeesh and Smetters, Kent, 2005. Fiscal and Generational Imbalances: An Update.' August 2005: http://www.philadelphiafed.org/econ/conf/forum2005/ Smetters-Assessing_the_Federal_Government.pdf.

20 http://www.philadelphiafed.org/econ/conf/forum2005/Smetters-Assessing_the_ Federal_Government.pdf.

21 In The Long Run, We Are All Debt: Aging Societies And Sovereign Ratings: Standard & Poors Ratings Direct March 2005: http://www2.standardandpoors.com/portal/ site/sp/en/eu/page/article/2,1,8,0,1112292523641.html.u

22 pp. 412–413.

Chapter 7

1 WEO Global Risks Network & Report: http://www.weforum.org/en/initiatives/ globalrisk/index.htm. http://www. weforum.org/pdf/globalrisk/report2008.pdf.

2 World Economic Forum Global Risk Network Reports: http://www.weforum.org/en/initiatives/globalrisk/Reports/index.htm.

3 Pacific Investment Management Company PLC.

4 http://www.pimco.com/LeftNav/PIMCO+Spotlight/2006/Secular+Forum+McCu lley+06-2006.htm.

5 Simmons, Matthew R., 2005. *Twilight in the Desert: The Coming Saudi Oil Sshock and the World Economy.* John Wiley & Sons, Ltd, p. 346.

6 http://www.simmonsco-intl.com/research.aspx?Type=msspeeches.

7 http://www.simmonsco-intl.com/files/ASPO%20World%20Conf%20-%20BW. pdf.

8 www.iea.org.

9 http://www.pimco.com/LeftNav/Featured+Market+Commentary/IO/2003/IO_ 07_2003.htm.

10 http://www.pimco.com/LeftNav/Featured+Market+Commentary/IO/2003/IO_ 07_2003.htm.

11 http://www.treas.gov/press/releases/hp611.htm.

12 http://www.rgemonitor.com/blog/setser/220986.

13 'Fear over Food Price Inflation' *Financial Times*, 23 May 2007: http://www.ft.com/ cms/s/0/7f8bccb8-0960-11dc-a349-000b5df10621.html.

14 Food Price Rises Cause a Cut in Bio Fuels: Times on Line: http://www.timesonline. co.uk/tol/news/world/asia/china/article1917927.ece.

15 http://www.statistics.gov.uk/pic/.

16 www.shadowstats.com.

17 http://www.bloomberg.com/apps/news?pid=newsarchive&sid=aJioZ1QNF3gw.

18 Paul McCulley, Global Central Bank Focus: http://www.pimco.com/LeftNav/Featur ed+Market+Commentary/FF/2007/GCBF+October+2007.htm

19 'Junk Mortgages Under the Microscope'. *Fortune*, 16 October 2007: http://money. cnn.com/2007/10/15/markets/junk_mortgages.fortune/index. htm?postversion=2007101609.

20 http://www.instrategy.com/pdf/NM011106.pdf.

21 Roche, David and McKee, Bob, 2007. *The New Monetarism.* Lulu Publishing.

22 www.independentstrategy.com. 'Wither, hither, dither & the black hole'. *Independent Strategy*; 'New monetraism and the currency accelerator'. *Independent Strategy*.

23 *Are we heading for an epic bear market?* Jon Markman interviews Satyajit Das: http:// articles.moneycentral.msn.com/Investing/SuperModels/AreWeHeadedForAnEpic-BearMarket.aspx.

24 http://research.stlouisfed.org/fred2/series/DTWEXB/ chart?cid=105&fgid=&fgcid =&ct=&pt=&cs=Medium&crb=on&cf=lin&range=10yrs&cosd=1995-01-04&coed =2007-10-12&asids=+%3CEnter+Series+ID%3E.

25 US Census Bureau http://www.census.gov/briefrm/esbr/www/esbr042.html.

26 Kindelberger, Charles P., 2002. *Manias, Panics and Crashes*. 4th Edition, Palgrave, p. 111.

27 Shiller, R.J. *Understanding Trends in House Price and Home Ownership*: Paper presented on 1 September 2007 at Federal Reserve Bank Kansas, Jackson Hole, Wyoming Symposium: http://www.kc.frb.org/publicat/sympos/2007/PDF/2007.09.27.Shiller.pdf

28 I question whether Shiller is right about construction costs in the UK not rising and rents not going up. The house price surge has been disproportionate to rising costs but costs have been rising and so have rents.

29 Grauwe, Paul de. *Central Banks Should Prick Bubbles*: http://www.ft.com/cms/s/0/479f24ba-8892-11dc-84c9-0000779fd2ac.html.

30 http://www.treas.gov/press/releases/hp681.htm.

31 http://www.mckinsey.com/mgi/publications/The_Coming_Oil_Windfall/index.asp.

Chapter 8

 1 http://www.washingtonpost.com/wp-dyn/articles/A38725-2005Apr8.html.

 2 http://www.ft.com/cms/s/0/33a4f754-95b3-11dc-b7ec-0000779fd2ac.html.

 3 www.asiatimes.com.

 4 http://www.project-syndicate.org/commentary/rogoff19.

 5 NBER Working Paper 10869: http://www.nber.org/papers/w10869.

 6 http://www.project-syndicate.org/commentary/rogoff35.

 7 http://www.project-syndicate.org/commentary/rogoff37.

 8 Frankel Jeffrey: http://sparky.harvard.edu/m-rcbg/papers/j.frankel_AssessingRMB4-6-07cbg.pdf.

 9 http://www.imf.org/external/pubs/ft/aa/index.htm.

10 IMF Staff Report on the Multilateral Consultation Between September 2006 and March 2007 on Global Imbalances with China, the Euro Area, Japan, Saudi Arabia, and the United States: http://www.imf.org/external/np/pp/2007/eng/062907.pdf.

11 China's Approach to Reform: http://www.imf.org/external/pubs/ft/fandd/2007/09/xiaolian.htm

12 http://www.treas.gov/press/releases/hp633.htm.

Chapter 9

 1 See Paul McCulley, Global Central Bank Focus: http://www.pimco.com/LeftNav/Featured+Market+Commentary/FF/2007/GCBF+October+2007.htm

 2 Gross Bill, 'Shadow Dancing'. *Investment Outlook,* November 2007: http://www.pimco.com/LeftNav/Featured+Market+Commentary/IO/2007/IO+November+2007.htm

 3 The phrase 'tsunami of red ink' comes from an article by Gillian Tett in the *Financial Times*.

4 www.lbma.org.uk.

5 www.usfunds.com.

6 The phrase 'muddle though economy' was introduced into the investor's lexicon by Pimco and popularised by the analyst John Mauldin.

7 www.gold.org.

8 http://www.bloomberg.com/apps/news?pid=newsarchive&sid=aF2znXjMMfEI.

9 Grantham, Jeremy. *The Blackstone Peak and the Turning of the Worms, 25 July 2007:* https://www.gmo.com.

10 www.boomdoomgloom.com.

11 http://www.measuringworth.com/uscompare/.

12 http://www.gata.org/.

Chapter 10

1 A data sheet on gold measured by fineness and by carats and a buyer's guide on the subject is included in the Fact Book.

2 www.virtualmetals.co.uk.

Bibliography

Books

Bernstein, Peter L. (1996). *Against the Gods: The Remarkable Story of Risk*. New York: John Wiley & Sons Inc.

Bernstein, Peter L. (2000). *The Power of Gold: The History of an Obsession*. New York: John Wiley & Sons Inc.

Bloomfield, Arthur (1959). *Monetary Policy Under the Gold Standard, 1800–1914*. Federal Reserve Bank of New York.

Bonner, William and Wiggin, Addison (2006). *Empire of Debt: The Rise of an Epic Financial Crisis*. New York: John Wiley & Sons Inc.

Das, Satyajit (2006). *Traders, Guns & Money: Knowns and Unknowns in the Dazzling World of Derivatives*. London: Prentice Hall/Financial Times.

Davies, Glyn (1995). *A History of Money from Ancient Times to the Present Day*. Cardiff: University of Wales Press.

Diamond, Jared (2005). *Collapse: How Societies Choose to Fail or Survive*. London: Penguin Books.

Duncan, Richard (2003). *The Dollar Crisis: Causes, Consequences, Cures*. Singapore: John Wiley & Sons (Asia) Pte Ltd.

Eichengreen, Barry (1992). *Golden Fetters*. New York: Oxford University Press.

Faber, Mark (2002). *Tomorrow's Gold: Asia's Age of Discovery*. CLSA.

Fergusson, Niall (2001). *The Cash Nexus: Money and Power in the Modern World 1700–2000*. London: Allen Lane/The Penguin Press.

Friedman, Milton (1962). *Capitalism and Freedom*. Chicago & London: The University of Chicago Press.

Friedman, Milton and Schwartz, Ana (1971). *A Monetary History of the United States, 1867–1960*. Princeton: National Bureau of Economic Research and Princeton University Press.

Friedman, Thomas L. (2005). *The World is Flat. A Brief History of the Twenty First Century*. New York: Farrar, Straus & Giroux.

Gates, Robert M. (1996). *From the Shadows: The Ultimate Insider's Story of Five Presidents and How They Won the Cold War*. New York: Simon and Shuster Paperbacks.

Greenspan, Alan (2007). *The Age of Turbulence: Adventures in a New World*. London: Allen/Lane/The Penguin Group.

Hormats, Robert E. (2007). *The Price of Liberty: Paying for America's Wars*. New York: Times Books/Henry Holt & Co.

International Energy Agency (2007). *World Energy Outlook 2007: China and India Insights*.

Jastram, Roy (1997). *The Golden Constant: The English and American Experience 1560–1976*. New York: John Wiley & Sons Inc.

Kepel, Gilles (2002). *Jihad: The Trail of Political Islam*. London: I.B. Tauris & Co. Ltd.

Keynes, John Maynard (1923). *A Tract on Monetary Reform*. London: Macmillan. Kindelberger, Charles (1996). *Manias, Panics and Crashes: A History of Financial Crises*, 3rd edition. New York: John Wiley & Sons Inc.

Krugman, Paul (2003). *The Great Unravelling: Losing Our Way in the New Century*. New York: W.H. Norton & Co. Inc.

Lowenstein, Roger (2002). *When Genius Failed: The Rise and Fall of Long-Term Capital Management*. London: Fourth Estate.

McCulley, Paul and Fuerbringer, Jonathan (2007). *Your Financial Edge: How to Take the Curves in Shifting Financial Markets and Keep your Portfolio on Track*. New York: John Wiley & Sons Inc.

McKinsey & Company. *$118 Trillion & Counting – Global Financial Stock* McKinsey Global Institute.

Officer, Lawrence (1996). *Monetary Standards in History*. London: Routledge.

Prestowitz, Clyde (2005). *Three Billion New Capitalists: The Great Shift of Wealth and Power to the East*. New York: Basic Books.

Ricardo, David (1811). 'The High Price of Bullion and the Depreciation of Banknotes'. In: *Economic Essays by David Ricardo*, E.C.K. Goner (ed.). London: G Bell & Sons.

Rashid, Ahmed (2001). *Taliban: Islam, Oil and the New Great Game in Central Asia*. London: I.B. Tauris & Co. Ltd.

Rees, Martin (2004). *Our Final Century: Will Civilisation Survive the Twenty-First Century?* London: Arrow Books/The Random House Group.

Roberts, Paul (2004). *The End of Oil: The Decline of the Petroleum Economy and the Rise of a New Energy Order*. London: Bloomsbury.

Rueff, Jacques (1972). *The Monetary Sin of the West*. New York: Macmillan.

Simmons, Matthew R. (2006). *Twilight in the Desert: The Coming Saudi Oil Shock and the World Economy*. New York: John Wiley & Sons Inc.

Stiglitz, Joseph E. and Bilmes, Linda J. (2008). *The Three Trillion Dollar war: The True Cost of the Iraq Conflict*. New York: W.W. Norton & Co.

Talib, Nassim Nicholas (2007). *The Black Swan: The Impact of the Highly Improbable*. London: Allen Lane/Penguin Books.

Temin, Peter (1989). *Lessons from the Great Depression*, Cambridge MA: MIT Press.

Triffin, Robert (1960). *Gold and the Dollar Crisis*. New Haven: Yale University Press.

Wiedemer, D., Wiedemer, R., Spitzer, C. and Janszen, E. (2006). *America's Bubble Economy: Profit when it Pops*. New York: Simon & Schuster.

International Energy Industry (2007). *World Energy Outlook 2007. China and India Insights*.

Papers and Reports

Auerbach, Alan J. et al. (2007). 'Still Crazy After All There Years: Understanding the Budget Outlook.' The Brookings Institution, April 2007.

Bernanke, Ben S. (1983). 'Nonmonetary Effects of the Financial Crisis in the Propagation of the Great Depression.' *The American Economic Review* 73: 3.

Bordo, Michael D. and Eichengreen, Barry (1998). 'The Rise and Fall of a Barbarous Relic: The Role of Gold in the International Monetary System.' NBER Working Paper No 6436, March 1998.

Cooper, Richard N. et al. (1982). 'The Gold Standard: Historical Facts and Future Prospects.' Brookings Papers on Economic Activity. Vol 1982, No 1.

Eichengreen, Barry and McLean, Ian (1944). 'The Supply of Gold under the Pre-1914 Gold Standard'. *Economic History Review*, 47.

Krugman, Paul (2007). 'Will there be a Dollar Crisis?' *Economic Policy*, July 2007. 435–467.

McKinnon, Ronald I. (2001). 'The International Dollar Standard and the Sustainability of the U.S. Current Account Deficit.' Brookings Papers on Economic Activity, 1/2001.

McKinnon, Ronald I. (2005). *Exchange Rates, Wages & International Adjustment: Japan and China versus the United States.* Economics Department: Stanford University.

Mundell, Professor Robert A., Department of Economics, Columbia University. http://www.robertmundell.net

    'The International Monetary System in the 21st Century: Could Gold Make a Comeback?' Lecture delivered at St Vincent College, Letrobe, Pennsylvania, 12 March 1997.

    'A Reconsideration of the Twentieth Century.' Nobel Prize Lecture, 8 November 1999.

    'The Monetary Consequences of Jacques Rueff'. *Journal of Business:* Volume 46, July 1973.

    'The Case for an Asian Currency.' Presentation at the Symposium on Monetary Affairs, Institute for International Monetary Affairs, Tokyo, 12 November 2005.

    'Currency Areas, Exchange Rate Systems and International Monetary Reform.' *Journal of Applied Economics* III:2 (2000).

    'The International Financial Architecture, The Euro Zone and its Enlargement in Eastern Europe.' Kozminski & TIGER Distinguished Lectures Series, NO. 1,2000.

    'One World, One Money?' Robert Mundell and Milton Friedman debate the virtues, or not, of fixed exchange rates, gold and a world currency. Policy Options. May 2001: http://www.irpp.org/po/archive/may01/friedman.pdf.

Obstfeld, Maurice and Rogoff, Kenneth (2004). 'The Unsustainable US Current Account Revisited.' National Bureau of Economic Research. Working Paper 10869, October 2004.

Summers, Lawrence H. (2004). 'The US Current Account Deficit and the Global Economy.' Per Jacobssen Foundation lecture. November 2004. www.perjacobssen.org.

Triffin, Robert (1979). 'The International Role and Fate of the Dollar.' *Foreign Affairs* 57:2; Winter 1978/79.

World Economic Forum (2008). Global Risks 2008. A Global Risk Network Report. http://www.weforum.org/pdf/globalrisk/report2008.pdf.

War on Iraq

Kaysen et al. (2002). 'War with Iraq: Costs, Consequences and Alternatives.' Committee on International Security Studies. http://www.amacad.org/publications/monographs/War_with_Iraq.pdf. *The Cost of Iraq, Afghanistan and Other Global War on Terror Operations since 9/11.* CRS Report for Congress. http://assets.opencrs.com.

Bilmes, Linda and Stiglitz, Joseph (2006). 'The Economic Costs of the Iraq War: An Appraisal Three Years After the Beginning of the Conflict.' Cambridge, Mass.: National Bureau of Economic Research, Working Paper No. 12054, February 2006.

Orszag, Peter (2007). 'Estimated Costs of U.S. Operations in Iraq and Afghanistan and of Other Activities Related to the War on Terrorism.' Congressional Budget Office Testimony Before the Committee on the Budget U.S. House of Representatives.

Oil

Simmons. Matthew: *20ᵗʰ Century's Most Enduring Event: Growth in Oil Demand.* http://simmonsco.intl.com.

Godley et al. (2005). 'The United States and Her Creditors. Can the Symbiosis Last?' The Levy Economic Institute of Bard College: http://ww.levy.org, September 2005.

The Economist (2007). 'The End of Cheap Food.' 8–14 December 2007.

Webliography
Essential websites

For updates, additional data and extensive listing of links to information resources please refer to http://www.thegoldwatcher.com

Daily Commentary on Supply, Demand, Prices, Prospects and Mining

Mineweb
http://www.mineweb.com
Resource Investor
http://www.resourceinvestor.com
World Gold Council
http://www.gold.org

Regular Commentary for Investors

US Global Investors
http://www.usfunds.com

Commentary on Economics and Macro Economics

Pimco
www.pimco.com
Northern Trust: Paul Kasriel
www.northerntrust.com; www.econtrarian.com
Neil Behrmann's Marketpredict commentary
www.marketpredict.com

Analysis on Gold Fund Performance for Investors

Eagle Wing Research
http://www.eaglewing.com

News, Comment and Analysis on Supply, Demand and All Industry Developments

World Gold Council
http://www.gold.org
Virtual Metals
http://www.virtualmetals.co.uk
GFMS
http://www.gfms.co.uk/

Prices, Volumes, Trade Statistics, Standards and Annual Price Forecasts

London Bullion Marketing Association
www.lbma.org.uk

Information on Gold Coins and Small Gold Bars

Coins: tax free gold
www.taxfreegold.co.uk
Gold bars large and small
www.goldbarsworldwide.com

Economic, Financial and Market News and Analysis

Financial Times
http://www.ft.com
FT Associate Editor and Chief Economics commentator Martin Wolf
http://www.ft.com/comment/columnists/martinwolf
FT Market Data overview
http://markets.ft.com/markets/overview.asp

CNBC – US, Europe and Asia
http://www.cnbc.com
Bloomberg worldwide
www.bloomberg.com
Wall Street Journal
http://www.wsj.com
Barrons
http://www.barrons.com
Dr. Marc Faber
www.doomgloomboom.com

Key Gold Information Web Sites

News, Charts and Commentary
Kitco
http://www.kitco.com
Gold-Eagle
http://www.goldeagle.com
Nick Laird's Sharelynx
http://www.sharelynx.com
The Privateer
http://www.the-privateer.com
The Bullion Desk
http://www.thebulliondesk.com
321 Gold
http://www.321gold.com
The Bullion Vault
www.bullionvault.com

Speculation and Investment
Zeal
http://www.zeallic.com
Kitco Casey
http://www.kitcocasey.com
Gold Editor
http://www.goldeditor.com
Stockhouse – commodities page
http://www.stockhouse.ca/commodities/index.asp
Commodity on Line
http://commodityonline.com/

National and Parastatal Organisations

Official US data
Bureau of Economic Analysis
http://www.bea.gov:
Economic data including Gross Domestic Product (GDP), personal income and
outlays, corporate profits, fixed assets, regional accounts and international balance
of payments, trade in goods and services, international services and investment
position and multinational companies.
Federal Reserve
http://www.federalreserve.gov
Statistics, releases and historical data
http://www.federalreserve.gov/releases/
Why gold is precious: Federal Reserve Bank of New York
http://www.newyorkfed.org/education/addpub/goldvaul.pdf
US Treasury
www.treasury.gov
2007 Financial Report of the US Government
http://www.fms.treas.gov/fr/index.html
US Government Accountability Office
www.gao.gov
GAO Note on differences between accruals and cash deficits in Budget
http://www.gao.gov/docsearch/abstract.php?rptno=GAO-07–117SP

US Census Bureau
Economic Indicators
http://www.federalreserve.gov/releases/
International Trade in Goods and Services October 07
http://www.census.gov/foreign-trade/Press-Release/current_press_release/
ft900.pdf

UK official data
UK National Economic Statistics
http://www.statistics.gov.uk/instantfigures.asp
Bank of England
www.bankofengland.co.uk

European Union official data
Official European Union Commission Statistics
ec.europa.eu/eurostat
European Central Bank (ECB)
http://www.ecb.int/

ECB Statistics
http://www.ecb.int/stats/html/index.en.html

IMF – International Monetary Fund Key Reports

IMF
http://www.imf.org
IMF Biannual World Economic Outlook Publications
http://www.imf.org/external/ns/cs.aspx?id=29
IMF Global Financial Stability Report
http://www.imf.org/external/pubs/ft/gfsr/2007/02/index.htm
IMF Data and Statistics
http://www.imf.org/external/data.htm
IMF 2007 Fact Sheet: Gold in the IMF
http://www.imf.org/external/np/exr/facts/gold.htm
BIS Bank for International Settlements
www.bis.org
BIS Quarterly Review with Financial Statistics
http://www.bis.org/publ/qtrpdf/r_qt0712.pdf
OECD: Organisation for Economic Co-operation & Development
www.oecd.org
OECD Key Statistics
http://www.oecd.org/document/15/0,3343,en_2649_201185_1873295_1_1_1_1,00.html

Comprehensive Information Resources

Eh Net Encyclopedia
http:// www.eh.net
Measuring Worth – adjusting historic prices to current prices
http://www.measuringworth.com

Futures and Technical Indicators

New York Mercantile Exchange: Comex Gold Futures
http://www.nymex.com/GC_spec.aspx
Technical Indicators
http//www.technicalindicators.com

Index

Note: Charts and Tables are indicated by *italic page numbers*